India Orientalis by Hondius, 1613

HARVARD EAST ASIAN MONOGRAPHS

76

TRIBUTE AND PROFIT: SINO-SIAMESE TRADE,
1652-1853

TRIBUTE AND PROFIT: SINO-SIAMESE TRADE,
1652-1853

by

Sarasin Viraphol

Published by
Council on East Asian Studies
Harvard University

Distributed by
Harvard University Press
Cambridge, Massachusetts
and
London, England

1977

This book is produced by the John K. Fairbank Center for East
Asian Research at Harvard University, which administers research
projects designed to further scholarly understanding of China,
Japan, Korea, Vietnam, Inner Asia, and adjacent areas. These
studies have been assisted by grants from the Ford Foundation.

Library of Congress Cataloging in Publication Data

Viraphol, Sarasin.
    Tribute and profit.

    (Harvard East Asian monographs ; 76)
    Bibliography: p.
    Includes index.
    1. China—Commerce—Thailand—History. 2. Thailand—Com-
merce—China—History. I. Title. II. Series.
HF3838.T45V57   382'.0951'0593   77-9447
ISBN 0-674-80915-7

FOREWORD

The early Ming voyages across the Indian Ocean under Admiral Cheng-ho in the early 15th century have long demonstrated that the expansion of China by sea antedated that of Europe. When the European adventurers and trading companies eventually reached southeast Asia in the 16th century, they found Chinese merchants active in all the ports and on the trade routes. The Chinese junk trade, as they called it, was well established in this region before the Europeans arrived. In short, there was a Maritime China active overseas in East Asia well before Maritime Europe expanded its influence into that region.

As the age of sail has given way to that of steam and now of air transport, the early achievements of Maritime China have been neglected. One of its staple trades was that in rice between Siam and South China. This was one of the principal economic interests that grew up under China's defensive tribute system for diplomatic relations. How international commerce was conducted within the tributary framework makes an absorbing study, and we are accordingly indebted to Dr. Sarasin Viraphol for his basic account of the two centuries of Sino-Siamese trade before the modern period.

To his attainments as a scholar of Chinese language and history, Dr. Viraphol adds his command of the Siamese materials and his knowledge of the Siamese end of the trade. His book opens the way for further studies of a complex political and economic relationship. Very appropriately, he has completed the revision of this manuscript while attached to the embassy of Thailand in Peking, where he is on leave from his post at Chulalongkorn University.

May 1977   John K. Fairbank

PREFACE

In January 1974, the Siamese (Thai) government formally announced its intention to rescind the controversial "Revolutionary Party Decree No. 53," which had been instrumental in suspending trade between Thailand and the People's Republic of China (PRC) since its introduction by the Sarit regime in 1959. It was almost eleven months, however, before the government and the National (Legislative) Assembly could remove this important obstacle and pave the way to the resumption of trade with the PRC through a state-regulated enterprise. In the course of the lengthy debate, two factors stood out. First of all, after so many years of diplomatic isolation from, and even open hostility toward, the PRC, the Siamese government again found it useful to establish a dialogue and a formal relationship with Peking, and seek trade as a major avenue toward the accomplishment of this objective. Secondly, trade with the PRC was considered desirable precisely because of its own inherent value: the PRC was a vital source of "strategic" materials (notably oil) while concurrently serving as a viable market for Thailand's agricultural and natural surpluses (especially tin, jute, and rubber). In addition the effort to escape a Japanese economic stranglehold was greatly aided by seeking an alternative in the China market.

That the prohibitive decree was so belatedly abolished was due, for one thing, to the apparent apprehension in some circles about the possible repercussions the action might have on Thailand's future economic and political well-being. A number of assemblymen feared that trade with the PRC would have adverse effects on the country's balance of trade, as well as providing a channel for political subversion—keeping in mind, among other things, the existence of a large, commercially oriented Chinese minority, and Peking's predominantly verbal endorsement and support of a war of national liberation against Thailand. This apprehension was also shared by a considerable portion of the public, as well as the armed forces.

For a country that historically maintained a close economic, political, and cultural tie with China, Thailand is appallingly deficient in knowledge of her giant neighbor, even though, commercially speaking, at one point in the early part of the nineteenth century the Sino-Siamese trade was a most important branch of the Eastern Seas trade. This ignorance contributed to the delay in the implementation of a positive policy toward the PRC.

The present study has grown out of an awareness of this problem. In a modest way, it attempts to bridge the information gap in the long and eventful history of the two countries' commercial intercourse. In dealing essentially with a crucial part, and as a matter of fact, the most crucial part, of this lengthy relationship, that is, from the seventeenth to the nineteenth centuries, the work can provide a historical perspective on the likely future course of development in Thailand's commercial contact with the PRC. At least it should serve as a reminder that trade between the two nations was traditionally cordial and mutually beneficial.

Above and beyond that, the study aims at presenting a vignette of economic conditions in premodern East Asia prior to the fateful impact of Western penetration into the region in the nineteenth century. More often than not, we tend to allow our perspectives of Asian history to be colored by what has happened since the middle of the last century. Notwithstanding the dramatic changes wrought by the introduction of Western capitalism into East Asia, the indigenous maritime trade, of which the Sino-Siamese junk trade was a part, was significant in its own right. Dutch historian J. C. van Leur has observed that one may be so hasty as to conclude that trade in pre-nineteenth-century Asia was "primitive in an economic sense and of no importance for modern times." But a more accurate picture, upon close scrutiny, is not deserving of such summary dismissal.

The present study also deals with a host of other issues. I attempt, for instance, to disprove the popularly held assumption that Siam's external trade stagnated in the period between 1688 and 1855 with the conspicuous absence of Western influence in the country. This study also investigates the Siamese tributary trade in its functional aspects, which in turn leads to a discussion of the organizational structure of the Siamese royal trade with China. In the same vein, a supplementary investigation is made to show the various organized activities at Canton, Amoy, and other Chinese ports, in the Siamese Chinese commercial context. The study also traces in some detail the historical development of the Sino-Siamese rice trade, which, in many ways, was catalytic in the further enhancement of relations between Siam and the southeastern Chinese society. Finally an effort is made to trace the stages of economic development of Siam in its transition from a basically self-sufficient agrarian economy to the semblance of a market economy: the increase of foreign trade in the second half of the seventeenth century, then the development of a commercial agriculture and commodity production economy, and finally a money economy in the nineteenth century.

In discussing the major topics in the Sino-Siamese trade, I have attempted to divide up the long history into essentially four chronological periods between 1652 and 1853, when tribute relations were actually maintained between the two countries. The four phases are: initial (1652-1717); developmental (1717-1776); flourishing (1776–1834); and declining (1834-1853). The height of the Sino-Siamese junk trade fell between the period when the Ch'ing government was at the apex of power (in the Ch'ien-lung reign, 1736-1795) and the start of its decline (in the Chia-Ch'ing, Tao-kuang, and Hsien-feng rules, 1796-1860). In the first few decades of Ch'ing rule, nascent foreign trade was severely suppressed, but from the last half of the K'ang-hsi period until the middle of Ch'ien-lung's administration, that is, roughly between the 1680s and the 1790s, the internal economy of China had advanced from the recovery to developmental stages, and this provided an impetus for foreign trade though, in the Chinese rationalization, not a justification for it.

This periodization is predicated upon watershed developments in both Siamese and Chinese history which affected the trend of the Sino-Siamese trade. Thus 1717 is picked as the dividing line between the initial and developmental phases because the second maritime ban imposed by the Ch'ing court that year provides a convenient pause to assess the first sixty years of the Sino-Siamese trade. This trade developed from a framework of legalized tributary trade to the beginnings of a relatively free-trade period accentuated by the participation of private merchants from the coasts of Southeast China. Though the ban in 1717 did not completely halt the Chinese trade to Southeast Asia as intended, it separates a period in which Amoy rose as the hub of the Southeast Asia trade and rice became an important staple in trade to China from the period marked by the dominance of Canton.

In the same vein, 1767 is picked as another dividing line because it represents the end of the old Ayudhya dynasty and the start of a premodern ruling period in Siam characterized by increasing pragmatism and rationalization in the Sino-Siamese trade. This attitude led in turn to the further intensification of this branch of trade and growing signs of the incongruity of the tributary trade framework.

These arbitrary divisions are not meant to portray separate, compartmentalized developmental parts, but rather provide one convenient way of viewing the course of the Sino-Siamese trade whose continuity transcended the periodization projected herein.

One difficulty encountered in the present study is that bibliographic materials were often unavailable. Owing to the undeveloped nature of the topic under question, and the fact that records were wanting for the large part of the junk trade, the sources consulted are diverse and fragmentary. Because as a rule the later Ming and Ch'ing emperors would not allow their subjects to trade and reside abroad, the Chinese who defied this order were more apt to be seamen and pirates not well-educated merchants who would leave written records. On the whole, Chinese materials constitute the most important references for this work, though efforts expended at archives in Thailand have also yielded some interesting, though much less voluminous, Siamese records including official court communications primarily of the Rattanakosin (Bangkok) era. Furthermore, Japanese sources may also be considered significant, particularly the collection of Nagasaki port reports entitled *Ka-i hentai* covering the seventeenth and early part of the eighteenth centuries.

My interest in this study was initially generated in the course of my study of Ch'ing dynasty documents under Professor John K. Fairbank at Harvard University. With his inspiration and guidance, the exposition emerged first as a seminar paper, then as a doctoral dissertation, and finally in the present form. I have learned a great deal from his invaluable comments and suggestions, for which I am most grateful.

I also owe a great debt of gratitude to Dr. Glen W. Baxter, Associate Director of the Harvard-Yenching Institute, and to the Institute itself for the general financial backing during my entire four-year sojourn at Harvard from 1970-1974. I am thankful to Professor Dwight Perkins for his thorough comments and criticisms, and to Professor Alexander Woodside for a similar contribution. Appreciation is also extended to Harvard's East Asian Research Center for publishing this study, and to Mrs. Olive Holmes for her invaluable editorial assistance.

This volume would have been impossible without the help of my wife, Nantana, who typed most of the draft copies and did other mechanical chores which ordinarily accompany the preparation of a thesis and a book. Her perseverance, understanding, and encouragement were also vital elements in the successful completion of the work.

I, of course, bear full responsibility for any factual and interpretative errors arising herein.

CONTENTS

FOREWORD   v

PREFACE   vii

INTRODUCTION   1

I.   THE INTERNATIONAL CONTEXT OF
      THE SINO-SIAMESE TRADE   7
      Rise and Decline of Dutch Trade with Siam   9
      Japanese Trade with Siam   15

II.   THE SIAMESE TRADING STRUCTURE   18

III. INITIAL PERIOD, 1652–1720: CHINESE
      RESTRICTIONS ON TRADE   28
      The Tributary Trade between Siam and China   30
      Illegal Trade between Siam and China   42

IV.   THE SINO-SIAMESE-JAPANESE TRIANGULAR
      TRADE   58

V.   THE ABROGATION OF THE SECOND MARITIME
      BAN AND THE ROLE OF THE RICE TRADE   70
      Rice Shortage and Population Increase   74
      Aid from Interprovincial Sources   79
      Encouragement of Rice Import   83
      Rice Trade in Late 18th and Early 19th Centuries   107

VI.   SOUTHEAST CHINA'S TRADE ORGANIZA-
      TIONS IN THE EIGHTEENTH AND EARLY
      NINETEENTH CENTURIES   121

VII. THE SINO-SIAMESE TRIBUTARY TRADE:
      FROM LATE AYUDHYA TO EARLY BANGKOK
      PERIODS   140

VIII. THE CHINESE IN THE ECONOMIC LIFE OF
      SIAM IN THE EIGHTEENTH AND NINETEENTH
      CENTURIES   160

IX. THE HEIGHT OF THE SINO-SIAMESE JUNK
TRADE IN THE SECOND AND THIRD
BANGKOK REIGNS, 1809–1833   180
Shipbuilding in Siam   180
The Siamese Royal Monopoly   181
Employment of Chinese   185
Ponts   189
The Third Reign   191
Siam's Regional Trade   202

X. CHINESE IMMIGRATION AND ITS ECONOMIC
IMPACT IN THE THIRD REIGN, 1824–1850   210

XI. DECLINING FORTUNES OF THE SINO-SIAMESE
JUNK TRADE   223
Change in the Third Reign   224
Disruption in the Fourth Reign   232

CONCLUSION   242

APPENDIX A. A Chronological List of Siamese Ships
Reported as Trading to Nagasaki   259

APPENDIX B. A Chronological List of Pattani Ships
Reported as Trading to Nagasaki   264

APPENDIX C. A Chronological List of Songkla Ships
Reported as Trading to Nagasaki   266

APPENDIX D. A Chronological List of Ligor Ships Reported
as Trading to Nagasaki   267

APPENDIX E. Dispatches of Royal Ships Trading to
Kwangtung in the Second Reign   268

APPENDIX F. Letters from the King's Adviser to the Ruler
of Songkla Concerning the Outfitting of Junks
to Trade with Amoy   270

NOTES   271

CHINESE AND SIAMESE DYNASTY AND REIGN
NAMES FROM THE SEVENTEENTH TO THE LATE
NINETEENTH CENTURIES   341

BIBLIOGRAPHICAL NOTE   342

BIBLIOGRAPHY   361

GLOSSARY   389

INDEX   403

TABLES

1. Some Chinese Ships Trading to Siam between 1689 and 1702   55

2. Price Differentials of Certain Items Quoted at Canton and Nagasaki at the Turn of the Eighteenth Century   68

3. Quantities of Rice to be Transported (1725)   73

4. The Fukien Encouragement Plan for Rice Importation from Siam (1754)   99

5. The Kwangtung Encouragement Plan for Rice Importation from Siam (1756)   100

6. Awards Granted to Kwangtung Importers of Foreign Rice (1758)   104

7. Awards Granted to Kwangtung Importers of Foreign Rice (1767)   104

8. Rice Prices of Siam in 1850   119

8A. Some Siamese Rice Export Figures for the Decade Following the Bowring Treaty   119

9. A Partial List of Siamese Junks Trading Overseas and Their Sponsors in the Third Reign   193

10. Ships from Kwangtung Engaged in the Coasting Trade for the Year 1831   198

11. Foreign Vessels from the Eastern Seas Trading to Shanghai, Ningpo, and Soochow in a Certain Year in the 1830s   199

12. Siamese Ships Calling at Singapore, 1829–1851   207

13. Ships Frequenting Siam in the Second Reign   207

14. Ships Frequenting Siam in the Third Reign   209

15. Chinese Population in the Third Reign   210

16. Chinese Population in Bangkok in the Third Reign   213

17. A Partial List of Farm Monopoly Fees Payable
     to the Government for the Year 1845   219

18. Estimates of Government Revenues from Selected
     Monopoly Farms for the Year 1832   220

MAP

East and Southeast Asia   xx

"[T]he temporary hegemony of Western European civilization [on Asia] has distorted our view of the past and made our interest one-sided. Because the world had been dominated by the West for a hundred twenty years—a short span of time yet, in retrospect, an eternity—the West came to consider itself as the focus of world history and the measure of all things."

—W. F. Wertheim, "Early Asian Trade,
An Appreciation of J. C. van Leur,"
Far Eastern Quarterly

EAST AND SOUTHEAST ASIA

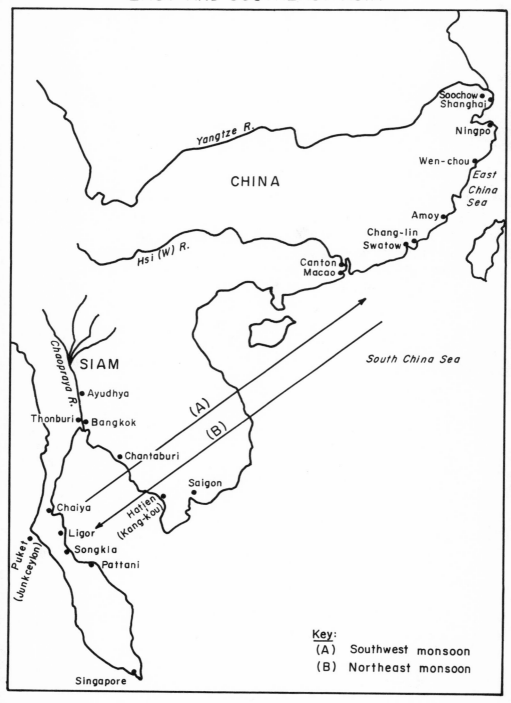

Soochow
Shanghai
Ningpo
Wen-chou
East China Sea
Amoy
Chang-lin
Swatow
Canton
Macao

CHINA

Yangtze R.

Hsi (W) R.

Chaopraya R.

SIAM

● Ayudhya

Thonburi ● ● Bangkok

● Chantaburi

Saigon

South China Sea

(A)

(B)

Chaiya

Hatien (Kang-k'ou)

Puket (Junkceylon)

● Ligor

● Songkla

● Pattani

Singapore

Key:
(A) Southwest monsoon
(B) Northeast monsoon

INTRODUCTION

Maritime trade between Siam and China had existed since the Yuan dynasty (A.D. 1278-1368), but it was not until the Ch'ing period (A.D. 1644-1911) that its political, economic, and social implications were fully manifested.

From the outset this trade was considered to be within the official tributary framework, measurable in one respect by the frequency with which tribute missions from the tributary state (*shu-kuo*) were dispatched to make obeisance to the Peking court, and hence ostensibly to maintain a political *modus vivendi.* Ch'ing China inherited both the basic Confucian disdain for commercialism (and the corresponding belief in the indispensability of agriculture) and the Neo-Confucian philosophy of national security based on self-imposed semi-isolation and nonequality in foreign intercourse. Underlying all this was the assumption that although China was fundamentally a self-sufficient agricultural economy and materially independent of the outside world, it was in a position to dispense material benefits to those foreign states willing to be subscribed as its tributaries.[1] In one respect, it may therefore be argued that both China and Siam shared the consensus that tributary and trade relations were essentially complementary. The concept that the Confucianized Manchu court allowed "barbarian" states to participate in the material excellence of Chinese civilization fitted the underlying Siamese assumption that intercourse with the Celestial Empire was pre-eminently commercial in character.

Underneath such mutual acknowledgment that tribute and trade formed an integral whole was, however, a basic divergence of official attitudes vis-à-vis the manner and extent of such interaction. So far as the Chinese government was concerned, trade was of course of secondary consideration, and, in the final analysis, conformed strictly to the general political principle of *chi-mi* (lit., control by a "loose rein," i.e. permitting the growth of trade as a vested interest of the foreigner, by manipulation of which he

1

could then be influenced). This in effect brought trade "within
the framework of politics."[2] To the Siamese court, which traditionally regarded overseas trade as one important means of enrich-
ment, commerce was an end in itself; tribute missions were just
one form of commercial investment. One of the most notable
proponents of such an interpretation was no less a person than the
colorful King Mongkut (Rama IV; r. 1851–1868) who regarded
tributes as indistinguishable from taxes for the privilege of trading
with China.

In the heyday of the Sino-Siamese trade in the late 1820s
Charles Gützlaff, who was visiting Siam as a preacher, characterized the Siamese approach to relations with China in the following
way: "Though the Siamese acknowledge, nominally, the sovereignty
of China, and show their vassalage by sending to Peking tribute of
all productions of their own country, yet the reason of their paying
homage so regularly is gain. The vessels sent on these expeditions
are exempt from duty."[3]

In no other period could the divergence in the conception of
the real function and purpose of the tribute presentation be viewed
so fully. Nevertheless, to conclude that the Chinese side in practice
adhered strictly to the above notions would not be totally accurate.
First of all, inasmuch as foreign trade benefited tributaries, its
profitability was also an enticement to the Chinese side. In periods
of tranquillity, the Chinese government permitted maritime trade
with Southeast Asia from the coasts of Southeast China often with
advocacy from local officials who stood to gain from the administered trade, while even in times of prohibition, merchants connived with local officials to venture forth to trade. Hence, it may
be said that although overseas commerce, in the sense of the regular
two-way intercourse, might not have conformed to the Confucianized world view of the Chinese state, its practical contribution to
the government both at the formal and informal levels and to certain sectors of the Chinese public was undeniable.

Furthermore, it is perhaps too simplistic to pass up, without
careful analysis, the notion that Manchu rulers became, in the
course of their rule, so Confucianized that their contempt for

commercialism distorted the underlying importance of trade in the tribute context. It seems that some policies and actions adopted by K'ang-hsi, Yung-cheng, and Ch'ien-lung demonstrated considerable pragmatism. Although they would never have gone so far as to accept outright the Siamese assertion of the real motive behind the sending of tribute missions, the emperors nonetheless responded to varying situations with enough imagination to acquiesce in a number of Siamese activities which were contrary to the prevalent assumption governing tribute relations. For instance, the Siamese employment of Chinese individuals to manage their trade to China was an act contrary to the proper Confucian order governing the relationship between Chinese and "barbarians"; nevertheless the Siamese were allowed by the emperors to do so with public sanction.

Thus in spite of the above dichotomy, tributary relations between Siam and China were maintained at a satisfactory level throughout this period. This intercourse revealed the existence of considerable adaptability within the limitations imposed by the Chinese system, which, in time even witnessed some growth and development. Part of this compatability was due, of course, to the nature of the Siamese state which was in its own right similarily structured on "administered" principles.[4] The Siamese kings were also predisposed to exploit the China trade to its fullest even to the extent of utilizing the resourcefulness of Chinese individuals.

For a long time, Southeast Asia's seaborne trade with China took place within the context of tribute relations. As far as Siam was concerned, the trade conducted under the auspices of tribute presentation, or tributary trade, was the most important part of its political interaction with China at least up to the middle of the nineteenth century. Such a system was, in practice, a means of legitimizing official trade, while at the same time accommodating private trade on the side. By the latter half of the Ming dynasty (circa the 1500s), this private trade was predominantly Chinese and came to outweigh the official trade both in volume and value. In the meantime, Siam was sending regular missions to China "to aid the highly developed local trade which it controlled."[5]

In economic terms, the junk trade provided the main channel

for Siam's foreign trade at the time. The country's supply of "luxury" goods (high-value-per-unit-weight items such as rhinoceros horns, elephant's teeth, sapan wood, pepper), and staples such as rice, could be unloaded on the lucrative China market; and its demands for Chinese goods, including a considerable amount of luxury merchandise such as silk and porcelain for the court and the rich, could be met. Siam, being basically a productive, under-populated, and generally surplus agrarian state, maintained a favorable balance of trade throughout the period under study. The junk trade was well adapted to this end, and with the impetus provided further by the royal monopolies, it flourished, particularly from the Yung-cheng period (1722-1735) until the Tao-kuang reign (1821-1850).

The magnitude of the growth in the Sino-Siamese trade is underscored by the fact that Siam's foreign trade at the time was largely concentrated on the China market. But although Siam depended on China for trade, she also helped to develop the Chinese junk trade. For example, by the early part of the nineteenth century, Bangkok had become the main junk port in the Eastern Seas where not only much of the regional trade was centered, but also where most of the Chinese-style seagoing junks were constructed.

Characteristically, one important "commodity" in this trade by the end of the eighteenth century was the immigrant Chinese who went from Southeast China to Siam searching for economic improvement.[6] As their numbers began to climb rapidly, these male immigrants came to have a significant impact on traditional Siamese society which hitherto had been relatively intact despite the presence of an influential but small circle of Sino-Siamese engaged in the junk trade through increased participation in the management of royal and private vessels. The Chinese immigrants developed commercial agriculture and mining on a sizable scale which, in one respect, also fed into the junk trade. As more Chinese spread through the interior of the country for such purposes, they were apt to produce an impact on the countryside. Because of the resourcefulness of these Chinese, taxes on various products, including taxes on gambling, the manufacture and sale of liquor, lotteries, and later, prostitution, were farmed out to individual Chinese under the patronage of the Siamese government and nobility. Chinese manual labor also came to be preferred by the Siamese government, which had traditionally relied on corvée labor recruited from among Siamese males. This shift to Chinese labor helped to undermine the existing social structure, which had based its wealth upon considerations of land and corvée rather than money. In other words, the role of the Chinese hastened the introduction of money economy into Siam by the early decades of the nineteenth century. Finally, intermarriage between the Chinese immigrants and Siamese women was another important factor modifying the traditional social fabric, and in itself helped to create a harmonious relationship between the Chinese and Siamese in times to come.

There is an apparent gap between word and action, policy and practice, underlying the Chinese official stand on foreign trade and the maritime ban. The junk trade contributed substantially to the material well-being of Ch'ing officialdom, but the basic Confucian anticommercial orientation and the traditional Inner-Asia orientation maintained by the Manchu leadership prevented the full realization of the Chinese foreign maritime trade. It is possible that the Ch'ing government never really imposed a tight ban on the junk trade, but adopted instead an ambivalent and precarious stand best described by T'ien Ju-k'ang's phraseology, "Not daring to grant complete laissez-faire they (the government) were unable to carry out the ban; nor were they able to administer efficiently" (*fang shih pu-kan fang, chin shih chin pu-liao, kuan yeh kuan pu-hao*).[7]

A pattern of official control over trade existed in both Siam and China, and turned out to be a basis for much corruption and lack of innovation in the Sino-Siamese trade. At a time when Thailand is seriously thinking about letting the government supervise and control foreign trade with states that also deal in foreign trade through their governments, it is perhaps worthwhile to examine this problem in a historical perspective. In China where merchants had traditionally been subordinated under officials, the only safe and profitable way in commerce was through collusion with those officials in charge of regulating trade. This is what made the monopoly system and the system of bribery possible. While collusion might actually have led to growth and development in some transactions, on the whole, such a trend led to exclusivism and lack of innovation and expansion. Merchants were constantly wary of official persecution and were unlikely to invest indefinitely or diversify their investments; instead, they were apt to concentrate on those few products that would bring them the quickest returns.

In the case of Siam, bribery and collusion was also the order of the day. Although the system served to ensure the dominance of certain groups of Chinese and exclude participation by others, it did not launch the country into capitalistic development. The mode of trade of Siam consequently remained essentially reactionary.

In the process, the Confucianized Manchu rulers clung to the myths of the tributary system, pretending that foreign trade could be safely and effectively contained within such a context in spite of the obvious prostitution of this system in later periods.

Chapter I

THE INTERNATIONAL CONTEXT
OF THE SINO-SIAMESE TRADE

The junk[1] trade may be defined as that branch of the maritime commerce of the Eastern Seas (East and Southeast Asia included) which encompassed Japan to the north and the East Indies to the south, and which was managed almost exclusively by Chinese. This trade was at its height at the end of the eighteenth and during the early decades of the nineteenth centuries.[2] The network of this maritime commerce, according to Chinese navigational charts,[3] emanated from the Taiwan Straits and branched out essentially in two directions: *hsi-yang* or the "western ocean" route covering Annam, Cambodia, Siam, and the Malay peninsula, and *tung-yang* or the "eastern ocean" route which included the Ryukyus (Liu-ch'iu), Japan, the Philippines, and the East Indies.[4] These two routes had of course been used by Chinese navigators long before the Ch'ing dynasty, but after the second half of the seventeenth century traffic picked up greatly, especially on the "western ocean" route during a time when the Eastern Seas trade was predominantly in the hands of the Chinese seafarers who often collaborated with various indigenous rulers. The comprehensive scope of this trade may further be viewed from the large number of ports and calling stations, and the wide range of exports and imports.

Siam occupied a central position in the junk trade in the "western ocean" branch owing to its geographical location; it served as a locus of both regional and East-West trade.[5] The various ports of Siam (the capitals of Ayudhya, Thonburi, Bangkok, and others such as Chantaburi, Pattani, Nakorn [Ligor], Songkla Chaiya) all maintained a vigorous trade at various times with China because they had an abundance of produce suitable for the junk trade, and because of the sailing range of the junk and the manner in which it was sailed. Larry Sternstein has observed that "Chinese 'navigators' much preferred an interminable coasting around

7

mainland Southeast Asia to the relatively short out-of-sight-of-land voyage, because junks were manned, not by 'efficient' seamen, but by so many independent entrepreneurs engaged in multifarious time-consuming deals."[6] These factors, in addition to the under-populated nature of the country, made Siam an ideal center for the junk trade.

This position was made even more favorable because by the second half of the seventeenth century Siam's status in the East-West trade was already well established. Political consolidation, receptiveness of the ruling court to such foreign trade, and the country's proximity to the coveted China and Japan markets[7] enabled Siam to play the crucial role as a transshipment point for East-West goods, thus further enhancing the junk trade. The capital at Ayudhya was then known as an "emporium of the East," serving as a vital crossroad for the flow of merchandise between Europe and China and Japan.

Another factor that favored a long and cordial commercial relationship between Siam and China, which in turn strengthened the position of the junk trade, was the atmosphere of informality in which business was conducted. The Chinese traders to Siam were invariably moved solely by commercial motives; hence they were almost always ready to go to any extent to accomplish a business deal. In contrast to the comparatively more systematic and legal-istic mode of Western trade, the casualness of traditional Asiatic societies prevailed.

Furthermore, not only were the Chinese more knowledgeable about sailing junks and about market conditions at the various ports of call (where merchants were more often than not Chinese compatriots), but the Siamese government policy of discouraging the participation of Siamese individuals in navigation and foreign trade, and the skill of the Chinese in bribery and other "wheeling-and-dealing" techniques enabled them to transact business with minimal cost and delay. Understandably, this commercial "adroit-ness" was consistently pointed out by Western traders as an asset only the Chinese themselves could fully enjoy.

The junk trade, nevertheless, did not flourish solely because of the above geographical factor and the character of the Chinese merchants (though such factors cannot be lightly ignored); it also came about as a historical accident. Precisely because of the considered importance of Siam's status as an entrepôt, as early as in the reigns of the Siamese kings Songtham (1611-1628) and Prasart Thong (1630-1655), Western (Portuguese, Dutch, British)[8] and Japanese traders were already active in the area. The fame of Chinese silks and gold, Japanese silver and copper, and spices of the East Indies, had been well established by the lucrative ventures of the Portuguese vessels in the sixteenth century, much to the envy of other European powers. The Portuguese captured Malacca in 1511, and commenced trading with Siam at Ayudhya, Pattani, Nakorn, Murgui, and Tenasserim after 1512. Following the acquisition of another base at Macao in 1557, the Portuguese clinched the European trade to China and Japan for the remainder of the century. They served as a main conveyor of Chinese silks to Japan, for indigenous Japanese ships were not permitted at Chinese ports by Chinese imperial decree.

Rise and Decline of Dutch Trade with Siam

Although Portuguese shipping in the Eastern Seas was, in the final analysis, only a fraction of the local Asian shipping at the time, it proved the value of the intra-Asian trade to other European states.[9] The first formidable competitors of the Portuguese were the Dutch who began to trade directly with the Eastern Seas after their independence from Spanish rule and after Philip II of Spain severed from the Dutch supplies of oriental goods normally available at Portugal in the latter quarter of the sixteenth century (after 1580). In 1602, the Vereeningte Oost Indische Compagnie (VOC) or the Dutch East India Company was chartered. One of its first acts was the establishment of factories (trading posts) at Pattani and Ayudhya for the purpose of competing with the Portuguese in the intra-Asian trade, and also to make up for the loss of supplies of pepper and fine spices by exchanging these products with European silver which was worth more in the East.[10] In the meantime, the British, impressed by news of successful Dutch voyages to the

East after 1596, formed the East India Company in 1600 to control and finance all English trade with the East. It differed from the Dutch counterpart founded two years later in that the British Company was entirely private whereas the Dutch was a national enterprise with full governmental support. In 1612, the British set up a factory at Ayudhya, and by 1615, another one at Pattani. Hoping to have a share in the Portuguese monopoly of Eastern goods, the British attempted to use Siam and Lower Siam as a base for acquiring Chinese goods brought in by visiting junks, and to send deerskin, buffalo horns, and sapan wood from Lower Siam to sell to Japan and China.[11] Direct trade between Ayudhya and Hirado was started by the British in 1614.

From the start, the Dutch schemed to push out the Portuguese from the Eastern Seas trade. In the first fifty years of their ventures, they established trading posts at Hirado (1609) and Nagasaki in Japan, founded Batavia in 1619 to control the spice trade of the Moluccas and Indonesia, and settled on the Pescadores in 1622 with the hope of establishing a home base to trade directly with Ming China and a halfway station for trade to Japan. (They were forced by the Chinese in 1625 to evacuate to Zeelandia on Formosa where they remained another thirty-eight years.) In addition, they finally wrested the control of Malacca from the Portuguese in 1641 thus eliminating the Portuguese commercial presence from mainland Southeast Asia. Although the Dutch were never able to capture Macao (they tried in 1622), the fall of Malacca marked a decisive end to Portuguese commercial power in the Eastern Seas; the Portuguese had earlier also lost the right to trade directly at Canton (1631), been expelled from Japan (1637), and lost the privilege of trading in the Philippines after Portugal broke off from Spain in 1640.

In the first few decades of the seventeenth century, the English profited from the intra-Asian trade. Direct trade with the Eastern Seas was not profitable because there was little demand for Western goods in the Eastern markets, except for specie and firearms, but growing competition from the Dutch, the unsuitability of principal British goods (woolen broadcloths) for the Asia market, loss of their trading stations in Japan in 1637, and failure to gain direct access to the China market eventually compelled them to concentrate on the development of India, and for the time being, leave the Dutch as the foremost Western traders in the region.

In establishing their commercial sphere of influence in the Eastern Seas, the Dutch also found Chinese merchants standing in their way. Since Western trade was actually grafted onto the junk trade, it was natural to find the ubiquitous presence of Chinese commercial interests. For instance, Chinese ships were active in the Japanese copper trade, bringing in Chinese silks to Hirado and Nagasaki to exchange for Japanese copper. This action undercut Dutch copper acquisition since Dutch ships could not go directly to China to secure the silks much coveted in the Japanese market. In addition their Western rivals, the Portuguese and the English, could naturally get Japanese copper at such places as Siam and Malacca where Chinese junks traded. So from the start the Dutch were decidedly anti-Chinese though they never abandoned their hope of trading directly in the Chinese market.

In Siam, the Dutch were also fully aware of Chinese influence as early as the 1630s (when they noted the practice by the Siamese king of using Chinese in the Japan trade), although the Dutch themselves managed to secure hides from Siamese kings. In the face of Chinese competition everywhere, the Dutch resorted to indiscriminate piracy and plunder of Chinese shipping on the high seas,[12] while setting up various obstacles against Chinese trade at Batavia, the center of their commercial empire in the East Indies. Their major attempt came in 1644 when, as a result of a brief armed confrontation with the Siamese court, they imposed an unequal treaty aimed specifically at controlling Siamese exports and stifling Chinese influence in the country's external trade. The imposed provisions included a guarantee that the Dutch would be assured of a continuous supply of desired items for their trade to Japan, Malacca, Batavia, and Holland, the right to trade anywhere in the country on payment of established duties, the Siamese king's pledge not to employ Chinese in the management of his royal ships engaged in trade, and the right of the Dutch to capture on the high seas any Siamese vessel found to be navigated by Chinese individuals.[13]

King Narai (r. 1656-1688) circumvented this unequal treaty with the Dutch in three ways. First, regarding the question of employing Chinese in royal ships, the king resorted to "hiring" Chinese-owned vessels to transport his cargo to China and Japan and sharing the profit with the vessels' owners. So, ironically, the Chinese traders, whose competition the Dutch had wanted to eliminate, became more entrenched than ever. Before long, the Dutch themselves decided not to press for the strict enforcement of this provision, one reason being that they feared that such a move would alienate the Manchus and jeopardize their attempt to open up direct trade with the new rulers in China. So, by the latter part of Narai's reign, the Chinese actively resumed the management of royal ships as before.[14] A second measure adopted by the shrewd monarch was the increased use of the machinery of the royal trading monopolies whereby the king became an active merchant competing with the Dutch. Lastly, the king turned to the French who, under Louis XIV (r. 1661-1715), established a trading company (1664) to compete with the Dutch and the English, and who extended their religious and military influence to the East, to counterbalance the Dutch through commercial, religious, and military concession. Narai pursued a pro-French policy principally with advice from his foreign cum financial minister (Praya Praklang), a Greek named Constantin Phaulcon (known in the Siamese annals as Praya Wijayen). Between 1683 and 1688, Phaulcon was the main architect of the Franco-Siamese military alliance.[15]

The death of Narai in 1688 and the abortive French attempt to seize control of the government with the aid of Phaulcon marked the abrupt decline of Western commercial fortunes in Siam. The French were expelled from Siam, and with them their nominal commercial influence. The British and the Portuguese also departed, having actually seen their commercial roles in the country decline to insignificance earlier. The only important group of Western merchants left were the Dutch who continued to be regarded with some favor by Narai's successor, Pra Petracha (r. 1689-1703) because they had not participated in the political intrigue that took place over the succession issue after Narai's death.[16] The new king even signed a new treaty with the Dutch East India Company confirming its monopoly of hides and adding another monopoly on tin.[17] Nevertheless, the Dutch Asiatic trade by this time was declining. The flow of gold, silver, and copper from China and Japan which had been the mainstay of Dutch maritime strength was being curtailed after the 1670s because of the forcible removal of the Dutch from Formosa by the Koxinga (Cheng Ch'eng-kung) forces, and the establishment of copper export quotas by the Japanese; the formerly lucrative spice trade was also suffering a setback. So by the close of the seventeenth century, the only Westerners with commercial interests who still remained in Siam were the Dutch, but what they had was only the semblance of formal representation.[18]

Toward the end of the century, some British ships were again calling at Ayudhya, but the lack of success of the British East India Company endeavors in Siam over the century (between 1623 and 1663, for instance, British trade with Siam was completely suspended) discouraged the British from reappointing a factor at Ayudhya.[19] They were by now fully entrenched in India anyway. As for the French, a reconciliation was attempted in 1698 with Siam when Father Tachard visited Ayudhya to conclude another treaty of friendship. According to historian W. A. R. Wood, the Dutch advised King Petracha against any rapprochement, playing on the king's fear of renewed French ambitions. This rejection presumably spelled an end to French interest in Siam, though French missionaries were allowed to remain on Siamese soil.[20]

By the beginning of the eighteenth century, the Dutch were still keeping factories at Ayudhya and Ligor, and were still buying tin and other products from Songkla to feed their trade with Japan. In 1706, however, the factories were closed down, and trade from Siam began to suffer steady losses at least until 1730, according to available statistics.[21] The Netherlands government repeatedly advocated complete withdrawal from Siam, but the Batavia government continued to recommend staying. The latter was interested in Siamese rice while also apprehensive that other powers might take the place of the Dutch should they pull out. So relations were maintained on a precarious level until the 1740s, when, as a result of a brawl between some Dutch sailors and Siamese at Ayud-hya, all the Dutch personnel, save for two, were withdrawn from Siam.[22] Their outposts were completely liquidated in 1762.

Contributing to the ultimate failure of Dutch commercial ventures was the fact that the Dutch were not receiving favorable treatment from the Siamese court, which by that time had grown almost exclusively pro-Chinese. For instance, in 1705, the head merchant of the Dutch East India Company complained that Dutch merchants had experienced much difficulty in securing sapan wood and tin, as well as in importing goods into Siam, since the government was not fulfilling its treaty obligations.[23] Commer-cial intercourse under the increasingly effective royal monopolies was growing more difficult, and as John Cady observes, "The suspicion of European traders in particular outweighed the court's interest in bribes and imported luxuries."[24]

The Dutch commercial decline in the Eastern Seas by this time had become general, and the character of the European market vis-à-vis Eastern goods was changing. In Asia, the Dutch liquidated their outpost at Tongkin in 1700, and abandoned their trading posts in Arabia and Persia in the 1750s. They never succeeded in estab-lishing direct trade with mainland China, for they also had to evacuate Formosa. As far as Japan was concerned, they maintained the small outpost at Nagasaki and carried out some profitable but limited trade. In the meantime, their hold on the East Indies with the exception of Java where considerable political expansion was carried out was also slipping. This situation was further com-pounded by the decline of Holland as a power in Europe particularly after the wars of the League of Augsburg (1689-1697) and the Spanish Succession (1701-1713) and the growing inefficiency and corruption in the Dutch East India Company, which ultimately led to the dissolution of the company in 1799.

Although for a moment in the seventeenth century it seemed that the Dutch would gain commercial hegemony in the Eastern

Seas, the eighteenth century was anything but a European century in Asia. The indigenous element that stood in the Europeans' way was, of course, the Chinese merchants insofar as that segment was affected by maritime commerce. Chinese merchants for some time also faced a challenge from the Japanese as well as from Western competitors. For the first three decades of the seventeenth century, Japanese maritime commerce with Siam was conducted in earnest, and although the Japanese vessels, the so-called *shu-in sen* or "ships with the red-seal authorization," were a common sight in the Eastern Seas they did not generally venture further south than Siam.

Japanese Trade with Siam

When the first Europeans (Portuguese) arrived in Japan in the 1540s, the various feudal lords (particularly of Kyushu) were already eager to trade with foreigners. Toward the close of the century, the development of Japanese overseas shipping had started, thanks to the following factors: unification efforts by Nobunaga and Hideyoshi; overseas expansion by Hideyoshi which created a sense of adventurism and a desire to seek material betterment, augmentation of knowledge about the world (the Eastern Seas in particular) brought about by the advent of the Portuguese and Chinese trading to Southeast Asia, improvement in shipbuilding and navigation; and closure of the Chinese market to the Japanese which compelled the latter to look south and eastward to Southeast Asia.[25]

In 1592, Hideyoshi began to dispense licenses (*shu-in*) to merchants of Kyoto, Nagasaki, Sakai, and so forth (backed by the various feudal lords), who had gained a great deal of economic power by the late Ashikaga period.[26] These licenses were for ships designated for Annam, Ligor, and Pattani. After the country finally became unified under Shogun Ieyasu, the policy of encouraging native shipping overseas continued. Siam soon became one of the principal areas of trade for such ships. Between 1604 and 1635, of the 355 *shu-in* ships which sailed to Southeast Asia, 55 were recorded as having traded directly with Ayudhya, while 7 went to Pattani. (Cochin China had 71–the highest number.)[27] Japanese ships trading to Siam hence were concentrated at Ayudhya. They usually left Nagasaki in late autumn and early winter, arriving at the mouth of the Chaopraya river (entrance to Ayudhya) in about a month. Normally with the help of the sizable Japanese settlement at the capital, these ships sold copper at the port, and acquired Chinese silks from junks there as well as Siamese produce, such as lead, deer hides, and sapan wood.[28]

At first, Japanese trade was strengthened by official sanction and encouragement. Ieyasu opened official contact with the Siamese court in 1606 for trading purposes, and, six years later, permitted the first ship from Siam to visit and trade at Japan. (Chinese junks of Siamese origin had actually traded to Japan as early as 1563, and with the Ryukyus even much earlier, but there had been no official approval as such.)[29] Under a system of partnership, feudal lords (daimyo), samurai associates of the Shogunate, and merchants put up considerable capital and actively invested in Siamese deer hides and sapan wood, which were shipped back to Japan in comparatively large vessels, to the consternation of the Dutch and even Chinese merchants. In these first years of the Shogunate, the country's economic position was strong, and the mining of silver and copper, the basis of Japan's wealth, prospered under government direction. At the close of the period, the Japanese enjoyed the fullest confidence of the Siamese court under King Songtham (r. 1611-1628), and Hirado and Pattani were dubbed "sister ports."[30] This period also coincided with the temporary setback in the Sino-Siamese trade brought on by the political upheaval in China as a result of the Manchu invasion. Thus the Siamese-Japanese trade was actually more important than the combined trade of Siam with other countries.[31] But misfortunes soon set in for the Japanese in their trade to Siam. In 1629, as a result of alleged Japanese complicity in the succession issue of the Siamese throne (an often tumultuous event), the sprawling Japanese settlements at Ayudhya and Ligor were uprooted, and in the following year, the Japanese fled the country or were massacred, shortly after Yamada Nagamasa, the former trusted lieutenant of King Songtham, died. The closure of Japan to foreign traders except for the Chinese and Dutch (at enclaves in Nagasaki) and for the Koreans (at Tsushima), coupled with this incident, sealed the fate of the Japanese trade to Siam. The reason for the *sakoku*, or closing of the country as the event is known in Japanese history, was that Hidetada, successor to the commercial-minded Ieyasu, feared the growing Western encroachment on Japan's sovereignty. The rivalry among the Spanish, Portuguese, Dutch, and English (who competed for trade privileges in Japan), and the growing influence of the Catholic Church and their conversion of the Japanese (including unemployed samurai) convinced the shogun that a defensive measure was necessary; hence, the decision to severely restrict outside contact.

These two events produced a profound effect on the future course of Siamese-Japanese trade. In the first place, Japanese were now forbidden to leave the country, and their three-masted vessels hitherto employed in foreign trade were broken up. The building of ships of over 500 *koku* or 2,500 bushels burden was forbidden. Furthermore, Japanese residing abroad were prohibited from returning to Japan. This decree, enunciated in 1636, was successfully implemented by 1641, and the closure was complete. In addition, since the Siamese court had committed offenses against Japanese nationals, Siamese vessels as such could no longer trade with Japan. After several efforts by the Siamese court to resume trade with Japan,[32] the Shogunate finally consented to permit ships from Siam to trade at Nagasaki, but they were to be Chinese ships or Chinese-style vessels managed by Chinese (*tōsen*).[33]

As far as Japan was concerned, the closure was not a major blow to the economy. The restriction of Japanese nationals with regard to overseas commerce and travel did not affect the majority of the people, nor did trade at Nagasaki which had consisted primarily of imports of Chinese silks, hides, spices, and so forth, and exports of copper and silver. Instead, the merchant class, which hitherto had been stimulated by the political unification of Japan and the ensuing peace, turned its energies to internal development.

Chapter II

THE SIAMESE TRADING STRUCTURE

Western and Japanese competition had been an obstacle to the Chinese junk trade in the Eastern Seas, but the peculiarities of the Siamese trading structure proved to be an asset. Since foreign trade was of considerable consequence for the Siamese court after the seventeenth century, its management inevitably became part of the state administration, though in the final analysis the court probably paid less attention to trade than it did to religious and military affairs. Actually, court-managed trade (or *wang-shih mao-i*) was characteristic of most Asian states. Where commerce was considered crucial, where gain, convenience, and control were the most important considerations, free trade was regarded as "non-beneficial" to the ruler; it was also a nuisance.

In a milieu where the king, theoretically the Brahminist-Buddhist Chakravatin or "Lord of the Universe," was the embodiment of the "state" and where commerce was regarded as a means of enriching his own domain, Praklang, or the Treasury, the bureau that dealt with trade, was formally organized to serve the king, the source of authority. As such, like the other departments in the elaborate bureaucratic structure, Praklang responded primarily to the king, and hence its effectiveness or survival depended entirely upon him. The Thai people on the whole had no part or interest in such a body.

When the Dutchman, Joost Schouten, was in Ayudhya in the 1630s, he observed that King Prasart Thong was "one of the richest Princes of India" (i.e. Southeast Asia and the Indian Ocean region), having acquired revenues in the millions from rice, sapan wood, saltpetre, tin, and lead. In addition, the king also had ships trading to Coromandel in India, and China, which brought him "incredible profit" at the expense of free merchants.[1] In the latter part of the seventeenth century, King Narai alone engrossed about one-third of the state income through royal monopolistic practices,[2] derived by the following means: measurement taxes on vessels calling at port for trade, import and export duties, profits from direct royal trading, right of pre-emption on imported cargoes, and the sale of export articles to calling vessels.[3]

The court-managed trade was consciously developed by Kings Prasart Thong and Narai, two able mercantilist rulers. (The former is generally credited with developing the trading monopolies to an advanced stage, and the latter was responsible for transforming them into an elaborate management.) The court-managed trade covered such areas as the acquisition and disposal of goods for foreign markets, the handling of imports, the assessment and collection of commercial duties, as well as the construction and staffing of royal junks.[4] The maintenance of this royal trading made the Siamese king dependent on Chinese who staffed the apparatus at all levels: royal factors, warehousemen, accountants, captains, seamen, and customs officials. According to G. William Skinner this cooperation came about during King Prasart Thong's reign,[5] creating in the royal trading organization, "a vested interest in the China trade."[6] The nature and scope of the Siamese court's intercourse with China not only fitted the prevailing mode of regulated and officially sanctioned trade of the day, but also made feasible a cordial and pragmatic trading relationship between the two countries under the ostensibly acknowledged framework of the tribute system. As shall be seen, tributary trade was justified and facilitated by the existence of royal trading practices which assured that all trade conducted was under official sanction and hence in proper order.

In the reign of King Trailokanat (r. 1488–1528), which may be said to have been the first period in which the Siamese court entered consciously into foreign trade, an Office of Ports (Krom-ta), was organized.[7] Within this office were three sections: Right Section (Krom-ta kwa) in charge of ports on the western side of the Malay peninsula and trade conducted primarily by Mohammedan (Persian) traders; Left Section (Krom-ta sai) in charge of ports on the Gulf of Siam and trade in the Eastern Seas conducted primarily by Chinese merchants;[8] and Central Section (Krom-ta klang) in charge of other foreign trade in general.[9] Prior to this time, the Siamese central civil administration was composed essentially of four working departments (Chatu-sadom, or, literally, "Four Pillars"): Treasury (Klang), Palace (Wang), Land (Na), and City (Vieng), apart from two other super ministries, Defense (Kalahom) and Civil Affairs (Mahattai) which were in charge of various outlying provinces, in addition to general civil and military duties. Originally, the Treasury or Praklang had few responsibilities since the income of the state was primarily in the form of corvée labor. When trade developed, however, it became one of the most important departments in the government. By the time of King Songtham, Chaopraya Kosatibodi (official title of the head of Praklang; he was commonly known among Westerners, however, simply as Praya Praklang or Barcelon, its Portuguese corruption; in Chinese official communications, he was called a *ta-k'u szu*) came to take charge of the department, and hence, was also referred to as Chao-ta, or "Port Master."[10]

The royal trading monopolies also dealt directly with foreign trade. They comprised, first of all, the royal warehouses (*klang sin-ka*) erected for the purpose of storing taxes from subjects and tributes from vassals. Since such collections were in kind, the court had to dispose of them by selling them to foreign vessels or transporting them to overseas markets (in junks outfitted by an official of Praklang known as Pipat-kosa). In return, with the help of the junk trade, desired goods were purchased and stored up in royal warehouses for use or for resale.

Furthermore, in the second half of the seventeenth century, King Narai maintained additional royal factories and collecting centers in the provinces under the direction of Praya Praklang. They were intended for the storage of "monopolized" items, commodities over which the court had declared sole rights or those that were required to be sold only to the government from particular areas. (Hence, tin was often taken from Lower Siam and deposited in the capital prior to its export, while lesser items could presumably be disposed of in provincial collecting centers by the king's appointed agents.) As a matter of course, large profits were derived from the sale of such prohibitive articles. Not only was there a usually exorbitant export duty levied on them, but it was alleged that the king charged exorbitant prices for them as well. For instance, George White, an employee of the British East India Company stationed at Ayudhya in the 1670s, observed that sapan wood, which was purchased by the king at the royal warehouse for 2.5 *salung* Siamese per picul, was in turn sold to foreigners by the court for 6 *salung* (3s. 9d.). Likewise, saltpetre, purchased by the king at 5 *baht* a picul (11s.3d/133.3lbs.) was in turn sold to foreigners at 17 *baht* (£ 2 1s.3d.).[11]

Simon de la Loubère, an observant French diplomat who visited Ayudhya in the 1680s, said that King Narai was engaged in wholesale and retail trade. The king maintained ships in the market places and was an export monopolist as well. He engrossed the sale of tin, saltpetre, elephant's teeth, sapan wood, and other products.[12]

There were important reasons for the royal monopoly on imports and exports. Apart from the obvious motive of maximizing profits, the control of exports was intended to restrict the flow of large quantities of scarce and valuable goods such as tin. Therefore the court made it mandatory that such articles could only be sold to the royal warehouses by indigenous merchants and bought from there directly by foreign merchants.[13] In the reigns of Kings Songtham and Narai, concern for the control of exports grew because of competition from the Dutch who, by written agreement at least, monopolized much of the country's export trade. They were thus in a position to feed their Japan market (part of the lucrative intra-Asian trade carried on at the time) where they sent sapan wood and deer hides, the main export commodities of Siam at the time. As a countermeasure, King Prasart Thong, also in order to increase state revenues, followed the example of his predecessor King Songtham, who placed foreign trade entirely under Praklang's supervision. Sa-nga Kanjanakapun comments on this mode of operation: "The purpose (behind the export monopoly) may have been to avoid any closure of the door to trade by the Dutch while the method employed would also have generated more state income.

It may be said that to have been a policy quite suited to the prevalent situation. As a result of it, the Dutch were quite angered by it, which led to later feuds [between them and the Siamese court]."[14]

King Prasart Thong further augmented the list of articles to be restricted to royal trading monopolies, and in spite of the treaties with the Dutch which supposedly granted later free trade (to an extent), even simple and insignificant items were declared goods on which the Siamese court claimed pre-emption on procurement. In this reign, rice also became a monopolized item in addition to the other articles already previous engrossed.[15]

As far as import monopolies were concerned, the logic behind the direct participation of the king was that those items imported were either of great strategic or commercial value or both. For instance, at this time the main imported articles brought in by Western traders in which the court had an interest were firearms and ammunition. Such items were considered strategic and hence had to be controlled solely by the authorities, as did copper, silver, and cowries, which were brought in from China and Japan. Furthermore, some luxury items, such as fine porcelain, screens, and silks, naturally appealed to the taste of the Siamese court which acquired them for its own use or for sale at a large profit.

Under King Narai, the monopoly system was developed even further to the point that the formerly lucrative Dutch trade suffered curtailment and only the Chinese seemed to thrive in this atmosphere.[16] In the meantime, Siamese trade is said to have increased a "thousandfold,"[17] for profits from the royal monopolies had grown considerably.

Such monopolistic practices also led to the arbitrary collection of duties and charges on goods for transaction. While benefiting the court's treasury immensely, a part of such levies undoubtedly went to line the pockets of individual officials in the Praklang. For example, in the time of Narai, Engelbert Kaemper described the head of the Praklang, one Praya Pipat, as an extortioner of foreign merchants.[18]

Traditionally in the Siamese government administration officials were remunerated not by fixed salaries, but by grants from the king which were based on the income of the court. Usually such payments were far from sufficient since with widespread polygamy traditional officials customarily supported large families, and hence had to seek extra sources of income. Those in charge of aspects of foreign trade either engaged themselves directly or indirectly in trade, or simply resorted to extortions from foreign merchants.[19]

In these circumstances, Simon de la Loubère expressed the frustration of Western merchants when he made the following observation concerning the "dilemma" faced by shippers: "[B]ecause that when the season of departure pressed on, the merchants choose rather to sell in great lots and dear to buy a new cargo, than to wait at Siam a new season to depart, without hopes of making a better trade."[20]

Siam's trade with China and Japan (as controlled by the Chinese), however, seems not to have been adversely affected, but, on the contrary, continued to flourish. One reason was that the Chinese had come to dominate the country's maritime trade to such an extent that the court could not afford to do without them. Increasing numbers of Chinese merchants went to Siam and collaborated with the Siamese court, to such an extent that in the second half of the seventeenth century, the Chinese quarters at Ayudhya and other coastal areas were bustling with commercial activities.

Siam's royal monopoly system also benefited the Chinese. It allowed individuals to attain the status of mandarin merchants through ennoblement as a reward for their services. This recognition served as an enticement for Chinese merchants whose status was officially downgraded in their indigenous society. Thus a sort of symbiotic relationship evolved to the extent that outsiders were effectively excluded from all areas of competition. This is a vital point in understanding the Siamese position in foreign trade, and explains why the junk trade was to remain the essential mode of Siam's foreign trade for many years.

One other important area of the royal trading monopolies was the construction of junks, to which the court naturally paid close attention because of its obvious value. Endowed with abundant raw materials, namely teak and other kinds of wood, Siam by the second half of the seventeenth century was already noted for its shipbuilding. Another reason for the boom in this activity, which took place toward the middle of the eighteenth century, was the active participation of Chinese. The Siamese court benefited in three ways from the construction of junks in Siam. First of all, it levied a *ka pak rua*, which was a tax payable upon the application for the construction of a vessel. In addition to this customary tax, which was calculated on the ship's breadth and length of 250 Siamese taels per *wa* (£125 for 6 ft.), the prospective builder was required to pay an additional *ka lim thong* (golden stake) fee payable to the king, members of the royal family, and various officials involved. The fee was usually computed in monetary equivalents with the value per stake per individual fixed beforehand.[21]

Last, but not least, the collection of duties on ships trading to Siam was also a major part of the monopoly system. In traditional Siam, four principal kinds of duties were assessed: *changkob*, levied on carriers of cargo both on land and at sea in accordance with their sizes; *akon*, assessed on the basis of the income of the people and as payment for concessions granted by the government to private individuals such as concessions for gambling or a liquor farm; *suei*, from the Amoy appellation of the Chinese term *shui*, levied on concessions on "essential" things, such as saltpetre, granted by the government to individuals who worked the concessions in lieu of the required corvée service; and *lucha*, a fee collected in return for the recognition by the government of interests belonging to private individuals for example, recognition of the right of a person over a piece of land or property.[22]

For the discussion on foreign trade, we are concerned primarily with the *changkob* duty. Meaning literally "the rudder of a vessel," *changkob* had been collected since the times of the Sukothai dynasty (A.D. 1238-1350, predecessor of the Ayudhya dynasty, A.D. 1350-1766) when Chinese junks went to Siam to trade. Customs officials at the entry point (to Chaopraya River and those along the river up to Ayudhya and elsewhere) obliged the junk to "raise its rudder," and when the tax or proper payment had been made, the vessel could then lower its rudder and proceed to the trading post. Later on, King Ramkamhaeng of the Sukothai dynasty (r. 1277–1317) decreed as a favor that this tax would no longer be levied on Chinese junks. In the Ayudhya period, the *changkob* tax was broadened to include duty on the cargo as well.[23]

Hence there were two kinds of *changkob* tax in the reign of King Narai. There was *changkob rua*, popularly known in Western terminology as a measurement fee, which was collected according to the size of the entering vessel.[24] H. G. Wales says that the distinction was made with regard to the assessment of this tax, according to the vessel's breadth and frequency of visits. Hence ships of four *wa* (26 ft.) and over, and accustomed to trading with Siam would be taxed 12 *baht* per *wa* (£ 1.5 per 6 ft. 6 in.) while another of the same size but not accustomed to trading with Siam would be assessed 20 *baht* (£ 2.5) per *wa*. The Chinese trader, since the Ramkamhaeng decree, paid no measurement fee.[25]

There was also *changkob sinka* levied on both import and export merchandise.[26] According to H. G. Wales, 3 percent of the assessed value of the cargo was levied as import duty for ships that called frequently while nonfrequent ones were taxed 5 percent.[27] In the second half of the seventeenth century, these rates were at one time or another increased from 8 to 10 percent.[28] Like China, Siam traditionally practiced the levying of duty on all cargo taken into the country, whether or not it was all eventually sold or some was carried back.[29] The export duty was, of course, contingent upon the kind of goods shipped out, and differed from one item to another.

In addition to the above duties, foreign merchants trading to Siam encountered another form of assessment called "extra-legal" exactions. For instance, when a Chinese junk called at a port, before any transaction could be carried out, the vessel was boarded by officials usually of the Krom-ta sai who had the right to select articles desired by the government. In the exercise of this pre-emption right, the officials could also demand "gifts" for both the court and themselves.[30] Western ships were similarily treated, as evidenced by an observation made by an Englishman visiting Siam at the turn of the nineteenth century.

He said: "The king is the principal merchant and engrosses the greatest part of the trade. When you have settled with the Datoo [*ta-t'ou* or "chief," referring here to the Siamese official in charge of the vessel] or the king's merchant [*sic*], what part of your cargo the king is to have (which is commonly called a present, unless he asks to buy anything in particular), some of the principal merchants of the place are called in to value them, and as they are valued, you are paid by the king, as a present, in the goods which he monopolises, at the highest price they will bring."[31]

Despite the rather elaborate structure within the Siamese government which dealt exclusively with foreign trade, and which was staffed largely by foreigners, namely Chinese and Mohammedans, it was of course not the most important part of the Siamese administration. Foreign trade on the whole did not significantly alter the closed, self-sufficient, indigenous village society that characterized Siam (and other parts of Asia) in the seventeenth and eighteenth centuries; it was only the occupation of a selected group or selected groups of people. But in spite of the limited basis of the money economy (or the rather slow turnover in trade compared with trade after the advent of Western or modern capitalism), those engaged in foreign trade helped ensure the supply of imported goods for the market in the intra-Asia trade, which in turn enhanced the well-being of the ruling class.[32] Specifically, the trading administration that existed in the Siamese government generated dynamism, though admittedly limited, for Chinese individuals and helped preserve a long-lasting relationship between Siam and China.

The trading structure also helped to provide the Siamese king with a source of revenue which he used to finance the country's administration and its frequent wars.

Finally, the Siamese trading structure enabled the Chinese junk trade to weather competition from other groups, and eventually to establish hegemony over the country's foreign trade. The Siamese government provided the sanction while Chinese junk traders carried out the actual operation of trading.

Chapter III

INITIAL PERIOD, 1652-1720:
CHINESE RESTRICTIONS ON TRADE

The Manchus, in conquering Southeast China, inherited an area that had supported an active junk trade with Southeast Asia and other locales in the Eastern Seas. But this territory also turned out to be the last secured area of the new dynasty in Peking. For close to forty years after their triumphant entry into the northern capital, the alien conquerors were to have a serious security problem along the coasts of Kwangtung, Fukien, and Chekiang, engendered by the continued existence of various anti-Manchu and Ming royalist groups which resisted the new regime.

It was in such a setting that trade between Ch'ing China and Ayudhya Siam commenced. For security reasons and for reasons tied to the principles of Ming dynasty foreign relations which the Manchus came to imitate, the beginnings of economic intercourse between the two countries were understandably in the form of tributary trade; only regulated and limited transactions through the medium of tribute presentation fixed at periodic intervals were officially permissible. The Manchu authorities apparently believed that only through such a mode of trade could possible abuses be controlled.

Working under such seeming restrictions, the Siamese court which controlled Siam's foreign trade was able to devise ingenious means to augment its volume of trade to the fullest extent the system would tolerate. Actually the Siamese deemed it appropriate to interpret liberally the allowances of the tributary trade system without destroying it. It seemed that from the early 1650s to the 1680s, prior to the stabilization of military and political conditions in Southeast China, the Siamese concentrated their efforts in the China trade on this tributary trade, though admittedly they also carried on some unauthorized trade to Fukien and Formosa (areas controlled by anti-Ch'ing elements) as well.

Nevertheless, the effort the Siamese put into developing the tributary trade provided a stimulus for private trade from the Chinese side (which had declined dramatically in the last years of the Ming dynasty), though such activity was, of course, banned. The fear of piracy and aid to and collaboration with various anti-Ch'ing elements were major motivations leading to the imposition. It may be said that such clandestine dealings also received both the direct and indirect blessings of the local authorities, particularly the government of Kwangtung under an autonomous Chinese general who pledged his support to the Manchus. The actual extent of this manner of trade with Siam cannot be fathomed, but it was certainly complementary to the ongoing tributary trade conducted at the official level, if not directly stimulated by it.

Soon after the Manchu conquest of China, a series of security measures were adopted as part of the new government's continued campaign against remnants of the Ming royalists in Southeast China, notably those under the Cheng family (first, Cheng Ch'eng-kung or Koxinga, and later, his son Cheng Ching). A ban on overseas travel and trade, known commonly as the *hai-chin* and patterned after the one instituted in the Ming dynasty, was imposed, outlawing the movement of ships from Kwangtung, Fukien, Chekiang, and Kiangnan (Chiang-nan), and efforts were made also to forcibly move settlements along the coast from Kwangtung and Fukien 30 to 50 li (11–18 miles) inland.[1] In such a situation, any foreign trade seemed virtually impossible. Nevertheless, through the resourcefulness of the Siamese court, and the willing cooperation it received from the Chinese side (via the authority of Canton officials representing the Manchu regime as well as the Chinese merchants), Sino-Siamese trade was made possible throughout the period. This trade as it then existed was in two forms: from the Siamese side, it was conducted mainly as tributary trade; on the Chinese side, it was handled by private merchants under the protection of the Canton regime of the Shang family (Shang K'o-hsi, conqueror of Kwangtung, who paid allegiance to the Manchus in return for rule over the province, and his son, Shang Chih-hsin). The other form, totally clandestine, was the trade between the Siamese court and the Cheng elements at Formosa and Fukien.

The Tributary Trade between Siam and China

Siam became the first tributary to be allowed to trade at
Canton when it presented tribute to the new dynasty there in
1652[2]—with the purpose of opening up trade. It was Shang K'o-hsi
who requested authorization from Peking to allow the Siamese
tributary vessels to conduct a limited trade at Canton. (Here we
see primarily Canton interests at work.)

The Manchu court had earlier adopted the previous Ming
model of tributary relations, when it issued an edict in 1647 inviting neighboring states in the Southeast Asian region to become
tributaries of the new regime. By and large, the Shun-chih Emperor
(r. 1644-1661) accepted the previous Chinese premise that "earnest
and respectful" vassal states should be allowed to conduct trade
accompanying the tribute presentation. It was probably due to
this precedent that the emperor readily approved Shang K'o-hsi's
request on behalf of the Siamese, with an understanding that the
trade would be carried out at Canton under strict tributary regulations.

In the first year of the dynasty, some regulations were laid
down pertaining to the procedures for receiving tribute envoys
arriving from across the ocean, the storing of tribute cargo, the
number of tribute ships and size of crew, a ban on the export of
materials considered to be of strategic value, including a provision
outlawing the presentation of gifts by the tributary to the governor,
governor-general, and other officials at port.[3] After the acceptance
of the first Siamese tribute mission, a series of additional regulations,
pertaining primarily to the conduct of tributary trade, was formu-
lated. In 1653, it was stipulated that goods brought in by tribute
ships were to be sold, and other business was to be conducted only
at the foreign envoy's residence (Ming's Huai-yuan i-kuan) in the
Hsi-kuan district outside Canton city for a period of three to five
days. The supervision would be the joint responsibility of the
governor, governor-general, and the provincial treasurer (*pu-cheng
shih*; his duties were formerly those of a provincial governor during
the Ming period, before newly created posts limited his status to
that of a treasurer). This was similar to the Ming practice of *tsai-*

kuan chiao-i (trade within the station) under the charge of the Bureau of Trading Junks (Shih-po-ssu).[4] In addition, Siamese cargo, in the form of ballast on board tribute ships, could not be sold upon its unloading from the ships, but instead was to be stored until permission for such a sale had been secured in writing from Peking. Furthermore, not only was private trade to be prohibited, the Ch'ing authorities also laid down more stringent regulations: when the main tribute ship (*cheng-kung ch'uan*) was not in port, no other types of official vessels connected in any way with the tribute presentation mission were to be allowed to carry out any form of commercial transaction, and local officials at Canton were also admonished to refrain from undertaking private business deals.[5]

After the K'ang-hsi Emperor (r. 1662–1722) came to the throne, the number in each suite of tribute ships from Siam was fixed (in 1664) permanently at three, designated as *cheng, fu,* and *hu* ships.[6] Three years later, the period for tribute presentation was also formally fixed at once every three years, with the size of the crew aboard each tribute vessel stipulated at no more than a hundred, included in which was to be a 22-member official entourage bearing the tribute from Canton to Peking for formal presentation to the Manchu emperor. Also it was made explicit that the three tribute ships were to be allowed.[7] The K'ang-hsi Emperor was particularly wary of any abuse arising from the tributary trade. In the beginning of his reign, King Narai dispatched a tribute mission to request permission to trade. But since the main tribute ship met a storm at sea, and only the accompanying *hu-kung* vessel made it to Canton, the local authorities refused to consider the request because the earlier Shun-chih stipulation required that the main tribute ship must be present in port before any trade could commence. Nevertheless, the Siamese sent another mission in three ships (including one designated as *pu-kung*, or "supplementary-tribute carrying") supposedly to make up for the previous unsuccessful one. Trade was subsequently permitted by Shang K'o-hsi after Peking had sent its approval of the tribute mission.[8] K'ang-hsi continued to reiterate the provision disallowing trade except within tribute presentation periods, and up to 1684 when the *hai-chin* order was rescinded, the Manchu court endeavored to enforce it stringently. In 1668, the Board of War, in trying to define the scope of trade permissible by the Siamese, as well as other foreign nations, made the following statement: "It has previously been ordered by the emperor that we meet with the Board of Rites to deliberate the question of trade by foreigners conducted outside of the tribute period. We have investigated and discovered that the *Collected Statutes* [or *Hui-tien*, the Ch'ing administrative code] has nothing on trade by foreign countries outside the tribute period, though in 1664 the Dutch were permitted to trade once in such fashion, and so were the Siamese in 1665. Nevertheless, by 1666, such (practice) was permanently stopped. Henceforth, if it is not in the tribute period, no trade is to be permitted."[9]

In 1667, in an effort to formalize the various regulations governing the tribute system,[10] K'ang-hsi reiterated the limitation of three ships to one suite of Siamese tribute ships, which, in addition, were required to pay measurement fees and duties on their ballast.[11] Also in an attempt to tighten the commercial conduct of the tribute system, he ordered a stoppage of such vessels as *chieh-kung* and *t'an-kung* which hitherto had been permitted to ply back and forth between Siam and Canton when the regular tribute ships were in China to present tribute; the rationalization was that this move was in accordance with the *hai-chin* policy then in effect.[12]

Up to this point, King Narai was able to maximize the commercial potentials of tribute missions by devising means to take advantage of the various allowances implicit in the mechanism of the tributary trade. Since the Ming dynasty different types of vessels involved in the tribute presentation rituals and the trade that followed were classified in various ways. Consequently, aside from the three "regular" formal tribute ships, a host of other vessels were attached, in one way or another, to the operation of the tribute presentation. Such carriers were variously known as *pu-kung ch'uan* (supplementary tribute ship), *chieh-kung ch'uan* (tribute-receiving ship) and *t'an-kung ch'uan* (visiting tribute ship). The *pu-kung* vessels supposedly carried supplementary tributes to make up for those that might have been lost or damaged in a previous mission. In the Chinese records, especially those pertaining to the early part of the nineteenth century, there was frequent mention of tribute ships wrecked at sea (especially in the vicinity off the Vietnam–Canton coasts) en route from Siam to Canton (or since they were not reported in official communications, some of the tribute supposedly lost could very well have found its way elsewhere through smuggling); and it may be assumed that the frequency of loss must have been high at any period, since sailing conditions and the constant threat of piracy made it a hazardous undertaking at the time. *T'an-kung* ships ostensibly "investigated" the irregular schedules of the sailings of the regular tribute ships. Finally, the *chieh-kung* vessels were so designated because they were assigned such duties as receiving the official tribute-bearing entourage returning from Peking, or imperial missives (*ch'ih-shu*) or imperial gifts (*shang-ssu*) from the Manchu court, or all of these.[13] All such vessels in one respect or another participated in the commercial venture of the tribute mission, for they were all considered part of the system and hence could carry out business transactions, a privilege denied to private ships.

Faced with the possibility of a sharp curtailment of tributary trade, Narai, nevertheless, was not about to be discouraged by such apparent restrictions. He had already, in 1664, secured Chinese approval to expand the market for Siamese business to include Peking, where the Siamese envoys were also at liberty to sell their ballast cargoes and to purchase anything they wished (Ch'ing authorities were following the Ming precedent of permitting tributary trade at the capital's T'ung-wen kuan for a maximum period of five days; this trade was under the supervision of the Board of Rites). Narai also continued to seek a relaxation of the instituted regulations.[14] As a result, the Siamese in time managed to get the Chinese court to grant duty exemptions on their ballast cargoes; K'ang-hsi eventually issued the following edict which was to remain the standard rule applicable to all foreign tribute ships regarding the question of taxation of all cargo accompanying the tribute ships: "The imposition of a duty on foreign ships' accompanying cargo is [actually] inappropriate . . . Goods taken on board the (regular) three tribute ships should no longer be taxed. But for the rest coming in to trade privately, officials shall assess them." [15]

Ballast Cargo

When Siamese tribute ships proceeded to China, they usually carried two cargoes, one for presentation to the Chinese court as formal tribute (or "tax") and the other for sale at Canton, known as "ballast cargo" (*ya-ch'ang huo-wu*).[16] The justification for carrying the second cargo, known sometimes as *chu-kung* (auxiliary tribute) cargo, was, of course, the Chinese court's expressed magnanimity to the tribute-presenting states. Such ballast cargo, especially in later stages of development like the eighteenth and nineteenth centuries, belonged not only to the Siamese king, but also to various members of the Siamese nobility whose interests were represented by certain members of the tribute mission. It would appear that in times when tributary trade was strictly interpreted and observed, many courtiers would attempt to utilize this channel for profit when other means were not as advantageous nor as easily available.

The returning Siamese missions had a good reason to demand a Chinese cargo shipment that would be used to "ballast" their vessels: insufficiently weighted carriers would be imperiled at sea. The first mention of the Ch'ing authorities allowing the Siamese to take aboard a Chinese "ballast" on the return voyage came in 1659 (in the reign of the Shun-chih Emperor) when a Siamese *t'an-kung* vessel dispatched by Narai to enquire after the well-being of his mission exchanged the ballast it had brought from Ayudhya to Canton for a Chinese kind, though the ship was required to pay measurement fees and taxes on the export cargo by the Board of Revenue.[17] This may be taken as a further breach in the Ch'ing system of tributary trade where commercial motives emerged as the prime consideration, where "tribute" (*kung*), initially stringently observed as the prime motive, gave way to the consideration for "market" (*shih*).

The question of the ballast becomes significant when one considers it in the following light. In conformity with the underlying principle of tribute mission with commercial aims, the Siamese court also sought another unique way to maximize the profits from the tribute missions. This involved essentially a "stretching-out" method which permitted tribute ships to trade at a maximum of four separate times in one mission. Ballast in such ships, ostensibly for the purpose of stabilizing the vessel, always constituted the bulk of the cargo for commercial transactions, and with the tax exemption status, was incorporated into a business scheme of considerable proportions. Both articles for presentation as tribute to the Chinese court and those for sale in China were usually collected from the royal warehouses at Ayudhya during this time, which had in turn drawn together such articles from other collection centers at Pattani, Songkla, and so on; in this respect the tribute system and the royal trading monopolies were complementary. Such shipments could be carried more than twice because of the loose interpretation of the standard rule governing the conduct of Siamese tribute presentation which was instituted in 1669, and which read in part: "Siam: one embassy every three years; the number in one suite of [tribute] ships shall not exceed three, with a crew not exceeding one hundred aboard each vessel. The envoy's party bound for Peking shall not exceed twenty-two strong . . . with the remainder [of the Siamese mission] staying behind at the frontier [Canton] . . . until the envoy returns and leads them back to their country."[18]

This narrow imposition on the movement of the Siamese tribute mission, insofar as the actual function of the ballast trade was concerned, was more apparent than real. First of all, when the Siamese mission reached Canton and as soon as the Peking-bound party set out from Canton (a journey involving about 7,000 li [about 2,500 miles] by water and overland and requiring normally three to four months [a round trip of six to eight months]),[19] many of those remaining behind at Canton did not settle down idly to wait for the envoy's return, as stipulated in the Chinese regulation above. Instead, as early as the first years of the K'ang-hsi reign, the

Siamese were already petitioning the Ch'ing authorities to permit some of the crew remaining behind at Canton to take the mission's vessels back to Siam for "reconditioning and refitting," and to be back at Canton in time to meet the returning party from Peking. In 1673, the Siamese king mentioned this subject in his gold leaf letter to the Chinese court, and the request was subsequently granted. In 1684, in an effort to reconfirm the initial request, the Siamese again brought up the subject, and the Manchu court once more approved the Siamese proposal.[20] These two instances created sanctions for all later practices. The process of sending tribute ships back and forth instead of having them wait at Canton naturally bore a marked commercial overtone. By making as many as four runs, the Siamese ships could secure several ballast cargoes for sale in one tribute mission. Each tribute embassy normally left Siam with the prevailing southwest monsoon in July or August and took from thirty to forty days to reach Canton.[21] While the Peking-bound official party took up to eight months to accomplish its mission, the Siamese ships would have ample time (two full sailing seasons) to return to Siam with the northeast monsoon, which starts in November, and to go back to Canton for the party in the following year, with the southwest monsoon.

Consequently, four possible portions of the ballast could be handled in the following fashion. The first consisted of Siamese goods taken aboard the three tribute ships when they carried the tribute embassy to Canton. Before 1684, as mentioned above, the Siamese ballast cargoes were usually stored up in Canton warehouses until the Board of Rites in Peking sent its approval for their disposal. The procedure for the transaction of such ballast cargoes was, first of all, for the linguist and captain of the Siamese ship to report the content of the ballast to the authorities of the Kwangchou prefecture, which in turn had to verify the report. A petition was then filed with the Board of Rites which took a minimum of ten days by fast imperial post carrier. When the approval came back, the Canton authorities, before allowing the goods to be sold, would have to ascertain which part of the ballast was taxable and which tax-exempt.[22]

This process naturally caused delay and inconvenience. King Narai, therefore, in 1684 when the political situation at Kwangtung had returned to normal, informed the Manchu government that when his tribute ships arrived at the Boca Tigris, the entrance to the city of Canton, local officials often hindered them and much time was wasted before the ships could finally proceed up the river to Canton. On top of that, officials also transferred the Siamese ballast cargo to warehouses where it was sealed up until the receipt of acknowledgment from Peking. Such practices had often caused the cargo to spoil, and great losses consequently resulted. Wishing to demonstrate his magnanimity, K'ang-hsi proclaimed an edict to the Canton officials declaring that thereafter Siamese ships reporting at the Boca Tigris could sail up to Canton immediately, and that their shipments could be taken ashore for proper transaction right away. In addition, the Siamese mission was to be allowed to purchase anything it desired beyond the list of restricted items.[23]

The emperor also ordered his Canton officials to let the Siamese vessels go back to Siam and to return the following season to pick up the Peking-bound party.[24] This move was in response to the Siamese request for the "reconditioning" of their ships. On this return trip, the vessels could load another ballast cargo consisting of Chinese articles for the Siamese market. Then, on the voyage back to Canton the following monsoon season, another ballast cargo of Siamese produce was taken for sale in China. Finally, when the mission had achieved its objective in China and was ready to return to Siam, yet another round of Chinese goods could be procured for "ballasting" the vessels.

Such a practice of loading four ballast cargoes in four runs for each mission must have been prevalent at the time, especially since these shipments were classified as duty-free. This leads Li Kuang-t'ao of Formosa's Academia Sinica to point out that the entire picture of the Siamese tribute presentation conforms with the official Ch'ing characterization of such undertakings as *hou-wang po-lai* (lit., "coming light, returning heavy," meaning that the Siamese benefited greatly from such a process), and was actually a kind of *wang-lai mao-i* (to-and-fro trade). Thus within this seemingly narrow and inflexible framework sizable economic opportunities were indeed to be found.[25]

A maximum of twelve loads of Siamese and Chinese goods could be traded by just three ships in one tribute mission. If we were to count the other types of vessels connected with the tribute presentation, such as the *chieh-kung* and *t'an-kung* which were also in time permitted to trade, the total of shipments per mission could reach as high as sixteen, assuming here that only one *chieh-kung* and one *t'an-kung* ship were also involved. Actually the number could be as high as twenty, if one also takes into account ships dispatched to supplement the regular mission on occasions such as the emperor's birthday, to thank the Manchus for extra-generous gifts accorded to a previous mission, and so forth. The same practice was carried out in the Ryukyuan trade. This trade, conducted by the Ryukyuan missions at Foochow, Fukien, the officially designated entry point for Ryukyuan embassies, reportedly fetched a handsome 100 percent profit under normal circumstances, but a profit as high as 500 to 600 percent was not unusual.[26]

An idea of the size of the ballast cargo may be derived from two vessels, one belonging to Li Ch'u and one to Yang Kuei, which had traded at Siam and called at Canton in the 1670s. Li and Yang, in their request to the Canton authorities for tax exemption on their ballast, revealed that such cargoes weighed 3,425 piculs (207 tons) and 2,547 piculs (154 tons) respectively, which actually represented only half of the ballast they had originally carried from Siam before they encountered a storm at sea, and in which losses resulted.[27] Li Kuang-t'ao is of the opinion that the size of these two vessels was about the same as that of the average Siamese tribute ship in the reign of King Narai, and feels it is safe to assume that each Siamese ship could have been carrying from 5,000 to 6,000 piculs (303 to 363 tons) as their ballast on each of their runs, which, indeed, is quite impressive.[28]

In short then, three elements made this scheme operational. First of all, the tribute ships had adequate time to make the necessary runs. During the eight or so months expended for the completion of the tribute presentation rituals in China, which included time for preparations, for the actual journeys to and from Peking, for the stay in the capital, and so forth, the ships could sail back to Siam and return to Canton in a matter of five months or so at the change of the sailing seasons. Two other elements were Siamese ingenuity in exploiting this scheme, and most importantly, Chinese acquiescence to such a practice under the *hou-wang po-lai* principle which actually prevailed up to the early decades of the nineteenth century.

The commercial worth of a tribute mission may be seen in the kind of gifts bestowed on the Siamese party at Peking, which supplemented the commercial transactions of ballast cargoes at Canton. Usually fine plain and wrought silks, porcelain, cash, and other types of high-value items were given to the Siamese court, as well as to the tribute bearers, in significant quantities.[29] The Ch'ing court, as a rule, accorded the Siamese party a generosity comparable to that given to envoys from Korea, Vietnam, and the Ryukyus.[30] Not only were such gifts highly prized by the Siamese aristocracy, they also fetched very attractive prices in the local market and for re-export to the West, considering that such things were normally restricted for export from China by private individuals at the time of the maritime ban and that individuals could only acquire them through the channel of tribute presentation. Chang Te-ch'ang thinks that some of the gifts received by the Siamese must have been resold by the Siamese before they left for Siam; the proceeds would then be accounted for as part of the overall tributary transactions by the Siamese court.[31]

Another advantage of trade conducted through tribute presentation was the procurement of "strategic" materials, usually copper, iron, and other metals prohibited for export from China under normal circumstances, by the Siamese mission; the Ch'ing authorities exempted these in the tributary context. There is no record of any attempt by the Siamese court at the time to use the tribute channel to acquire any specific strategic material, though it is possible they could have obtained some iron implements from

Canton in this manner. Nonetheless, the Siamese were to use the tributary channel to secure the desired metals more and more, especially in the second half of the eighteenth century when the country was at war with neighboring Burma, and weapons were needed.

Chinese Management

One crucial element in the Siamese tributary trade in the early part of the Ch'ing dynasty was the already total involvement of Chinese individuals in the management of the tribute ships and the handling of the trade. In the fifteenth and sixteenth centuries, the Chinese had begun to act on behalf of the Siamese court, conducting tributary trade with the Ming dynasty. One notable example was Hsieh Wen-pin, a Fukienese merchant from the Ting-chou prefecture in southern Fukien, who served under the Siamese king for this specific function. In spite of the Manchu-imposed ban on overseas travel and trade, the Siamese tributary trade must have been profitable enough for a good many Chinese to handle it. Consequently, the early Chinese settlers in Siam were principally merchants from Ch'üan-chou prefecture in southern Fukien and Canton in Kwangtung, who were connected with the Siamese tributary trade.[32] They were joined by a number of Ming loyalists and former ranking Ming officials who had fled to Southeast Asia and Siam.

Kularb Krisananon, a noted biographer and writer in the Rama IV reign of the Chakri dynasty (r. 1868-1909), mentioned two such officials who were surnamed Wang (in the original Fukienese appelation, Ong) and Ch'en (in the original Fukienese appellation, Tan) who became prominent at Ayudhya for their role in the court trade and their own privately conducted trade to Vietnam, China, Japan, Java, and the Malay peninsula, which was sanctioned by the Siamese court.[33] From a dispatch by George White, one learns that Narai sent annually a few vessels to trade not only at Canton, but sometimes clandestinely at Fukien also. Such an undertaking must have been the inspiration of adventurous Fukien merchants who apparently did not seem to run into any sort of official obstruction from the Chinese side. George White further noted that "the navigating and commercial affairs of the royal ships, whether at Siam or outside, are managed by Chinese. This place's merchants who are keepers and traders for the king are all Chinese. Among the king's merchants, the highest ranked and extremely capable is Okphra Sivepott (of Krom-ta sai)."[34]

In the thirty-odd years before the resumption of private trade was permitted by the Manchus, the Siamese under King Narai were able, with help from Chinese merchants, to manipulate the tribute system so that its commercial aspect could be fully exploited. When he came to the throne in 1657, Narai understood perfectly well from past precedents that tribute could be used as the tool to open up trade with China officially, as well as facilitating trade at Canton through the lessening of the frequent interference from local authorities. This arrangement would, besides, have served the political purpose of appeasing the Manchus and thus maintaining a state of political *modus vivendi*, if nothing more.[35]

In his reign, Narai dispatched a total of five formal missions to the Manchu court, averaging about one mission every six years. Although this number was by no means large, the techniques employed by Narai inevitably laid a sound foundation for later phases of the Sino-Siamese tributary trade. There are other factors to consider: first, in the two decades leading up to 1644, the year the Ming dynasty officially expired and the Ch'ing dynasty was proclaimed at Peking, Sino-Siamese trade had been on the decline. Second, the civil and military strife that ensued in Southeast China in the four decades after this date was responsible for restricting trading prospects in the area. Third, the Siamese court during this period was preoccupied with the growing political and economic encroachments on Siam by the Dutch. Still it is to be noted that the Siamese ships were not only the earliest to present tribute but also their ships called more frequently than any other foreign ships at Canton in the reigns of Shun-chih and K'ang-hsi.[36] Under the conditions of restrictive trade and the constant threat of civil disorder, what King Narai managed to accomplish through tributary trade may be seen as at least[37] a minor personal triumph.

Illegal Trade between Siam and China

In the decades of the *hai-chin* restriction, one should also consider the clandestine trade which was never totally suppressed, for the Chinese maritime bans were never as deliberate nor as exclusive as in the Japanese instance after 1636. Somehow the Ch'ing authorities could never totally control illegal trade primarily because of their lack of effective supervision and the ubiquitous collusion between merchants and certain local officials. In the first decade of Narai's reign, private merchants from China were already trading in rather large numbers at Ayudhya, Bangkok (farther south and gateway to Ayudhya), Ligor, Songkla, and Chantaburi. The Chinese traders were primarily from two sources: Canton and South Fukien.

At Canton, trading activities were within the sanction of local authorities. For instance, Shang K'o-hsi, the Canton ruler and one of the three Liaotung generals named "feudatory princes of the southern provinces" by the Manchus, was eager to enrich himself through foreign trade despite the *hai-chin*. Soon after he successfully sought the authorization for tributary trade at Canton for Siam in 1652, Shang proceeded to organize an "official merchant" system, and under his son, Shang Chih-hsin, the system was carried even further. A central guild (*kung-hang*) was created, which had a monopoly over the fishing and internal and external trade, as well as salt production and iron implements manufacturing (for example, the making of iron pans, *t'ieh-kuo*, whose exports were significant in the last part of the seventeenth century). One Hun-shunquin (Sheng Shang-ta), a salt merchant by profession, was appointed to head the organization.[38] Under him, a sub-guild (under the central guild) was formed which dealt specifically with foreign trade and was known in Chinese as *yang-hang*. Besides being in charge of the tributary trade, Shen Shang-ta also authorized some Chinese merchants to carry on illicit private trade,[39] and several of these ships were trading regularly with Ayudhya seven or eight years prior to the rescinding of the maritime ban in 1684.[40]

When the Shang regime was taken over by the Ch'ing court in 1680 (after the failure of the Revolt of the Three Feudatories in which Shang Chih-hsin participated), the commercial organizations established by the Shang family were also abolished, and for a brief period until 1684, active, free, and untaxed trade flourished through the greater part of Fatshan (Fo-shan), southwest of Canton, with all official controls on foreign trade, except for the dryland customs between Macao and the mainland, momentarily suspended.[41]

The majority of Chinese merchants trading to Siam at this time were South Fukienese. In the days prior to the Manchu conquest, Amoy (not to be taken in its restricted sense as meaning the city alone, but also, in a broader sense, the bay area serving the two adjacent prefectures of Chang-chou and Ch'üan-chou)[42] had been a prosperous trading center. Its significance in foreign trade came after the sixteenth century when it served as both a commercial center and a receiving point for the goods of its hinterland prefectures of Chang-chou and Ch'üan-chou.[43] From the early part of the seventeenth century, Fukienese trade with Southeast Asia was conducted mostly by families from these two prefectures, with many more going southward to Canton, Cochin-China, Siam (where they served the Siamese court as handlers of the tributary trade) as well as the Malay peninsula.[44] Chang-chou merchants reportedly had the most intimate commercial relationship with Siam in Narai's time, where they traded such Chinese products as silks, fine china, paper umbrellas, paper, and nankeen, for sapan wood, lead, and so forth.[45]

At the height of the Cheng rebellion, in the 1600s and 1670s, residents along the Fukien coast were forcibly moved inland, which at first had the effect of sharply curtailing foreign trade in the area. Then in 1674 the rebel forces recaptured Amoy temporarily and reopened it once again to foreign trade. Between 1674 and 1680, the Cheng forces under Cheng Ching also established themselves at various locales on the mainland from Hui-chou prefecture in northeastern Kwangtung to Amoy in southern Fukien.[46] This move had the effect of luring back such countries as Annam and Siam to trade with the returning population.[47] Siam at this time was noted by the Fukienese for its abundant rice, and for such items as tin, gems, rhinoceros horns, elephant's teeth, pepper, sapan wood, and wood for ship construction, which were all brought to Amoy for sale.[48] Even before this, the Manchus, in spite of their strict maritime ban, permitted ships from Fukien to sail to neighboring northeastern Kwangtung and Chekiang, where they procured rice to make up for the shortage of staples in South Fukien. Chang-chou and Ch'üan-chou supplied a number of rich merchants who were strongly backed by local officials.[49] A censor named Fu Yuan-ch'u gave the following account (probably in the early 1680s) in the Fukien-Formosa area in his petition to the Manchu court to make Amoy a port of entry for international trade. Noting that this area was already taking part in an active overseas trade in the 1640s, he described foreign trade in the Fukien-Formosa area for the K'ang-hsi Emperor: "Besides the traffickers from the Western Seas [Cambodia, etc.] and the Japanese, there are also the Siamese who bring products much needed, and consumed, by China, such as sapan wood, pepper, ivory, and rhinoceros horns, whereas the Franks, Portuguese, and Spanish bring coins very dexterously cast. Our people when trading with these different foreigners, in one case, barter their goods in exchange for those above-mentioned, whilst from the Spaniards and others, they receive nothing but silver dollars." He added that the foreigners were pleased to get raw silk from Hoochow (Hu-chou) and Kiangsi porcelain and Fukien preserved fruits and other delicacies from the Chinese.[50]

Concurrently, the Cheng faction on Taiwan exploited the products of Chang-chou and Ch'üan-chou, as well as those of Ch'ao-chou and Hui-chou, the two northeastern Kwangtung prefectures, in their trade with Siam.[51] In the early 1650s when Cheng Ch'eng-kung was still entrenched in South Fukien, he had five major commercial firms (*hang*) in Fukien, Soochow (Su-chou), Hangchow (Hang-chou), and Shantung engaging in foreign trade on his behalf. Up to 1656, there were several ships sailing annually to Formosa to trade with the Dutch who still maintained their stronghold on the island at Zeelandia. Cheng traded with Japan, Luzon, Siam, and Annam as well, in such items as silks (wrought and unwrought), sugar, gold, and porcelain. He also acquired silver, lead, and coins in Japan and sold these to Southeast Asia, getting in return important strategic materials such as tin and salt-petre for military use.[52] Cheng's overseas trading activities presented a threat to the Ch'ing government (for among other things, they sustained a large fighting force), leading, as we have seen above, to the government's adoption of measures to discourage trade by moving coastal inhabitants inland, and to the maintenance of cordial tribute relations with Siam and other countries. After the death of Cheng Ch'eng-kung, Cheng Ching retired to Formosa in 1664 (where he also forced the Dutch out), set about to reorganize a civil government on the island and opened up foreign trade. The Fukien coast during this period was relatively quiet, and some of the former coastal inhabitants were gradually slipping back. A good many traders in South Fukien became active supporters of the Cheng cause. With their help, Cheng Ching, in 1665, dispatched twenty junks to trade to Southeast Asia (ten of which went to Siam).[53]

Essentially, then, it seems that the *hai-chin* as a security measure had limited success in severing trade relationships between China and Southeast Asia. On the contrary, it has been demonstrated that the Ch'ing court, its officials, and other groups all had a vested interest in keeping commercial channels with foreign nations open, and the adoption of the Ming model of tributary trade actually created a loophole in the *hai-chin* control. By continuing to regard foreign trade as a form of concession the Celestial Empire was obliged to dispense to tributaries, the Ch'ing court could never hope to completely control and effectively restrict trading contacts between China and abroad.

So the situation by the 1670s resembled the time of the late Ming when commerce along the coast of Southeast China had developed to such an extent that the *hai-chin* that was officially proclaimed was never fully enforced or enforceable.

The 1680s was an eventful decade as far as the Sino-Siamese trade was concerned; during this period the junk trade began to flourish. Two events merit our attention in particular: the so-called

1688 Revolution, mentioned in Chapter 1, and the legalization of the private junk trade from Chinese ports in 1684-1685.

Historians have traditionally interpreted the 1688 episode as the death-knell of Siam's once prosperous foreign trade, and the beginning of a period of stagnation in the country's economy which was to last for over one and a half centuries. It has been commonly asserted that the two immediate successors to Narai, Pra Petracha (r. 1688-1703) and Prachao Sua (r. 1703-1709), allowed foreign trade to decline; even in the following reign of King Taisra (r. 1709-1733), the country's trade supposedly worsened. The following account by a French missionary entering Ayudhya in 1713 is often cited to support this argument: "I am surprised to see that the country has become quite stagnant throughout. Siam now is not like the Siam of fifty years ago [i.e. during Narai's reign] when we saw it for the first time. At present one does not see the many foreign ships or Siamese vessels engaged in foreign trade as they used to be."[54]

But records have tended to present the opposite of a sharp decline in foreign trade in post-Narai times. Although between 1689 and 1709, there was only one formal tribute mission from Siam in 1708 it does not mean that trade between Siam and China had been seriously curtailed, but rather that the tributary trade could have temporarily been subordinated by the rapid growth of private trade after the opening of China in 1684. The rise of the Chinese population in Siam at the time may serve as one indication of the proportional increase of the Sino-Siamese trade. In the beginning of the 1690s there were already some three thousand Chinese at Ayudhya and probably many more in other areas of the country. This number is significant when one considers that all foreign trade now came under the Chinese, and the fact that the entire Siamese population then did not exceed two million. By 1720, an English visitor to Ayudhya was saying that the Chinese residents there were "very numerous."[55]

A mid-eighteenth-century Japanese source, the *Tsūkō ichiran*, mentions that in the 1700s Siam was the gathering place for all sorts of shipping and was very prosperous. A report filed with the Nagasaki authorities in 1706 by the Dutch captains resident there concerning the general situation of trade in Siam, clearly underlined Chinese influence in Siamese trade.[56] And the Savary brothers of Bruslon, France, writing in the first two decades of the eighteenth century, noted that "the Chinese annually export large quantities of merchandise to Siam, and the imports from there at the same time are not small either."[57] Hence, what is perhaps nearer to the truth on Siam's foreign trade after Narai may be reflected in the following statement by W. A. Graham: "After the sea-borne trade with Europe was stopped, commerce with other Far Eastern countries increased rapidly, and soon a large junk fleet was devoted solely to the Chinese-Siamese trade. Concurrently, the king built a number of ships for foreign trade."[58]

As in the case of Manila in which there was continued Chinese-Spanish economic intercourse, the Chinese junks supplied Ayudhya with wealth and enhanced its status as a prominent Chinese settlement. Increasingly the annual sailings of junks to and from China may be said to constitute the basis of the country's prosperity.

In the meantime the Siamese court continued sending junks to trade with China regularly, both directly and to Japan via China. Siamese junks throughout the last quarter of the seventeenth century and early part of the eighteenth century were calling regularly at Chinese ports en route to and from Japan, while some Chinese vessels were also visiting Siam in their Japan trade. Available records also show that Siam maintained a constant direct trade with Chinese ports. In 1700, for instance, two Siamese ships traded to Namoa (Nan-ao, an island off Ch'ao-chou prefecture in Kwangtung) and Amoy, and in 1709, the Siamese monarch dispatched another ship to trade at Ningpo under a Fukienese shipmaster named Chou Hsiang.[59]

One important factor in the development of trade between China and Siam was, of course, the growing influence of the Chinese in Siamese officialdom. A contemporary French missionary observed in 1714 that a Chinese who became Praya Praklang in charge of the country's foreign relations was a favorite of the king. He appointed Chinese to important positions in government, including those dealing with trade. The missionary comments that, because of this close relationship between Praya Paklang and king, trade at this time was in the hands of the Chinese. "Even though the Siamese, Malays, and Moors [Mohammedans]," he comments, "are dissatisfied that Siam had been made to lean toward the Chinese in such fashion, they dare not raise their voices to object, knowing that the king listens to the Chinese with the Praya Praklang acting as the go-between."[60]

These conditions in Siam were further aided by the internal political developments of China. When the Cheng rebellion was finally suppressed in 1683 and Southeast China came under the full control of the Manchus, a basis existed for the re-opening of the region to Southeast Asian trade. K'ang-hsi declared in an edict in 1684 justifying his rescinding of the maritime ban that "The ocean had been opened for trade because allegedly this can benefit the livelihood of the people residing along the coast of Fukien and Kwangtung."

The edict went on to say that as the needs of people of these two provinces were met and there was a flow of money and goods, trade could benefit other provinces as well. It pointed out that large duties could be assessed and the revenue could be used by the government to supply the needs of the military at Fukien and Kwangtung, which would, in turn, lighten the tax burden of provinces in the interior. And so the reopening of the ocean to trade was ordered.[61]

The Manchu court also expected that trade from the Chinese side would directly benefit the imperial coffers. Not only would the court acquire expensive products (often of medicinal value) from foreign lands, such as bird's nests, elephant's teeth, rhinoceros horns, and the like, but by establishing customs houses to tax the foreign trade it would also acquire some extra income. Consequently, as soon as the *hai-chin* decree was rescinded, customs posts were erected in Kwangtung, Fukien, Chekiang, Kiangnan, and Shantung —with the headquarters for the first three provinces at Macao (later transferred to Canton), Chang-chou (later transferred to Amoy), and Ningpo respectively. A customs superintendent was stationed at each main customs post. He was known popularly as the hoppo, and his appointment was made through the Imperial Household (Nei-wu fu) in Peking. His constitutional powers included the handling of customs revenue for the government, both for the Board of Revenue and the Imperial Household. The Ch'ing revenue was of two types: the regular quota or *cheng-erh* to go to the Board of Revenue as part of the regular governmental earnings, and the surplus quota or *ying-yü* to go directly to the Imperial Household.[62] He was also empowered to supervise the movement of trade at port, for instance, to give chop for the ship to enter the river to go to Canton or another port, to grant freedom of access for merchants coming to trade, to assess measurement fees and so on.[63] Besides such constitutional powers, the hoppo also performed the function of collecting duties for the maintenance of his own office, for his appointment from Peking had to be bought in most cases.

The establishment of the customs superintendency signified the entrenchment of Ch'ing authority over the area, and some semblance of official control of foreign trade, eclipsed after the fall of the Shang fortunes in 1680, returned. But this time the influence was not in the hands of one single authority. There were other sources of power in the region as well as the hoppo. The governor, governor-general, and even the tartar-general, who exercised local administrative and military duties as set down by Peking, emerged to play a role in foreign trade. In a milieu where local government was still far from settled, such personages represented several loci of autonomous power which tended to stand behind their own commercial interests. Hence, H. B. Morse cites British East India Company sources as mentioning that in 1699 at Canton, some merchants were classified as the king's, viceroy's (governor-general's), and tartar-general's merchants, each "engaging in trade with the power of their respective masters behind them."[64] In 1700 there was also mention of a merchant representing the governor. In 1702, both Canton and Amoy are said to have had a king's or emperor's merchant. But by 1703-1704, apparently owing to the growing subordination of other kinds of "mandarin" merchants by the emperor's merchant, only the latter was mentioned. This occurrence, according to Morse, represents the consolidation of power by the hoppo. Most historians consider the hegemony of the emperor's merchant the first significant step toward the eventual monopoly system of foreign trade seen in the establishment of the hong system at Canton and Amoy. It is said that in this period after the rescinding of the *hai-chin*, the emperor's merchant at Canton was actually a salt merchant who had presented 42,000 taels (£14,000) to the Ch'ing court for the appointment.[65] And, during this time, even brokers belonging to the defunct foreign trade organization formed under Shang Chih-hsin also managed to re-emerge.

Despite official pronouncement of the liberalization of foreign trade, the continuation of the licensed or privileged merchant scheme after the lifting of the maritime ban shows that the action of the Ch'ing court toward foreign trade (as exemplified by the establishment of the customs superintendency) was geared toward official control. The system did not differ much from that of the Shang regime (except that the conduct of trade was now legally recognized).[66] This phenomenon reflects the basic Chinese official attitude of the governmental subordination of commerce.

Despite the continued presence of such a system of trade within restricted circles and other manifestations of a controlled system (such as that merchants trading overseas did not have complete freedom of action, but were subjected to a host of restrictions, including the amount of capital, tonnage of vessel, and so on), the lifting of the ban drew a large number of Chinese merchants to Canton. Most of them were from Ch'üan-chou prefecture, because these Fukienese had organized guilds for overseas trade ever since the Ming dynasty, and they did so with branches in Canton as well.

Another reason for the large number of Chinese overseas merchants in Canton was that, at this time, Canton was an active trading center, especially under Liang-Kuang Governor-General Wu Hsing-tso (from 1685-1689)—the first person to take charge briefly of the Canton customs superintendency—who was a known advocate of the resumption of foreign trade. From contemporary sources, we know that Canton was being frequented by foreign ships which came mainly from Southeast Asia and which also traded at Macao. A ship from Ch'ao-chou prefecture reported to the Nagasaki authorities in 1697 that Canton had been a flourishing trade center with many commercial vessels from different parts of the province (Kwangtung has the longest coastline in China) trading to various parts of the Eastern Seas, including Japan. A variety of products were manufactured in the vicinity of Canton city, products that were in demand abroad. Ch'u Ta-chun mentioned that Canton merchants traded sugar, metal tools, and other articles up and down the coast from Macao to the south, to Kiangnan in the north, as well as "traversing the 'eastern ocean' and the 'western ocean.'"[68] Among the goods carried, metal tools were perhaps the most popular. These articles, comprising iron pans, axes, spades, cast iron, metal tubes, and metal wire, had actually long been exported to Southeast Asia from the time of the Sung and Yuan dynasties, though historically they had been restricted officially, along with the export of unwrought iron (which, nonetheless, significantly enhanced their value in the neighboring markets).[69] Places with which Canton maintained the most prosperous commercial relations at this time were Japan, Manila, Indo-China, Achin (Sumatra), Malacca, Siam, and Batavia.[70]

Trade from Canton to Siam could have gone direct or via the island of Hainan. Active trade between Canton and Hainan was already in motion at this time, and judging from the commodities exchanged, it would seem that Hainan could very well have served as a middle point. Hainan sent to Canton products of Southeast Asia, while the latter sent back iron tools, Fukien cotton, and the like. The Savary brothers again provide us with a rather detailed list of exports to Siam around the turn of the eighteenth century: iron, tutenage, alum, cane sugar, copper tools, iron tools, copper wires, copper basins and pails, silks, sweetmeats, dried fruits, quicksilver, nankeen, marelle die, gum raisin, and golden threads. Such articles as metal tools fetched at least a 50 percent profit at the Siamese market, while sweetmeats brought as much as 60 percent.[71] French Jesuit l'Abbe de Choisy, writing from Ayudhya in 1685, indicated that the best Chinese raw silk sent from Canton could fetch a handsome 100 percent profit.[72] Canton also exported a much-coveted fine porcelain china to Siam. By the end of the Ming dynasty, the Siamese court had begun sending designs both for shapes and ornamentation to be carried out in porcelain, for excellent workmanship and designs were available at Canton.

Amoy was perhaps next to Canton in foreign trade. After the suppression of the Cheng factions from South Fukien and the Formosan Straits in 1683, Shih-lang, Manchu admiral and con-queror of Formosa, pointed out to the Ch'ing court the advantage of the resumption of overseas trade at Fukien.[73] His petition was approved, and Amoy was chosen as the main site for foreign trade of the province.[74] The Amoy customs superintendency was also established in 1685 upon the recommendation of Shih-lang. Until 1728, for over forty years, its administration was jointly under two customs superintendents: a Manchu and a Chinese.

Since the South Fukienese were from a rather unproductive area and imbued with a strong pecuniary interest and an adventur-ous spirit, they were quick to take advantage of the legalization of foreign trade which hitherto had been conducted clandestinely. George Hughes, Amoy commissioner for the Imperial Maritime Service in the nineteenth century, wrote that "a large and flourish-ing trade arose in consequence, and, indeed, the dimensions it attained, in so short a space of time, are quite remarkable."[75] The *Hsia-men chih*, local gazetteer for Amoy, records that Amoy authorities permitted local ships to trade to Batavia, Achin, Ayudhya, Chaiya (Siam), Ligor, Songkla, Johore, and other places in Southeast Asia.[76] Ships of Amoy trading overseas were known as *yang-ch'uan* (ocean ships) as opposed to those trading within the China waters, which were classified as *shang-ch'uan* (commercial ships.)[77] From the start, Amoy merchants (both native Fukienese and those from neighboring Chekiang province) trading to Southeast Asia were principally small-time capitalists, or to use J. C. van Leur's term, "pedlars." Eighteenth-century documents indicate that the outfitting of ships for foreign trade in Southeast China, as was also the case with Japan in the seventeenth century, was the basis of the "commenda" system. Under such a system, wealthy financiers in Fukien cooperated with handlers of ships in trading ventures. For the financiers, it was a matter of occasional investment of capital, but for those conducting the actual operation of trade overseas, it was in most cases an occupation. In later periods, particularly in the nineteenth century, small-time financiers would also pool their resources and operate shipping of their own, but it would seem that in the seventeenth century, the commenda system was most prevalent.[78]

The system of licensed merchants under official supervision also sprang up in Amoy. We have mentioned that Morse refers to an emperor's merchant (*huang-shang*) who organized the Amoy merchants into a close corps of a selected few, while the hoppo and tartar-general (the Manchu military governor) also had their own groups dealing with foreign trade. These officially backed merchants had more power than capital, but they made up for what they lacked by soliciting those wealthy merchants who were unlicensed and yet wished to engage in foreign trade. Under this arrangement (which caused British attempts to open up trade with Amoy to fail repeatedly throughout the seventeenth and early part of the eighteenth centuries), Fukienese shipping to Siam developed well, partly because South Fukienese had long maintained a cordial relationship with the Siamese court and knew local conditions. In addition the Fukienese junk trade to Siam was not served just by the port of Amoy, but also by other smaller ports in the area.[79] (Cities in Chang-chou and Ch'üan-chou were all situated near mouths of rivers connecting with the hinterland.) Finally, the commenda system was well suited to the mode of trade under official supervision.

Besides Canton and Amoy, Ningpo in Chekiang province in the last part of the seventeenth century also maintained a noticeable trade with Siam both at Ayudhya and Lower Siam. This trade was both direct and indirect in the form of the China–Japan–Siam triangular trade (as with Canton and Amoy). For awhile after the rescinding of the maritime ban in 1684, more Ningpo than Cantonese ships trading to Siam appeared in extant records. There was an intimate relationship between Fukien and Chekiang merchants, for, as we have mentioned, many Amoy merchants had originally come from Chekiang.[80] Western ships with a large investment did not fare better at Ningpo than they had at Amoy, for the benefits derived from the business venture were too small. Nevertheless, the junk trade was able to sustain itself because the investment (its mode and amount) corresponded more or less to the rate of return to be expected.[81]

After 1685, the number of Chinese ships calling at Siam increased steadily. According to one ship report at Nagasaki in 1686, several ships from China went there annually to trade. Another Chinese ship by 1707 was still reporting at Nagasaki that various provinces in China had ships trading to Siam.[82] In addition, vessels trading to Japan from Siam often supplied information about the movement of Chinese ships at Siam. Table 1 represents a record of Chinese ships trading to Siam as supplied to the Nagasaki authorities at various times. Although the data presented are by no means complete, one can at least get a partial picture of what transpired in the Sino-Siamese junk trade during the first few decades after the lifting of the maritime ban.

The Savary brothers summed up the spirit of trade from the Chinese side during this period:

> At present . . . by opening a commerce with other countries the Chinese have increased the means of enriching their own. They now not only suffer, but encourage both near and distant nations . . . to come and trade with them; and bring them the most valuable commodities; and, at the same time, allow their own people to disperse themselves unto a great number of foreign parts, whither they carry their silks, porcelain, Japan, and other curious manufactures and knicknacks, as well as their tea, medicinal roots, drugs, sugar, and other produce. They trade into most parts of East India; they go to Batavia, Malacca, Achen, Siam, etc. No wonder then that it is so opulent and powerful, when all the four parts of the globe contribute to make it so.[83]

In spite of a relatively vigorous start in the Sino-Siamese trade, participation in it by the Chinese side soon became affected by the erratic and restrictive policies of the Ch'ing government, a phenomenon

Table 1

Some Chinese Ships Trading to Siam between 1689 and 1702

Year	Number of Ships	Remarks
1689	14-15	from Canton, Chang-chou and Amoy; eventually proceeded to Japan.
1695	8	five from Amoy; 2 from Ningpo; and 1 from Canton.
1697	"at least" 4	called at Ayudhya.
1698	7	
1699	6	four went back to China; 2 to Japan.
1701	1	
1702	"over" 10	

Source: Hayashi Harunobu, Hayashi Nobuatsu, comps., Ura Ren' ichi, anno., *Ka-i hentai* (Tokyo, 1958), I, 633; II, 1271; II, 1274; II, 1736; II, 1947; II, 1998; III, 2081; III, 2205; III, 2232.

which remained ever-present in an official-controlled situation. After over thirty years of relatively free trade (notwithstanding various official inhibitions which were injected into the otherwise normal commercial intercourse between the two sides in most instances), the Chinese authorities at length reintroduced the maritime ban to Southeast Asia. One apparent cause leading to this move in 1717 was the fear among officials that foreigners and opportunistic Chinese would impoverish China by smuggling large quantities of rice (particularly to Luzon and Batavia), which had allegedly been carried aboard three to four hundred ships in former years.[84] K'ang-hsi himself was not totally convinced that the staple was being taken out of the country at such an alarming rate, but he wanted to prevent such an occurrence.[85]

More importantly, there were one or two other factors, both long-range and immediate, that led the Manchu court to finally reimpose the ban. The government had all along been wary of the activities of Chinese engaged in overseas trade, though the profit from such ventures allowed it to continue. For instance, the Ch'ing authorities, with characteristic suspicion, had often entertained the notion that such places as Luzon and Batavia might be havens for up to several thousand pirates and other "undesirable Chinese."[86] In 1716, K'ang-hsi was informed by local officials that many Chinese had gone to these ports and were not likely to return. Fearing that they might endanger national security, the emperor ordered the viceroy of Min-Che (Fukien and Chekiang provinces) to request the Dutch and Spaniards to repatriate them for execution. When this request fell on deaf ears, he proceeded to issue a decree ordering specifically Fukienese who had sailed abroad prior to 1712 to return under the mutual guarantee of shipping firms (ch'uan hu); those failing to comply after the enactment of the decree into law would face legal action if they should sneak back.[87]

Perhaps the most immediate reason for the closure of Southeast Asia to Chinese trade in 1712 stemmed directly from the discovery by the emperor during his southern tour at the Suchou (Soochow) shipyards that annually some thousand or more junks were going abroad, ostensibly to trade, but that only 50 to 60 percent of them managed to return with the remainder presumably sold. This discovery immediately stirred up imperial concern. In the first place, the emperor was led to believe that unscrupulous merchants took the ships and sold them overseas for large profits because the construction of such vessels required iron wood (t'ieh-li-tao or mesua ferrea L) for their keels, and such wood was grown only in Kwangtung. Secondly, the construction of junks was expensive, each large one requiring a capital of over ten thousand taels (£3,333).[88] This kind of expenditure would mean a severe drain of money from the country. K'ang-hsi thereupon imposed the death penalty (by decapitation) on those Chinese selling ships abroad, as well as a sentence of three months in the cangue for those who knew of such activity but did not report it.[89] As a firmer measure, the emperor banned private trade to Southeast Asia.[90] This ban applied to all ships from Kwangtung, Fukien, and Chekiang.[91] However, as ships from Southeast Asia continued to be allowed to trade with China, suggestions were also made to gain control over them—for instance, to limit the number calling at Canton annually.[92] Furthermore, areas along the coast considered "strategic," such as the island of Namoa,[93] were placed under tight surveillance in conformity with another imperial edict resorting to the re-enactment of the Ming practice of erecting forts and government posts along the Southeast China coastline.[94]

The imposition of the 1717 ban and the other restrictive measures of course did not stop the flow of the Chinese junk trade overseas entirely. For one thing, when the various decrees went into effect, many local Chinese merchants rushed to Macao which was still unaffected by the ban, in order to carry on their trade with Southeast Asia. Nevertheless, in the following year, the Manchu government managed to include Macao, still under China's nominal sovereignty though actually run by the Portuguese. Under the ban Liang-Kuang Viceroy Yang Lin forbade ships to trade to Southeast Asia and declared that although foreign ships could still trade at Macao they were forbidden to take Chinese on board. The edict banning trade did take into consideration the fact that Southeast Asia was abundant in rice on which China might eventually depend, indicating that the ban might not be permanent.

Nevertheless, the reimposition of the maritime ban was detrimental to the normal development of Chinese overseas trade. Although by the end of the eighteenth and the beginning of the nineteenth centuries the Eastern Seas were still served predominantly by Chinese junks, such vessels came to be owned primarily outside of China and trade was conducted for the benefit of the various tributaries of the Celestial Empire. In the face of the ever-present threat of official repression, the development of the Chinese junk trade was deprived of any assurance of success. As Chang Te-ch'ang comments, "Not only did the Chinese overseas merchants lose an [important] requisite of development, it became increasingly difficult to reverse the former position [of maritime supremacy]."[96]

Chapter IV

THE SINO-SIAMESE-JAPANESE TRIANGULAR TRADE

In order to understand the size of the Sino-Siamese trade, we must consider, apart from the direct two-dimensional trade between Siam and China, the three-way intercourse between Siam, China, and Japan which was conducted during King Narai's reign up to the first decades of the eighteenth century. Not only were Siamese ships trading to Japan manned and staffed by Chinese (as was the case with ships trading to China) and calling at Chinese ports on the way to or from Japan, but vessels from China frequently sailed to Siam to procure cargoes for their trade to Nagasaki as well. This triangular trade served the vital function of extending the scope of Siam's foreign trade and the Chinese junk trade in the Eastern Seas at a time when Sino-Siamese trade was still in a nascent state (in the Ch'ing period).

Political events in the first half of the seventeenth century necessitated a reclassification of ships trading from Siam to Japan as "Chinese" vessels, *tōsen*.[1] By the 1660s, the Siamese *tōsen* trade to Japan had become established, which in turn meant that the Chinese, who along with the Dutch were the only foreigners permitted to remain trading with Japan after the latter's closure in 1636, had also gained a decided advantage. Western observers in Siam in the 1670s and 1680s all attested to the strong Chinese control of that branch of trade.[2] Nicholas Gervaise himself said: "As the king of Siam has numbers of Chinese in his domains, it is by their means that he continues to carry on the commerce with the Japanese, which has always been so profitable to him. Every year he sends to Japan several of his vessels manned by Chinese and accompanied by some Siamese mandarins, who have an eye to all that goes on."[3]

In Narai's time a number of ships were sent in this manner to Japan; it must be said that ships from other parts of Southeast Asia were permitted to trade at Nagasaki under the same *tōsen* system. In the Tokugawa reckoning after the country's closure, Chinese ships were given three distinctions: hence, ships from the China ports of Kiangsu and Chekiang were classified as *kuchibune* (mouth ships), those from the southern ports of Fukien and Kwangtung were known as *nakaokubune* (middle-inner ships), and Chinese-style junks from Southeast Asian ports were called *okubune* (inner ships).[4] Iwao Sei'ichi says that between 1661 and 1688, a period of twenty-eight years, Siam dispatched some forty-three ships (*tōsen*) to Nagasaki. Among them, thirty-five belonged to the king, the rest were owned by the queen, princes, and other high-ranking officials and rich merchants.[5] According to Ch'en Ching-ho, sixty-four Siamese ships traded to Japan between 1657 and 1688,[6] and between 1689 and 1723, no fewer than forty-one called.[7]

Siamese goods were handled by the Chinese guild at Nagasaki which usually sold them to the Japanese by auction (with a commission given to the Japanese Treasury department which approved the sales). Of the Siamese exports, deerskin was the most important; other articles were sapan wood, buffalo skin, elephant's teeth, rhinoceros horn, betel nut, tin, lead, and rosewood which were not too divergent from exports to China.[8] Siam also reshipped raw silks it acquired from Canton and Macao to Japan. Siamese *tōsen* ships acquired desired goods from Japan through the Japanese Treasury (Hiokwan) in exchange for the cargoes brought in (that is, in the barter system). Copper, Japan's principal export and a monopolized item of the government, was the main import for Siam (the Siamese king also engrossed its sale in the kingdom).[9] Other imports included pearl shells, iron, screens, camphor, and crockery.

The rescinding of the 1684 maritime ban had a significant impact on the Siamese-Japanese trade. One immediate result was that it led to a tremendous upsurge of Chinese shipping in general to Japan. For example, in 1684, just prior to the opening of overseas shipping, 24 vessels visited Nagasaki; in 1685, the number jumped up to 73. It was 84 a year later, 111 in 1687, and 117 in 1688.[10] This phenomenon in turn produced three additional factors important to the course of the Siamese-Japanese trade. First, more ships from Siam came to be managed by Chinese as more manpower was made available owing to increased Chinese immigration into the country. This increase had the effect of making Siamese shipping to Japan appear even more a part of the *tōsen* shipping, while the same development was taking place in other parts of Southeast Asia.[11]

Between 1651 and 1700, 130 ships, managed by Chinese, are said to have visited Nagasaki from various parts of Siam.[12] These were royal ships from Ayudhya, as well as those sailing from Lower Siam ports such as Ligor, Songkla, and Pattani, which, in actual fact, were originally Chinese ships sailing from China.[13] The Shogunate had made it a mandatory requirement after the first half of the seventeenth century for foreign ships calling at Nagasaki to make detailed reports pertaining to certain information about the ship (i.e. its place of origin, its crew, and the name of the captain, etc.), including any occurrences that the ship might have witnessed or experienced on its way to Japan. The purpose was ostensibly to keep tabs on what was happening in the world outside.[14] The reports given by Siamese ships were collectively known as the *Shinra tōsen fusetsu* (Reports from Siam's China ships). Two recurring features in these reports are: the presence of a Chinese shipmaster (*ch'uan-t'ou*) and a Chinese crew often 90 to 100 strong (with the exception of those from Lower Siam, Siamese ships were among the largest at the time) accompanied by some Siamese officials, and the calling at Chinese ports on the way to or from Japan, notably in the vicinity of Amoy and Namoa Island.

There are one or two points to be noticed in these reports. First, the Siamese ships frequently called at Chinese ports on the way to and from Japan, either for repairs, to seek shelter from storms, or simply to load and unload cargoes. These Chinese ports had an important function in the triangular trade because on all such occasions goods were exchanged among the three countries. For instance, one Siamese ship in 1699, supposedly damaged on the way back from Nagasaki to Siam, disposed of the copper acquired in Japan at Amoy and took a local cargo in its place. There was a similar case in 1700. Amoy, Canton, and Namoa were frequently stopping places for Siamese junks trading to Japan (Amoy in particular), which may reflect the pervasive influence that the South Fukienese had with Siam at this time; silks and sugar could be had in abundance there and they fetched excellent prices in the Japanese market.[15] Shipmasters in charge of royal Siamese ships, as we have mentioned briefly, were often Fukienese from the Amoy area.[16] A good illustration is one Ch'en Chao-k'ua who was born at Amoy and settled in Siam for a number of years; he eventually served the court with the title of Luang Chinchuli-samutpakdi.[17]

The Chinese management of Siamese ships never met with any official objection from the Chinese government at this time, although a policy existed prohibiting Chinese from serving in such a capacity for foreigners. This prohibition was a part of the overall effort to prevent contact between Chinese and foreigners on an intimate level, which was viewed officially as a source of potential trouble. This objection ultimately became an important issue in Sino-Siamese relations in the early part of the nineteenth century when the Ch'ing court sought to put a curb on such a practice by the Siamese king.[18] There is no evidence that Siamese ships trading to Japan and frequenting Chinese ports ever ran into trouble with the local Chinese authorities over this issue. Two explanations may be offered herein: either those managing the Siamese ships had ways to strike up an understanding with local officials, or, since such ships were classified by the Japanese as *tōsen,* it could be argued that they were not exactly foreign ships run by Chinese. Nevertheless, the point is that since the Manchu government had cast a suspicious eye on the so-called "unstable elements" going abroad to Southeast Asia, official policy would naturally have been averse to such a practice.[19]

In addition to the Siamese ships from Ayudhya, there were a number of other ships which originally belonged to merchants in China and came from a Chinese port, but nonetheless were treated as being from Siam because they had visited Siam and were out-fitted with Siamese goods before proceeding eventually to Japan. Such a class of ships formed an important segment of the triangular trade as well as serving a supplementary role in the direct Sino-Siamese trade. The practice must have dated back to the first part of the seventeenth century when ships from Fukien and Chekiang started sailing to the Lower Siam ports of Pattani, Songkla, and Ligor, where the Dutch had already established trading contacts and where they maintained centers for trade with Japan. After the maritime ban was lifted in 1684, it follows that the merchants of these two provinces would resume conducting this branch of trade in full force, especially since Lower Siam traditionally offered an abundant supply of hides and tin which were in demand in the Nagasaki market.[20]

Pattani (known to the Chinese as Pei-ta-nien), a dependency of Siam, at various times in the seventeenth and early eighteenth centuries participated in an active trade conducted by Fukien and Chekiang ships. Considered by the Dutch as the "door for China and Japan,"[21] Pattani allowed Chinese to trade there with a special provision of duty exemption on local produce taken aboard the junk (a practice granted as early as 1566 when the notorious Chinese pirate Lin Tao-ch'ien of Ch'ao-chou prefecture settled there with his gang).[22] In the seventeenth century, apart from the Dutch traffic, the Pattani trade with Japan was in the hands of the Japanese and South Fukienese.[23] With the rupture of relations between Siam and Japan, the trade from Pattani to Nagasaki involved essentially ships originating from China which carried Pattani produce to trade at the Japanese port. Kanemitsu Kanazawa's *Wa-Kan senyo shu* (a work published in 1761) says in its description of Pattani that the place did not send ships directly to Japan, but rather that Chinese went there and transported its produce to Nagasaki.[24] Nishikawa Tadahide, writing about half a century earlier, also commented that Chinese ships that went to Pattani were called "Pattani ships," and that local inhabitants did not send out vessels of their own.[25] The first "Pattani ship" is said to have traded to Nagasaki in 1648.

According to information from the *Ka-i hentai*, the usual operation between Pattani and Nagasaki was that the Chinese vessel from either Fukien or Chekiang sailed for Pattani, discharged its Chinese cargo in exchange for an indigenous one, organized a new crew, and then set sail for Japan.[26] Sometimes, such ships were also sold to Pattani Chinese upon their arrival. Like the Ayudhya ships, Pattani ships were required to give reports to the Japanese authorities upon their arrival at Nagasaki.

In all, no less than eighteen ships from Pattani traded to Nagasaki, mostly in the last two decades of the seventeenth century.[27] This was a period when trade was liberalized by the Manchu court and Chinese merchants of Chekiang and Fukien could sail to Pattani and Japan legally.

Lying north of Pattani, the port of Songkla (known to the Chinese as Sung-k'a) also played a role in the triangular trade particularly in the last two decades of the seventeenth century. Its birds' nests, tin, dried shrimp, hides, sea slugs, and cotton had been well-known articles of trade to Chinese merchants.[28] But trading relations with Japan were initiated by the Dutch who maintained a factory there—and who tried to keep their rivals, the British and Chinese, out of both Pattani and Songkla.[29] South Fukienese, however, who traded to Pattani also stopped by to trade at Songkla on the way, and increasingly they came to supplant the Dutch in the direct trade between Songkla and Nagasaki, just as in the case of the Pattani-Nagasaki trade. As an established practice, Fukien traders usually secured hides from Songkla, stopped by at Amoy for another cargo of sugar, and finally proceeded to trade both articles at Nagasaki. In addition to the Fukienese merchants, there were occasionally some ships' traders from neighboring Ch'ao-chou prefecture in Kwangtung who undertook the triangular trade from Songkla, but on the whole, as in the case of Pattani, the ships from Chekiang and Fukien were dominant.[30] In the two decades of trade to Japan by Songkla ships, a total of seven vessels were recorded.

Ligor (Nakorn Si Thammarat or Nakorn for short; known in Chinese as Liu-k'un) is another important port in Lower Siam which maintained a role in the triangular trade.[31] Its proximity to Songkla and Pattani—and hence relative accessibility—and the similarity of products gave Ligor a share in the prosperity of its neighboring southern ports. Similarly, in the last two decades of the seventeenth century, Chinese ships from China frequented the port before going on to Japan, and consequently were designated as "Ligor ships." In Hayakawa Junsaburo's *Tsūkō ichiran* he says: "Chinese came, to this state [*sic*], buying its products, and setting sail for Nagasaki in vessels designated as Ligor ships."[32] Nishikawa Tadahide wrote at the turn of the eighteenth century: "This state's [*sic*] ships had never ventured to Japan; only Chinese who had gone there brought ships to Japan."[33] From a report given to the Nagasaki authorities by a Ligor ship in 1693, we discover that every year one or two ships from China traded with Ligor.[34] As far as the trading to Japan done by Ligor ships, this trade is said to have commenced in the 1660s with ships from Fukien and Chekiang proceeding to Ligor to acquire an indigenous cargo for the Japanese market.[35] Ligor ships, as in the cases of Pattani and Songkla ships, were owned by private Chinese merchants and not by the Siamese court. Hence, there is no mention of Siamese officials accompanying Lower Siam ships to Nagasaki as they did with vessels from Ayudhya.

Japan had several items desired by foreigners, particularly silver and copper. Until the 1720s China attempted to import copper from Japan for coinage, in order to supplement the inadequate supplies from the mines of Yunnan, Szechwan, and Kwangtung. Chinese traders, especially those from Chekiang and Soochow, took wrought silks, sugar, medicine, books, and embroidered goods to Nagasaki to exchange for copper, while others from Fukien and Chekiang went to Southeast Asia to secure hides for the Japanese market—as in the cases of Ligor, Songkla, and Pattani ships.[36] In the same fashion, Siam, which wanted Japanese copper both for domestic consumption and for re-exports, sent their ships to Nagasaki under the fictitious designation of *tōsen*, to secure the valuable item. In 1685, the Tokugawa Shogunate, alarmed over the serious drain of copper (as well as silver coins) in the light of increased Chinese shipping as a result of the abolition of the Chinese maritime ban, imposed a limit of 600,000 silver taels a year on the volume of trade permitted the Chinese.[37] In addition, all export of specie, both copper and silver, was banned, and only merchandise, such as refined copper in bulk, was exportable.

This official action had an effect on Siamese shipping. In the following year, a Siamese junk, one of a group bound for trade at Nagasaki, was allowed to dispose of only a limited portion of its cargo, just enough to pay the expenses of the return voyage. Two other Siamese vessels that year reported to Ayudhya that they had received the same treatment.[38] Nevertheless, Siam's trade with Japan continued. Contemporary observers like de Chaumont (French envoy to Siam in 1685-1686) and de la Loubère all mentioned the continued Siamese importation of Japanese copper, though its amount must have been considerably less than in previous years.

In the meantime, the tremendous upsurge in Chinese shipping to Japan created an additional problem of smuggling and illicit trade which had been in existence since the country's closure in the 1630s. Kyushu and the southern approaches to Nagasaki were centers for such activities. (*Ka-i hentai* reports, of course, do not contain information about Chinese ships' involvement, but such a possibility existed, even for Siamese ships.) In 1689, in order to strengthen supervision, fixed quarters called the *tojinkan* (Chinese quarters) were assigned to Chinese merchants trading to Nagasaki. In that same year, the Shogunate laid down a restrictive schedule of the time of the voyage and the number of Chinese ships from various places allowed to trade at Nagasaki:

1. "Spring" ships (those permitted to trade in the spring season): twenty in number, comprising five ships from Nanking, seven from Ningpo, two from P'u-t'o-shan (off Chekiang), and six from Foochow;
2. "Summer" ships: thirty in number, comprising three ships from Ningpo, three from Chang-chou, two from Batavia, one from Cambodia, one from P'u-t'o-shan, five from Amoy, five from Pattani, four from Foochow, and two from Canton;
3. "Autumn" ships: twenty in number, comprising two ships

from Nanking, three from Annam, two from Siam, two
from Kao-chou, three from Foochow, one from Ningpo,
four from Tongkin, and two from Ch'ao-chou.

The total number of Chinese ships allowed came therefore to
seventy annually. There were also to be issued permits (*shimpai*)
specifying their periods of trade.[39]

This effort to control Chinese shipping, which after all was
similar to the system used by the Manchu court in dealing with
foreign tributary trade, had a stifling effect on the normal development of the triangular trade. Although by 1698 the number of
Chinese ships permitted to trade at Nagasaki each year was raised
to eighty (an increase of ten), there was still a limitation imposed
on the amount of wrought copper, which was to be no more than
the equivalent value of two thousand taels per Chinese vessel—even
though this amount actually represents at least twice the value of
copper allowable according to the 1685 regulation.[40]

By the turn of the eighteenth century, Japan continued to
experience a serious strain in copper production, a problem that
necessitated further restrictions in its export. Songkla and Ligor
ships became the first casualties; thenceforth, records concerning
their trade to Japan ceased. The next in line were the Pattani ships
which suffered the same fate after 1709. In 1715, a new series of
restrictions was further instituted. Known officially as the Shotoku
shinritsu (New regulations of the Shotoku reign), the new measures
further limited the number, tonnage, and value of Dutch and
Chinese ships (both the *kuchibune* from mainland China and the
okubune from Southeast Asia). Of a total of thirty Chinese ships
permissible per year (a reduction of fifty) with a total value of
6,000 *kan* (about 4 million lbs.) of copper, Siam's allotment was
an annual vessel with a copper cargo not exceeding 300 *kan*
(200,000 lbs.) of silver in value.[41] Ships from Pattani, Songkla, and
Ligor were not allotted any quota at all. The new measures were
to further slow down the Siamese traffic which, as shown, had
already started to decline in the first decade of the eighteenth
century. In addition, the value allowed the single annual Siamese

vessel for copper export suffered an additional reduction after 1715: it went down to 150 *kan* (100,000 lbs.) of silver for a quantity of copper fixed at 36,000 catties (as compared to 63,000 catties allowed in 1715).[42] As far as overall Chinese shipping was concerned, in 1717 its quota was temporarily raised to forty and the export value to 8,000 *kan* (4 m. lbs.), but thereafter both were reduced.[43] In 1719, the number of Chinese ships was cut back to thirty and the copper export value rolled back to half of 1717. While Siam was steadily curtailed in its copper supplies from Japan, it found a new source in China—even though it was not a phenomenally large one. Exports of copper had been banned by K'ang-hsi in 1683, but after Southeast Asia was reopened to Chinese merchants, Chinese copper flowed into the region.[44]

At this juncture, it may be relevant to consider briefly the profitability of the triangular trade as conducted from Siam. We may from the start safely assume that Siamese and Chinese ships became involved in transactions in order to make the great risks and long distances of navigation worthwhile. There are no readily available sets of figures to show the extent of profits in this branch of trade; however, an idea may be formed by examining Table 2 which gives the price differentials of certain merchandise quoted at Canton and Japan. Siamese ships and others engaged in the triangular trade more often than not stopped at Chinese ports en route to secure additional cargoes for sale at Nagasaki.

The big price differences for most of the items appearing in the table show that it was indeed profitable to trade with Japan at the time.[45] Had it not been for the tight restrictions imposed by the Tokugawa Shogunate, Siam's triangular trade would have continued strong or at least would have lasted much longer.

In the triangular trade, there were sometimes Chinese ships that traded with Japan first before proceeding to Siam, then returned eventually to China. Such ships would as a rule visit Ayudhya. There is no information as to how frequently Chinese ships conducted the triangular trade in such a manner, but we are fortunate to have a record of one such trip around the time of the abolition of the Chinese maritime ban in 1684, which indicates the dimension of the three-way trade.

Table 2

Price Differentials of Certain Items Quoted at Canton and Nagasaki
at the Turn of the Eighteenth Century

Item	Original Price at Canton	Selling Price at Nagasaki
Sugar (white)	1.6 taels/picul	4.5 taels/picul
Sugar (brown)	9 mace/picul	2.5 taels/picul
Agullah (best)	90 taels/picul	410 taels/picul
Iron	1.6 taels/picul	4.5 taels/picul
Tutenaque	2.8 taels/picul	5.5 taels/picul
Areca	1.4 taels/picul	1.6 taels/picul
Wax	12 taels/picul	40 taels/picul
Quick silver	40 taels/picul	115 taels/picul
Nanking raw silk	125 taels/picul	230 taels/picul

Source: Jacques and Philemon-Louis Savary des Bruslons, "Shinsho Kanton bōeki kansuru ichi shiryo," tr. Miyazaki Ichisada, *Tōa keizai kenkyū* 25.6:54 (November-December, 1941).

The ship in question was an Amoy ship named the *Tung-pen-tao* with a crew of 83 and a shipmaster named Liu Kuo-hsien. It set sail from Amoy for Nagasaki with a shipment of 2,500 piculs of white sugar and 150 piculs of sugar crystals, which fetched the ship a sum of 13,520.5 taels (£4,507) at the Japanese market. After subtracting 3,518.5 taels (£1,173) for provisions and the crew's pay, the ship used the balance to purchase copper, wine, chestnuts, pickles, soy sauce, cuttlefish, dried jelly, and fish, for the Siamese market. The ship was able to earn 8,312.775 taels (£2,771), with an unsold portion of copper (160 cases). Upon paying 1,529,225 taels (£510) for provisions and the crew's remuneration, the shipmaster was left with 6,783.52 taels. For the voyage back to Amoy from Ayudhya, the ship acquired, among other things, over 40,000 catties of sapan wood, 162,000 catties (215,946 lbs.) of pepper, 1300 catties (1,730 lbs.) of elephants' teeth, 1,386 catties (1,860 lbs.) of lead, about 3,000 catties

(4,000 lbs.) of gum benjamin, 4,000 catties (5,332 lbs.) of birds' nests, and some ells of cloth. The crew also secured a cargo of its own which included: 25,000 catties (33,250 lbs.) of sapan wood, 2,500 catties (3,325 lbs.) of corn, 1,500 catties (2,000 lbs.) of dried shrimp, 1,500 catties of sandalwood, 1,000 catties (1,333 lbs.) of lakawood (incense); the crew also retained 1,500 catties (2,000 lbs.) of the unsold Japanese copper. The record does not mention how much profit was finally generated at Amoy, nor does it mention how much capital the ship invested when it commenced the voyage from Amoy.[46]

The Chinese took over the Siamese-Japanese trade which lasted over a century and contributed to the support of the Siamese court by enhancing the royal trading monopolies. Chinese participation made the continuance of Siam's trade with Japan possible, and also the three-way trade involving Chinese ports, which was firmly held in Chinese hands.

A great deal of information about political and economic conditions in Asia (the Eastern Seas) may be discovered from the triangular trade. Both the Siamese court and the Chinese—private merchants as well as those serving the Siamese king—kept very few records. Thanks to the Shogunate's efforts at gathering intelligence, we are able to learn many details that otherwise would not have been mentioned.

The triangular trade, particularly in the last decades of the seventeenth century, strengthened considerably the economic bonds between Siam and China (especially at Kwangtung and South Fukien) through mutual economic cooperation, and served to accelerate trade relations between the two countries in subsequent eras.

Chapter V

THE ABROGATION OF THE SECOND MARITIME BAN
AND THE ROLE OF THE RICE TRADE

The basic problem the Ch'ing court faced over the closure of the country was the discrepancy between political desires and economic realities. In 1727 in China there were continued widespread crop failures causing distress among the people as well as a breakdown of the ban on travel and trade to Southeast Asia which had been imposed in 1717.[1] Min–Che Governor-General Kao Ch'i-cho, in a direct effort to stimulate new means of livelihood through trade and emigration, petitioned the Yung-cheng court for the reopening of Fukien to trade with Southeast Asia. His reasoning was that this trade would increase the provincial treasury as well as secure rice from abroad, two factors that weighed significantly in the thinking of Peking.[2] In addition, he emphasized that shipping would open up another means of livelihood for people of the province, especially those living along the coast. Since one ship could hold a hundred persons, these people would not consume locally grown rice and would be able to support their kin. He also allayed the fears of the court about rice smuggling by arguing persuasively that there was no need to smuggle rice to Southeast Asia because rice was grown in the region.[3] Finally, Kao raised the point that even though overseas trade essentially benefited the rich,[4] a hundred poor peasants of Kwangtung and Fukien could also derive advantages. The poor people of Chang-chou and Ch'üan-chou would have jobs[5] and the problems of piracy and banditry, caused primarily by economic depression and unemployment, would abate. All in all, the viceroy contended that the reopening of trade with Southeast Asia would indeed be beneficial.

A report was sent by the Board of War to Yung-cheng recommending the opening of maritime navigation as a result of the Kao memorial.[6] The recommendation was subsequently approved, and hence the nascent maritime trade with Southeast Asia from Amoy developed between 1684 and 1717 was revived. It was to last officially for forty more years. George Hughes observed, "His [Kao's] prayer was granted, and from this date sprung up a flourishing and lucrative trade with the South [Southeast Asia]."[7]

The reopening of Amoy to Southeast Asia trade by local merchants was followed less than a month later by a similar petition for the reopening of Canton which was submitted by the viceroy of Liang-Kuang, Ch'ang-lai. Like Kao Ch'i-cho, he cited the fact that the annual rice production of Kwangtung could satisfy only half the total consumption, and that relief from neighboring Kwangsi was at best slow and difficult. Consequently, as most ships formerly trading to Southeast Asia were from Kwangtung and Fukien, the reopening of Canton would mean an immense benefit to the livelihood of the people in the province, and could offset the rice problem as well, for rice could be brought back by local merchants.[8]

Two years later, merchants of Chekiang and Kiangnan were also permitted to trade to Southeast Asia. This permission was principally due to the effort of Min-Che Governor-General Li Wei who pointed out that Fukien had already been permitted to resume the importation of foreign rice. Since the coastline of Chekiang is contiguous to that of Fukien, he thought that Chekiang should also be reopened in order to prevent unscrupulous Chekiang merchants from proceeding to trade secretly with Southeast Asia via Fukien—thus incurring losses in rightful revenues. Li also cited the problem of rice deficiencies in Chekiang and the need for foreign imports.[9]

In the later years of the K'ang-hsi reign, as the productive forces of Chinese society gradually regained momentum after years of turmoil, trade in various places picked up. The lifting of the ban on trade to Southeast Asia in the mid-reign of Yung-cheng therefore represents a mark of recovery for China's overseas trade. External trade with Siam from Kwangtung, Fukien, and to some extent Chekiang, also accelerated after a brief snag. Amoy and Canton became the focal points of the Sino-Siamese maritime trade between 1729 and 1757, with a number of other smaller posts along the two coastlines of the two provinces feeding from these two major ports. Siamese tributary trade (and whatever venue of trade on the Siamese side that came under such a designation) together with that conducted by local merchants was actively pursued at these ports, so much so that by 1742, the Min–Che governor-general estimated that of all Amoy ships trading overseas, 70 to 80 percent of them went to Siam and the Malay peninsula.[10] According to Ts'ai Hsin, an official at Fukien and native of Chang-chou, the number of ships trading to Southeast Asia from Fukien and Kwangtung was not less than 110 a year.[11]

Actually, as was the case with the first maritime ban before 1684, in the period between 1717 and the time Peking finally approved Kao Ch'i-cho's petition, Chinese foreign trade was by no means inactive; some was even carried on with the sanction of the Manchu court. Japanese records have indicated that Chinese ships did indeed continue to conduct the triangular trade between China, Siam, and Japan at that time.[12] In addition, due to the shortage of rice, the Yung-cheng Emperor (r. 1723-1735) did show a degree of pragmatism when he permitted certain Chinese ships to trade to Southeast Asia, ostensibly to acquire the staple.[13] In 1725, he authorized Amoy ships to trade overseas with the condition that they carry back specified quantities of rice, depending on destination and size. Table 3 indicates the scheme subsequently adopted, showing varying amounts of rice to be carried back.

Medium-sized vessels trading to such places as Chaiya, Nakorn, and Songkla in Siam, Tringganau on the Malay peninsula, Sulu in the Indian Archipelago, and Annam, were each to take back 100 piculs (13,330 lbs.). Upon entry into Fukien, the ships were to be examined, and merchants would be allowed to sell any excess quantity at the regular current market prices. Should they for any reason be less, and should there be any attempt at misinterpretation, criminal punishment would be meted out.

Furthermore, in 1726 Fukien Viceroy Kao Ch'i-cho reported that at least 21 ships from Amoy were permitted by the local authorities to trade to Southeast Asia, and by the following season, 12 of them had returned with over 11,800 piculs (1.6 m. lbs.) of

Table 3

Quantities of Rice to be Transported (1725)
(in piculs)

Trading to	Large junks	Medium junks
Siam	300	200
Batavia	250	200
Luzon	250	200
Cambodia	200	100
Johore	200	100

Source: *Fu-chien t'ung-chih cheng-shih lüeh*, comp. Liu Chien-shao (n.d.),
    14:29a-b.

rice (or averaging over 8,000 piculs [106,640 lbs.] per ship—together
with other articles: birds' nests, biches de mer (sea slugs), sapan
wood, and water buffalo hides. The trading activities of the Amoy
ships were further confirmed by a memorial in 1716 by Fukien
Governor Mao Wen-ch'uan stating the presence of several Fukien
firms dealing in overseas trade, which had quick communication
with foreign merchants.[14]

In addition to this activity, officials like Kao Ch'i-cho who
were in favor of continuous overseas trade by people along the
Southeastern China coast constantly made their views known to
the Chinese government. Lan Ting-yuan, a contemporary official,
argued against the wisdom of banning Southeast Asia trade. He
said that such a measure hurt the livelihood of people on the coast,
and that the allegation of Chinese rice and ships being sold abroad
was inaccurate since foreign ships could be built better and more
cheaply, and that prior to 1717, Luzon had frequently sent rice to
relieve Fukien.[15] Such officials therefore played a role in finally
convincing the court to revamp its isolationist stand.

In the final analysis, the regeneration of the Sino-Siamese trade
in the period between the 1720s and 1760s owed most to the importation of rice from Siam into Southeast China, the single most tangible
factor for the rescinding of the second overseas travel and trade ban.[16]

Rice Shortages and Population Increase

Importing staples from abroad for the Ch'ing government was a serious admission of economic difficulty, but rice shortages in Southeast China in the early decades of the eighteenth century were grave, and foreign rice (*yang-mi*) was considered an important source of relief. Beginning in the eighteenth century, the problem of a deficit in and of high prices for rice was becoming more and more vocalized, as the population increased. Reports on the problem were most numerous during the reigns of Yung-cheng and Ch'ien-lung (1736–1795). According to Dwight Perkins, the southeastern coastal provinces of Kwangtung, Fukien, and southern Kiangsu/northern Chekiang (at the mouth of the Yangtze) were major chronic areas in the Chinese grain-marketing pattern in the eighteenth and early nineteenth centuries.[17] The reasons for such deficiencies are varied, but all the above-mentioned provinces invariably encountered the following realities: population pressure, physical limitations in rice cultivation, including such factors as the unsuitability of the soil, famine, and other natural calamities, and the existence of a vast nonagrarian, "nonproductive" population—for example, the large military forces. The single most fundamental reason for the shortage of rice, and hence also for the high price of the grain, is the phenomenal population increase that China had in the eighteenth century. One estimate[18] is that the population tripled, from 105 million in 1721 to 313 million in 1794 as compared to the population figures in Russia in the comparable period, which doubled from 14 million in 1722 to 29 million in 1795. During the period from the Revolt of the Three Feudatories (1675–1681) to the end of the Yung-cheng reign (1735) the fastest growth occurred, since it was a peaceful and prosperous period after over half a century of turmoil. The rice problem was first consciously noted by Yung-cheng, who realized that the dearness of rice was caused primarily by the increase in population which production could not keep up with.[19] His successor, Ch'ien-lung, was to become equally concerned with the effect of this population increase on China's rice supplies.

In essence, the population increase in a pre-industrial society was serious because there was no technology to alleviate the worsening material conditions, in this case the production of rice, the main staple of Southeast China and elsewhere.

Fukien

Fukien was perhaps the area most seriously deficient in rice, particularly when one considers only the eight prefectures within mainland Fukien and not the island of Formosa, which did not become a part of Fukien until 1747. Much of the province was mountainous; its sandy soil, unsuitable for growing rice, was more favorable for root crops such as sweet potatoes. Certain areas near Foochow, the administrative capital, were comparatively rich, but elsewhere, especially in Chang-chou and Ch'üan-chou prefectures in South Fukien, less than half of the land mass was suitable for rice cultivation. Even when the weather was conducive to a good crop, the typical rice harvest was usually not enough even for half a year's consumption. Hence people of the two prefectures traditionally had to rely on foodstuffs imported from overseas.[20]

In addition, flooding of the coastal land was particularly severe in Yung-cheng's reign. As a result, starvation was chronic in the area. For instance, in the fourth and fifth years of the reign (1727 and 1728), severe famine in the two prefectures left many dead and many had to live on tree bark (similar occurrences also took place in the reign of Ch'ien-lung). Fukien's population around the 1700s must have been no less than two million (Nishikawa Tadahide, a contemporary, gave the population figure of Fukien at the time as 1,820,000 [510,000 households]; he apparently quoted these figures from official tax records, and to get closer to reality, one might have to add 10 percent). By 1761, the population had quadrupled to over eight million, while cultivable land stood at 174 persons per square mile. The land expansion could not have been that much though productivity per acre could have risen to some extent. In the reign of Yung-cheng, Fukien happened to have the smallest area of cultivable land per capita: 9.1 *mou* or about 1.4 acres (as compared to the highest at Hupei, which was 120 *mou* or about 18 acres). To aggravate this trend of shrinking availability of land due to population increase, there existed a sizable contingent of "nonproductive" people who were "parasitic" on the province's rice supplies. Owing to the strategic position of South Fukien, a large military force had been stationed there since the seventeenth century. Prior to the reign of Yung-cheng, there were no less than 100,000 men in the land and sea forces of the Green Standard (*lu-ying*) and Manchu Banners in the entire province. They depended on their rice rations from some areas on mainland Fukien namely Yen-p'ing, Chien-ning, Shao-wu, Ting-chou, and Hsing-hua, which in addition had to supply other rice-deficient areas within the province. Consequently mainland rice was never sufficient to meet the demands of such troops, who, with the exception of those stationed at Namoa, usually received only half rations. From the end of the reign of Kang-hsi to that of Yung-cheng, the inadequate rice supply was felt particularly in the Amoy area because the region had strategic value and was, consequently, feeding a large number of troops.[21]

During the 1720s and 1730s the general trend of rice prices in Fukien shows that rice was most expensive at Chang-chou and Ch'üan-chou and cheapest at Formosa; the prices at Foochow fell in between.[22]

Kwangtung

Kwangtung was one of the few areas in China where two crops of rice a year could be cultivated,[23] and the province's farmland ratio per capita was better than Fukien's.[24] Nevertheless, such advantages were offset by a variety of adverse factors, many of which were similar to those found at Fukien. The fertile rice basket of the province lay at the delta area comprising the prefectures of Kao-chou, Lui-chou, and by the beginning of the Yung-cheng period, these prefectures managed to store up some 300,000 piculs (40 m. lbs.) of rice. However, they had to supply most of the rest of the province that was rice-deficient, a very difficult task because, for one thing, the transport network was ineffective, and, for another, they had to be mindful of the possibility of natural calamities like floods occurring in their own locales.

The entire province produced over four million piculs (240,000 tons) annually, but this was only adequate for a half year's supply. In particular, Canton city, Hui-chou, Chao-kuang, and Ch'ao-chou prefectures were most deficient in rice, with Ch'ao-chou being perhaps the worst of all. For instance, in 1727, Ch'ao-chou was hit by famine, with the rice price at Ch'ao-yang district soaring up to 1,000 *wen* per *tou* (7 s. per 316 cu. in.). Three years before that, the price of rice in Namoa, then administratively with Ch'ao-chou prefecture, and Ch'ao-chou itself rose to 2.8–3 taels a picul, because there was too little land for too many people.[25] Chuan Han-sheng and Wang Yeh-chien consider that rice prices in the Yung-cheng period were highest at Hui-chou and Ch'ao-chou, the lowest at Kao-chou, Lui-chou, Lien-chou, and Ch'iung-chou (Hainan); those at Canton city were in between. In this period, rice prices in the province ranged from 0.47 to 2.85 taels (3.5 s.- 19 s.), with highly erratic fluctuations.[26] For instance, in the famine years of 1726–1727, the price at Canton city doubled its normal level, from 1.20 to 2.85 taels (9 s.-19 s.). But because of its more developed marketing system, Canton faced comparatively less drastic fluctuations which in some other areas could have reached as high as seven times or more their normal level. But conditions were still far from favorable at Canton, especially when the city and its immediate environs had a large number of nonagrarian, "nonproductive" people who were in the military and other areas such as trade and crafts. For instance, one thriving commercial area important to the livelihood of Canton was Fatshan where people were engaged exclusively in cotton weaving, iron mongering, and trade. In addition, Canton was obliged to pay to the court at Peking on an annual basis 120,000 piculs (16 m. lbs.) of rice (plus 20,000 piculs [2,666,000 lbs.] of salt), of which 32,000 (3.1 m. lbs.) of rice (and 8,000 piculs of salt) reverted to the military garrisons in the province.[27] Dwight Perkins states that in Kwang-tung in the early eighteenth century there were wide fluctuations in the price of rice and that therefore, a farmer who depended on cash crops could lose both savings and land. "Peasants with no land as security for a loan (which was more than half in number)

either grew sweet potatoes or fled to the city with slim hope of
work there, or stayed and died."[28]

Chekiang

Chekiang province, though lying close to the fertile rice-
producing region of Kiangsi and the main artery of transport,
the Yangtze, faced a serious rice shortage in the early decades of
the eighteenth century.[29] In 1713, one picul of rice was quoted at
3.3 mace (2.3 s.) at T'ung-ch'eng in Chekiang, which was much
higher than at Fukien and Kwangtung. In 1717, partly as a result
of the "rampant" smuggling of rice from Fukien to Luzon and
Batavia by local Chinese, and also as an effort to arrest the deterio-
rating rice situation in Chekiang, the K'ang-hsi Emperor imposed
a rice ration in that province. In the beginning of the Yung-cheng
period, ships trading to Nagasaki from Nanking and other provinces
were all reporting the shortage and high price of rice in the province.
In the following reign of Ch'ien-lung there was no let-up in the
general condition, aggravated further by chronic famines.[30] In 1743,
the people of Chiang-yu allegedly had to resort to mud to satisfy
their hunger. They called it *"Kuan-in-fen"* (lit., "the flour of the
Goddess Kuan-in").

The causes of the rice deficiency in Chekiang were similar to
those of Fukien and Kwangtung, with population pressure accentu-
ating the seriousness of the problem. Chekiang's land had been
devoted principally to hemp, cotton, and mulberry (sericulture),
which was, of course, much more profitable than rice growing.[31]
It is therefore not difficult to appreciate the delicate balance between popular consumption and the demand for staples which
could easily be upset by a sudden growth of population accompanied
by natural calamities.

Within provinces, the government used three general methods
to deal with the problem: the diversion of tribute grain, the prohibition of rice export, and the establishment of public granaries.[32]
Still, it was not sufficient to alleviate the crisis, and obviously outside sources of supply needed to be tapped to supplement these
efforts. There were two outside sources to which the government

could turn: interprovincial and overseas. Although the interprovincial source proved in the long run to be more vital in meeting the chronic rice crises in the southeastern provinces, its significance had to be complemented by the overseas sources, which were a more novel and yet more difficult way of securing grain for deficient areas on a sizable scale. Let us first examine briefly the interprovincial sources.

Aid from Interprovincial Sources

Fukien sought the bulk of its interprovincial rice relief, by sea, from two sources: the rice-growing region of the Yangtze and the island of Formosa. Rice supplies were also transported overland to Fukien from Kiangsi, but this mode of transportation was not as prevalent as the one by sea. As early as the first part of the eighteenth century, shipments were secured from Szechwan, Hukuang (Hunan and Hupei), and Kiangsi via the Yangtze to Soochow. And from there tens of thousands of piculs were transhipped to points on the Fukien coast. Soochow was a most important rice market for the Yangtze region. By the mid-Ch'ing period it served as a vital distribution center of rice for both Fukien and Chekiang, perhaps because Suchow lies at the outlet of the Yangtze River valley which was at this time the most important rice producing as well as the largest exporting area of China. In the famine year of 1727 for instance, both official and private ships conveyed tens of thousands of piculs from Soochow.[33]

But this source alone was far from adequate, and supplies had to be sought further afield (even from rice-deficient Chekiang, which at least was still, relatively speaking, much better off than its southern neighbor) chiefly for the purpose of *p'ing-tiao*,[34] and hence only in times of grave want. For instance, in 1721, K'ang-hsi ordered some 30,000 piculs (4 m. lbs.) shipped from Chekiang to Amoy, which would eventually be used by Fukien. The same was repeated by Yung-cheng some time later when 24,000 piculs (3.2 m. lbs.) were ordered shipped for Amoy, Chang-chou, Ch'üan-chou, and Foochow.[35] So imports from Chekiang seem to have been resorted to primarily as a stop-gap measure.

Fukien received most of its relief, however, from Formosa, which was only one day away by junk. Since it was near rice-deficient Chang-chou and Ch'üan-chou, Formosa would seem the most logical provisioner for South Fukien, or for that matter the entire province. But because of restrictions imposed by the Manchus, the smooth flow from Formosa was obstructed at various periods. First of all, after the "pacification" of the island in 1683, Formosan rice had been officially designated for military consumption, and its function as a commercial commodity for popular consumption was thus subordinated. The government moved to stipulate further that each private vessel could take no more than 60 piculs (8,000 lbs.) of rice from Formosa at a time. Toward the end of K'ang-hsi's reign, partly because of the popular revolt that had erupted again on Formosa, the nervous Ch'ing court imposed a ban on rice export from the island, taking the advice of some official circles that such a measure would also stabilize the Taiwan rice price. So it was decreed in 1717 that no rice from Formosa was to be exported unless conditions in southern Fukien were acute enough to warrant it. It would be up to the governor and the governor-general to determine the amount needed, and to forward the requests to the Formosa authorities. The rice shipment was to be escorted by military ships to Amoy for storage and eventual distribution. Furthermore, local officials were required to supervise the sale and submit details of transactions to the governor-general. With this restriction, the rice that was going from Formosa to Fukien in the remainder of the K'ang-hsi rule and in Yung-cheng's reign continued to be composed basically of military shipments, which by the 1720s were reaching some 85,000 piculs (11.3 m. lbs.) per month; between 1739 and 1745, annual exports to the Fukien military forces from Formosa amounted to 80,000 to 100,000 piculs (10.7–13.3 m. lbs.) annually. Nevertheless, in times of extreme want, efforts were made, though necessarily sporadic, to bring in some rice to relieve the general populace. For instance, in 1729, some 120,000 piculs were brought over for sale to the public.[36]

In 1746, the governor of Fukien, Chou Hsueh-chien, memorialized Ch'ien-lung for permission to have private ships transport

Formosa rice to the various provincial storages for the government. This was the beginning of the commercial transportation of Formosa rice. In the following year, when the island officially became an administrative part of Fukien, private merchants were again allowed to transport rice from Formosa, with the following restrictions: that official permits were required, that the period in which trade was to be conducted must be between the tenth and first moons, and that in years of need on Formosa, private purchases and transportation were to be suspended. In that year, a total of 200,000 piculs of Formosa rice was imported into Fukien.[37]

But Fukien in the eighteenth century continued to suffer from an inadequacy of rice. It became increasingly evident by the end of the K'ang-hsi period that with existing conditions, namely: shrinking acreage, population pressure, famine, policies adopted by the government, and the essentially underdeveloped means of land transportation, Fukien had also to look overseas for additional supplies.

In the eighteenth century, Kwangtung occasionally received supplies of rice from surplus areas on the Yangtze, but the province, particularly the city of Canton, was primarily dependent on the resources of neighboring Kwangsi. Unlike the commercial areas of the lower Yangtze it could not rely on the great rice bowl of the upper Yangtze during a poor harvest, and hence had to hope for the surpluses of the single underpopulated Kwangsi. As pointed out by Mao Wen-ch'uan, the governor of Kwangtung, to Yung-cheng in 1726, the main problem was that transportation over stretches of mountainous areas was indeed difficult and slow. Nonetheless, there was a real need for Kwangsi rice, and the task had to be carried out. For even when there was a good harvest in Kwangtung, which for all practical purposes was seldom, Canton and other large urban centers on the Pearl River delta received one to two million piculs (about 60,000-120,000 tons) annually from Kwangsi, according to a memorial presented to the Peking court in 1737. We can get an idea of how much rice Canton and its environs consumed annually at this time from a memorial written in 1727 by a Canton official in which it was stated that Canton had stored 1.6 million piculs (97,000 tons) from Kwangsi to make up for the inadequacy.[38]

Still Kwangsi was not a completely satisfactory source to fulfill the growing needs of neighboring Kwangtung. For one thing, Kwangsi was never completely willing to send its staple on spiraling scales to feed another province, in accordance with the traditional thinking of ensuring certain reserves for needy periods. For another, land transport costs and risks were high. Difficult terrain, danger from wild animals and bandits, all compounded to make rice transportation problematic, not to mention the fact that travel overland for long distances was on the average approximately three times as expensive as by junk.[39]

The other rice-deficient areas of Kwangtung, notably, Hui-chou and Ch'ao-chou prefectures in the northeastern part of the province, however, relied less directly on Kwangsi rice. On the one hand, Ch'ao-chou junks drew rice from Ch'iung-chou (Hainan) which by itself was not a rice-surplus area but could obtain rice relatively economically from the rice-surplus area of Kao-chou and Lui-chou prefectures, in addition to Formosa, and Southeast Asia. On the other, Ch'ao-chou obtained rice from neighboring South Fukien for subsistence, particularly from Chang-chou prefecture. Normally, rice from Formosa for South Fukien was first stored at Amoy. In 1726, a year of severe food shortage, people from Ch'ao-chou went to Amoy in large numbers along with Fukienese from the interior of Fukien, numbering altogether tens of thousands a day to purchase rice, and thus hiking the already soaring rice prices even more.[40] So throughout the Yung-cheng period at least, there were considerably higher demands than could be met by any supplies available. The fact that Ch'ao-chou had to seek rice from South Fukien, which itself was in great need of the grain, is one indication of the shortage in that region of Southeast China, where people could still at least manage to turn to neighboring areas for minimal help, thanks to the accessibility of water transportation. Despite the apparent advantage, however, in a famine year, the grain market was usually so thin that grain prices skyrocketed. This situation was the same in Canton, which was also close to water transportation.

Chekiang was more fortunate, in one respect, than Kwangtung and Fukien, but it also had to depend on outside relief, no matter how unsatisfactory. The province relied primarily on grain ships from Kiangsi and Anhwei, and from Hukuang, which was nearly nine hundred miles away, via Suchou (Soochow), apparently like Fukien. Chekiang also obtained relief from neighboring Fukien in times of emergency, mainly from Formosa and Foochow, amounting in the 1720s to tens of thousands of piculs a year. These amounts were sent under special authorization for the purposes of relieving famine and of *p'ing-t'iao*.[41]

Encouragement of Rice Import

Faced with the gloomy prospects of a chronic rice shortage, the Ch'ing government resorted to a combination of measures to control the situation. It encouraged people to expand acreage and plant root crops, such as maize, potatoes, and peanuts, as a long-term policy. But as short-term measures, the authorities in the reigns of Yung-cheng and Ch'ien-lung used two methods simultaneously: regulating the outflow of rice, and encouraging the importation of foreign rice.

In 1683, when foreign trade was first legally sanctioned, the Manchus had instituted a regulation forbidding merchant ships from China to take along more than 50 piculs of rice for sale; the penalty was confiscation of the excess. In addition, the rice rations of the crew were also specified. One crewman was allowed one *sheng* or pint (31.6 cu. in.) of rice per day, with an additional pint as reserve in case of delay due to bad weather or other natural causes.[42] These official stipulations were to remain in force throughout the eighteenth century. The ban on trade and travel to Southeast Asia reintroduced in 1717 and lasting for ten years was ostensibly to curb the smuggling of junks and rice to Luzon and Java, but it also reflected the rising concern of the Chinese government for the growing insufficiency of rice along the southeastern coast and therefore the need to control the outflow.

About this time the Chinese began to seek foreign rice. Toward the close of the seventeenth century, for example in 1697,

Chekiang, Nanking, and Ch'ao-chou ships were still taking rice to sell at Nagasaki, as well as reporting successful crops in several places.[43] The abrupt population increase after the turn of the eighteenth century quickly put an end to such practices. Nevertheless, it was not until the end of the 1710s that foreign rice was reported as coming into China, brought in from Luzon by private merchants and probably destined mainly for Fukien. Ch'en Fen-jen writing in his *Ch'üan-nan pi-chi* in the late seventeenth century said: "All of the prefecture of Ch'üan-chou relies entirely on the rice from overseas; wherever and whenever the rice price is lowered, i.e. competitive, merchants must proceed there."[44] According to a contemporary official, Lan Ting-Yuan, the rice production of Kwangtung was not sufficient: "Every year, half of Fukien's rice-for popular consumption—comes from Formosa, and help from Chekiang also has to be sought. Prior to the ban to Southeast Asia, rice was being imported from there into Fukien annually."[45]

The first official mention of the import of rice from Siam came in 1722, the last year of K'ang-hsi's reign, a year in which all of China seems to have been suffering from a general rice shortage and phenomenal price hikes.[46]

As early as the 1670s the Chinese were already reporting that Siam had a surplus of rice.[47] George White of the British East India Company commented in 1679: "This country [Siam] is the general granary for the adjacent parts, equally if not exceeding any part of the world in abundance of rice, where in the neighboring Malayan coast is yearly supplied as far as Mallaccah [Malacca], and when it happens to be scarce and dear about Java, as it did anno 76-77, the Dutch and others transport several ships loading thither."[48] The abundance had also been noted by the Chinese back in the second half of the seventeenth century. For instance, Chinese crewmen aboard a Siamese *tōsen* reported to the Nagasaki authorities in 1690 that rice was abundant in Siam. The Siamese did not have to worry about rain because of the annual floods, they explained, and since rice was grown so easily the price was much lower than in other countries.[49]

The Siamese were also annually transporting rice in the king's ships to trade at Nagasaki at least since the end of the seventeenth or beginning of the eighteenth centuries.[50] But K'ang-hsi apparently did not learn of the cheapness of Siamese rice until 1722 when he received the Siamese tributary envoy who informed him of it. He thereupon gave the Siamese permission to transport 3,000 piculs to Canton, Amoy, and Ningpo, a shipment that would not be subject to duty of any kind.[51]

Since the ban on travel and trade to Southeast Asia for local merchants was still in effect, the emperor specified that rice shipments were to be transported in Siamese bottoms. K'ang-hsi also stated that the unit of weight and type of currency to be used was to be Chinese. When the shipments arrived the emperor granted further favors by buying the Siamese rice at 5 Chinese mace (3.3s.) with no duty assessment.[52] At the time, the price of rice in China was averaging about 1.8 tael (12s.) at the highest, and 1 tael (7s.) at the lowest, so the rice from Siam would indeed represent a good bargain for the Chinese side.

When the Siamese responded favorably to this first official request for a large rice shipment, the Siamese king at once took advantage of the opportunity by asking the Chinese court to grant the Siamese full rights to undertake trade outside the regular tributary missions. To this the Chinese emperor could only give his approval and thereafter Siamese merchant vessels commenced trading to China in sizable numbers.[53]

K'ang-hsi's approval of Siamese rice shipments was precedent-setting. In the next few decades, the Chinese court welcomed Siamese rice in large quantities. During this period there was a genuine demand in the Chinese market for Siamese rice, and since Siam itself was in a period of peace which was often not the case with states on mainland Southeast Asia, and the Siamese kings' dispositions were favorable, there was every indication that Siam would be in a good position as a significant grain supplier. James Ingram estimates that for 1850, the total yield of rice in Siam was roughly 23.3 million piculs from a total area of 5.8 million *rai* (about 2.9 million acres), about 4 piculs per *rai* or about 732 lbs. per 0.49 acre. Assuming that there was little or no change in the basic technique of cultivation, and that the total area under rice cultivation in the first part of the eighteenth century was about half that of 1850, one may conjecture that the representative yield per year at that time could reach 6 million piculs (about 370,000 tons). And as the population then was much smaller than in 1850, an export of several hundred thousand piculs to China a year was entirely credible.[54]

During the reign of Yung-cheng official interest in Siamese rice continued, and there were even more endeavors to promote this trade.[55] Two years after K'ang-hsi's significant order, Kwangtung Governor Nien-hsi-yao memorialized that Siam had transported rice to China and also presented grain seeds. The emperor, expressing his appreciation of the Siamese action, instructed his local officials to sell it speedily at the current price in Kwangtung.[56]

In the same edict, Yung-cheng made a few additional statements. First he ordered rice transport from Siam to be temporarily suspended and the areas in need of rice (in China) to wait for his further rescripts before ordering rice from Siam.[57] This decree seems to have reflected the emperor's momentary hesitation in relying on Siam's rice indefinitely; the "wait-and-see" stand adopted was perhaps his way of maintaining options regarding the importation of foreign rice though he must have realized its importance, as his other statements in the same edict would indicate.

There could be three possible reasons for such a move. First of all, Yung-cheng was fearful that the rice transported over a long distance from Siam might fall into the hands of pirates and other anti-Ch'ing elements which were still infesting the waters of Southeast China.[58] The second reason for suspending rice imports under the *kung-yun*, or official, arrangement may have been Yung-cheng's doubts about the wisdom of relying on foreign sources for staples. A third explanation may be the displeasure expressed by local customs officers and other high-ranking provincial officials over an arrangement that did not seem to fill their pockets, especially when such officials had a quota obligation to their patrons in Peking, particularly the hoppo who had to constantly resort to "squeeze" in order to make sure that he would have enough to forward to his patrons in the capital each year.[59]

Notwithstanding the above order, Yung-cheng granted a duty exemption on the accompanying ballast aboard the Siamese vessels, noting that under normal circumstances such items were taxable. The rice was ordered sold at once. And, finally, apparently appreciative of the distance and the risks taken by the Siamese king to transport rice to China, Yung-cheng made an exception (contrary to the established law governing the migration and employment of Chinese individuals abroad): the 97 Chinese crewmen, including the shipmaster Hsu K'uan, could return with the ship to Siam and would not be repatriated to their ancestral villages in China. The rationalization offered by the emperor was that these individuals had resided in Siam for generations and that they all had families with them in Siam.[60]

At the same time, the emperor made an addendum to the regulations governing tributary envoys from Siam, namely that shipmasters (ch'uan-chang) and foreign crewmen (fan-shao) of Siamese tribute ships were in the future to be considered in the same class as linguists (t'ung-shih) and attendants of the Peking-bound tributary envoy respectively, meaning that they would be entitled to imperial presents. Although the shipmaster could in no way measure up to the ambassador in status, he should be awarded with ten bolts (1 bolt had 40 ch'ih or about 14.3 metres) of silk, in addition to another ten bolts of cloth for transporting rice to China over a long distance.[61]

We gather from the above pronouncements that Yung-cheng's policy, in spite of his order for the temporary suspension of further shipments (which will be seen presently as lasting only a couple of years), clearly favored Siamese rice importation. What is most significant here is the fact that he acknowledged that the rice trade was an indispensable part of the tributary system.

The untenability of the imperial order for temporary suspension became apparent as soon as it went into effect. Fukien and Kwangtung continued to face a severe famine in the next two years, while Siam on the other hand was apparently having good harvests. Under such circumstances, shipments could not be kept from reaching China. In 1726, two Siamese t'an-kung vessels shipped rice for sale in China. In spite of his previous order, Yung-cheng accepted the Siamese explanation that the two ships had not known of such an order when they left Siam, an unlikely story since the order itself had gone out two years before, and the traveling time of ships from Siam required at the most only a few months. Subsequently, the emperor consented to the unloading of the rice, reasoning that the ships had come a long way.[62]

In 1726 Yung-cheng issued a rescript ordering a temporary halt of *kung-yun* of Siamese rice.[63] But in the following year, he again invited the Siamese, and others willing to do so, to send rice to China. The reason for this modification in his stand is not difficult to understand. Fukien had just experienced one of its worst famines in the previous year, and the crisis was continuing unabated for a second year. The urgency of the rice shortage in Fukien and neighboring Kwangtung was consistently reported by local officials to Peking, particularly by the governor-general of Fukien, Kao Ch'i-cho. Implying that transporting rice from adjacent provinces within China was not necessarily economical, Kao proposed to the emperor that a renewed import of rice from Southeast Asia would enable large supplies of grain to reach China, while generating a source of revenue for the local area, since the Southeast Asian market would once more be subject to taxation. Also, a memorial by the viceroy of Liang-Kuang dated 1742 recalled that in 1727 local officials at Canton, citing the problems of overpopulation and congestion, successfully petitioned for the reopening of the port of Canton to rice shipments from Southeast Asia.[64]

Shortly after the emperor made known his intention of favoring renewed rice importation from Siam, Liang-Kuang Governor-General Kung Yü-hsun memorialized that a Siamese junk came into port and was told that "Our Celestial Dynasty does not have to rely on your country's rice but is considerate to people from afar." Whereupon the Siamese replied that they had had to put into Canton because of unfavorable winds, that they had lost two ships out of three, and that their profit was limited. But they expressed their appreciation of the imperial magnanimity.[65]

There are some interesting implications in this memorial. First of all, it is evident that Yung-cheng wanted the continuation of the rice import from Siam, though he made it appear that the allowance was actually for the benefit of the Siamese. The Chinese side did not have to depend on Siam's supplies, but simply wanted to show imperial kindness to distant foreigners. Secondly, the Siamese shipmaster mentioned that transporting rice alone was not always profitable, and that it was necessary to take along other articles for sale as well, for example, the highly marketable sapan wood which, in this case, made the shipment pay. Nevertheless, rice remained a desirable article for trade, as long as there were large demands for it by China. Furthermore, the shipmaster also quoted the rice in his shipment as 3 mace per *chin* which would appear to be considerably higher when compared to that quoted in 1722, then 2 to 3 mace a picul. The rice trade in the eighteenth and nineteenth centuries, in which prices depended both on conditions in Siam and the nature of demand in the China market, was precarious. A good rice harvest in Siam in a given year and a bad one in another could make a difference in the price of rice, regardless of how large a demand existed in China at a given moment. The time of this particular rice shipment was apparently not a very favorable one.[66] Still, its cargo of rice seems to have been accepted rather easily by the Chinese, thus reflecting the extent of the demand in Southeast China at this juncture.

The change in Yung-cheng's stand in permitting Siamese rice shipments prompted another shipment to Amoy in the following year 1728. The Chinese authorities took the opportunity to reiterate the provisions governing rice transport from Siam as announced in 1722 by K'ang-hsi, as well as declaring that the duty exemption on Siamese rice was to become a standard policy.[67]

The official sanction of the tax privilege prompted more imports. In the same year, the Board of Rites memorialized the emperor that the governor of Fukien had submitted a report stating that the Siamese king, in his earnestness, had ordered merchants of his country to take rice and other articles to Amoy. The governor asked that they be allowed to dispose of their cargoes at Amoy with tax exemption. The Board recommended that thenceforth Siamese merchant vessels taking rice to Fukien, Kwangtung, and Chekiang should be uniformly treated, that is, the duty assessment was to be waived. The imperial rescript on this request was that although rice was not to be taxed, other goods accompanying it must be.[68] This policy remained in force until the beginning of Ch'ien-lung's reign, when, with the worsening of the rice crisis, further allowances were made.

The Siamese king (Taisra) dispatched another rice shipment to Canton in the same year (1728). In 1729 yet another Siamese ship visited Amoy loaded with rice, and the ballast acquired at the port for the return trip to Siam was granted tax exemption.[69] In the following month, a Siamese tributary mission arrived and was very well received by the Chinese: it was granted lavish gifts and permitted to purchase whatever articles were desired (by the Siamese court), including several hundred horses, which were normally restricted for export due to their military value.[70]

Siamese rice continued to be imported to Fukien in 1730. The Siamese kept up the dispatch of rice to Southeast China up to the end of Yung-cheng's reign, for demand was increasing, and there was a noticeable abundance of rice production in Siam.[71] It is almost impossible to estimate the amount of rice transported by Siam to China in the thirteen years of Yung-cheng's rule since adequate figures are unavailable. Some writers have postulated that the amount could have been maintained at a hundred thousand piculs a year at least following K'ang-hsi's request in 1722 for three hundred thousand to Canton, Amoy, and Ningpo. If we are to agree with James Ingram who thinks that before 1850, if the harvest was a good one and the Siamese king was willing, and if nearby countries (including China) had a need for rice, Siam could probably have exported several hundred thousand, or perhaps as much as one to one and a half million piculs a year, the total amount for the entire reign might have reached at least one million piculs. Assuming that one vessel carried an average of 5,000 piculs (665,000 lbs.) of rice (Siamese ships were generally large and had a carrying capacity of over 10,000 piculs), it would take a total of about 200 junks, or an average of 13 to 14 a year. These figures seem credible despite the fact that only a few Siamese shipments in a year were officially recorded. Wei Yuan said in the mid-nineteenth century that since the end of the K'ang-hsi period, several hundred thousand piculs of rice were brought into Fukien and Kwangtung annually.[72]

For at least the first decade or so of Ch'ien-lung's reign (1736-1795), Siamese rice imports flowed steadily, in spite of the court's initial consideration in 1740, as a result of the Dutch massacre of Chinese residents in the East Indies that year, to reimpose the ban on Chinese trade with Southeast Asia. It seems that local officials at Kwangtung and Fukien were against the reintroduction of such a measure. For instance, Liang-Kuang Governor-General Ch'ing-fu reasoned that China could gain a great deal from Southeast Asian rice, and the incident (known as the "Batavia Fury") should not cause a complete ban on the entire region since many in Kwangtung depended on trade with Southeast Asia where rice was then cheap. Reportedly one picul cost only between 2.6 to 3.6 mace (1.7 to 2.4 s.); many merchants took back several hundred to a thousand piculs apiece and made great profits from its sale at Canton. Foreign ships also imported the grain annually, which did much to alleviate the food shortage in Kwangtung. The Peking court again admitted that Southeast Asia was able to provide surplus rice much needed in Southeast China, and this acknowledgment continued to encourage the various countries in the region to transport the staple when they traded to China. In 1742, Ch'ien-lung decreed that all rice ships from Southeast Asia were to receive specific privileges at customs in order to facilitate the flow of rice.[73] Renewed generosity was shown to all Siamese rice shipments, culminating in 1743 when the Peking court instituted another scheme to induce the importation of rice from abroad. Prompted by the continual flow of Siamese rice into Fukien and Kwangtung, the emperor issued an edict that year saying that, starting from 1743, cargo vessels from overseas coming to Fukien, Kwangtung, and so on, with ten thousand or more piculs of rice would pay only half of the normal cargo duty (ch'uan-huo-shui), and those carrying five thousand or more piculs would pay only 70 percent of it.

In this edict, Ch'ien-lung promised that the Chinese government would see to it that the rice transported would be sold at fair prices. However, if there were plenty of grain among the people at any given time and hence no demand for rice purchase, the government would undertake to buy the rice for its various public granaries or to distribute it among various coastal garrisons as military supplies, or both. The local officials and the Siamese king were to be informed immediately.[74]

Another bad year for Fukien came in 1743, and local officials had to go where rice was cheap to secure whatever was possible.[75] This was perhaps one valid reason for Ch'ien-lung to favor rice shipments from Siam as well as from other parts of Southeast Asia. Nevertheless, this new guideline generally represented an extension of the emperor's encouragement of foreign rice importation.

The new measure made possible further shipments of Siamese rice to Amoy in 1744.[76] Ch'ien-lung even made further concessions to demonstrate favors to Siamese shipments. For instance, in 1746, Hsin-chu, who was the Fukien tartar-general cum Amoy customs superintendent, memorialized that in the seventh moon of that year a Siamese ship registered to one Fang Yung-li (a Sino-Siamese merchant) transported 4,300 piculs (573,190 lbs.) of rice to Amoy, followed closely by another registered to one Ts'ai Wen-hao (also a Sino-Siamese merchant) which had on board 3,800 piculs (506,540 lbs.) and other articles such as sapan wood, lead, and the like. Hsin-chu felt that since the two vessels did not carry the minimum five thousand piculs to be eligible for any special customs treatment they ought to be assessed the proper taxes. The emperor's rescript, however, cited that since the vessels had traversed a long distance, which was itself an indication of earnestness, their *ch'uan-huo-shui* should be reduced by at least 20 percent and the ship's measurement fees by one-fourth to demonstrate the gratitude of the Chinese.[77]

Such exceptions were, of course, not granted indiscriminately, and each shipment of rice below the prescribed minimum was subject to individual scrutiny by the emperor himself. For example, in one case where a Sino-Siamese merchant named Wang Yuan-cheng called at Amoy with a rice cargo, Hsin-chu memorialized the court that the fleet of merchant ships under Wang, which carried in addition sapan wood, lead, and tin, was required to pay a measurement fee and a *ch'uan-huo-shui* of 1,000 and 1,010 taels (£33 and 337) respectively. Wang however claimed that previous shipments by Fang Yung-li, Ts'ai wen-hao, and Hsueh Shih-lung, and so on (five shipments altogether), had been granted a special imperial favor in the form of a reduction in both kinds of duties. They had subsequently returned to Siam and reported this to the king, who then proceeded to order more rice to be officially transported to Fukien for sale and asked the Chinese for a reduction of the measurement and cargo duties. Because Wang's shipment was one result of the previous imperial act, it should be entitled to similar preferential treatment. Hsin-chu reported to the emperor that Wang's shipment was much less, and therefore ought not to receive any consideration at all.[78] The emperor concurred with his official's recommendation.

All the rice ships from Siam mentioned thus far, that is, since 1722, had been associated with the king's name, which leads to the conclusion that all shipments in the span of these two decades had been assumed to be under royal sanction. It appears that the Siamese king and certain Fukienese merchants (residents of Siam or trading there regularly) had taken advantage of the imperial encouragement of rice imports, and devised a system whereby the Fukienese merchants would transport rice, along with other goods, to trade at Kwangtung and Fukien in the king's name. (Rice shipments to Chekiang, which officially commenced in 1729, were not as important as the other two provinces.) Profits may have been split between the merchants and the king, or the merchants may have been hired for a fee.

There were, under normal circumstances, rather exorbitant charges levied on foreign ships entering Amoy. Since both Yung-cheng and Ch'ien-lung had instituted a string of exemptions and reductions of the various levies they must have wished to show imperial favor toward the Siamese for their part in supplying the much needed grain. There is, of course, no way of computing exactly how much the Siamese saved in these arrangements, but whatever profits were made certainly provided a strong incentive for a more or less steady and continuous flow of Siamese rice into Southeast China.

With the close of the 1740s rice importation from Siam seems to have gradually been given an added dimension: the growing participation by the Chinese merchants from Fukien, Kwangtung, and Chekiang. Chinese official records (memorials to Peking by local authorities and imperial edicts and rescripts) mention the new role of these local merchants with greater frequency; and, conversely, give less information about the participation by mandarin merchants from Siam. This phenomenon has been interpreted by some as an overshadowing of the role of the Siamese side by the Chinese counterpart in the purveying of Siamese rice.[79] But rather than indicating an eclipse in the Siamese role, it could well mean an added dimension to the expanding Siamese rice trade with China, since the demand grew in proportion to the worsening food situation in Southeast China.

Rice prices throughout China after 1748, notably those applicable to the Yangtze region, were high (owing primarily to the population increase). Riots resulted in such provinces as Kiangsu and Fukien (Amoy) in 1748, for public granaries could not supply the demand. Chuan Han-cheng says also that when compared with those of the K'ang-hsi and Yung-cheng periods, rice prices after 1748 in the reign of Ch'ien-lung were much higher.[80] Before 1748, Siamese rice quoted at 3 mace (2.1s.) a picul in 1722, and below that in the reign of Ch'ien-lung, continued to hold at an attractive price (just over 2 mace), and this undoubtedly ensured the continuation of rice imports from Siam.

One general characteristic of rice importation from Siam between 1722 (when K'ang-hsi invited the official transportation of 300,000 piculs) and 1729 (when Yung-cheng again allowed local merchants to trade in Southeast Asia, and thus rescinded the 1717 ban instituted by K'ang-hsi) was that all legal rice importation was to be carried out in Siamese bottoms (though managed by Chinese crews). The first Chinese port, Amoy, was officially reopened for local merchants to Southeast Asia in 1727. However, it appears that Amoy merchants still participated, to a relatively small extent, in the rice trade; one apparent reason was that local merchants were yet to be accorded comparable privileges for transporting rice to China, which naturally put them at a disadvantage vis-à-vis Sino-Siamese merchants from Siam. The lack of full official support in the initial period was, perhaps, more important. This lack of support is partly evident from the time (1743) when Ch'ien-lung proclaimed tax privileges for rice-bearing Siamese ships, in which he also stated a concern regarding the possible exploitation of this scheme by local merchants. Expressing his apprehension of the Chinese merchant, he said in part: "It is feared that crooked merchants of the interior, hoping to gain profit from the tax exemption [granted to foreign rice shippers], may in the future use this [opportunity] to bring back cargoes, which upon reaching port, will be falsified as rice transported by [Siam]."[81]

The emperor was thus admonishing local officials to supervise carefully, so that local merchants would not abuse the privilege accorded foreigners transporting rice to China. This apparent move to "discriminate" against local merchants perhaps fell in line with the overall Manchu policy regarding foreign trade. The Peking government, however, found itself unable to stop overseas trade by local merchants, partly because of the rice shortage which required the reopening of ports for the importation of rice and the creation of opportunities for the people's livelihood. Another reason was simply the connivance between resourceful southeastern Chinese merchants and corrupt local officials eager to line their pockets. As a result, in time the court had to compromise. Beneath the periodic stern warnings against foreign trade was an attempt to regulate the movement of local merchants (perhaps also as a way for local officials to "squeeze" the merchants) through selection, the granting of permits (licenses), and the prescription of fixed periods of absence for vessels trading overseas. In 1727, certain hong merchants at Amoy were granted a monopoly of trade to Southeast Asia.

Even though such restrictive provisions became in time a dead letter, the Manchu policy of "trade with Southeast Asia with little or no local merchants' participation" nevertheless hindered the normal development of the junk trade by local merchants—many of them having chosen to render their services to Southeast Asian principals, notably the king of Siam.

In 1739 the authorities at Fukien recommended to Ch'ien-lung that local merchants be permitted to return from Southeast Asia, where rice was cheap and plentiful, without any limit imposed on their rice shipments. In the 1740s and 1750s, further conditions emerged that would encourage the participation of local merchants in the transport of Siamese rice. First of all, in the early 1740s, Amoy merchants discovered that timber was abundant in Siam and that seagoing junks could be commercially built in the country.[82] Ch'en Ta-shou, the governor of Fukien, told the Peking court that local merchants since 1744 had reaped immense profits by going to Siam to construct vessels and bring them back to Amoy along with rice. This enterprise had proven even more advantageous than transport by the Siamese side itself. Hence he urged that the court authorize the granting of licenses to the newly built ships brought back from Siam by local merchants.[83] The Fukien governor, mindful of the primary importance of rice importation from Siam, also recommended that if local merchants went to Siam to acquire ships and did not return with a quantity of rice, they should be penalized by heavy taxes. Therefore, considering all of these activities, it seems likely that it was a very profitable venture on the part of the local merchants. The governor did not forget to add that despite the abundance of rice in Siam, local merchants had hitherto maintained little interest in the trade because of its small profits. No doubt, they, without the same privileges accorded foreign carriers, stood no chance of competing with the latter.[84] At first the Ch'ing government regarded shipbuilding overseas by Chinese as illegal. But because Fukien and Kwangtung needed Siamese rice, the governor's request was conditionally accepted.[85]

As far as dealing in both ships and rice from Siam by local merchants was concerned, Ch'ien-lung did not act upon the recommendation of the Fukien customs superintendent who emphasized the desirability of the combination.[86] Apparently the emperor was still wary of encouraging private merchants to go into this lucrative venture, because of constant reports he received on rampant rice smuggling and hoarding by local merchants, not to mention the possible abuses from shipbuilding. These activities were partially responsible for the continual soaring of rice prices in China.

In the midst of such uncertainty, one group of officials, namely those in the coastal provinces of Fukien and Kwangtung, was openly advocating the management of the rice trade with Siam through official channels (*kuan-yun* or "official transporting"). Such a mode was employed in the conveying of rice from surrounding provinces into Fukien when the latter's 1743 harvest failed. For fear of smuggling and other abuses, private merchants were not allowed to have any part in the venture and only government ships were used.[87] Some now felt that this method would be equally applicable to shipments of rice from Siam. In 1751, Fukien Governor P'an Shih-chü memorialized this recommendation to Ch'ien-lung, stating that since Fukien and Chekiang were desperately in need of rice, official management of the Siamese rice shipment might actually be more beneficial to the livelihood of the people there. But Ch'ien-lung felt that the planning of official management might generate suspicion among foreigners. The Siamese might attempt to hoard the rice or resort to blackmail which would cause prices to soar. He ordered the Min-Che viceroy, K'a-erh-chi-shan, to deliberate the matter and send a detailed memorial to him about it.[88]

The governor-general soon reported to the emperor that since Siam was small and thinly populated and the rice surplus unpredictable, officials would find it difficult to avoid immediate hoarding and high prices; he recommended that private merchants rather than officials should handle the trade.[89]

There were two schools of thought among Fukien officials on the advisability of official management of the rice acquisition, each side obviously with its own vested interests. The emperor himself was more inclined toward the position adopted by K'a-erh-chi-shan, that is, to let the rice trade continue under private handling. The main concern was the abuses that would hinder the Sino-

Siamese rice trade. And the image projected by the opponents of official management of the Siamese was that the latter were opportunists ready to extort outrageous prices from Chinese officials. Nonetheless, by 1753, Ch'ien-lung seems to have made up his mind to discard the idea of official handling altogether. In that year a Siamese embassy arrived to present tribute, and the governor-general of Liang-Kuang memorialized that in recent years rice had been shipped from Siam which helped make up for the local deficit. In order to supplement public granaries, a special commissioner ought to be deputized to purchase and transport rice from Siam directly; but the rice transported from overseas in commercial ships should be sold immediately upon their arrival at port, since the grain would not keep in granaries for long. The governor-general and other local Kwangtung officials therefore concluded that it would still be better, that is, more practical, to allow local merchants to continue to do the buying and shipping in any amount that would benefit local rice relief.[90]

As a matter of fact, back in 1751 Ch'ien-lung had already informed Fukien officials that local merchants sailing to Siam for rice should be encouraged: those transporting two thousand piculs (266,000 lbs.) or more would be rewarded. The emperor considered that official handling would indeed be costly, and handling by the Siamese side might be uncertain and unreliable; hence, the best alternative would be to encourage local merchants to trade in Siam. Shortly afterward, K'a-erh-chi-shan memorialized a scheme aimed at inducing local (Fukien) efforts to import rice from Siam, ostensibly to aid the population of the province. Honorary titles would be bestowed on those who brought back certain amounts of rice.[91]

The proposal struck the emperor's fancy, and in 1754 he approved a formal plan to encourage rice importation from Southeast Asia (explicitly from Siam), as shown in Table 4.

A similar scheme was introduced for neighboring Kwangtung two years later in 1756, after the governor-general of Liang-Kuang, Yang Ying-chü, and others had memorialized the court that people from the province were also similarly engaged in shipping rice from

Table 4

The Fukien Encouragement Plan for Rice Importation from Siam (1754)

Amount of rice transported (in piculs)	Award for degree holders, sheng and chien (national and local academy graduates)		Award for merchants
1,501-2,000	*li-mu*	title	9th rank button
2,001-4,000	*chu-po*	"	8th " "
4,001-6,000	*hsien-ch'eng*	"	7th " "
6,001-10,000	*chou-p'an* (Second class Assistant, Department of the Magistrate, 7b)	"	*pa-tsung* (Sub-lieutenant, 7a)
Over 10,000	The governor/or governor-general would make special considerations as to the appropriate award(s) to be given.		

Source: Feng Liu-t'ang. *Chung-kuo li-tai min-shih cheng-ts'e shih* (Taipei, 1970), pp. 226-227.

overseas to relieve conditions, and hence were entitled to the encouragement granted to Fukien as well. The emperor therefore pronounced that thereafter eastern Kwangtung individuals and merchants who proceeded to Annam, Siam, and so forth, with their own capital to ship rice back to Kwangtung would be eligible for the scheme of awards indicated in Table 5.

Furthermore those carrying more than the maximum amount prescribed would be entitled to additional awards but no more buttons. Each merchant transporting rice to Kwangtung would sell at the current market price, and no hoarding was to be allowed.

One common feature may be observed in the above: Fukien through this period had seemingly received "preferential" consideration over the other provinces (Kwangtung included) in matters pertaining to the maritime transportation of rice. The inducement schemes above indicate that higher rewards were given to the Fukien merchants than those from Kwangtung for comparable

Table 5

The Kwangtung Encouragement Plan for
Rice Importation from Siam (1756)

Amount of rice transported (in piculs)	Award for degree holders, sheng and chien (national and local academy graduates)		Award for merchants
Within 2,000	governor/or governor-general to consider appropriate award(s) in individual cases		governor/or governor-general to consider appropriate award(s) in individual cases
2,001–4,000	*li-mu*	title	9th rank button
4,001–6,000	*chu-po*	”	8th ” ”
6,001–16,000	*hsien-ch'eng*	”	7th ” ”

Source: *Ming-Ch'ing Shih-liao* (Taipei, 1960), *keng* (7th part), 8:736b-737a.

quantities of rice imported. This difference may be due, in one respect, to the greater urgency of rice demands in Fukien, and, consequently, to the need for greater inducement. At the same time, however, one must mention the importance of Fukien to the rice trade conducted since the early 1720s. With Amoy as the hub of the Sino-Siamese rice trade and, as a matter of fact, of the general trade between the two countries, it is only natural that precedent-setting measures and decrees would emanate from Fukien. Fukien merchants and local officials at southern Fukien involved with international trade must have been active in promoting measures thought to be beneficial to their undertaking.

Records of the amounts of rice imported by local Chinese after the proclamation of the inducement schemes are few, but from what is available a general idea may be derived as to the general effect of the new measures. For instance, the governor of Fukien reported that in 1757 local merchants transported over 39,000 piculs (5,198,700 lbs.) from Southeast Asia.[92]

During the years 1754, 1755 and 1758, the annual rice imports by local merchants of Fukien ranged from 90,000 to 120,000 piculs (approximately 12-16 million pounds), which undoubtedly was a major aid to the province's rice situation. Fukien's governor-general commented in 1765 that such transport had been steadily increasing, and was indeed quite effective.[93] Back in 1759 Min-Che Governor-General Yang T'ing-chang memorialized the court emphatically about the necessity of the encouragement scheme which he said was responsible for a steady flow of rice into China. Also from this memorial, we learn that local merchants venturing to Siam for rice had first to obtain an official permit. Upon the ship's return to Amoy, the customs and port authorities would inspect it for the quantity of rice and would then notify the proper channel for the disposition of the cargo to help feed the people of Chang-chou and Ch'üan-chou. Also, any mention of the involvement of degree holders (*sheng* or *chien*) in the rice importation was conspicuously absent.

Thus foreign rice imports by local merchants reached the hundred thousand picul (13.3 m. lbs.) mark by the middle of the 1750s, only a few years after the official encouragement plans went into effect. But as quickly as it rose, this branch of trade also took a plunge after 1757-1758 when the annual import rate went down from 90,000-120,000 to 60,000-10,000 piculs. By 1759, the decline became marked, as reported by Min-Che Governor-General Yang T'ing-chang, who tried to persuade Ch'ien-lung to extend the encouragement scheme. By the middle of the following decade, Su-teng, the Min-Che governor-general, memorialized that the amount of outside rice imported had become rather small, so much so that it could not fill the need at the two South Fukien prefectures. Despite the allowance for a limit of 200 piculs (26,660 lbs.) of rice for each ship seeking grain relief at Formosa (which supplied about half of Fukien's rice each year) and freedom to carry back unlimited amounts of rice from Southeast Asia (to which was added an inducement scheme), the handling of foreign rice from Southeast Asia had become erratic.[94]

The governor-general offered some explanations for the decline. First, prices had fluctuated because of harvesting conditions in the rice-producing regions in Southeast Asia from one year to another. Secondly, those few merchants who had sufficient capital to transport rice from abroad, had already carried out the venture and had duly received their awards. Only those small merchants who could not afford to undertake such a venture were left and they were not eager to plunge into this trade. Consequently between 1759 and 1765, no awards were given out for Fukien. The governor-general personally felt that the second reason was a more significant cause for the drop in foreign rice imports.[95]

Su-teng went on further to report that rice was crucial, especially along the coast and the hinterland of Chang-chou and Ch'üan-chou prefectures, and additional means must be devised to encourage further importation of foreign rice or the shortage would eventually compel local prices to soar even more. He added that for 1765, rice was abundant in Southeast Asia and prices low. So the opportunity should be seized to enable the local people to benefit from its supplies. He therefore proposed that if the amounts of imported rice that were entitled to various types of awards as specified in the inducement scheme of 1754 could be somewhat modified (i.e. lowered), then big and small merchants would have an added incentive to gather their capital and endeavor to go to Southeast Asia to seek supplies. He also proposed giving additional numbers of honorary ranks of *pa-tsung* (sub-lieutenant, 7a) for commoner-merchants, and ranks of *chou-p'an* (second-class assistant, Department of the Magistrate 7b) to the degree holders (the local and national academy graduates).[96]

Finally, Su-teng recommended that since all the *yang-hang* (firms engaged in overseas trade) were based at Amoy, Fukien vessels trading to Southeast Asia would have to leave from, and return to, Amoy only. No other ports were to be opened for the purpose of conducting this trade, with the exception of the provincial capital Foochow which served as the assembly point for trade with the "eastern ocean" (*tung-yang*), and which had a dense population and little farmland; hence commerce must be kept open for the sake of the people's livelihood, and rice from abroad would also be much needed.[97] The emperor granted his vermillion endorsement to this recommendation designed to bolster the handling of rice imports from Southeast Asia by local Fukien people.

Starting from 1756, when Kwangtung was authorized to adopt an inducement plan similar to that of Fukien, a sizable number of local merchants there also went to Southeast Asia to secure rice. Again since only partial records are available, we do not know the real amounts of rice imported into the province in such a manner. Still in 1758 it was reported that a total of 24,776 piculs (3,282,650 lbs.) of rice was taken into Kwangtung from Siam, Cambodia, and the Dutch East Indies. Table 6 shows the individual merchants eligible for awards under the encouragement plan in that year.

Liang-Kuang Governor-General Li Tsou memorialized that apart from the seven vessels managed by the above-mentioned merchants, there were also nine other junks which carried less than 2,000 piculs of rice apiece; they were awarded accordingly (but not awarded any mandarin buttons) by the local authorities. Rice shipments were carefully checked by the Canton provincial financial administration (Pu-cheng-shih ssu) which also supervised their sale to the public. All the merchants involved also reportedly purchased the rice with their own capital and at their own risk.[98]

Table 7 represents the next available set of statistics for rice importation by local merchants into Kwangtung, dated 1767. It was provided by the Canton financial administration for the court at Peking.

The attitude of the government at the local and national levels toward these awards was favorable: they considered that rice importation was beneficial and should be encouraged by bestowing awards on those who undertook it with their own capital. Apparently Kwangtung was not eligible for the revised inducement plan instituted by the court for Fukien in 1765, but those merchants transporting under 2,000 piculs were given awards by local officials, just as under Fukien's first plan in 1754.[99]

If the above is representative of rice importation from Southeast Asia by local merchants of Kwangtung, it is interesting that at first the merchants were mostly from the environs of Canton city, the Nan-hai district; Ch'ao-chou merchants (notably those

Table 6

Awards Granted to Kwangtung Importers of Foreign Rice (1758)

Name	Amount transported (in piculs)	Award
Chiang Wang-t'ing of Nan-hai	over 3,840	ninth-rank button
Ch'en Ch'eng-wen of " "	3,110	"
Ch'ü Yu-t'ang of " "	over 2,710	"
Ch'en Kuan-ch'eng of " "	" 2,300	"
Yeh Chien-ch'en of " "	" 2,660	"
Lin Kuang-ch'ao of " "	" 2,220	"
Kuo Chun-yin of " "	" 2,330	"

Source: *Ming-Ch'ing shih-liao* (Taipei, 1960), *keng* (7th part), 6:526b-527a.

Table 7

Awards Granted to Kwangtung Importers of Foreign Rice (1767)

Name	Amount transported (in piculs)	Award
Lu Tsan of Fan-ü dist.	over 2,857	ninth-rank button
Chih Kang of Nan-hai dist.	" 2,521	"
Yang Li-ts'ai of Ch'eng-hai dist.	" 2,700	"
Ts'ai Chih-kuei* of " "	" 2,200	*li-mu*
Ts'ai Ch'i-ho of " "	" 2,200	ninth-rank button
Lin Ho-wan of " "	" 1,800	"
Ts'ai Chia of " "	" 2,600	"
Yao Chün-ho of " "	" 2,200	"
Ch'en Yüan-yu of " "	" 2,200	"

*Listed as a National Academy graduate.

Source: *Ming-Ch'ing shih-liao* (Taipei, 1960), *keng* (7th part), VIII, 736b-738a.

from the Ch'eng-hai district) in eastern Kwangtung did not become engaged in this trade until the 1760s. When Kwangtung authorities requested the adoption of Fukien's encouragement plan (in 1756), this was ostensibly for the benefit of the eastern Kwangtung merchants, who lived in an area more deficient in rice than the rest of Kwangtung. The merchants in the Canton area were more actively involved in the rice trade at this time perhaps because the Canton city market was better equipped to handle large volumes of rice, especially when the rice had to be transacted upon its arrival at port; one would naturally be apt to find more merchants with adequate capital to invest in trade congregating at the main international trading center of the province. Nevertheless, from the 1760s onward, Ch'eng-hai merchants were to play an increasingly vital role in the rice trade with Siam and eventually went on to become the most important Chinese merchants there. Ch'eng-hai ships reportedly started to trade to Siam by the early 1760s and were directly responsible for later influxes of Ch'ao-chou people into the country.

It seems that the rice imports for Kwangtung were smaller in volume than those of Fukien, probably for several reasons. Fukien's ability to import more rice because of a greater demand for the grain, the virtual dominance of Amoy merchants in the Southeast Asia trade, larger and better organized capital, and so forth. After the 1760s, however, rice importation from Southeast Asia into Fukien declined due to the closure of the latter to foreign trade. Conversely, rice continued to flow into Kwangtung (after short periods of disruption), when Canton became the sole international trading port.

Another point to note is that it is impossible to discern exactly what portion of the total rice imports from Southeast Asia into Kwangtung came from Siam. It can, however, be generalized that until the fall of Ayudhya in 1767, Siam continued to be an important rice source for local merchants from both Fukien and Kwangtung. Nevertheless for the few decades after the mid-1760s Siam played a lesser role mainly because of internal warfare. Annam and Cambodia were mentioned more frequently than Siam, and during this period, the supply center of foreign rice for Kwangtung was probably Annam, while Fukien relied increasingly on Luzon and Batavia. Siamese rice importation in Kwangtung was not mentioned again until after the 1780s. By then Annam was involved in a long civil war, and new forces had emerged to affect the mode of rice importation from Southeast Asia by the Kwangtung merchants.

In analyzing the role of the inducement plan instituted for local merchants, one has to remember the basic differentiation made by the court at Peking between the rice trade conducted by local merchants and that assumed by the Siamese side. As we have seen the importers of Siamese rice to Southeast China had been accorded many privileges, including the reduction of various taxes, ostensibly as a kind gesture toward a distant tributary state. Although local Chinese merchants also contributed substantially to famine relief in Fukien and Kwangtung by investing in the shipping of rice and although the court had demonstrated some willingness to encourage their action local merchants never had a free hand in fully developing this trade. The standard official reason may have been true that the decline of rice imports by local merchants was due to the lack of local capital, for although the encouragement plans of the Chinese government were indeed helpful, the absence of judicious governmental assistance prevented any strong possibility of storing up large enough sums to invest in rice transportation. The Ch'ien-lung government also followed its predecessors' policy of granting no tax break to the local merchants.

An edict of 1752, in response to a previous memorial by A-li-kun, the viceroy of Liang-Kuang, reflects the official stand regarding the question of granting import duty exemption on rice shipments by local merchants. Although this edict came two years before the special schedule for awarding honorary ranks to the local importers, the pronounced policy apparently remained unchanged through the eighteenth century. In essence, the edict reflects both the court's apprehension about letting local merchants at Kwangtung and Fukien have too much freedom or too great an influence concerning the Chinese maritime trade, and the local officials' jealousy in clinging to the vital means of their livelihood, that is "squeeze," through their perogatives. The edict pointed out that much revenue would be lost if local merchants were "subjected to the same treatment." The encouragement of rice imports was the reason for tax favors to foreign ships. It finally stated that "to have customs is to collect taxes from merchants."[100]

The incentive plans were meant at best to be a temporary measure while the situation in Southeast China remained precarious. K'ang-hsi at the end of his reign experimented with Siamese rice import. His son Yung-cheng relied further on this trade by encouraging the Siamese side to sell more rice by giving them special privileges. Although his successor Ch'ien-lung continued this practice, he also allowed additional participation by local merchants. The incentive plans were consequently his pragmatic approach toward solving the food problem of Southeast China. Although all this represents the ability of Yung-cheng and Ch'ien-lung to respond realistically to the economic conditions of the day, it also reflects a certain amount of ambivalence toward permitting full-fledged Chinese participation. The rice trade in the early decades of the eighteenth century, nevertheless, represents a significant stride in the development of the Sino-Siamese trade.

Rice Trade in Late 18th and Early 19th Centuries

The shortage of food in Siam became very serious during the first decade after the fall of Ayudhya in 1766. War naturally disrupted rice production, and even after Taksin emerged as the unifier of the new Siam, the struggle with Burma and other rival principalities—which had formerly paid allegiance to Ayudhya—continued unabated. Added to this was the misfortune of famine, a serious drought, for instance, in 1769. Turpin, using records of the French missionaries present in Siam at the time, wrote that "the price of rice in Siam after 1767 had risen to such an extent that it had ceased to become a marketable commodity. Wildroots and bamboo shoots were the staple articles of diet."[101]

Siamese chroniclers lend authenticity to Turpin's statement, in spite of the fact that Turpin has been regarded by some as biased, because he was sympathetic to French missionaries who were mistreated by Taksin. Prince Damrong Rajanubhab, the "Father of Thai history," said that when Taksin ascended the throne, rice was so scarce that he had to send vessels to ship it from as far as Pontemeas (Kang-k'ou) for sale in Thonburi at 3-5 *baht* (at least .75 to 1.25 Siamese taels or the equivalent of 1.2 to 2 taels Chinese) per barrel, and also to distribute it to the needy. The price eventually rose to 2.3 taels Siamese per picul (3.7 taels Chinese, £1.15, a much higher price than that during the crisis years 1720s-1750s in Southeast China), and more vessels were sent to the south for additional stocks.[102] By 1770 the capital still had to continue importing rice from far-away places.[103] Still, Siam had all the natural assets for a speedy recovery toward at least an adequate production. Dr. Jean Koenig described the potential abundance of rice in Siam in 1779-1780 in the following way: "The soil in these parts, the capital and its adjoining areas [or the so-called Central Plains] is very fertile, and particularly suitable for the cultivation of rice. . . There are generally two harvests of rice yearly, the first one being in December. Along the banks of the river only there is woods, from 100 to 1,000 feet wide, and behind this woods begin the never ending rice fields."[104] With the normalization of the country's sociopolitical conditions, much rice could again be produced.

In the meantime, local officials of Fukien (whose population had grown to 8,063,671 or 174.09/sq. mile by 1761, as compared with Kwangtung's 6,797,587 or 68/sq. mile)[105] continued to encourage the local importation of rice from Siam. The existing incentive plan was again amended in 1774, with a further provision that those who had already obtained the highest decoration available, that is, the honorary rank of *pa-tsung* for shipment of 6,000-10,000 piculs (800,000-1,330,000 lbs.), and who continued to import rice would be entitled to additional awards (though no further honorary ranks), and that they could also continue selling at Foochow in addition to Amoy.[106]

There are reasons to suspect, however, that the role of Fukienese merchants in handling the importation of rice from Siam (and from other places in Southeast Asia) declined from this time on.

One major cause may have been the closure of Amoy to trade by foreigners in 1758, which had a direct effect in curtailing the role of the *yang-hang* licensed to do business with Southeast Asia. While Amoy was still open, the *Hsia-men chih* noted abundant profits from goods transported in foreign ships from abroad. But now that profits had been slashed, the *yang-hang* found it increasingly difficult to meet the annual tributes payable to local officials. So by 1769, the number of *yang-hang* had dropped to seven.[107]

Concurrently, a new area emerged to assume the leadership in the Sino-Siamese rice trade and, later, other trade: the Ch'eng-hai district of Ch'ao-chou prefecture. This geographical shift was to have significant consequences in the history of the overall Sino-Siamese trade.

We learn from a memorial by the Liang-Kuang governor-general, Wu Hsiung-kuang, in 1807 that for forty-odd years between the 1760s and 1800s, the merchants of Ch'eng-hai had been allowed by the Kwangtung authorities to ship rice from Siam to Kwangtung. During this period, though such ships had been keeping up a steady supply, of every ten vessels that sailed for Siam, no more than five or six had returned. Moreover, there were discrepancies in the supposed and actual quantities of rice shipped back, which led officials to conclude that the ships might have collaborated with pirates who had their lairs at Kao-chou and Lui-chou in Kwangtung. The governor-general therefore recommended an end to the granting of licenses to local merchants for trips to Siam to ship rice. Chia-ch'ing, fearing abuses of the privilege, readily consented to issue an edict to this effect.[108]

This memorial reveals that, in the latter half of the eighteenth century, residents of Ch'eng-hai apparently dominated the Sino-Siamese rice trade. This predominance continued officially for forty years, and was evident from the time of Taksinon: Taksin himself was from Ch'eng-hai. By the beginning of Rama I's reign, such Ch'eng-hai merchants settled on the site of the present-day Chinatown and business district in Bangkok and are said to have occupied the prime commercial positions in the capital district.[109]

In Rama I's reign, rice production within Siam recovered

somewhat. Rice exportation to China must have resumed by the 1780s though the amount could still have been small, owing to the need within the country itself.[110] In the 1790s, after he took Saigon, Nguyen Anh, contender for the Vietnamese throne, notified Bangkok of a rice shortage in Saigon, and invited merchants from Siam to ship rice there to aid the war effort. This was the beginning of a series of Vietnamese requests for Siamese rice in the Gia Long and subsequent Min Mang periods (1802-1841). In the last quarter of the eighteenth century, there were periodic famines and floods such as that in 1794 which caused extensive damage to farmland and forced the rice price up to 20 taels Siamese per *koyan* (0.72d./lb., or one-third of the highest price during Taksin's time), as well as making it necessary for the Krom Na or Department of Agriculture to release surplus stocks of unhusked rice from government granaries in large quantities for distribution to the public.[111] But the country's production as a whole was on its way to recovery.

It would seem, therefore, that with the exception of the few years of rice shortage due to natural calamities, Siam, in the last two decades of the eighteenth century, was once again in a good position to resume sizable exports to China. In the reign of Rama I, exports to Canton, Amoy, and Ningpo continued to flow, with Siamese rice carriers bringing back large quantities of bricks and building materials for the construction of the new capital at Bangkok.[112]

In the 1780s and 1790s the Chinese government declared an expanded plan aimed at increasing the sources of foreign rice importation into Kwangtung. The chronic high prices of rice in eastern Kwangtung compelled the court to proclaim in 1786 and 1795 that any foreign merchant willing to transport rice to sell at Canton would receive a waiver of measurement and import duties.[113]

Between that time and 1806, since all foreign vessels taking rice to Canton were exempt from tax, and since rice from such places as Luzon and Manila was only three to four mace a picul, Canton rivers were filled with rice ships while other types of ships numbered about the same. In 1806 the Liang-Kuang governor, Wu Hsiung-kuang, and other local officials recommended that thereafter foreign merchants transporting rice to Whampoa or Macao should not be permitted to take away any cargo at all. Other goods accompanying the rice shipment were also to be taxed, and measurement fees for the vessel re-established. To Wei Yuan this move was an attempt by local authorities at Canton to hinder rice importation (though its professed benefit was harped on consistently) because the tax exemption privilege accorded earlier to foreign rice shipments had not benefited the authorities and would explain the motive behind their recommendations.[114]

The Canton officials, however, had a way of manipulating existing rules and regulations to their satisfaction. For a brief period, the recommendations were put into effect. Prior to 1826, the governor-general also imposed a restriction, though not sanctioned in writing by the Peking court, as to the specific quantity of 4,050 piculs (about 533,200 lbs.) to be taken into Canton by foreign vessels.[115] This impractical restriction was not meant to be enforced literally, but more as a means of extortion. At any rate, in 1826, this regulation was rescinded along with the previous recommendation, and a provision stipulated in its place that ships with a full cargo of rice would not be subject to measurement duties at Canton.

In time of real need, local officials were ready to revert to any inducement that would bring about the importation of the desired quantities of foreign rice. In 1806, for instance, the governor-general and customs superintendent, concerned with the high price of rice that year (4 to 5 Spanish dollars a picul and rising) which could cause a food riot, solicited the importation of rice from Bengal. As an inducement, the customs superintendent offered to waive all port charges, and hong merchants (Mowqua, Puiqua, and Conseequa) were prepared to subscribe 25,000 Spanish dollars. The British responded by importing over 300,000 piculs (20,000 tons), conveyed both by country and Company ships, to Canton.[116] In 1809, the governor-general made another inquiry for rice importation from Bengal, with the similar offer that all dues would be waived and the carriers exempt from measurement fees. The request was renewed in the following year, but since the British representatives at Canton insisted on both occasions that a satisfactory minimum price guarantee be made before shipment was acceded to, no actual order was filled in both instances.[117]

There is hardly any available record pertaining to rice importation into China from Siam during the 1800s and 1810s, so it is rather difficult even to guess at the state of the rice importation. One may be certain, however, that rice shipments were made in the latter part of the reign of Rama I, because the population of Kwangtung and Fukien had grown so phenomenally by this time (by about 30 percent in the two provinces between 1787-1812, with the average national percentage for the comparable period being only 24 percent).[118] It may also be reasonable to expect continued profitability in this trade in spite of expanding competition from other sources on which China could depend (such as Bengal);[119] the source of demand itself was increasing and was large enough to accommodate all available foreign rice imported. The only problems would be, that, first of all, the supplying source, Siam, in certain years might not have any rice for export due to the shortage caused by natural calamities (for example, in 1811 when Siam reportedly had to import rice from Vietnam).[120] Furthermore, the avaricious conduct of local officials at Canton, particularly the recommendations for terminating inducements to foreign rice ships, had the effect of curtailing the number of rice shipments into China.[121]

Ever since the recovery of production from the time of Rama I, Siamese rice was popular in China and even today it is still considered the best by Chinese. An Englishman observed in the late 1810s that part of the popularity was due to its competitive prices. "I know nowhere that rice is so cheap as in Java " he said, "except in Siam, and here it is exported as low as 10 Spanish dollars per *koyan* [26 Siamese piculs], or for one third the price even of Java rice. A great deal of the rice of this country is therefore exported to China by the junks."[122]

John Crawfurd added an interesting note on the lucrative trade in Java rice, which he said could fetch a 150 to 200 percent profit at the Kwangtung market.[123] Also, it may be said that Siamese rice fetched at least this much profit at Kwangtung, if not more, since by 1847, the Siamese nobility was making as much as a 320 percent profit in exporting rice to Singapore, then dependent on the staple for subsistence.[124]

At the beginning of the Third Chakri Reign, rice in Siam was reportedly very plentiful. This abundance coincided with a renewed effort by the Chinese government to import more rice into Southeast China. In 1825, in an attempt to encourage greater importation of foreign rice, local officials at Canton again tried to modify the existing regulations. In that year the Liang-Kuang governor-general (Juan Yuan), the governor, and the hoppo, jointly memorialized the Peking court about the continued rice shortage in Kwangtung, stating that though the previous rules allowed for the exemption of measurement duties for vessels with a full cargo of rice, they did not permit such vessels to take away any Chinese ballast. In recent years, therefore, the amounts of foreign rice coming to Kwangtung had been small, for though foreign lands were vast with small populations and much grain, to transport rice without a cargo to ballast the vessel was considered "dangerous" (and unbeneficial).

Consequently, the officials recommended that the existing policy should be modified, and cargoes of goods be permitted to be carried on board for the return. They were to be subject, however, to taxation just like other cargoes exported by foreigners, but with the rice imported still to be duty free and salable at current market prices. The memorialists rationalized that by enacting this measure, more shipments of foreign rice would steadily flow in, and though no duties were to be assessed, the export duties (on other articles acquired to ballast the ships) would more than make up for the apparent loss of the tax revenue and both local people and foreigners would benefit. The emperor concurred, noting in the process that since those foreign ships transporting rice to Canton and Macao more frequently carried small rice shipments of 300 to one or two thousand piculs, the recommended scheme would not drastically affect the collection of customs.[125]

A few years later Wei Yuan saw this as another move by local officials to put a squeeze in foreign rice importation, this time by making foreign importers pay duties on export cargoes. But, in spite of the new measure, which now allowed for duty exemption on the rice cargo as well as on the port charges in order to encourage rice imports, rice shipments by foreigners did not increase greatly in this period. Although rice was the only article of trade free from duty, the exemption must have been qualified for many reasons including highly fluctuating prices due to unforeseeable demands. Also, due to strict governmental control along the Chinese coast, foreign importers found it difficult to sell articles (including rice) except those that yielded huge profits, such as opium, which the Chinese were willing to risk purchasing. Rice shipments hence had been used to cloak opium import.[126] There were other instances in which foreign merchants exchanged their contraband opium for rice outside of Canton and then resold the rice obtained without duty at the port, as was mentioned in a British dispatch in 1826 and quoted by H. B. Morse: "Some instances have occurred of a cargo of rice the produce of the country being smuggled on board of vessels at Lintin from Macao and the adjacent islands and ultimately brought to Whampoa and forming a protection from the Port Charges."[127]

In the 1830s, rice, even though carried to the thickly populated and almost barren districts of northeastern Kwangtung and western Fukien, did not have a ready or remunerative market. Dealing with local officials was a persistent problem which made foreign merchants even more hesitant to send rice shipments. The supposed exemption of rice importation alone from duties was never fully implemented in the absolute sense; in actual fact fees, both those that were professedly legal and those that were in effect illegal, were still being demanded. A British correspondent for the *Chinese Repository* commented on this issue in his review of a book entitled *Considerations Respecting the Trade with China* (1835), authored by one Joseph Thompson: "The remarks as to the exemption of ships importing rice alone, from all port charges, is another proof of how loose is the information on which Mr. Thompson gives to the British public as 'fact' . . . The fact is that ships 'importing rice alone' are yet subject to charges, legal and illegal . . .

the imperial edict, no doubt, says that 'ships entering the port [Canton] with rice alone' are to be no longer charged with the 'enter port dues,' but as nothing is said of the 'go out port dues,' they are yet levied; this may be taken as a fair specimen of the mode in which the imperial orders favouring foreigners are obeyed in Canton."[128]

In the 1830s foreign vessels importing rice alone were exempt from a measurement charge (the usual measurement charge on a 300-ton vessel was 650 taels, and that on a 1,200-ton vessel was 3,000 dollars) and part of the *cumsha* or "gift" (of 1,950 dollars normally), as well as from the linguists and compradores' fees. However, such vessels were still liable, after an announcement by the Peking court in May 1833, for the legal charges of port clearance fee ("opening of the bar" at Canton), and the fee to the superintendent of grain, which amounted to, with the percentages, about 620 taels Chinese. Apart from these legal fees, the court forbade local officials to levy other charges. Nonetheless, as matters naturally turned out, the rice ships were assessed various other illegal fees which totaled about 1,000 Spanish dollars.[129] In addition, as soon as the incentive regulations were put into effect minor local officials expressed dissatisfaction. For instance, the linguists complained to the Kwangtung governor that although they received nothing from the ships importing rice, they were still obliged to pay the charges to the customs house officers who, having to purchase their posts, would not forego the usual fees. According to J. R. Morrison, the governor, who had actually been behind the exemption plan and had duly notified the foreigners, could not retract his word. He therefore directed the customs house to be satisfied with half fees, and in order to make up for the rest, security merchants (*pao shang*) at Canton were forced to contribute 150 taels. Still this was not sufficient and the linguists had to pay something in addition. Consequently, the hong merchants repaid themselves out of the price of rice, while the linguist, "not having that resource had to make up his loss by increased profit on other vessels."

The local government itself was aware of this practice, for in 1833 the governor (and others) sent a communication to the hong merchants stating that because of the need for rice from foreign countries they had "implored the [imperial] favor to promise the barbarian ships of all nations, that if they come without any other cargo but rice, to the port of Canton, as formerly, they shall not pay the entry port duties. Let the hong merchants report how much rice they have brought, store it up in their hongs, and sell it according to the market price. After having disposed of this, allow these ships to take in export duties according to the same laws as apply to other barbarian ships. This will benefit the revenues, suit the people, and bring foreign business upon a firm footing; and all parties will be equally benefited."[130]

This request was granted. But not many rice vessels called at the port of Canton in 1832 and the governor expressed his fear that there had been extortions and illegal duties which prevented the "barbarians from trading." He therefore commanded the hong merchants to see to it that rice ships pay export duties and customs "according to the established imperial tariff" and if they dared to disobey the merchants would be "punished, prosecuted, and all banished." "When the rice has entered the harbor," the proclamation read, "and passes the customhouse, let it be entirely disposed of, and let the hong merchants and shopkeepers give notice of it, for the advantage of the people. But every shopkeeper who retails it and sells it in small quantities, ought to confine himself to this province, to dispose of it (exportation is not permitted). Everybody ought to obey this implicitly and not slight this special proclamation."[131]

In spite of the above impediments, some foreign rice shipments did arrive in the 1830s. In 1833, American shipping alone brought to Canton more than 125,000 piculs (16.7 m. lbs.), while the British, Spanish, Dutch and Portuguese imported about 270,000 piculs (26 m. lbs.). Altogether the rice imports from these sources came to over 53 million pounds. Lin Tse-hsu said in the late thirties that since China did not produce sufficient rice, it had to depend partly on foreign rice importation, which in recent years, was conducted by American and British mainly from Singapore, Batavia, and Manila. Siam had shipped a great deal of rice to Singapore, and part of this must have been reshipped to China by the Westerners.[132]

As far as Siam was concerned, good rice harvest continued to be reported throughout the 1830s. In Rama III's reign no unhusked or husked rice could be exported without the express consent of the Siamese government as the court followed past precedents and prohibited the export of rice unless there was at least a three years' reserve on hand in the country's granaries.[133] O. Frankfurter explained the rationale of this ancient policy: "As in other countries of the Far East the economical ideas prevailing were absolutely against the export of rice, as there was always the fear that a dearth might occur, and thus the export of rice was as a rule absolutely forbidden."[134]

To Frankfurter's note one may add the fact that the Chinese had traditionally been favored by the Siamese, and that the Siamese king had usually taken part in the exportation to the lucrative China market. Since the country was most of the time abundant in rice and since the tropical climate normally did not permit storage of the grain for a long period, the king expanded the years of non-export to the Westerners to meet the ever-increasing demands of the China market.

With the possible exception of the years 1831-1832,[135] shipments abroad were still regularly authorized by the king.[136] Chinese junks trading to Siam usually took back rice as a returning cargo, since its export duty was much lower compared to that of another popular Siamese export commodity, sapan wood.[137] Charles Gützlaff observed in the early 1830s that Siamese rice was very popular, for crewmen of Chinese junks all took bags of it to give their families in China on their return voyage.[138]

By the early 1840s the rice situation at Kwangtung and Fukien was still such that continued reliance on foreign rice was inevitable. And at this time, Fukien's rice trade with Southeast Asia had again become significant. From Amoy (which was an important opium smuggling center), Chinese junks sailed to Siam and other places to trade, bringing back rice. Rice in Siam was still very cheap: 3 mace a picul (or 3s. per 133.3 lbs.) and much of it was sent to Fukien both by Fukien merchants or resident Chinese in Bangkok who were engaged in illicit trade beyond the port of Canton. The volume of rice imported from Siam was great enough to cause a decline in the sale of Taiwan rice, though the latter's importance to Fukien as a main rice granary continued. By the beginning of the 1850s, rice was certainly Siam's principal crop; its position as the number one crop of the country had been challenged by sugar, whose production in the 1830s actually surpassed that of rice. In 1850, Siam produced sufficient rice for local consumption as well as for export to China, enough to feed the population of Southeast China when the rice crop failed. Meanwhile, the Siamese nobility were making as much as a 320 percent profit by collaborating with resident Chinese at Bangkok in transporting rice to Singapore.[139] Until the Bowring Treaty in 1855, British merchants, desirous of participating in the lucrative rice trade from Siam to Singapore, were outclassed by Chinese merchants who held a monopoly.

D. E. Malloch quoted the rice prices of Siam in the early 1850s as shown in Table 8.

This rice, of various grades, is said to have been exported to China annually at 200,000 piculs (or 800 *koyan*) at 18 sicca rupees per *koyan* of cargo rice, making the shipment worth 36,000 taels Siamese (£18,000) or 57,600 taels Chinese.[140]

Lastly, the opening of Siam also had a favorable effect upon the export of Siamese rice. The implication of free trade as stipulated by the Bowring Treaty provided for the further augmentation of the rice trade, which in turn brought the Chinese to prominence as middlemen. Independent Chinese went directly to the Siamese farmers and sold their procurements directly to millers. The middlemen also made loans, advanced supplies, and rented out land, as well as selling imported merchandise. Homan Van der Heide gave the breakdown of rice export from Siam in the Fourth Reign after the treaty (Table 9).

James Ingram's estimates, however, vary significantly from the above. He postulates that the volume from 1857-1859 was 990,000 piculs (about 133 m. lbs.), averaging 330,000 piculs (44 m. lbs.) a

Table 8

Rice Prices of Siam in 1850

Koyan of 25 piculs	Highest/in taels Siamese	Lowest/taels Siamese
First quality	8 (£4)	7.0 (£3.5)
Second quality	7 (£3.5)	6.5 (£3.25)
Inferior quality	5 (£2.5)	4.5 (£2.25)

Source: D. E. Malloch, *Siam: Some General Remarks on Its Productions* (Calcutta, 1852), p. 43.

Table 8A

Some Siamese Rice Export Figures
for the Decade Following the Bowring Treaty

Year	Volume	
1857	60,000 piculs	(7.0 m. lbs.)
1858	70,000 "	(7.3 m. ")
1859	50,000 "	(6.7 m. ")
1860	95,000 "	(12.7 m. ")
1861	128,000 "	(15.0 m. ")

Source: H. Homan Van der Heide. "Economic Development of Siam during the Last Half Century," *Journal of the Siam Society* 3.2:82n (1906).

year. That for 1860–1864 is given at 1,840,000 piculs (about 240 m. lbs.) or 368,000 piculs (58 m. lbs.) annually.[141] Ingram's figures perhaps lend a greater degree of credibility.

China remained the most important market for Siamese rice. Aside from the recurrent population pressures and natural calamities in Southeast China, in the 1850s and early 1860s, the entire country was feeling the effect of the Taiping Rebellion and other popular uprisings (such as the Nien and the Moslem revolts). In 1856, the Taiping forces seized control of the middle and lower reaches of the Yangtze, and the traditional artery of the rice transport to Fukien and the tribute rice (ts'ao-mi) transport to North China was severed, causing widespread starvation. The Peking court frantically sought a large-scale importation of foreign rice for relief, designating Canton as the assembly point. The court instructed the Liang-Kuang governor-general, Yeh Min-shen, to acquire at least several hundred thousand piculs (upwards of 6,000 tons), presumably from Southeast Asia. The export of Siamese rice to China during this time was earning Siam a large income; she ranked first, with Singapore in second place. By 1870, the main market for Siam rice continued to be China, but the country was also sending the staple to Japan, the East Indies, and even Australia. The rapid expansion of rice cultivation for commercial export enabled Siam to meet the increasing demands from most sources; those from China alone during T'ung-chih's reign (1862-1875) amounted to over ten million piculs (over 660,000 tons) a year. By the end of the 1850s, Nakorn Pathom alone had up to three or four hundred rice mills, and after 1855, Western companies such as Borneo (1885), J. S. Parker (1856), Markevald (1858), Pickenpack Thies, and Remi Schmidt (1858), also established themselves in the Siamese rice industry and trade. The American firm of The American Steam Rice Milling Company was the first mill to use the steam engine in 1858.[142]

In time, however, the rice industry and trade of Siam was again dominated by the Chinese, a situation that has continued up to the present day.

Chapter VI

SOUTHEAST CHINA'S TRADE ORGANIZATIONS IN THE EIGHTEENTH AND EARLY NINETEENTH CENTURIES

There has been little research on Chinese commercial organizations in the premodern period, partly because there is not much written record available. This is especially so with companies that traded to Southeast Asia because they were comparatively less organized, smaller, and transitional. Following the imperial repeal of the second maritime ban, Kao Ch'i-cho proposed in 1728 that ships of Fukien and Kwangtung merchants be closely checked by officials for proper registry and size of crew. For every vessel putting to sea, three more owned by related concerns were to be presented as a guarantee for the sailing ship's return, in accordance with the *lien-huan-pao* mutual guarantee system designed to cope with smuggling and illegal emigration. Furthermore, it was stipulated that Fukien and Kwangtung ships could leave from and return to Amoy and Canton respectively only. Finally, the vessels had to conform to a fixed sailing schedule to facilitate inspection. The restriction worked in such a way that local vessels could leave for Southeast Asia in early spring with the northeast monsoon, and return in the following summer at the latest with the southwest monsoon. Fukien ships drifting into Canton on the way to and from Amoy were allowed to take another season for trading purposes. This is the so-called "three-year-maximum" rule applicable to all local ships.[1]

Upon the re-opening of Amoy local ships trading to Southeast Asia during the period up to the last of 1728 numbered upwards of twenty. From the twelfth moon to the third in the following year, twenty-five more left.[2] The *Hsia-men chih* comments on the commercial situation at Amoy at that time:

Commercial activities of the *yang-ch'uan* ships trading overseas to Southeast Asia at Amoy commenced in 1727 and flourished during the first years of Ch'ien-lung rule in the 1730s and 1740s. The trading situation then was: for Sulu, Johore, Batavia, and Siam, ships left in (late) winter and returned in the summer, once a year; at first the profits ranged from several times to several tens of times; the number of sailors engaged on a regular basis was in the ten thousand mark.[3]

After the rescinding of the second maritime ban in the 1720s Kwangtung vessels resumed trade to Southeast Asia in the following decades. Kwangtung merchants took embroidered fabrics, tea, porcelain, metal, and cotton goods, and returned with pepper, medicine, elephant's teeth, and so forth. Negishi Tadashi states that large profits were the incentive for Kwangtung merchants to trade to Siam, despite the fact that communication then was by no means easy. A 100 percent profit on such items as embroidered fabrics of Kiangsu (which would in turn have sold for triple the price at Kiangsu itself) was sufficient to induce a sizable number of merchants to venture forth to Siam.

Liang–Kuang Viceroy Ch'ing-fu lent further testimony to the burgeoning overseas trade of Southeast China in the 1730s, saying that every year ships left port with many sailors and merchants. Junks from various ports due north of Canton had to pass by the Boca Tigris and the viceroy could notice numerous ships from Fukien, Chekiang, and Kiangnan heading for Southeast Asia. At Canton alone, "several tens of thousands" were engaged in one facet or another of the foreign trade. Owing to the rapid increase of traffic, ships from Chekiang, Fukien, Kiangnan, and Kwangtung were officially marked after 1731 for identification purposes. Thus, Fukien ships trading to Siam were distinguished by their green prows and known accordingly as *lu-t'ou-ch'uan* (green-headed ship). Chekiang ships had their prows painted white, and subsequently adopted the designation of *pai-t'ou-ch'uan* (white-headed ship). Junks of the Kwangtung registry, on the other hand were called *hung-t'ou-ch'uan* because their prows were painted red. Finally prows of the Kiangnan vessels were painted blue, and thus were known as *ch'ing-t'ou-ch'uan* (blue-headed ship).[4] In the 1740s, according to one local official's estimate, the value of the one hundred odd junks trading with Southeast Asia from Amoy and Canton alone was in the millions of taels, while local merchants at these two ports amassed goods equivalent to several million taels.[5]

Local shipping from Southeast China to Southeast Asia involved a complex organization of merchants, capitalists, seamen, navigators, and officials, banded together to make it operational. The Chinese maritime trade of this period, as it had been before, was built upon a system of mutual cooperation, which in a sense enabled the Chinese merchants to survive in the most adverse circumstances. Often official extortion and the specter of bankruptcy necessitated the continued existence of some form of mutual organization for self-preservation (which of course also served the official purpose of mutual control).

The mode of the junk trade did not basically change in the nineteenth century. Since the costs of construction and investment in trade were astronomical, involving tens of thousands in gold (and very few Chinese merchants with such a large capital were ready to invest in a risky enterprise), T'ien Ju-k'ang estimates that around 1804, a junk of less than one thousand tons was often fitted out by pooling together capital from some one hundred small merchants and traders, and those over a thousand tons required participation from as many as two to three hundred individuals. In Kwangtung ivory craftsmen, painters, ironmongers, and gold and silver dealers kept storage spaces aboard the vessel where they deposited their articles for sale, goods that were often acquired on borrowed capital.[6] John Crawfurd obtained the following information on the arrangement of a junk cargo in the late 1810s: "The cargo of Chinese junks is not property of an individual but many. Proprietors had their own compartment in the vessel and had exclusive control. Principal adventures usually were joint property of a family, some lived in China and others in Southeast Asia."[7]

One of the reasons for the prevalence of this system of joint investment apart from the financial arrangement was the lack of support and the studied disdain of the Chinese government. Their contempt for commerce with foreign countries was also responsible for the lack of a large and permanent capital investment in the development of the junk trade. The following report by the British written in the early part of the nineteenth century summarizes quite well this perennial problem: "It is true that Keen Lung [Ch'ien-lung] at the commencement of his reign issued an edict by which he allowed his subjects to visit foreign ports, especially in order to buy rice, but not-withstanding this wide stretch of imperial favor, a merchant returning from India may be brought before a court of justice and sentenced to death as a traitor to this country for having commercial intercourse with foreigners."[8]

Within Kwangtung, Fukien, and Chekiang were several major groupings of merchants distinguished on geographical and dialectical bases, and known as *pang*. At Fukien there were notably the Ch'üan-Chang (Ch'üan-chou and Chang-chou) and Fu-chou (Foochow) *pang,* at Chekiang the Ningpo *pang,* and at Kwangtung the Kuang-Chao and Ch'ao-chou *pang,* all of which were also established actual trading bodies or guilds known as *hang* (hong) denoting both the ship and the organization (*hui-kuan,* a collective organization of ships and concerns bound together for mutual purposes). The hong was sometimes referred to as *chiao* or *kao.* Although primarily economic in outlook and purpose, the hong defined its memberships by locales and their functions often included social rituals similar to family and regional associations. Like all other Chinese guilds, these Southeast Chinese bodies lacked capital reserves, with a large proportion of membership fees collected going for "non-productive" use. The lack of a legal guarantee for guild privileges deprived them of independence and placed them under perennial official mercy. Hence a vicious circle was formed when the guilds, faced with constant official intervention and extortion, were reluctant and unable to truly build up a strong economic base through capital investment, which in turn lessened their bargaining power and made it impossible for them to challenge the officialdom and assert their independence. It followed that truly free and cooperatively regulated organizations of commerce such as the Western city guilds were not to be found in the Chinese setting.

As far as Siam was concerned, it is not likely that there existed any formal economic organization on this pattern among Chinese residents at this juncture in the eighteenth century. As far as can be ascertained, Chinese guilds were not formed until the second half of the nineteenth century. Prior to this date, any semblance of organized economic activities outside of the family centered around the temple, and they usually did not include overseas trade. So it appears that the Chinese in Siam at the time were individual capitalists around which the maritime trade evolved.[9]

Of the various hong bodies which appeared after the reopening of Southeast Asia to trade by local Chinese, those at Amoy and Canton seem to have been the most significant insofar as trade to Siam was concerned. In the first few decades, when Amoy merchants were predominant in the Southeast Asia trade, the hong at the Amoy area, established in 1727 and known as *yang-hang* (ocean guild), dealt almost exclusively in the Sino-Siamese trade. Before this, no organized body at Amoy was mentioned officially as maintaining trade relations with Southeast Asia, though according to British East India Company records business was already organized at Amoy as far back as 1684, and by the turn of the century, the licensed merchant system, seen as a precursor to the co-hong system at Canton by H. B. Morse, was already operating at full force. What relationship this body had with the *yang-hang* is, however, not clear, though the system of licensing could have set a precedent for the organization of the co-hong system.[10] We know that most of the licensed merchants at the main trading centers in Fukien, Kwangtung, and Chekiang at this time were natives of South Fukien.[11] The Amoy *yang-hang,* unlike the pre-1760 hong organization at Canton, managed both shipping to Southeast Asia and trade conducted by Southeast Asia to Amoy.[12]

One important function of the *yang-hang* was the handling of local ships trading to Southeast Asia (classified as *yang-ch'uan* or ocean ships). The shipowners (*ch'uan-hu*), including the owners of ships from other locales using Amoy as a point of departure for trade to Southeast Asia, had to seek cooperation from the *yang-hang,* which was responsible for establishing a mutual guarantee (the *lien-huan-pao* process) and for paying necessary customs dues on the vessels' behalf. In addition, as part of the obligation to the government which granted the trading monopoly, the guild annually presented tribute to the customs superintendent and the tartar-general; this tribute consisted of a fixed amount of *yen-ts'ai* (birds' nests?) and graphite. In 1755, this so-called *yang-kuei* (ocean fee) was reduced by 50 percent, but the guild was further required to give 4,000 taels (£1,333) for the maintenance of military craft.[13]

It appears that the mutual guarantee system for Amoy ships was first specifically recommended by the Fukien governor, Ch'ang-lai, in 1727, in connection with official attempts to stem illegal entry into Formosa by people from mainland Fukien. Nevertheless, some sort of mutual control, in which a vessel trading overseas was required to produce a guarantee by home-based commercial guilds, had always been in existence in the Chinese scene. In the seventeenth century, Fukien junks trading to Manila were observed sailing in groups, though not together in the form of a fleet. This was apparently part of the Chinese maritime regulation stressing a mutual guarantee.[14] (Chinese local administration, the institution of *pao-chia* or tithing in the village, was part of the same concept of mutual control.)

Under normal circumstances, Amoy vessels trading to Siam, three-masted and from several thousand to over ten thousand piculs (over a million pounds) in displacement, were constructed with the bulk of funds supplied by financiers (*ts'ai-tung*), who, in addition, put up part of the cargo.[15] These people, also known as *ch'u-chih-che* (ones who put up the capital), were resident merchants who formed a partnership (*ho-ku*) which included the *yang-hang*. The actual conduct of sailing and trade, however, was the responsibility of a separate group of operators comprising the shipmaster (known variably as *ch'uan-chu, ch'uan-chang,* or *ch'uan-t'ou,* who was also a merchant) and seamen, though the largest financier would sometimes assign his adopted son or son-in-law to oversee the ship's operation as well. Despite the fact that somewhat later the operators were also permitted to take their own goods aboard for sale, the practice of *hsing-che ju-hai chu-che fu-chih* (those who manage enter the ocean; those who finance stay home) was prevalent at the time.[16]

This mode of operation, noted previously as the commenda system, had been prevalent in Japan (known there as *nagegane* or "investment") in the seventeenth century, and was also widespread in Siam and elsewhere in Southeast Asia.

The business of organizing the junk for overseas trade inevitably involved dealings with local officials. For one thing, financiers had to allocate 20 to 40 percent of their investment to "patrons" in the local yamen (government office) for overall "protection." Also, the shipmaster on shore had to deal through a ship's broker (*chu-shang* or "chief merchant") who supervised trade for the government. Market clerks (*shih-huo*) who were attached to the customs office or district yamen would often set a fee or tax, which was then doubled by the broker who took his own squeeze.[17] Organizing junks for trade was no mean task because besides the great cost of constructing the vessel, there was the expense of staffing and outfitting. The entire organization of the Amoy junk operation may be diagramed as follows:

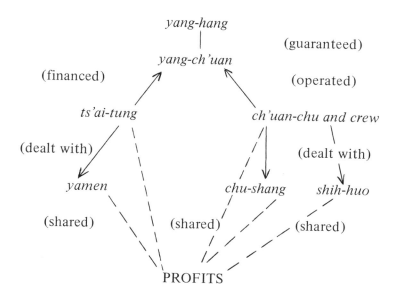

Amoy *ts'ai-tung* assumed the *nom de commerce* of Chin.[18] But around Amoy, in the prefectures of Chang-chou and Ch'üan-chou, there were apparently other groups with different *noms de com-merce* who were also engaged in trade to Southeast Asia. For instance, in T'ung-an district, a short distance from the port of Amoy, ships with the designation of Shun traded to Siam and other locales.[19] Nevertheless, Chin vessels seem to have been the most numerous as far as the Sino-Siamese trade was concerned.

The *yang-hang* organizations (numbered at this time at about a dozen or so) flourished in the Yung-cheng years and the first decades of the Ch'ien-lung period.[20] They reaped great profits from their positions as guarantors and brokers for all local ships of Fukien trading to Southeast Asia, as well as sole contact for Southeast Asia ships calling at Fukien. Such ships were then coming in great number to Amoy.[21]

But, inasmuch as the *yang-hang* and local vessels enjoyed prosperous trading relations with Southeast Asia, the prosperity itself in time became an important cause of their decline. Since their monopoly was so lucrative, it soon gave rise to smuggling or illicit trade. According to government regulations, only those vessels designated as *yang-ch'uan* and properly guaranteed by the *yang-hang* could trade to Southeast Asia; soon, however, guilds known as *shang-hang* (commercial guilds), *yang-hang*'s counterpart which acted as guarantors for ships (called *shang-ch'uan* or "commercial vessels") and engaged exclusively in domestic, interprovincial coastal trade, connived with *shang-ch'uan* in transporting cargo to Canton and other places where such cargo was transferred to larger ships bound for Southeast Asia or sold directly to foreign merchants. On the return voyage such vessels usually carried a nonvaluable cargo to avoid suspicion and possible detection, while more valuable goods acquired from overseas sources were often transported overland. In the 1750s such illegal activities were apparently rampant enough to constitute a serious setback for the *yang-hang* concerns.[22]

A series of official actions in the 1750s hastened the breakdown of the regulated trading system through the *yang-hang*. In 1755 the Ch'ien-lung Emperor increased the customs duties at Amoy and Ningpo, following it up with an edict restricting activities of foreign trade to the port of Canton in 1757. His moves were primarily designed to discourage foreign trade at Amoy and Ningpo, and to concentrate it instead at Canton. The restriction was also the effort of local Canton officials who had considerable influence with the Peking court; they wished to monopolize foreign trade with the further collectivization of the co-hong. The court and the local officials were also determined to end the constant controversy with foreign (Western) merchants, as exemplified by British attempts to trade to Chusan and Ningpo in the Flint episode.[23] It may also be argued that the basic scorn for commercialism and feeling of self-sufficiency also played a part in the imperial decision.

Though the closure measure did not directly stop local shipping to Southeast Asia, it affected the fortunes of Amoy and the Chinese firms dealing with foreign trade. In the second half of the eighteenth century and the early part of the nineteenth, the local Amoy trade increasingly veered toward Luzon, Batavia, and finally Singapore (after 1819). According to the *Hsia-men chih,* up to 1796 there were still eight *yang-hang* companies (along with some thirty *shang-hang* firms), and over a thousand vessels licensed to use Amoy as the exit or entry port in foreign trade.[24] Nevertheless, in addition to the problem of illicit competition,[25] the *yang-hang* concerns suffered from the all-too-common symptom of financial instability owing to the relatively weak capital foundation. (In no way were they comparable to the larger hong organizations at Canton which dealt with Western trade, and as shall be seen, even such "giants" suffered chronic insolvencies.) Part of this stemmed of course from governmental exactions. In addition to the annual purchases of materials for the military in the province, and the annual tributes payable to the civil and military authorities (viceroy, governor, and tartar-general) which were known then as "spring" and "autumn" tributes respectively, *yang-hang* heads were often asked to contribute to other causes. For instance, in 1796, they were asked by the Amoy Defense Bureau (Hsia-fang t'ing) to donate 20,000 taels yearly to be used in campaigns against smugglers and other law breakers; in 1825, it was reduced to 7,400 taels in view of the financial troubles plaguing the organization of foreign trade. Various forms of official restriction curtailed the profitability of foreign trade at Amoy. For example, when Amoy was opened to trade as an international port in 1728, *yang-hang* firms were permitted to ship tea overseas. In 1857, tea was banned for export (though local vessels could still carry it to Kiangnan, Tientsin, and other coastal areas) because the court feared that too much of this profitable commodity would flow overseas.[26] Another crucial factor in the decline of the Amoy *yang-hang* was that Siamese ships managed by Chinese residents increasingly frequented the various ports of China after the second half of the eighteenth century, thus taking over partially the role performed by local ships engaged in overseas trade. These local ships, as we shall see, could not compete adequately due to governmental restrictions and the comparatively higher cost of building and outfitting vessels for overseas trade. By about 1820, the Sino-Siamese trade had fallen into the exclusive domain of Chinese residents in Siam, which meant the eclipse of the direct role of *yang-hang* and *yang-ch'uan.* It was a blow to the Amoy-administered trade.

Only one *yang-hang* firm was then reportedly still in operation; the number increased to three by 1820. But by the following year, in the early nineteenth century, all of them had been closed down, and the Amoy Defense Bureau requested that the *shang-hang* firm of Chin Yuan Feng and three others assume the affairs of the defunct *yang-hang* guild.[27] Trade under the new arrangement again declined when foreign ships, in order to avoid the heavy levies at Amoy, bypassed it and went instead (clandestinely) to smaller ports such as Chao-an; by 1832–1833, the number of *shang-hang* firms had fallen to a mere five or six.

Like Fukien, Chekiang also established hong to handle the province's foreign trade after its reopening in 1729. By that time there were a number of Fukien merchants active in the province, particularly in the silk trade, and apparently they built ships to trade with Southeast Asia as well as Japan. Wang Chih-ch'un mentioned that a central guild or *tsung-shang* was set up at Ningpo; one of its duties was to check local ships trading overseas and to handle foreign trade calling at the province.[28] Beyond this, little information is available on Chekiang's role in the Southeast Asia trade at this time. In one sense, this lack of information may reflect the state of the trade that existed between the province and Southeast Asia. After the end of the seventeenth century, there was hardly any mention of Chekiang merchants trading to Siam or Siamese ships trading to Chekiang.[29]

There had always been a variety of licensed merchants at Canton from the time of Shang K'o-hsi. In the early days it was a rather unorganized system, with different local officials vying for and engaging indirectly in the lucrative foreign trade. By the second decade of the eighteenth century, some kind of order was established with the formation of a central guild (Shih-san hang or "Thirteen Hong"), dealing exclusively with foreign trade at Canton and ensuring the flow of revenues to both Peking and local authorities, as well as providing better control of foreign trade by the government.[30] According to H. B. Morse, co-hongs were organized specifically to prevent the formation of a monopoly of foreign trade at Canton by the then two most influential merchants, Linqua and Anqua, who were solidly backed by local officials.[31]

Unlike the *yang-hang* at Amoy, however, the co-hong of Canton, during its first decades, did not deal directly with ships of provincial merchants trading to Southeast Asia, but handled only trade at the port by foreign vessels, which included the tributary ships of Siam. A viable institution concerned directly with foreign trade, the co-hong may best be described as "a regulated company." Minor merchants could be licensed (by the handful of prominent merchants in complete control of all foreign trade) to trade with foreigners. It had no corporate capital (except the Consoo fund, established in 1779, out of which certain debts were paid, and presents for the emperor and officials were provided), each merchant trading separately and independently with the foreigners upon his own capital. It had a nominal head, but did not always unite in a policy of corporate bargaining and uniform price-fixing... Despite its loose organization, the co-hong was in a better position to enforce its demand... because the foreign traders had to come to it."[32]

The co-hong at this early stage already comprised many Fukienese from South Fukien, said to have been almost 90 percent.

According to H. B. Morse, such merchants, mainly of Ch'üan-chou, were skilled and became partially responsible for the boost in foreign trade at Canton; the co-hong was considerably influenced by the one in Fukien.[33]

Until 1736, the first year of the Ch'ien-lung period, foreign trade at Canton did not distinguish between Southeast Asia and the West (or elsewhere). The Siamese trade at Canton was probably handled by the firms within the co-hong, because before that time, Chinese records refer to the *yang-huo hang* (firms of foreign goods) as handling Siamese tributary trade. (The co-hong at Canton was sometimes called Wai-yang hang or "Outer-ocean Guild.") The absence of any differentiation may reflect the predominance of the Southeast Asia trade conducted at and from Amoy; it was not until 1760, with the eclipse of Amoy, that a separate guild dealing exclusively with the Sino-Siamese trade came into being. Outside Canton, particularly at Ch'ao-chou prefecture in northeastern Kwangtung, there was a commercial guild engaged in trade with Siam whose designation was Chin, the same name as that of the Amoy guild. According to Ch'u Ta-chun's *Kuang-tung hsin-yu,* several areas of the province were already trading actively with Southeast Asia by the late seventeenth century. Hence, it is not surprising that such a guild should exist in Ch'ao-chou, and be destined to play an important part in later Sino-Siamese trade.[34]

We noted that in 1736 a new guild of eight concerns came into existence at Hui-ch'eng, outside Canton, under the name of Hai-nan hang. Its origin has never been fully established. P'eng Tse-i has argued that the new body was actually an off-shoot of the former *chin-szu hang* (classified in 1686 as a body dealing with domestic trade, as against the *yang-huo hang* which handled external trade), whose name had been changed.[35] Frederic Wakeman, however, asserts that the Hai-nan hang was a group dealing with the Southeast Asia as well as the domestic coastal trade. Apparently it constituted a body of local merchants, notably from Ch'ao-chou prefecture, who also conducted business with Siam. But it is unlikely that this body had any direct part in the handling of Siamese tributary trade at Canton, which seems to have been in the domain of the co-hong.

The Hai-nan hang was, nevertheless, most likely an organization responsible solely for licensed private merchants of Canton trading to Siam (though probably on a smaller scale than the Amoy *yang-hang*). Unfortunately not much more is known about the organization, though one can safely assume that it represents a further specialization of the hong monopoly system as the dimension of the Canton trade grew.

The "localization" of trade by foreigners to Canton in 1757 had a direct effect upon the subsequent reorganization of the existing guilds, crystallizing the so-called "Canton system" which was characterized by the tightening of trade monopolies through bureaucratic actions. In 1760, the Liang–Kuang governor-general ordered the formation of another co-hong to consolidate the position of the hong merchants at Canton.[36] Hence the twenty-odd-member co-hong and the eight-firm Hai-nan hang (including a five-firm security guild, or *pao-shang* formed in 1745 whose main purpose was to prevent defaults in transactions) were up for reorganization. In the following year P'an Chen-ch'eng (Puankhequa) of the firm T'ung-wen hang, an important Canton merchant and native of Ch'uan-chou prefecture,[37] and eight other hong heads requested the establishment of a new co-hong (Wai-yang hang) to handle exclusively the Western trade. They also petitioned that the Hai-nan hang be renamed as Fu-ch'ao hang to handle goods and duties from transactions by Ch'ao-chou and Fukien merchants. Concurrently, another category of hong named Pen-chiang hang was formed to manage exclusively Siam's tributary trade and taxation.

A memorial by the Canton Hoppo Chi-shan to the Chia-ch'ing Emperor in 1800 states that there were in 1800 "three categories of hong: the Wai-yang hang, Pen-chiang hang, and Fu-Ch'ao hang... Functions of the Wai-yang hang and Pen-chiang hang previous to 1751 had been managed collectively by the *yang-hang*, i.e., the first Wai-yang hang... though (at the time) the designation of the Pen-chiang hang had not yet existed. Nor was there the Fu-Ch'ao hang, but only the eight firms composing the Hai-nan hang. Then in 1760, P'an Chen-ch'eng and eight other firms' merchants petitioned for the formation of a new co-hong to specifically manage foreign ships.

This request was granted. From then on, the Wai-yang hang ceased to manage affairs belonging to the Pen-chiang hang (i.e., the handling of Siamese tributary trade at Canton). It was noted (in 1760) that the individual firms of Chi-i hang, Feng-chin hang, Ta-feng hang, and Wen-te hang, specialized in the handling of the Pen-chiang hang affairs, but additional information about this guild is lacking. Documentation is also wanting about the seven firms making up the Fu-Ch'ao hang which had been transformed from the previous eight-firm Hai-nan hang."[38]

With the new arrangement, government control of Canton's foreign trade was complete, since most trade, both domestic and foreign, at Canton was now placed under genuine collective monopolies. Nevertheless foreign trade at Canton had probably grown to such a proportion that further specialization was called for. The *Kwangtung t'ung-chih,* or gazetteer of the Kwangtung province, notes that as of 1760 the number of ships engaged in foreign trade at Canton increased steadily. Those commercial firms with large capital usually handled the affairs of the Wai-yang hang, while those with comparably smaller capital were engaged in the Pen-chiang hang matters. Finally, merchants with the smallest capital of the three groups normally dealt with Fu-Ch'ao hang affairs.[39]

Comparing the functions of the *yang-hang* at Amoy and their counterparts at Canton between the 1720s and 1750s, we have already noted that, first of all, the Amoy guild dealt almost exclusively with the Southeast Asia trade; the co-hong at Canton was engaged more significantly with the Western trade—though they also handled the official Siamese tributary trade at the same time. This leads to the conclusion that during this period Amoy played a much more dominant role in trade to Southeast Asia. Secondly, although the Amoy guild handled both the foreign trade from Southeast Asia to Amoy and took charge of Amoy vessels trading to Siam and elsewhere in the region, the main part of the Canton system seems to have played no direct role in the trade from Canton to Siam. After 1736 the Hai-nan hang might have been responsible for guaranteeing local ships trading to Siam, but there is no documented proof of this. However, with the establishment of the Pen-chiang hang dealing exclusively with Siam, one is inclined to believe the new body handled not only the Siamese tributary trade at Canton as stated in Chi-shan's memorial, but that it took part in the general trade to Southeast Asia (and hence its functions were more like those of the Amoy foreign trade guild). According to Hsiao I-shan, the Pen-chiang hang and the Fu-Ch'ao hang were both engaged in trade with Southeast Asia in addition to other small-scale internal trade activities along the coast. Official communications also mention ships belonging to the Pen-chiang hang which were conducting trade to such places as Siam, Hatien, Batavia, and Cambodia.[40] The Pen-chiang hang may have shared with the Fu-Ch'ao hang the role of conducting trade with Southeast Asia. The new guilds probably represented a takeover of functions previously exercised by the Amoy foreign trade guild in regard to the Southeast Asia trade. In the first half of the eighteenth century, Amoy seems to have specialized in Southeast Asian trade, Canton in Western, and Ningpo in Japanese.

In the second half of the eighteenth century, Canton developed its monopoly trade further. For eleven years after its inception in 1760, foreign merchants looked upon the new system with considerable displeasure; the British were particularly vocal in their opposition. The new monopoly arrangement also magnified the perennial problem of insolvency among hong members: in 1770–1771, the bankruptcy of several members of the guild indicated the extent of the paucity of credit in the system.[41] After allegedly receiving a bribe of 100,000 taels (£30,000–35,000) offered by the British,[42] Liang–Kuang Governor-General Li Shih-yao petitioned for the suspension of the new co-hong and the temporary reversion of foreign trade management to individual firms.[43] So between 1771 and 1780, it is apparent that the Wai-yang hang, Pen-chiang hang, and Fu-Ch'ao hang were temporarily eclipsed, and Siamese trade to Canton was probably handled, as in the case of the Western trade there, by individual firms. But in 1780, the Pen-chiang hang was definitely back on the scene, because at the time of the arrival of a Siamese embassy that year, a collective body of four hong concerns, presumably the Pen-chiang hang, took charge of it. In addition, the

Fu-Ch'ao hang must have also been restored by then. (Though there is no mention in the record that these two hongs were suspended during the 1770s along with the Wai-yang hang, one presumes that the entire co-hong was affected.) By 1782, the co-hong system was firmly re-established with all its former privileges and was under the supervision of the hoppo.[44]

The precarious history of the Fu-Ch'ao hang and Pen-chiang hang in the latter part of the eighteenth century was characterized by the same malaise that was found in the *yang-hang* system of Amoy: official extortion, insolvency, and competition from clandestine dealers. Among these problems, financial difficulties seem to have been the worst for the Canton organizations. Between the 1770s and 1790s, stories of indebtedness could be heard with great frequency. Ch'ien-lung's order of 1760 prohibited the making or taking of loans by and from foreigners and by or from Chinese under the penalty of banishment to Ili for Chinese and the forfeiture of loans for foreigners. In spite of that order and the "consoo (*kung-so*) funds,"[45] because interest at Canton was exorbitant, the firms dealing with Westerners, for instance, owed the latter over four million Spanish dollars.[46] Not a single firm was able to stay on in the Pen-chiang hang (as well as the Fu-Ch'ao hang) for very long, as the periodic changes of firms and their numbers in the decades of their existence reflect. In 1771, there were only three firms in the guild, the Ju-shun hang (headed by Liu Ho-hsin), I-shun hang (headed by Hsin Shih-tuang), and Wan-ch'u hang (headed by Teng Chang-chieh). A decade later, there were four. Financial instability by the 1790s had become a crisis as evidenced by heavy borrowing from Siamese merchants, and, as a result, the guild went bankrupt. Hirase Minokichi comments that the financial basis of the Pen-chiang hang was still comparatively weak. One reason was that the Siamese tributary trade (the guild's mainstay) had not been developed fully enough to be immensely profitable for the guild.[47] The heads of the Ju-shun hang, I-shun hang, and Wan-ch'u hang had accumulated so much debt that they could not resolve the problem. Another equally important cause was that the merchants involved were apparently unable to stand the increasing pressure by Canton's hoppo who was demanding a number of things from the foreign trade guilds, including a two and a half million tael (£833,000) contribution to famine relief in North China. Consequently, between 1795 and 1796, with the Pen-chiang hang dissolved, the local authorities entrusted the management of the Siamese tributary trade to the Wai-yang hang. But this did not mark a definite end to the notion of maintaining a separate management for Siam's tributary trade. The Wai-yang hang eventually discovered that the profits from handling the functions of the Pen-chiang hang were not worth the large responsibilities involved, and so they relinquished the obligation.[48]

In 1796, one year after the dissolution of the Pen-chiang hang, the merchants in the Fu-Ch'ao hang proposed to the government that one of its principals, Ch'en Ch'ang-hsu, be authorized to assume all the former business of the Pen-chiang hang. No sooner was Ch'en permitted to do this than differences developed between him and the rest of the Fu-Ch'ao hang merchants, and he was subsequently accused of trying to monopolize the Siamese trade.[49] His eventual ouster did not end the inherent problems of separate management, and, consequently, the arrangement was permanently discarded, after the Chia-ch'ing Emperor approved a recommendation by Canton Hoppo Chi-shan in 1800 that the management of Siam's tributary trade be reverted back to the Wai-yang hang.[50] A new scheme was also devised for the actual handling of this trade whereby the existing eight firms in the Wai-yang hang were charged with the management by rotation, so that in each year, two separate members would take the turn jointly. Hence, in 1801, the task went to the T'ung-wen hang (headed by Puankhequa "the Second" or P'an Chih-hsiang, chairman of the co-hong in 1797) and Kuang-li hang; in 1802, the responsible concerns were the I-ho hang and I-ch'eng hang; in 1803, the Tung-sheng hang and Ta-ch'eng hang took charge; and in 1804, it was the turn of the remaining two members, the Hui-lung hang and Li-ch'uan hang. Then the rotation began anew. The Canton customs superintendent stressed the necessity of this approach in order to avoid any possibility of monopoly by one particular firm, which could, in turn, lead to irresponsibility and other difficulties—for instance, the incurring of debts. In this connection, he noted that the importance of Siam's trade to China necessitated such a step.[51]

Hence, from 1800 till the Opium War, the new arrangement persisted apparently without any major modification, and proved quite adequate in meeting the needs of the Siamese tributary trade. An indication of this may be seen first of all in Liang–Kuang Viceroy Juan Yuan's report to the Peking court in 1826. However, there is one curious matter concerning Siam's continued use of the name "Punkang" in the first half of the nineteenth century, which was an obvious reference to the supposedly defunct Pen-chiang hang ("Punkang" being a Siamese transliteration based on either the Ch'ao-chou or South Fukien appellation for the guild). For instance, the annals of the Fourth Reign (1851–1868) mention the delivery of an official communication from Canton to Praya Praklang in the 1850s which bore the following reference: "There were two letters from the storekeeper [sic] at Canton whose name was Punkang who was in charge of affairs concerning Siam."[52] Although the reference was obviously to the two members of the Wai-yang hang who were supposed to handle Siamese matters for that particular year, the name of the former Pen-chiang hang was retained. Unfortunately, we do not have written proof of how much interest this guild still had in the management of Siamese affairs by the Wai-yang hang. It is possible that members of the Pen-chiang hang managed ultimately to gain control over the management within the general co-hong.

There appears to have been a close relationship between the Pen-chiang hang and Fu-Ch'ao hang, as seen by the fact that the latter was mainly responsible for the brief revival of a semblance of the former; also the Ch'ao-chou and Fukien merchants at the time were the most active in the Siamese trade, and many of these individuals inevitably belonged to the Fu-Ch'ao guild. The relationship between the Pen-chiang hang and Wai-yang hand was, however, less obvious, though it may be noted that Puankhequa (P'an Chench'eng), who originally petitioned for the establishment of the new co-hong in 1760, was Fukienese. Born in 1714 near Ch'üan-chou, he established himself in Canton around 1740 and worked in a foreign trade firm until he opened up one of his own in 1750.[53]

The maintenance of a separate body for Siamese trade did not, in actual fact, imply any differences in their duties from the undifferentiated management under the Wai-yang hang, although a separate existence could have implied a special status insofar as trade from Siam was concerned. The general responsibilities of acting as guarantors, agents for merchandise transaction and the payment of customs duty, procurers for the tribute embassy, hosts for foreign merchants and envoys, and so forth, remained unchanged.

Chapter VII

THE SINO-SIAMESE TRIBUTARY TRADE:
FROM LATE AYUDHYA TO
EARLY BANGKOK PERIODS

In the Siamese tributary trade to China in the eighteenth and nineteenth centuries, there were "formal" and "semi-formal" embassies. The two embassies were equally official, for both were dispatched in the name of the king. The "semi-formal" can be distinguished from the "formal" ones in that the usual rituals of tribute presentation at Peking were conspicuously absent, and they were normally sent under a special pretext of some kind, for example, on the occasion of the emperor's birthday. Yet the treatment accorded the semi-formal envoys did not vary greatly from that given to formal ambassadors, particularly when it came to the dispensation of trading privileges (tax exemption, preferential treatment for official merchants, and so forth).

The number of formal Siamese missions to the Ch'ing court between 1700 and 1766 (the last phase of the Ayudhya dynasty), stood at twelve, or approximately one embassy for every five years. Regulations required the Siamese to present tributes once every three years[1] and, although there were no tribute presentations between 1708 and 1720, at first glance, these seem to be fewer than were required. Nevertheless, Siam had, between formal tribute presentations, managed to send four other semi-official embassies.[2] If we include such missions, the number for this period would stand at sixteen, or one embassy each in slightly less than four years. Such a frequency alone is remarkable in view of the distance and risks involved in the journey, without taking into consideration other means employed to supplement this mode of trade through formal tribute embassies.

The following account is typical of the pattern of trade conducted by a regular tribute mission in 1748. A Siamese *cheng-kung* vessel arrived at Canton escorted by a *hu-kung* ship. This *cheng-kung* ship had been recently built to replace the one in the previous year that had been forced to put in at Annam because of strong winds while en route to Canton. (The accompanying *fu-kung* vessel, the third in the suite, nevertheless made it to Canton.) The ship merchant was named Ma Kuo-pao, that of the *hu-kung* was named Fang Yung-li; both held Siamese feudal rank. The provincial treasurer at Canton, Heh-ch'ing, made certain that the mission conformed with established regulations regarding the proper number of ships and size of crew on board each ship. It was found that the crews of both ships consisted of 186 men, including a great many Chinese who, however, were not repatriated because they had lived in Siam for many years and their families were still there. A party eventually set out for Peking, while the *hu-kung* ship under Fang was permitted to sail back to Siam on the day of the party's departure for the Chinese capital. The Siamese bought 500 catties (666.5 lbs.) of copper from which they had copper plates, bowls, and candle holders cast (items not considered prohibitive). It was stated explicitly that the ballast aboard all the vessels, as allowed by regulation, would be tax exempt. The Siamese on that occasion also presented the emperor with two elephants.[3]

On a regular tributary mission, trade opportunities were not necessarily limited to the king's enterprise. There was also participation by members of the Siamese nobility, whose interests were represented by certain individuals on the mission. When the K'ang-hsi court announced in 1708 that all cargoes carried by the foreign embassy could be traded in any way and without duty, or when the Ch'ien-lung edition of the *Collected Statutes* (1764) declared that the mission could take any amount of merchandise into Canton duty-free, a legal basis was provided for a practice that intensified by the close of the eighteenth century. The usual items sent under such a category were pepper and wood which the Siamese nobles normally received in the form of taxes from territories assigned to them by the king.[4]

Trade conducted under semi-official auspices was usually carried out by *t'an-kung* (visiting tribute) vessels. Between 1729 and 1766 their activities were becoming noteworthy. By this time, their mission was no longer confined only to enquiring after the well-being of the regular tributary mission, but their functions had become all-purpose with the commercial role accented. For instance, in 1761, a *t'an-kung* ship called at Canton to deliver the Siamese king's thanks for Ch'ien-lung's magnanimity in not demanding compensation for several items of tribute lost at sea in the previous year. On that occasion, it also received authorization to sell its ballast at Canton without duty.[5] The *t'an-kung's* importance in trade was emphasized further by the Chinese concession in allowing Chinese management, a practice allowed by Yung-cheng and Ch'ien-lung because of Peking's desire to encourage rice importation from Siam[6]

The primary motive behind the dispatch of *t'an-kung* ships had in fact become commercial. Although their frequency was not as high as that of the regular tribute ships, their commercial significance should be noted. Secondly, the Ch'ing government seems to have officially acknowledged that the activities of the *t'an-kung* ships were in the proper bounds of tributary trade relations only in the 1750s. In addition to the regular tribute missions, by the 1760s, Ch'ien-lung further permitted the Siamese court to trade annually at Canton during the summer months in the form of *sui-kung* or "annual tribute presentation." This should be taken as a significant expansion of the scope of the tributary trade sanctioned by Peking itself.

Siam's tributary trade was not only conducted at Canton and strictly by defined categories of tribute ships, but also at Amoy and Ningpo. This trade, though conducted during off-tribute seasons, was nevertheless treated as part of the tributary trade of the Siamese court. In 1722, at the start of at least three decades of a continuous flow of Siamese rice into Southeast China, the Siamese were granted permission for such trade to Amoy and Ningpo. Records indicate that between 1723 and 1751, several vessels of this type traded regularly to the three major Southeast China ports.[7]

In the context of the tributary trade, the Chinese authorities throughout the period had also shown considerable leniency toward Siamese requests for commodities normally prohibitive for export as a form of favor-granting. These were usually strategic items such as copper and silver.[8]

In 1729, the Fukien governor memorialized that the Siamese king had instructed his envoys to purchase from China, among other things, some copper cash and a quantity of copper wire. The Yung-cheng Emperor, in noting that such articles were restricted for export, nevertheless gave his authorization. Again in 1736, the Siamese mission petitioned the purchase of copper ingots to be used in connection with the construction of a new temple named Fu-sung szu. Ch'ien-lung authorized the sale of eight hundred catties (1,066.4 lbs.) of the item, stressing that the approval was not in accordance with established rule, and hence was not to be taken as a precedent.[9]

Again in 1748 Kwangtung Governor Yueh Chun memorialized that the Siamese tributary mission had brought with them five hundred catties (666.5 lbs.) of copper with which they wanted copper plates, bowls, and candle holders made for them at Canton. Approval was granted with the usual admonishment that it was not to be taken as a precedent.[10]

Although the quantity of strategic materials acquired through the tributary channel in Late Ayudhya might not have been great, the fact remains that Siam during this time had to depend on China as the source for these materials, especially copper. After the restriction of the Japanese market, Siam had to acquire copper solely from China; it was mined in Yunnan's Tung-ch'uan district and marketed at Canton.[11]

In 1767, Burmese forces sacked the city of Ayudhya and ended the old regime. As an important part of his concern for revitalizing the Siamese polity after the removal of the immediate Burmese armed threat in 1767, Taksin entrenched himself in a new capital some sixty kilometers nearer to the mouth of the Chaopraya river than the former Ayudhya city. This new site had strategic value, good commercial facilities and closer links to China. Concerned with revitalizing the Siamese polity after the removal of the immediate Burmese armed threat he resorted to the resumption of trade with China as a means of securing state revenue.[12] This was a logical step, because in his reign, and later in those of Rama I and Rama II of the Bangkok dynasty, the country was still not fully consolidated, and it was difficult to obtain revenues through taxing the people. The government was in tenuous control over many parts of the country, and the imposition of exorbitant taxes could create unrest among the people and upset the delicate political balance. According to Rama IV (Mongkut) in 1853: "At that time there was no tax given the little authority (the government) could assert and the tendency of the populace to revolt. The state was newly reinstituted. They therefore resorted to the junk trade, the income from which was then used to defray the expenses of the state and for the upkeep of the individual royal, noble, and wealthy commercial families."[13]

In addition, Taksin needed weapons and strategic materials in his continuing struggles against the Burmese and other independent Siamese forces in the North and South, and the only way he could secure such items was to send emissaries, in all cases Chinese merchants, to China to ask for them from the Manchu court. As a matter of fact, local mines producing primarily iron and salt-petre had been put out of operation or exhausted as a result of continued engagements with the various Burmese forces since 1759.

Although he was not recognized officially by Peking (upon the recommendation of Liang–Kuang Governor-General Li Shih-yao who claimed that he was a usurper of the Siamese throne),[14] Taksin exerted pressure on the Chinese and dispatched an embassy to request the purchase of salt-petre and iron pans (two items prohibited by Peking for export back in 1731) citing the Burmese invasion as the pressing reason. When the request was readily filled by a Ch'ing court which itself was involved in a campaign against the Burmese over a minority people in the Yunnan-Burma border area, Taksin was encouraged and ordered more salt-petre, iron pans, and even some cannon purchase, but continued to grant the other items. This apparently prompted other requests for similar articles in 1776 and 1777.[15]

With the end of the Sino-Burmese conflict in sight and the resumption of tribute presentation to Peking by Burma in the late

1770s, the Ch'ing court became less "considerate" about granting strategic materials to the Siamese. This reluctance is reflected in the outcome of Taksin's next mission in 1780 when he requested over a thousand copper and silver articles, ostensibly for religious use. (His reign was noted for the casting of cannon, and the articles could therefore be used for military purposes.) Ch'ien-lung refused, though three years earlier he had sent instructions to the Kwang-tung officials to honor future Siamese requests for salt-petre and iron pans.[16]

Nevertheless, tributary trade was a major part of the Sino-Siamese trade under Taksin. One interesting aspect of the tributary relationship in the Ch'ing dynasty is the pragmatic approach adopted by both sides. It was fully recognized by the Chinese that aside from acknowledging Chinese suzerainty the motive for the tribute mission was profit, and hence the applicability of the *hou-wang po-lai* principle. To the Siamese, commerce was an indispensable part of each embassy.[17]

Under the mutual acknowledgement that trade formed an integral part of the tribute mission was, however, a basic difference between Siamese and Chinese attitudes regarding the manner and extent of such commercial intercourse. The Siamese, with their uninhibited language about their trade interests, appeared as "opportunists" preoccupied with "petty economic gains."[18] Although ready to grant whatever economic interests were in accord with the time-honored principle of *chi-mi,* or the concept of control and regulation of "barbarians," the Chinese deemed it more vital to keep tributaries in their proper place vis-à-vis the Celestial Empire. The interaction between the convention and the reality of the tribute system leads to the obvious conclusion that what was set down in the regulations was, largely, interpreted and applied to suit varying circumstances.

The embassy that Taksin sent to the Ch'ien-lung court in 1780–1781 not only demonstrates the economic significance of one particular embassy and clearly reflects the commercial overtures of such undertakings, but also indicates some of the economic potentials in the dynamics of Sino-Siamese relations.

The eleven-ship fleet[19] dispatched in 1780 was Taksin's first and only full-fledged official mission to be accepted by the Chinese authorities. In his businesslike letter to Ch'ien-lung, Taksin outlined the various purposes of the mission, which may be summarized as follows: a) a protest against extortion by the governor and by officials of the Board of Rites in their demand for thirty catties (40 lbs.) of silver as a "tribute-receiving" fee from the previous Siamese envoy dispatched in 1766, against the curtailment of the envoy's freedom of movement at Peking, and against the deliberate action by Canton officials in frustrating the envoy's return to Siam aboard their own ships, and charging the envoy silver when the latter lodged a complaint; b) a request for the return of certain Ai-i prisoners of war whom the Siamese had sent to China in connection with the war of both countries against Burma; c) a notification concerning the favorable treatment of certain shipwrecked Chinese fishermen by the Siamese king who subsequently sent them back to China; d) a request for the immediate dispatch of nine additional ships, in three three-vessel fleets to trade rice, wood, and other Siamese produce for Chinese bricks and tiles (which were classified as "nonrestrictive" items) at Canton, Amoy, and Ningpo; e) a request for approval to employ a Chinese pilot to guide two Siamese ships from Canton to Nagasaki to procure copper ingots; f) a presentation of "supplementary tribute" (*kung-wai chih kung*) to the emperor, in addition to the regular tributes (*cheng-kung*).[20]

Aside from demands set forth in the above letter to Ch'ien-lung, the Siamese, in two other separate letters intended for the viceroy of Liang–Kuang, also inserted the following: a request for the issuance of permits for two newly constructed Siamese vessels; a solicitation for the viceroy's help in locating a pilot to whom the Siamese would pay any price (to guide Siamese ships to Japan); a presentation of gifts to the viceroy, the heads of the four hong (of the Pen-chiang hang), and officials of the Board of Rites; a request for permission to purchase over one thousand items of copper and silver utensils; and a request for the hand of a Chinese princess.[21]

The protests in the letters did not appear to be central, for the simple reason that they actually concerned an embassy that had been sent some fifteen years earlier and in a different Siamese dynasty of Ayudhya. Nor did the second point have much significance: the request for the return of prisoners of war, for the Chinese had settled their conflict with the Burmese in the 1770s. The third point on the favorable treatment of the Chinese fishermen was again meant merely to present the Siamese favorably in the eyes of the emperor. Li Kuang-t'ao sees it as indicative of Taksin's eagerness to present himself in a favorable light to the Chinese court so that the latter might grant him recognition. What is further noteworthy was the exclusion of the above three points, together with the one on the request for a Chinese princess, from available Chinese official correspondence.[22]

Thus, it may be argued that the remaining points, the list of requests and demands pertaining to commercial transactions, indicated the main motive behind the 1780 embassy.

In light of the official provision, stipulated in the *Ta-Ch'ing hui-tien,* that no more than three tribute vessels could be permitted at Canton in one tribute presentation season, the fact that this embassy had eleven ships became significant. The number is important when one considers the commerce that was part of the actual practice of tribute presentation.

We are led to believe by the *Ta-Ch'ing hui-tien* that while the official Siamese entourage was being escorted to Peking (a process requiring several months, as mentioned above) the remainder of the Siamese crew simply waited at port for its return. This was, as we have seen, not a totally accurate picture of what really happened. In the 1780 mission, according to Siamese sources, the envoy had been instructed by Taksin to send the ships back with the copper and silver utensils as soon as such items could be secured at Canton, and the ships would then sail back to China in time to receive the returning envoy from Peking. This procedure (contrary to the written rule, but always practiced since at least 1684) was an important feature in this particular mission, for ships could return to Thonburi with the prevailing northeast monsoon as soon as the

Siamese set out for Peking in January 1781, and journey back to Canton in the summer (with the southeast monsoon) of the same year, well before the envoy's return.

All tribute ships from Siam were entitled to carry a cargo classified officially as duty-free ballast composed of the remainder of the goods after portions for the "supplementary tributes" and the presents for the officials and merchants had been deducted which in monetary value, came to 9,000 taels Siamese (£4,500) or 14,400 taels Chinese.[23]

In addition to the tribute ships (which exceeded the number allowed by regulation), Taksin also attempted to send three other groups of three ships each to trade at Canton, Amoy, and Ningpo. However, Ch'ien-lung refused any authorization, not on the basis of an excessive number of ships being permitted to trade in the tribute system, but because foreign trade could then be conducted only at Canton and the hiring of a Chinese pilot was prohibitive.[24]

The commercial value of the mission can further be seen in the presentation of "supplementary tribute." It was an established tradition that for each state bearing tribute to the Ch'ing court, the latter made a fixed list of items to be accepted as the proper tribute, or *cheng-kung.* As far as Siam was concerned, precedents had pointed to the strict observation and enforcement of this rule. Consequently, the "supplementary tributes" of the 1780 embassy were naturally explicitly declined by the emperor, who remarked, "Regarding the supplementary tribute, as the tribute items are all fixed, how can we permit (the Siamese) to increase them at will"? One would not have been surprised had it not been for the volume of the supplementary tribute intended for the emperor, which actually rivaled that of the *cheng-kung,* and this gives rise to a justifiable speculation about the real motive of King Taksin in making such a presentation. Was Taksin hoping that the Chinese would automatically reject the supplementary tribute which the latter, for all practical purposes actually did, but still permit the Siamese to dispose of the rejected goods in China rather than make them transport them back to Siam (a practice which would ordinarily be deemed by the Chinese

emperor as putting an unfair burden on tributary states demon-
strating their sincerity and respect by traversing long distances to
present tribute)? It may not be totally incorrect to harbor such a
suspicion, especially when one notes the value of the supplementary
tribute, which was recorded in the Siamese accounts to have been
about 37,320 taels Siamese (£18,660) or the equivalent of 59,172
taels Chinese.[25] As it turned out, perhaps anticipated by King Taksin,
the emperor rejected the supplementary tribute, but nonetheless
allowed the Siamese to sell it at Canton, along with the other goods
as a gesture of his magnaninity. In passing judgment, the emperor
actually said: "As to the supplementary items, to order them to be
shipped back would not be in accordance with the principle of
treating men from afar with tenderness. It is therefore ordered that
the elephants should be sent on to Peking but that the (Siamese)
envoy should be at liberty to sell the other items at Canton, and
should also be permitted to unload the rest of the cargo of their
vessels free of import duty. The Board of Rites is also instructed to
reward them liberally, in accordance with the Imperial wish that
envoys are to 'come empty and go back full' (hou-wang po-lai)."[26]

Even if this supplementary tribute had been accepted by the
Ch'ing court along with the regular one, it would still have meant a
sound investment for the Siamese in this particular mission. For one
thing, the tribute consisted essentially of local produce and did not
cost the Siamese king much since most of it was actually presented
to him in the form of tribute from states and persons paying him
allegiance. But more importantly, by presenting this tribute, which
in one respect, may be deemed a "tax,"[27] the Siamese hoped to
acquire certain materials, such as bricks. King Taksin's letter explicitly requested Chinese bricks and tiles which were destined for the
construction of Thonburi city. He also asked for copper and silver
utensils, but being aware of the official ban on their export, Taksin
made the excuse that such articles were to be used for religious
purposes. The same pretext had been successfully employed by
previous Siamese kings, such as King Taisra, in circumventing the
Chinese prohibition against the exportation of strategic materials.[28]

Although this particular request was refused by Ch'ien-lung (primarily because of the lack of endorsement by the viceroy at (Canton), the Siamese acquired many vital materials from China.[29]

The presents bestowed on the Siamese by the emperor on this occasion should not be overlooked. Past occasions had seen lavish presentations; the one in 1780 amounted to over one hundred valuable gifts, such as fine silks and porcelain, prized particularly by the Siamese court and fetching tremendous prices in the royal monopoly market.[30]

The letter from the king of Siam in 1780 indicated that the authority of the viceroy at Canton ranged from the customary receiving of, and caring for, the Siamese embassy at Canton, preparing it for the eventual journay to Peking, to the granting of licenses for newly constructed ships trading with China. Another important duty of the viceroy was the translation of official Siamese letters to the Chinese government and his paraphrasing of its contents in the form of a memorial, thus accounting for frequent deletions or editing as he saw fit. The alteration of the style and tone of the tributary state and the elevation of the emperor's position was very well illustrated in the case of the 1780 mission.[31] Furthermore, it is natural that whatever was presented to the emperor by the viceroy was bound to have considerable influence on the court's decisions, as was indeed evident in the reply of the emperor to the Siamese king in the form of an imperial edict.

Because of this situation, the Siamese paid particular attention to the viceroy. The large gift intended for him, 500 piculs (66,650 lbs.) of sapan wood and 500 piculs (66,650 lbs.) of red wood, or the equivalent in monetary terms, of 750 taels Siamese (£375), and separate letters to him indicated the Siamese awareness of his vested authority as the emperor's highest-ranking official at the frontier. But when it came to the actual handling of trade at Canton, the Siamese had to deal through the hong organization (then the Penchiang hang) which the Siamese called *nai-hang*. Consequently, the mention of presents to the four hong concerns in the 1780 embassy represented also the Siamese awareness of this body's significance— 100 piculs (13,330 lbs.) of sapan wood and red wood to each of them.[32]

The Siamese envoy in 1780 also provided presents for the personnel of the Board of Rites at Peking; sapan wood: 1,000 piculs (133,300 lbs.); black wood: 300 piculs (40,000 lbs.); red wood: 1802.3 piculs; or the equivalent of about 1,120 taels Siamese (£560).[33] These gifts could again have some commercial meaning, since the Ch'ien-lung Emperor explicitly permitted the Siamese to trade at the capital in addition to the frontier if they so chose.[34] Under such circumstances, supervision would obviously fall under the jurisdiction of the Board of Rites. But it cannot be ascertained if the 1780 envoy did attempt to carry out trade at Peking as well, for there is no available evidence to substantiate this.

We have thus far attempted to indicate the connection of the tribute system and trade between China and Siam, carried out essentially through the administered machinery at Canton. The 1780 mission shows concretely the commercial significance of China to the Siamese foreign trade (a truism throughout the eighteenth century and the first half of the nineteenth century). Because private trading per se was officially restricted, commerce with China had to naturally assume the form of the tributary trade, and hence, the dual aspect of diplomacy and commerce as explained above. Siam was further able to satisfy part of its demands for external goods through the port of Canton, one reason being that despite the restricted nature of the tributary trade, Siam's demands were compatible with it. For, after all, Siam itself was operating under a royal monopoly system, and in such a mutual orientation, supply and demand could easily be kept in balance.

As far as the Chinese were concerned, the dual aspect of the tribute system was, as mentioned above, a Confucian way of applying the principle of *chi-mi*. Although the Ch'ing court saw comparatively less worth in external trade, it did permit the tributary states to partake in the various commercial advantages of the Celestial Empire—though within an administered framework, of course. But the framework, often subjected to the human element within it, was by no means rigid. Canton was the scene for the interaction of the convention and the reality of the tribute system, where the various actors staked out both common and personal gains.

The 1780 mission further demonstrated the realistic attitude taken by the Siamese toward the tribute system, bordering at times on an opportunistic approach, in accordance with the well-known principle of *yu-shih chih kung* ("missions dispatched with an aim," a principle that was officially acknowledged by the Ch'ing court). King Taksin had never been officially recognized by the Chinese court as Siam's legitimate ruler, but this fact did not prevent him from exploiting the opportunities of the Chinese trade—as evidenced by his employment of a large number of Chinese to conduct the royal and private Siamese maritime trade with China both within and without the tribute system.

In 1781, Taksin, allegedly suffering from some form of mental disorder, was deposed and succeeded by his trusted lieutenant, Praya Chakri, who became Rama I and founder of a new Chakri or Bangkok dynasty. Rama I was quite familiar with the advantages of external trade,[35] particularly of that with China. He had served under Taksin and noted the great wealth of private Chinese traders and the symbiotic relationship that existed between them and the Thonburi court. Also, his parents were part Chinese.[36] As in the previous reign, Rama I had to depend on the China trade for the main part of the state's revenues, since he was unable to levy much direct taxation. Rama IV stated years later that the founder of the Chakri dynasty sought revenues for the royal treasury by resorting to trade by Chinese junks as before and that the profits derived from the junks were disbursed to meet government expenses. This *modus operandi* was carried on through that reign.[37]

Individual courtiers also secured part of their income from the trade. For instance, when the younger brother of Rama I (who served Rama I as his first Maha uparat or "Second King") complained in 1796 that the annual grant of 20,000 Siamese taels (£10,000) from the government was insufficient since he needed to take care of his own household and officials, the king advised him to outfit some junks to trade to China to find supplementary revenues, claiming that the state itself had to resort to this so the government could make annual grants to all its grandees.[38]

Because Rama I saw its usefulness, the China trade was subsequently filled with both royal and private junks. The official annals of the First (Bangkok) Reign speak of the customary practice of the junk trade then: "In the junk trade at that time, from which great profits were derived, there were numerous junks of Chinese style painted green and red with breadths from five to seven *wa* (32.5–45.5 ft.) which belonged to the government, nobles, officials and merchants. Such ships were constructed both in Bangkok and at provincial centers. They loaded goods to trade to China every year, and some sold only the cargo while others sold both the cargo and the ships. Profits from this trade were tremendous."[39]

The Rama I court fully exploited the channel of tributary trade. By this time tributary trade had grown to such an extent that Manchu government, uncomfortable with the "heightening of commercial motivation" on the part of the Siamese, proceeded to institute measures to curb it. In 1786, the year Rama I was formally invested by Ch'ien-lung (four years after his accession), Canton Customs Superintendent Mu-t'eng-o proposed the taxing of all ships in the tribute mission save the single *cheng-kung* vessel, since he had noticed that the number of Siamese "tributary" ships coming to Canton each year was increasing.[40]

Tribute missions accelerated considerably starting with the reign of Rama I. Between 1782 and 1800, or the first twenty years of the reign, formal embassies multiplied dramatically; eleven were accounted for, or a rate of over one mission for every two years. Apparently apprehensive about the real motive behind Siam's action, Ch'ien-lung suggested in 1790 that thereafter the Siamese should not be obliged to carry out the established three-year-per-tribute rule, but should perhaps present tribute at ten-year intervals instead.[41] Undeterred, Siamese missions continued arriving, and in addition to the formal tribute embassies, semi-formal, yearly annual tribute (*sui-kung*) missions with the privilege of trade at Canton continued unabated.

At least three additional missions were sent on special occasions: one in 1790, as well as a regular embassy sent in the same year, on the occasion of the eightieth birthday of Ch'ien-lung; another in 1796 in connection with the coronation of Chia-ch'ing; another in 1788 sent ostensibly to thank the Ch'ing court for

generous gifts given the embassy that had visited Peking in 1787.
All in all, the frequency of all types of formal missions dispatched
from Siam for this period not counting the annual tributes to
Canton was actually one in less than two years, showing thus a
deliberate intensification of the use of such a medium to accelerate
trade with China.[42] All this led Li Kuang-t'ao to describe the busy
tribute traffic from Siam at the time in the following way: "Hardly
had the one ship before returned when another set sail; it was in a
circular and continuous fashion" (*ch'ien-che wei huan, er hou-che
chi, hsun-huan lo-i, wu yu hsiu-hsi*).

Rama I endeavored to use the formal tribute presentation,[43]
to acquire articles that were primarily "restricted" by the Chinese
authorities. The 1786 embassy is one illustration. Rama I informed
Ch'ien-lung in a letter that Siam could not send all the tribute that
was by regulation applicable to the former Ayudhya dynasty, since
his own capital had just been settled and with continuous political
unrest and warfare, trade was at a minimum. In addition, the king
requested 2,000 pieces of copper armor for use against the Burmese.
He noted that he was fully aware that the export of copper was
forbidden, but he hoped the emperor might grant him a special
favor. Ch'ien-lung wondered why the Siamese king asked for copper
armor when the steel kind was far superior. Suspecting Rama I of
harboring ulterior motives,[44] he rejected his request.

Thus, Siam had persistently asked for the relaxation of the
ban on the export of strategic materials, and the Ch'ing court up to
the 1780s had usually continued to make exceptions and allow the
amounts requested. The Chinese may have wished to show good
will, but they had other reasons. By that time, domestic production
and imports of copper had finally become sufficient to meet the
internal need for copper cash and hence the monetary situation
had stabilized (contrary to the period between the 1740s and 1750s
when the empire was faced with a copper crisis),[45] and although the
Siamese claimed that they needed copper and other metals for
defense, articles made of such metals were of significant commercial
value in the Southeast Asian market. They could always be melted
down, too, for their metal content, which was apparently what the

Siamese were doing in this period with some of these imports from China.

Furthermore, what aroused the apprehension of the Manchu government was not only the number of missions, but also the number and kind of vessels that the Siamese side managed to lump together under the category of tributary trade. As we have seen, the usual composition of an official tributary embassy was a group of three vessels, designated as *cheng-kung, fu-kung,* and *hu-kung,* but as illustrated by the Taksin mission of 1780, this rule in reality had come to be violated openly. In the memorial by the Liang–Kuang governor-general in 1786, it was stated that upward of ten "formal" tribute ships from Siam were calling at Canton every year.[46] In addition to this, hosts of other ships also tagged along under the sanction of the formal embassies. Such vessels were generally categorized or designated by the Siamese as *t'an-kung,* or "visiting tribute" vessels, but as a rule were actually ships owned by Chinese merchants. Eventually, the Manchu government moved in to deal with such practices so as to "set right" the tribute system as well as for security reasons. The Ch'ing court's action was two-fold: to tax all ships except for the three designated as belonging to the formal tributary embassy, and to prohibit the Siamese from continuing to employ Chinese hands in managing Siamese vessels, a practice that was thought to encourage the perversion of the tribute system.

The commercial role of the *t'an-kung* grew much larger and more obvious in the second part of the eighteenth century—partic-ularly after the accession of the first Chakri king in 1782. In that year, a Siamese *t'an-kung* mission arrived at Canton under one Tseng Tzu-sheng, ostensibly to inquire after the fate of Taksin's 1780 mission.[47] Tseng was sent back to Canton on another *t'an-kung* mission in 1785, and in one part of the memorial to Ch'ien-lung by the Liang–Kuang governor-general, Fu-le-hun (Furgun), it was stated that: "Again the king of Siam dispatched merchant Tseng Tzu-sheng to carry out the *t'an-kung* mission at Canton. After an investigation, it was discovered that in 1782 the Siamese king had sent Tseng with a ship to Canton with a letter to perform the *t'an-kung* duty. The Siamese requested that the accompanying ballast of the ship be duty-exempt as before."[48]

Taxation was waived on the ship's ballast and the crew, predominantly Chinese, received provisions from the date of the ship's arrival at Canton until the return of the envoy from Peking, the same treatment accorded to the regular tribute *cheng-kung* vessel.[49] What is perhaps noteworthy here is that emphasis seems to have been placed on the status of the ballast, which undoubtedly put commercial considerations before anything else, including the supposed mission to inquire after the well-being of the regular tributary embassy.

Owing to the marked increase in the number of *t'an-kung* ships, coupled with the prospect that regular tribute missions were becoming capitalized for commercial ends, the official Chinese reaction was at last forthcoming, as may be seen in the imperial edict of 1786 responding to Mu-t'eng-o's memorial, asking him and the other responsible officials to devise tax procedures against the proliferating Siamese ships. The edict read in part: "Mu-t'eng-o has said that every year when the *cheng-kung* and *fu-kung* ships come to Canton they also bring along up to ten ships of other descriptions. There are others designated as *t'an-kung* ships, which all belong to local merchants and carry a great many goods. The Canton customs superintendent is to investigate and recommend the amount of tax that should be assessed on such ships." The governor-general and the governor proposed that apart from the two *cheng-kung* and *fu-kung* ships, all the others with a cargo ought to be taxed. The court seems to have swayed to the side of the governor-general and the governor, agreeing that the Siamese *cheng-kung* and *fu-kung* vessels should, of course, be waived of duties, but the rest of the private ships should be taxed.

The emperor ended the edict by admonishing the customs superintendent to follow the discretion of the governor-general and governor (Sun Shih-i) who would decide which ships were the regular tributary vessels, and hence be exempt from duty, and which were craft belonging to local private merchants, and hence to be fully assessed, and to act accordingly with promptness without having to wait for further edicts from the emperor.[50]

This new stand adopted by the Chinese government was considerably tougher than any previous one. Ch'ien-lung himself had previously heard his Canton officials argue that though the *t'an-kung* vessels' heads and crewmen were of Chinese origin, they had resided in Siam for a long time with their families, and he had allowed for this practice every time in the case of Siam. Perhaps owing to the "abuse" of the system by the Siamese court which allowed private Chinese merchants to disguise their trade under the identity of *t'an-kung,* the Ch'ing court was finally jolted into action. The *t'an-kung* system had been so commercialized that the emperor and his officials finally decided to restrict its activities. Thereafter, the role of *t'an-kung* ships seemed to decline, as trade outside the tributary framework was rapidly building up.

Liang–Kuang Governor-General Wu Hsiung-kuang, who helped to formulate the policy of granting no special favors to foreign rice shippers, memorialized Peking in 1807 to the effect that two Siamese trading ships registered to the firm of Chin hsieh shun (a Fukien trading firm headed by a merchant with the *nom de commerce* of Chin Hsieh-shun) called at the port of Tung-lung at Ch'ao-chou prefecture; the viceroy noted that the port was supposedly out of bounds for foreign vessels.[51] Although the two vessels were eventually permitted to discharge their goods and also allowed to load a Chinese cargo there, the viceroy felt that some measure must be taken to stop this. He found further from the Ch'eng-hai authorities that for several decades Siamese ships had taken sapan wood, tree bark, and other articles to the port of Tung-lung, and, besides, Chinese authorities had not issued licenses to such vessels. Even worse, those vessels that could not sail back to Siam in time (with the right monsoon season) usually loaded sugar instead at Kiangnan and Chekiang, after having been issued the proper papers by the Ch'eng-hai district. All of this was going on despite the fact that in 1796 Amoy's admiral had issued an order to officials of Fukien and Chekiang to reiterate the standing imperial ban on trade by foreigners to provinces other than the port of Canton, and had admonished them to keep barbarian ships from coming near the coast or to anchor for even one moment.[52]

The viceroy was informed that a short time before there had

been at least three more vessels registered to the firms of Chin ch'ü shun and Chin kuang shun (Ch'ao-chou concerns) which had put in at Tung-lung port supposedly because of bad weather and could not return to Siam in time. They were subsequently given permits to proceed to Kiangnan and Chekiang to trade. The viceroy considered that Siamese vessels trading up and down the China coast exploited imperial kindness to foreigners and must be stopped immediately. He then sent word to Kiangnan and Chekiang authorities instructing them to order the Siamese ships to sail back to Siam and not to linger on any longer to trade, though the ships, along with that of the Chin hsieh shun, would be permitted to load a new cargo at Canton on their return journey. Finally, the viceroy, suspecting that there would be more Siamese ships doing this, ordered a thorough investigation by the Canton customs superintendent in an effort to stem the practice altogether.[53]

Professor John K. Fairbank considers the arrival of Siamese tribute at the Chinese court to be a precursor of the invasion of the Middle Kingdom by the West. In his view, the "rising tide of maritime trade conducted by Chinese merchants" was an ill omen, for the "prostitution of the tribute system for commercial ends seems to have confirmed the Chinese idea of superiority just when it was most urgently necessary to get rid of it."[54]

It would seem, from the discussion above, that the Manchu authorities were at least aware of the apparent perversion of the tributary system by the Siamese, and had even explicitly ordered a halt to various improper practices. Nevertheless, the main problem was one of inertia and inability to enforce the regulations. As Manchu power weakened at the end of the eighteenth century, it became difficult to enforce prohibitive measures. In the meantime, some local officials continued to flout imperial decrees, choosing instead to seek personal gain from "illicit" Siamese practices. But above all, the Manchu government continued to ignore the anachronism of the tribute system since it still believed that trade could be controlled within the narrow framework set up long before.

By the second decade of the nineteenth century, the tribute system was giving way to commercialism. Many areas in Southeast

Asia, formerly known in Chinese annals as "tributaries" (*kung-kuo*), were now called "trading states" (*hu-shih chu-kuo*). The 1818 edition of the *Ta Ch'ing hui-tien* itself named Chaiya, Ligor, Songkla, and Pattani as such. Professor Fairbank gives as a probable reason that it was no longer the rulers of these places who "came to China, but the Chinese who went to them." He sees the list of ports as "a catalogue of ports of call on the two great sea routes of the Chinese junk trade."[55]

All this would eventually bring down the last vestiges of the tribute system, with its myth of "restricted" but "legal" trade, which actually had never been truly endorsed by the tribute-presenting states such as Siam in the first place.

Chapter VIII

THE CHINESE IN THE ECONOMIC LIFE OF SIAM
IN THE EIGHTEENTH AND NINETEENTH CENTURIES

It has been evident all along that partly because of the participation of Chinese individuals. trade between Siam and China was flourishing during the eighteenth and nineteenth centuries. We need only remind ourselves that conditions at that time were favorable to such an undertaking: the removal of potential and real competition in trade with the Chinese resulting from the eclipse of Japanese and Western influences in Siam; the continued existence of a royal monopoly trading structure largely because of the China market; the existence of a pragmatic Siamese court eager and ready to exploit the willingness and talents of those Chinese merchants, who were equally, if not more prepared to render services for reciprocal advantages; and the presence of a favorable economic tributary framework best suited to all the above factors. Finally, the acquiescence of Chinese authorities in the Siamese practice of employing Chinese for official and semi-official trade was another vital element that cannot be overlooked.[1]

In the official tributary trade, Chinese were hired by the Siamese court to staff the various positions: from the Ratakosa-tibodi (in charge of outfitting junks for trade) to linguists (*t'ung-shih*), ship merchants, shipmasters, and crewmen. One noted Ratakosa-tibodi in the first half of the eighteenth century was Ong Heng-chuan (probably the South Fukienese pronunciation of Wang Hsing-ch'üan) who was authorized by King Taisra to outfit several royal junks annually for the China trade, a task later inherited by Ong's son Lai-hu (Lai-fu?) in the succeeding reign of King Boromakot. (Lai-hu was also put in charge of collecting measurement fees from foreign ships trading to Ayudhya.)[2] *T'an-kung* ships were notably under exclusive Chinese management, as seen in the instances of missions by Ts'ai Hsi-wang, Wu Shih-chin, and Tsang Tzu-sheng during this period.

160

Chinese also undertook official, but outside the tribute presentation period, trade on behalf of the Siamese court. In the 1720s and early 1730s none was more prominent than Ong Heng-ch'uan. Chinese records also mention several Chinese merchants trading in Siam's behalf at Canton, Amoy, and Ningpo: Yeh Shun-te at Canton in the 1720s; Chang Ts'uan in 1734; Hsu Shih-mei in 1745; Fang Yung-li and Ts'ai Wen in 1746; Kuo I-kung in 1749; and Wang Yuan in 1751.[3]

One characteristic shared by most of these Chinese merchants was that their supremacy in the Sino-Siamese trade was undisputed, and was strengthened by the ennoblement bestowed upon them by the king for meritorious services. Their economic privilege seemed to grow as time progressed. Also known by their popular designation *tso-sua* (South Fukienese appellation for *cho-shan,* indicative of someone in the position of a philanthropist), these mandarin merchants found economic security in the Siamese court, and often passed it on to their offspring, a factor contributing directly to the growth of the employment of Chinese in the tributary trade. Further, it is to be noted that though they might have become identified with the Siamese court economically, most of the merchants of the first generation usually retained their Chinese identity (characterized by the retention of Chinese attire and the queue) even after ennoblement.

The Siamese practice of employing Chinese to manage Siamese royal vessels was approved by the Ch'ing court throughout the first half of the eighteenth century. Although K'ang-hsi ordered the repatriation of the Chinese crewmen aboard the Siamese tribute ships calling at Canton in 1722,[4] the Chinese court, in its effort to encourage Siamese rice importation, soon acquiesced in the Siamese argument that the employed Chinese were "long-time residents with families in Siam." The first reference to this came in 1724 when Yung-cheng pronounced in an edict regarding the crewmen on board the Siamese tributary vessels at Canton that "though the (ninety-five) crewmen aboard the (Siamese tributary) ship are actually people from Kwangtung and Fukien, they have lived in Siam for a long time and have also got their families there. [So] in reality it is difficult to detain them. They should be permitted to go back (to Siam) as requested."[5]

Despite the official position that long-term Chinese sojourners (let alone Chinese under foreign employment) in foreign lands were "unstable elements," the Yung-cheng court stuck to the guideline laid down in the above edict throughout in the case of Siam. For instance, in 1734, the emperor allowed the two Chinese crews aboard the Siamese ships managed by Chang Ts'uan and Hsu K'uan to return to Ayudhya. Two years later, the new emperor, Ch'ien-lung, followed established precedents of the previous reign and approved the suggestion of Min-Che Governor-General Chi Tseng-chun to let the 167 Chinese crewmen of two Siamese ships (man-aged by Ch'iu Shou-yuan and Lin Yen) sail back to Siam. In another instance twelve years later, the emperor executed a similar policy regarding another Chinese crew of a Siamese vessel.[6] Hundreds of Chinese had in fact served on Siamese ships at this time with Chinese acquiescence. People (particularly the economically hard-pressed) of Fukien and Kwangtung continued to venture to Southeast Asia in spite of the unsympathetic attitude of the Ch'ien-lung court toward the fate of Chinese residing abroad. Ch'ien-lung's reaction to the massacre of Chinese by the Dutch authorities in the East Indies in 1740 was that "he was little solicitous for the fate of unworthy subjects who, in pursuit of lucre, had quit their country and abandoned the tombs of their ancestors."[7] He also issued a standing order that those merchants in Southeast Asia were to return to China within three years.[8] The emigrants of Kwangtung used to avoid these regulations during the Ch'ien-lung period by boarding foreign vessels for Southeast Asia via Macao. Some also took the land route from Kwangtung's Shih-wan-ta-shan (Ch'in-chou district) through Vietnam. Those in South Fukien also clandestinely boarded foreign ships to go to such destinations as Siam and Johore, as noted by Fukien Governor P'an Shih-chü in 1751.[9]

The "leniency" shown by the court toward Siam was, of course, not uniformly applicable to all other states.[10] As a matter of fact, records show that it was an exception rather than the rule.

For instance in 1750 a Fukienese merchant (native of Lung-ch'i district) named Ch'en I-lao, who had previously left Canton for Batavia to trade, was punished by the Ch'ing authorities for the services he had rendered to the Dutch as a Chinese captain and emissary. His possessions were impounded and he himself was sent into penal servitude on the frontier.[11]

Ch'ien-lung also reacted strongly to another case in 1754 in which the state of Sulu employed Chinese individuals in the state's tribute presentation. Subsequently, a Fukienese named Yang Ta-ch'eng who acted as the deputy ambassador for the Sulu mission in that year was banished to Heilungkiang (a severe punishment). Fearful that the practice would lead to irregularities, Ch'ien-lung admonished the Chinese serving foreigners in various capacities that they would be subject to stern sanctions. In the reign of King Taksin (1767–1781), Chinese, especially Ch'ao-chou kinsmen of the king, enjoyed the highest privileges. Known as *Chin luang* (royal Chinese), many of them were Ch'ao-chou merchants encouraged to go to Siam to engage in foreign trade. They quickly established hegemony over the Sino-Siamese trade, a position previously enjoyed primarily by the South Fukienese group.[12]

The king authorized his mandarin merchants to sell not only the usual goods at Canton but also junks which were being con-structed in large numbers under royal patronage. One such mer-chant was Mua Seng, son of Ong Lai-hu, who himself had a deep respect for Taksin and served under him with the honorary title, Luang Apaipanit. Mua Seng was authorized to outfit at least ten to fifteen ships a year to trade at Canton on the king's behalf, and was also given permits to build two ships annually at Chantaburi. (These newly built vessels in turn had to have permits issued by provincial authorities in China before they could legally call at Chinese ports.) Other Chinese merchants were also allowed to take the king's vessels, as well as some of their own, to trade to China. Among them were another one of Ong Lai-hu's sons, Chin Ruang, a million-aire of Cholburi in eastern Siam, a wealthy Chinese named Lin Ngou (Lin Wu?), whose surname was the same as that of Taksin's queen, and who was appointed Pra Pichaiwari in charge of outfitting royal junks that he personally escorted to trade at China annually.[13] In addition, Chinese merchants were given monopolies in other areas related to the China trade. For instance, some grandsons of Ong Lai-hu, the mandarin merchant in Taisra's reign, were enfranchised to secure produce along the coast on the Gulf of Siam, from Cambodia to the Malay peninsula. In the 1760s they had over thirty ships transporting pepper from Chantaburi to the royal junks at the capital which were trading mainly to China.[14] In Lower Siam, Taksin made one Wu Yang, a Fukienese from Hai-ch'eng district a tax farmer of birds' nests at Songkla. Because of his economic influence he was eventually named governor of Songkla.

Nevertheless, as the Siamese continued to employ the tactic of Chinese management with greater frequency toward the end of the eighteenth and nineteenth centuries when they fully exploited the tributary trade scheme, Manchu sensitivity became aroused. (After all, when approval was first given in the 1720s to Sino-Siamese trade volume was comparatively less and relatively manageable.) In 1807, in the reign of the Chia-ch'ing Emperor (1796–1820), Peking finally took a stand on this issue after Liang–Kuang Governor-General Wu Hsiung-kuang urged the court to curb the abuse before it got out of hand. In his edict handed down to the Grand Council-lors in the ninth moon of that year the emperor said that foreigners from various countries who outfitted commercial ships to trade at Kwangtung should send their own people to trade themselves, and could not order local (Chinese) merchants to do it for them. "As for the two ships of the firm of Chin hsieh shun, since they have now reached China, they should be allowed to discharge and their cargo taxed, and to load a new cargo with an official permit to sail back [to Siam]. But after this prohibition, should there be any more Chinese managing foreign ships, it is to be investigated, delib-erated, and [proper] action taken at once."[15]

There actually existed a case in which Chinese merchants swindled the Siamese king of a cargo he had entrusted them to sell in China. It took place around 1806–1809, but was not reported by the Praklang to the Chinese authorities until 1815. According to the report, the Siamese court in 1806 hired two Chinese merchants named Hsu Mou and Ch'en Chin to take a vessel owned by the firm of Lin yung fa (based in Siam) and chartered by the king to trade at Shanghai. The merchants took a cargo at Shanghai with the king's money (proceeds from the sale of the royal cargo) and sailed to Ch'ao-chou prefecture, leaving it there with a firm named Wang yu chi. Hsu subsequently never bothered to return to Siam, thus swindling the Siamese king of several thousand taels.[16] It was this kind of incident that Chia-ch'ing allegedly wished to prevent.

In addition, the emperor's concern over the issue stemmed from his apprehensions about the danger of the coastal waters, in light of reports from provincial authorities that piracy had been rampant. He obviously considered that the practice of Chinese managing Siamese ships would lead to connivance between the merchants and pirates. By 1804 pirates around the Canton waters alone numbered from seventy to eighty thousand men with four hundred craft, and local officials had had a difficult time suppressing them. There were altogether five dominant bands of pirates in the Kwangtung waters from Ch'ao-chou prefecture in the northeastern corner to Canton city by 1807, and several merchants were in collaboration with them, supplying them at various points in the province, including Hainan island.[17] The situation was aggravated by the Chinese who, in the service of the Siamese king, had taken Siamese ships to trade not only at the port of Canton, but also at other smaller ports along the China coast, adding to the aura of clandestine activities feared by Peking.

From the middle of the eighteenth century, smaller inland ports, suitable for the junk trade, grew up along the coasts of Kwangtung and Fukien. The most notable ones in Kwangtung were located in the northeastern corner of the province: Chang-lin (Chang-lim), Tung-lung in Ch'eng-hai district, Lung-tu in Jao-p'ing district, and Namoa, all of which were within the prefecture of Ch'ao-chou. With heavy Ch'ao-chou influence introduced into Siam by the rice trade and King Taksin, it is small wonder that such ports played an important part in the Sino-Siamese trade.[18] Another locale that figured importantly in the enterprise was Hainan which, as shall be seen, pursued active direct trade with Siam in the early part of the nineteenth century. The Fukien inland ports, Lung-ch'i, Hai-ch'eng, Chang-p'u, T'ung-an, and Ma-hsiang were frequented by ships (Chinese junks) from Siam. But in an age dominated by Ch'eng-hai commercial interests, such ports played a lesser role than those in the Ch'ao-chou district. Finally, Siamese ships also traded as far north as Kiangnan province.

The Siamese tributary party that arrived in Peking in 1807 was handed a copy of an edict for presentation to the Siamese king, Rama I, which pointed out that two Chinese merchants were carrying Siamese goods to Kwangtung and requesting Chinese goods for the return journey, although such trade had been forbidden. The edict promised leniency in this particular case and stated that the cargo could be unloaded and a Chinese cargo loaded for the return journey. But the edict proclaimed, "Henceforth, should the said king have his own ships come [to China] manned by his country's subjects and accompanied by his officials, they would be [considered] in good order. He may no longer entrust this task to Chinese subjects. But if after this declaration the king still asked [Chinese] merchants to come in disguise, and should the local officials find out, not only would the ships be barred from entering port to discharge cargo, the merchants would be punished, and accordingly, the said king would also be shamed by the accusation of his having [willfully] violated the [imperial] regulation!"[19]

Rama I's reply to Chia-ch'ing's new order reiterated the fact that indigenous Siamese were not experienced in navigation and transport, and that he had no choice but to hire Chinese, pointing out at the same time that the cargo was always legitimate. Praya Praklang also addressed a letter to the Board of Rites imploring for reconsideration of the new order, arguing that the Siamese themselves would be unable to transact business due to the language barrier. The new Liang–Kuang governor-general, Pai-ling, apparently bribed by the Siamese side, endorsed the Siamese position, for he said in his memorial to the Peking court showing "sympathy" toward the Siamese that the latter would have difficulty in communicating, and besides, they carried no contraband cargoes. Suggesting to the court that all the points raised by the Siamese side were "legitimate," the viceroy proposed an alternative with emphasis on control rather than complete prohibition." Thereafter those local merchants hired to trade on behalf of the Siamese should report to the local officials who will give everyone of them an identification tag."[20]

Peking did not share the viceroy's view, and instructions were issued through the grand councillors to Pai-ling that Siam's request could not be approved, for if it were allowed "bad elements would be difficult to check."[21]

The local authorities accordingly intensified their surveillance over Siamese trading ships. The following is one report of such activity by Amoy officials in 1810, which reveals the degree of seriousness of the synarchic relationship between the Siamese king and Chinese merchants in trade. The report further indicates that many a Fukienese merchant had migrated to Canton since the closure of Amoy to trade from outside, and many of these people were managing Siamese royal shipping to China.

Min–Che Viceroy (cum Governor) Chang Shih-ch'eng memorialized Peking that the Fukien authorities had investigated some Fukien-Chekiang people who had gone to Siam to bring back cargoes to Kwangtung, but whose ship had afterwards drifted into Fukien due to storms. In 1809 one Yang Yu, a Fukienese of T'ung-an district, had been hired to navigate a newly constructed vessel of the Siamese king, the *Chin hsieh shun,* to trade to Kwangtung. The Kwangtung viceroy, Wu Hsiung-kuang, thereupon memorialized that foreign vessels should be managed by foreigners themselves when they traded to China, but the *Chin hsieh shun* along with the other ships was allowed to unload, acquire a new Chinese cargo, and return to Siam.

The emperor authorized Wu Hsiung-kuang to send an inquiry to Fukien to ascertain the date of departure of Yang Yu from Fukien. According to the report by the Amoy Maritime Defense quoting the *yang-hang* sources, Yang Yu left for Siam from Amoy in 1804. When Yang arrived back at Amoy with another Fukien friend, Siamese cargo was offered for sale there (indicating that the arrival in Fukien might have been deliberate and not due to storms, after all). Upon interrogation, Amoy officials found out from Yang's friend, Wu Ching, that people from Chang-chou's Lung-ch'i district had all along done business at Kwangtung. He had bought goods from them at Kwangtung and left for Siam aboard a tribute ship. After selling the cargo at Siam for four thousand Spanish dollars, he was told by a Kwangtung merchant in Bangkok, Ch'en K'un-wan, that since the Peking ban on the practice of hiring Chinese hands on Siamese royal vessels, the Siamese king wished to sell his newly built ship, the *Chin hsieh shun,* for a sum of five thousand Spanish dollars, and to reserve a space aboard the vessel for shipping his articles to sell at Kwangtung. Ch'en thereupon took Yang and Wu with him (all were originally from the same district in South Fukien). Subsequently, the ship encountered winds and drifted into Amoy and was detained there. The local Amoy authorities also discovered that the vessel had previously been granted licenses to trade by the Canton customs and Nanhai (Namoi) district.[22] The fate of the *Chin hsieh shun* and its crew is unknown but it may be assumed that the Amoy authorities eventually let the vessel and crew return to Siam.

In the reign of Chia-ch'ing, the question of Chinese managing Siamese tributary ships (including those vessels participating in the Canton trade) again came up though the Chinese court had definitely ruled that such a practice be discontinued. In that year Praya Praklang sent a petition to the Chinese government asking for a reconsideration to exempt the tribute ships. The governor and governor-general at Canton memorialized the emperor to that effect, with their own recommendation that although tribute and commercial ships were in different categories, the practice should not be continued. To the Siamese argument that Siamese ships would otherwise encounter difficulties with storms, the Canton officials replied that such natural factors were beyond the control of either Chinese or Siamese navigators. The Canton authorities told how the Siamese king had hired Chinese merchants to transport his embassy to Canton in 1782, and the ship encountered difficulties at sea in a storm just the same, proving that natural events bore no relation to skill in navigation. The emperor, again fearing abuses, acted on the local officials' suggestion.[23]

Thereafter the Siamese were officially forbidden to employ
Chinese to take either their commercial or tributary ships to China,
after the Ch'ing court had acquiesced to such a practice (officially)
for almost a century. However, how strictly the new regulations
were observed and enforced cannot be truly ascertained. Indications
are that Chinese continued to manage Siamese royal vessels, for no
sizable numbers of indigenous Siamese emerged to replace the
Chinese. As a matter of fact, the issue is not raised anywhere in
Siamese documents at all. In addition, the entire subject seems to
have faded from Chinese official documents just as swiftly as it
appeared, except for a brief reference to one instance in 1822 when
Liang-Kuang Governor-General Juan Yuan reported to Peking that
a Siamese *cheng-kung* ship en route back to Siam that year was
shipwrecked off Kwangtung's Hsin-an district, and among those
rescued was one Chinese named Huang Tung, who was eventually
repatriated to his original domicile in Kwangtung. Aside from this,
the viceroy made no mention of any form of penalty meted out to
the Siamese for the alleged violation of the existing regulations.[24]

John Crawfurd, writing in the late 1810s and early 1820s,
said that the Siamese court was hiring Chinese to man its junks to
trade to Chinese ports more than ever. In his opinion, the Siamese
were apparently officially forbidden, like the Westerners, to trade
anywhere in China except Canton. Hence it was necessary for the
Siamese, in spite of the official sanction, to continue hiring Chinese
to do the trading for them at other ports which only they knew.
Finally, another bit of evidence to this effect appeared in 1823, in
the reign of Tao-kuang, when the Siamese Praya Praklang had the
"audacity" to send a letter to the Board of Rites asking the latter
to memorialize the emperor on behalf of the Siamese requesting an
award for one of their linguists (*t'ung-shih*, official translator on a
tribute mission), a Chinese named Weng Jih-sheng. The memorial
was to suggest that a mandarin button be given to Weng by the
Chinese court for meritorious services performed for the Siamese
side. The Ch'ing authorities, discovering that Weng was in fact a
native of Yung-ting district of Ting-chou prefecture in Fukien,
ordered the Liang–Kuang viceroy, Juan Yuan, to "sternly" investigate Weng when the next Siamese embassy arrived at Canton, as

the Siamese recommendation was indeed completely out of line.[25] Although the outcome of this small episode is unknown, the above evidence may be sufficient to indicate the continued employment of Chinese individuals by the Siamese court. Thanks to the growing participation of Chinese individuals in the Siamese royal trade, Siamese vessels were able to trade to the various ports of Kwang-tung, Fukien, Chekiang, and Kiangnan, where the Siamese them-selves as foreigners would not have been able to enter.

The development of the Sino-Siamese trade also increased the involvement of Chinese individuals in the overall economic life of Siamese society in the eighteenth and early nineteenth centuries. As a matter of fact, Chinese economic influence in Southeast Asia was established by the second half of the eighteenth century in spite of the misfortunes suffered by the Chinese there between the 1740s and 1770s.

The Batavia incident in 1740[26] greatly thinned the ranks of Chinese in the Netherlands Indies; the Dutch spared only some three thousand Chinese merchants, cultivators, craftsmen, and workers in sugar and timber.[27] In 1775, the Spaniards in the Philip-pines expelled all non-Christian Chinese as part of their policy to uphold the Philippine polity through self-imposed isolation.[28] In Siam, another important Chinese center, though the authorities did not practice discriminatory measures against the Chinese, war with neighboring Burma and other internal strife that accompanied it left the Ayudhya dynasty in ruins.[29]

But these disasters were only a brief and temporary setback for entrenched Chinese influence. At Batavia and Luzon, the services of Chinese as middlemen and procurers for the European colonials were indispensable. The Batavia government had attempted to get rid of Chinese influence, but ironically the Chinese economic position grew stronger. By the last half of the eighteenth century, when the Dutch East India Company took to farming out large tracts of land, the Chinese had become dominant again in the colony's economic life. At Manila, for the benefit of the galleon trade to the Spanish New World, the authorities had to continue permitting Chinese traders to come annually to Manila, to sell their cargoes (though under the restriction of an old sixteenth-century law), and to catch the monsoon back to the China coast. Then finally in 1778, the Chinese were once again allowed to return to the colony.[30]

As far as Siam was concerned, in one sense, the war with Burma from 1765 onward actually provided a further impetus to Sino-Siamese cooperation. Young Chinese volunteers rallied around Taksin during and after the fall of the capital at Ayudhya. The half-Chinese Taksin[31] also received economic and financial assistance from Chinese merchants, especially at Trad and Chantaburi in eastern Siam. In 1767, against this background, he formed a Sino-Siamese synarchic bureaucracy following his establishment of a new dynasty at Thonburi, across the river from the town of Bang-kok.[32] The war had left the country ruined, and much rebuilding and consolidation needed to be carried out. For this task, Taksin turned primarily to the Chinese, as a contemporary French mission-ary residing in Siam had occasion to observe: "The Chinese have put gold and silver into circulation in Siam in the 1760s and 1770s, and it is to their industry that one owes the prompt recovery of this kingdom. If the Chinese were not so eager for gain, there could be neither silver nor money in Siam."[33]

In his new capital which was less agrarian-based and more commercial than Ayudhya, Taksin employed Chinese artisans and craftsmen to help build the city, which accounts for the beginning of a great influx of technicians from China lasting through the reign of Rama II in the early part of the nineteenth century.[34] Bricks and other building materials were secured from China. According to a contemporary French writer, F. Turpin, Chinese in Siam equipped at least forty ships a year to bring back brick-clay, cement, and shell-lime which constituted a brisk trade at Thonburi. By the end of the 1770s the Chinese had become the most influen-tial economic force in the new dynasty. Basing his observation on French missionary records, Turpin said: "The Chinese colony is the most numerous and flourishing by the extent of its commerce, and

172

by the privilege it enjoys. Its compliance to received customs, a
conformity of character and manners, seem to ensure it continuance
of its privilege and prosperity."[35]

Chinese also acted in private capacities to bring Chinese products to the Siamese market, with the blessings of King Taksin
himself. Rama IV was to comment in the 1860s that "the King
[Taksin] collected money in a variety of ways based on his devices,
influence and ability. The then usual and prevalent method was to
secure goods from the forests and sell them to the [Chinese] junks
and receive goods from the junks which he in turn sold to the
inhabitants."[36]

According to an eyewitness account by a European missionary
in Siam, Chinese junks put in at Thonburi regularly during the
entire dynasty. After 1770, about a dozen Chinese vessels a year
were said to be calling there. Dr. Jean Koenig, a Danish botanist
wrote from Siam in 1780, saying: "This country . . . is amply
provided with all sorts of articles from China . . . The most important
trade is made by the Chinese living there, the king himself favouring
it . . . The king wants to be the first seller of the products of the
country, and buys the best goods imported at very low price, selling
them again to the merchants of the town at one hundred percent
interest [profit]."[37]

When Rama I came to the throne, he transferred his capital to
Bangkok across the Chaopraya river from Thonburi. His new palace
was to be on the site of a large settlement, a market gardening zone
which was subsequently moved to the present-day Wat Sampreum-
Sampeng area (where Chinese, particularly of Ch'eng-hai district
who are well-to-do merchants, still congregate).[38] From the outset
he retained many Chinese who had been in the employ of Taksin,
while taking in many of their descendants as well.[39] For example,
the son of Lin Ngou, Boonchoo, was authorized to be the fitter and
appointer of all the royal junks for the court, a position later filled
by his son, Chim. A great-grandson of Ong Heng-chuan and a prominent merchant in Taksin's reign, Chin Gun, who had earlier turned do
Taksin's offer for a position in the Krom-ta sai, was persuaded to

become the third Praya Praklang under Rama I, and was subsequently known as the "Wealthy Junk Trader" (Setti Ka-sampao).[40] Mua Seng of Taksin's reign remained an important official in the Krom-ta.[41] Finally, there was also one Chim Cho-cho, son of a Chinese merchant named Si, who was put in charge of the royal warehouses and monopolies.[42]

For the sake of economic development and royal trading, the Siamese court under the First Reign encouraged Chinese to settle in the country, fully realizing their potential in providing the necessary skills in navigation and management of trade, as well as their ability to earn for the government a substantial sum in passage fees.[43] Rama IV was to comment again on his predecessor's endeavors in this field: "The Siamese built junks and exported articles for trade in China. On their return they brought *nangke* [Ch'ao-chou dialect for *jen-k'e* or "guests," referring here to Chinese passengers emigrating to Siam]."[44]

The two-year construction of Bangkok (from 1783 to 1785, just shortly before the first major Burmese attempt to invade Siam in the First Reign) and the revival of Siamese influence set off waves of Chinese immigration. As in the case of the construction of Thonburi, but on a grander scale, Chinese were engaged as skilled and semi-skilled laborers to supplement the masses of Laotians and Cambodians recruited to dredge canals and erect city walls. Since timber was abundant and conditions were ideal for shipbuilding, Chinese, especially of Ch'ao-chou prefecture, came to Bangkok to build junks along the Chaopraya river at a much lower cost, and also to export timber to China for the shipbuilding in the southeastern provinces. Both these activities, whose foundation was laid in the mid-eighteenth century, continued to flourish during the first three decades of the nineteenth century.[45]

Bangkok had the largest concentration of Chinese at this time, but sizable settlements were also spread out throughout the country, especially in areas close to the sea and along major rivers, where Chinese pursued the various tasks connected with the general internal economic development as well as feeding the flourishing junk trade with China. Outside Bangkok, in Lower Siam Rama I continued to give clientships to Chinese headmen, whose power in some cases was tantamount to that of an autonomous local ruler.[46]

The mining of tin was already established in the First Reign, and was attracting a great many Chinese to the eastern side of the peninsula.[47] Trade with China previously carried on from here was also drawing Fukienese in great numbers. Pattani, an important ancient port in the China–Japan–Siam trade, had many Chinese, among them several gold prospectors.[48] Songkla, with its Fukien governor, became one important center of Chinese trade with Malacca and Johore on the tip of the Malay peninsula, as well as with China. Ligor continued to export its elephants, elephant's teeth, tin, gold, wax, and so forth, to the Kwangtung market.[49] On the eastern coast of the Gulf of Siam, Chantaburi, which had a sizable Chinese settlement, no longer traded directly with China. Instead, much of its produce, notably pepper, was now usually sent by Chinese to the capital for transhipment to China.[50] Ponta-meas (Hatien), which up to the early part of Rama I's reign was still under the nominal control of Siam, continued to maintain a vigorous trade with Kwangtung; it also had many Chinese residents. The currency was Chinese and the export and import business was entirely in the hands of Chinese merchants.[51]

G. William Skinner has argued that the bulk of eighteenth-century immigrants to Siam had been Fukienese; this assertion is well substantiated by various documents. However, the reason he has provided for his observation that "Fukien, closed to foreign vessels from the end of the seventeenth century with the advent of the Manchus, provided an added incentive for Chinese merchants there to venture out to trade in Chinese junks"[52] is not convincing. His statement was in error for Amoy was subsequently opened for foreign vessels for three full decades in the eighteenth century and a flourishing foreign trade was taking place there during that time. It is more probable that Fukienese were dominant in Siamese society because Amoy was open to Southeast Asia traffic in the 1720s through the 1750s and the Amoy hong organizations and those in South Fukien came to specialize in the trade with Siam;

there were other reasons for this dominance, such as the long relationship maintained between the Chang-chou merchants and Siam
and the history of large imports of Siamese rice into Fukien. In the
latter half of the eighteenth century, however, the number of
Fukienese in Siam declined in proportion to those of other dialect
groups of Kwangtung, particularly the Ch'ao-chou group, which
rose very sharply.

There are several reasons for this change in the composition of
Chinese in Siam. First of all, the imperial restriction of foreign trade
to Canton was a setback for the Fukien–Siam trade, though Fukien
merchants could still trade to Siam from Fukien (as Ts'ai Yuan-ma
and Fang Hsien did in 1781). A British visitor to Amoy in the 1790s
remarked: "The inhabitants of Fukien carry on a considerable
trade with Japan, the Philippines, Java, Cambodia, Siam, and the
Isle of Formosa, which renders this country [sic] extremely opulent."
Nevertheless, the Sino-Siamese trade gradually veered to neighboring
Kwangtung province, shown perhaps by the establishment of the
specialized hong organization of the Pen-chiang hang and Fu-Ch'ao
hang at Canton to deal exclusively with the expanding Siamese commerce to China. In addition, in the early part of the eighteenth
century, the Ch'ao-chou waters had been kept under strictest
military surveillance by the Manchus; one reason was that the area
was supposedly infested with pirates and other dangerous elements.
In fact, the Manchu hero General Shih-lang (1621–1696), toward
the end of the seventeenth century had also prohibited people of
Ch'ao-chou from going overseas to such places as Formosa.[53] Hence,
it was only after the 1730s that Ch'ao-chou merchants assumed
active trading activities to Southeast Asia as seen in the organization
of the Hai-nan hang which was later reorganized as the Fu-Ch'ao
hang. Another important reason was, of course, the special favors
shown toward Ch'ao-chou merchants by Taksin, a policy which was
continued under Rama I.

The two other dialect groups which came into Siam in considerable numbers at this time were the Hainanese and Hakkas, both
of Kwangtung province. The Hakkas emigrated from Hui-chou and
Ch'ao-chou (primarily from Hai-feng district) prefectures, but did

not play any direct part in the junk trade because they were, for the most part, agriculturists and laborers by profession, while the Hainanese from the island of Hainan participated significantly in the Sino-Siamese trade as navigators and shipbuilders and also as saw millers and small-time traders in the country's interior. For some reason, the Canton group in Siam at this time also dropped in number along with the Fukienese, though previously they had made up the two most dominant dialect groupings in the Chinese settlements in Siam. As artisans and mechanical tradesmen, Cantonese were to be found primarily in major towns.[54]

Perhaps owing to the overall decline of the Ch'ing regime, Chinese authorities began to find it increasingly difficult to stem the tide of emigration to Southeast Asia from Kwangtung, thus aiding the continued influx of Chinese into Siam. H. B. Morse cited the case of Chinese emigration to Penang after 1785 when the British East India Company ships were taking Chinese artisans and farmers recruited by the Canton supercargoes. There was also one case of a Chinese captain at Penang who came to Canton in 1804 to recruit additional Chinese by himself with blessings from the British.[55] If such emigration aboard British vessels could not be curbed, it is doubtful that any control could be effectively exerted over Siamese vessels which resembled Chinese junks in almost every detail.

Passages to Siam at this time must have been relatively cheap. A passenger from Kwangtung around 1805 paid 20 Spanish dollars (about 15 Chinese taels or £5) for a passage to Penang; that to Bangkok would have been lower in all likelihood.[56]

Ch'ao-chou ships sailing for Siam from the 1780s on usually set sail from the ports of Tung-lung and Chang-lin (Changlim) where they were assessed duties and checked for proper registration by the local authorities. The commonest commodities taken aboard included passengers, sugar, and sweetmeats.[57]

In the reign of Rama I the administration of the Sino-Siamese trade continued to be the responsibility of the Krom-ta sai—which in turn was under the Department of the Praklang. However, its status was elevated during this time, especially when administrative control of several coastal areas also increased, and as the royal junk fleet became the main factor in the royal monopoly system as well as in Siam's foreign trade from this period onwards.[58] As before, but perhaps more than ever, officials in the Krom-ta sai were actively engaged in the trade themselves, a prerogative given them by their official station.[59] In addition, the chiefs of the various departments of the governments, including the Maha uparat, were all engaged in the China trade. Hence, it seems that all major government officials had appropriate access to sources of independent income which relieved the government of responsibility for the entire financial undertaking.

In Rama I's time, apart from foreign trade, the government also tried to find other means to secure revenues though these alternatives yielded a comparatively smaller income. One important means was the farming out of taxes to Chinese individuals which became established later in Rama III's reign. In the Rama I and II period, there were ten kinds of taxes established: distilleries, fisheries, grain production, large gardens, gambling, bird's nest collections, lead, ship construction, "fields in which were cultivated short-lived plants," and "petty" trading.[60] The list of taxes would be considerably expanded in the times of Rama II, III, and IV when they would be used as an alternative to the junk trade in the securing of state revenues.

By the turn of the nineteenth century and over the last years of the first Chakri reign, Siam had completely recovered from the Burmese menace, and had also emerged perhaps more powerful than at any previous period in its history. Its overseas commerce as well as its domestic business came now under the nearly exclusive control of the Chinese.

Chinese immigration into Siam at this period continued to climb rapidly, because of favorable treatment of Chinese by the Siamese court, economic opportunities, and famine in China in the 1790s and 1800s, such as the one at Ch'ao-chou.[61] The area in which the Chinese made a notable contribution during this period was in the development of commercial agriculture particularly the cultivation of pepper and sugar for the Sino-Siamese trade. The

Ch'ao-chou group had already cooperated with the Siamese court since Taksin's time especially in assisting the Siamese in building junks and manning them for trade to China. They now also contributed to plantation agriculture, a skill brought with them and developed in Siam.[62] William Skinner observes: "Perhaps as early as the first decade of the nineteenth century, Teochiu [Ch'ao-chou] agriculturists began to settle in rural areas back from the seaports and river towns. As plantation agriculture expanded, the rural Teochiu population increased, but this settlement was for the most part limited to the areas around the earlier settlements of Chinese traders. The most rapid rural development was in the valleys of Janthaburi [Chantaburi], Bangpakong, lower Jaopraya [Chaopraya], Thajin [Thachin], and Maeklong river."[63]

Pepper cultivation was one of the chief occupations of the Ch'ao-chou agriculturists at the beginning of nineteenth century. Chantaburi, the main pepper-producing area, produced as much as 90 percent of the total output of the country, though fields were also located at other places, such as Trad, Bangplasoi, Nakorn Chaisi, and in Lower Siam. Until 1910 pepper cultivation provided the steadiest employment for Chinese agriculturists, for pepper, in great demand abroad, was a chief item of export.[64] At this time, the king monopolized much of the export of pepper which was bought up at Chantaburi and sent on to the capital for transhipment abroad. Almost all the pepper produced annually was destined for the China market.[65]

Another product in plantation agriculture at this period was cane sugar, important in the manufacture of spirits whose export in the first decades of the nineteenth century became most important for Siam.[66] Back in the seventeenth century, the export of "raw sugar" from Siam to China and Japan was already noted, but this was not cane sugar.[67] By the close of the eighteenth century, Ch'ao-chou agriculturists had already planted sugar cane at Chantaburi, as witnessed by Dr. Jean Koenig, who, however, did not say if it was grown on a commercial basis. By early 1810, the commercial production of cane sugar had definitely started, and, in a little over a decade, it had become a strong export of Siam. For instance, in 1822, a total of 60,000 piculs (about eight million pounds) of the white best-grade cane sugar was exported.[68]

The largest sugar plantations were to be found at Chantaburi, Chachoengsao (eastern seaboard), and Nakorn Pathom. There were also smaller ones located at Bangplasoi (eastern seaboard), and Paet-riu.[69] Prices of cane sugar at these producing centers were naturally cheaper than at Bangkok, but apparently no other foreigners except the Chinese could go there to obtain it.

Chapter IX

THE HEIGHT OF THE SINO-SIAMESE JUNK TRADE
IN THE SECOND AND THIRD BANGKOK REIGNS,
1809–1833

The Chinese junks were supreme in the Eastern Seas during the first few decades of the nineteenth century, in spite of a lack of Chinese governmental encouragement and often restriction and hostility, the absence of a truly rationalized organization of the junk trade, and little improvement in equipment. Not only were they in control of the markets in the area,[1] but numerically speaking, Chinese junks around 1820 had an edge over their most important rival, Britain. About 300 were active in the Eastern Seas between 1805 and 1820; their tonnage amounted to over 85,000 tons a year, as compared to ships of the British East India Company (which monopolized the British Eastern trade until 1833) which never exceeded 30,000 tons annually. In this period Chinese shipping was then close to three times as much as that of Britain in the Eastern Seas.[2]

Shipbuilding in Siam

By the beginning of the nineteenth century, shipbuilding in Siam, which resumed in Taksin's reign, was invigorated by the acceleration of the Sino-Siamese trade. Virtually all the ships in the trade, including a large number of vessels engaged in China's external trade, were constructed in Siam. This was attested to by John Crawfurd in the late 1810s: "Almost all the junks employed in the commerce between the Indian islands and maritime Southeast Asia are built at Bangkok on the great river [Chaopraya] of Siam, and the capital of that kingdom. This is chosen for convenience, and the extraordinary cheapness and abundance of fine timber, especially teak, which it affords. The parts of the vessel under water are constructed of ordinary timber, but the upper works of teak."[3]

180

In the early 1820 Crawfurd stated that six to eight junks of "the largest description" (the size of junks depended on which port in China the junks were calling at) were annually constructed at Bangkok at 6.25 Siamese taels (3.2.6.) per ton, as compared to 42 and 32 Spanish dollars at Amoy and Chang-lin respectively. He stated elsewhere in the late 1820s that a junk of 8,000 piculs or 476 tons burden cost 7,400 Spanish dollars to build at Siam, 16,000 at Changlin, and 21,000 at Amoy. One important reason for the large difference in costs was the scarcity of wood along the Southeast China coast during the period.[4] Besides, ships trading with Siam that were built in China were generally of inferior wood, usually fir. (However, they imported masts, anchors, and rudders from Siam.) Ships constructed in Siam were on the average about two hundred tons in displacement, and known as the "Ch'ao-chou traders." With a few as large as 1,200 tons,[5] they were more maneuverable than those built in China, and had a smaller crew of about 16 hands to each 100 tons.[6]

The Siamese Royal Monopoly

Rama II[7] found himself in a situation similar to that of his predecessor when he discovered that the bulk of state revenues still had to come from the junk trade; otherwise, the king did not have enough to pay grants to his courtiers and officials.[8] (In some years, the grants had been reduced by as much as a half or two-thirds when revenues from the junk trade dropped.)[9]

As a prince, Rama II already owned several junks trading to China, and sometimes he even personally managed the preparation of their cargoes. As king, he naturally pursued Rama I's policy of encouraging trade with China. In his reign, he sent a total of thirteen missions to China (vis-à-vis Rama I's twenty-two in twenty-seven years), all of them with the primary aim of extracting commercial benefits. He was aware, as were his predecessors, of how tribute missions would facilitate the trade to China and lessen the likelihood of interference from avaricious officials as well as provide official sanction for other forms of trade. As early as 1812 he tried to point out in a letter to the Chinese emperor the favorable treatment accorded to foreign traders in Siam in an effort to demand reciprocity in the treatment of Siamese merchants by the Chinese authorities, making clear that Sino-Siamese relationships were predicated for the most part upon commercial considerations.[10]

In the reign of Rama II, the royal monopoly system was developed on an unprecedented scale. For one thing, in addition to the royal monopolies on import and export articles, and the management of the junk trade, the Praklang sin-ka also assumed the new task of distributing tax farms, indicating a notable expansion of its economic sphere.[11] That Rama II was inevitably a royal monopoly trader by circumstance (since the system was intimately connected with the tax structure) was observed by Captain Henry Burney who arrived in Siam in the mid-1820s:

> The late king of Siam [Rama II] monopolized the exclusive sale of the stic-lac, sapan wood, irovy, gamboge and pepper... Unfortunately the king of Siam receives a great portion of his revenue in kind. The Siamese troops when not otherwise engaged, are employed in cutting timber and sapan wood for his Majesty. The people of Laos pay their tribute in stic-lac ivory, gum benjamin, and other articles. The inhabitants of the Siamese portion of Cambodia send gamboge, pepper, and cardomons. To get rid of this produce his Majesty is obliged to become a merchant, and his officers of course try to dispose of it to foreign merchants on the highest possible terms.[12]

Rama II was also a royal monopoly trader by choice. Trade with China as engaged in by royal junks and those vessels chartered by the king had by this time become so vigorous that the royal warehouses could not provide all the goods desired from what had been collected and deposited as taxes and tributes. So under the royal monopoly system, the government tried harder than before to monopolize the acquisition of certain goods from commoners. The king took about two-thirds of the annual production of pepper, for instance. A dispatch to the ruler in Ligor in 1818 shows to what extent the king exerted his right to acquire supplies for his junk trade to China. He asserted the need for a large quantity of articles to load the vessels, articles that cannot be found at the capital. He reminded officials at Ligor that the government had a monopoly on pepper and it was illegal to sell this item to permanent customers. "The ruler of Ligor is to use the money from taxes on gambling and liquor manufacturing to purchase all the pepper from the citizens [of the three places] at 2 *salung* [1s.3d.] per picul, which is that paid [for the royal purchase at Chantaburi, the main pepper-producing center in the country at this time]. Do not let [any amount of] the pepper be sold to anyone else. After buying any available amount of the pepper, state the amount of money paid and the quantity of pepper acquired, and have the pepper sent immediately to Bangkok within the fifth moon, in time for the sailing monsoon season."[13]

The above dispatch shows how eager the court was to acquire pepper, no matter what amount, and how much in demand it was for the junk trade. The king also purchased large sums of the following articles: cardamum, eagle wood, gamboge, birds' nests, turtle eggs, and sapan wood. These were also monopolized by him—that is, he had pre-emption over their acquisition; they were normally given to the government as a tax by commoners exempt from corvée labor (in lieu of the latter and called *prai suei*). Nevertheless, John Crawfurd was of the opinion that the royal monopoly was not rigid, for when specified quantities of desired articles were met, the king allowed others to transact the leftovers freely.[14] Still it is noticeable that the amounts demanded by the king to feed his China junk trade kept growing.

In real value, the system (believed by Crawfurd to constitute the most extensive source of revenue since it covered the principal items demanded in the Chinese market) netted the king substantial sums.[15] Income was also generated from the levy of duties on vessels trading to and from Siam. In Rama II's reign, a 3-tael (£6/6 ft. 6 in.) fee was levied on ships from friendly states as a measurement charge (5 taels Siamese for non-frequenting ships). Three-masted ships were assessed a measurement charge of 20 taels per *wa* (£10/6 ft. 6.6 in.) while ships with two-and-one-half masts were assessed at 10 taels. The Rama II administration collected 3 percent *ad valorem* on imports by frequenting ships, and 5 percent for non-frequenting ones. As for the export duty, it is believed that the rate varied according to items to be exported—for instance, one-half *baht* (1.2.s.) was levied for every picul of cane sugar. Ships trading to China, which by this time were mostly built at Siam, owned and operated by the Siamese nobility and Chinese merchants resident in Siam, were exempt from both cargo and measurement fees. Chinese junks trading to Siam, which were at this time principally smaller vessels from Hainan island, were required to pay a measurement fee at a fixed rate per fathom (*wa*) of the breadth of the beam, which was half of that levied on Western ships.[16] Junks trading with the Malay peninsula were, however, levied 130 *baht* (£16) each. They were owned by officials and merchants residing in Siam.

In addition to the regular assessments on the trading ships, extra-legal exactions were also made by the government and officials. But as far as Chinese junks were concerned, there seems to have been fair treatment on the whole. According to John Crawfurd, "I have heard it from some of those engaged in conducting the trade that they have no room to complain of extortion or oppression."[17] With Western ships, however, the picture was different.

Revenues were also derived from the construction of junks which by then had become a bustling activity in the country. The king received timber for making junk masts as tribute and gifts from his vassal-rulers, notably the ruler of Pitsanuloke.[18] In addition as we mentioned earlier, a fee, the *ka-pak-rua,* was levied on those individuals, taxing the construction of junks. In all, the royal coffers must have been filled by substantial revenues from this source.

Revenues generated directly from the junk trade, which was conducted mainly with China, netted the government 565,000 taels Siamese (£232,500 in 1823. In addition to the two royal ships specifically identified by Siamese historians as the principal royal tribute-bearing and tributary trading ships to China (as in the case of Rama I), the *Malapranakorn* and *Herakamsamut,* each of 1,000 tons burden,[19] there were several other royal vessels engaged directly in the Sino-Siamese trade, including one or two of 13,000 piculs (1.73 m. lbs.) burden based at Nakorn ithamarat (Ligor), and one or two at Songkla. There was another at Chantaburi of 4,000 piculs (533,200 lbs.) burden.[20] Altogether these vessels formed part of a considerable trade in the Eastern Seas which had come to center around Bangkok by the late 1810s and early 1820s. After some first-hand observations on this period, the perceptive British envoy John Crawfurd concluded that the foreign trade at Bangkok "far exceeds that of any other Asiatic port not settled by Europeans, with the single exception of the port of Canton in China."[21] A large portion of the east coast trade (traffic along the eastern seaboard of continental Southeast Asia) had come to center at Bangkok, making it an important entrepôt in the South China Sea. At a time when Macao was on the decline as a port and Hong Kong had not yet gained prominence, there was no other significant port dominated by the Chinese lying as close to South China or as centrally located as Bangkok.

Employment of Chinese

When Rama II ascended the throne in 1809, he continued the practice of employing Chinese, and those favoring the China trade, to carry out his external trade. At the time, Ch'ao-chou natives were the most numerous, and were in the forefront of those holding state power and ennoblement, though a number of Fukienese and Cantonese were also used by the king. For instance, Rama II put Gun in charge of the Ministry of Civil affairs (Mahattai) with the title of Praya Rattanatibet. Gun was the son of a Chinese merchant named Gui (who had won recognition as an outfitter of junks to trade to China), serving in all three reigns of Taksin, Rama I (as Praya Praklang) and Rama II. He was subsequently elevated to the position of close adviser to the king, the Samuhanayok. In addition, Rama II also put a descendant of the Mohammedans, Dit Bunnag, in charge of the Krom-ta. A fervent advocate of the junk trade with China, he was subsequently promoted to the position of the Praya Praklang in this reign.[22]

Chinese influence in government outside the capital was also growing. For instance, in Lower Siam, where the Fukienese rule of Songkla was being handed down to a descendant of Wu Yang, a Cantonese (originally of Macao) named Lim Hoi (Lin Hai?) was also made a ruler of the Chinese settlement on Junkceylon (entitled Luang Ratcha-kapitan) as well as chief collector of taxes (royalties) in kind on the island's tin mines for his part in helping to thwart a possible combined Burma-Kedah (Malay sultanate on the Siamese border) attack on Siam.[23] This was, however, only a part of the growing Chinese influence in the political-economic sphere of Lower Siam.

Where Chinese influence was pervasive in the rule and adminis-tration of the country, it is not surprising to find the Chinese domi-nant in the country's economic activities particularly in those relating to trade. Crawfurd, in pointing out the inconveniences the European traders experienced in Siam during the reign of Rama II, observed nonetheless that the Chinese were the only foreigners accorded a "fair footing." There were no inconvenient restrictions on selling and buying for the Chinese. He gave an example of the arrival of fourteen to fifteen Chinese junks from Penang and Singa-pore in 1822 behind a batch of English and American vessels: the Chinese were able to dispose of their cargoes (which was supposed to have been a consignment of contraband opium worth at least 100,000 Spanish dollars) much more quickly than did the Western ships.[24]

The trade with China, managed exclusively by Chinese hands, was indisputably of the greatest volume and value. Captain Henry Burney observed that "the China trade is necessary and extensive not only because of the wants of the Chinese themselves who all use Chinese crapes, porcelain, teas, and sweetmeats."[25] On the Siamese side apart from the twenty-odd junks owned by the court, nobility, and officials, Chinese residing there also owned a fleet of some 136 junks, 32 of which operated in the trade with China, while 54 traded to other parts of Southeast Asia.[26]

In addition to the royal vessels at Bangkok, the Siamese king also had ships at other ports including Chantaburi, Ligor, and Songkla. Ships of the Lower Siam ports, where Fukienese predominated, appear to have been trading principally with the port of Amoy, and to have been directed by the local rulers on behalf of the Siamese king. From available documentation (in the form of dispatches from the king to the rulers of Ligor and Songkla) it is evident that these ships loaded articles belonging to the king as well as those of the local overlords; the latter were required to submit the proceeds and details of transactions to the court periodically. Thus it would appear that there was close cooperation between the king and his trusted officials at the various ports, particularly at Ligor and Songkla, the two most important ports for the junk trade at this time.[27] Other high-ranking officials, especially in the Krom-ta sai, continued to participate directly in the trade to China. Among the courtiers and officials privately engaged in the China trade was no less a person than Prince Chetsada-bodin, the future Rama III. He was reportedly a magnate of the junk trade.[28]

Crawfurd said that at the end of the Second Reign Siamese shipping per year amounted to about 393,000 piculs (24,562 tons) and employed about 4,912 Chinese hands, an average of 20 hands to each hundred tons. The tonnage was impressive considering the fact that only an average of three British and American ships (or one or two thousand tons in all) called annually, and much of the trade conducted was incidental. The largest vessels, about eight in number, traded to Kwangtung; smaller ones, usually over thirty of them (of about 1,000 piculs [133,300 lbs.] each), went to Fukien, Chekiang, and Kiangnan. Siamese junks of even lesser tonnage, from 7,500 piculs (933,150 lbs.) to a mere 850 piculs (113,305 lbs.) traded to Batavia, Malacca, Penang, Singapore, and Saigon. Singapore was rapidly becoming the most important of these ports.[29]

As we mentioned previously, foreign trade conducted by local Chinese merchants was by no means clandestine, or unacknowledged by Chinese authorities. Local officials of the coastal provinces had the power to specify the number of vessels and even the kinds of cargo to be exported and imported. In many instances, however, these Chinese vessels seem to have engaged in "improper" procedures. John Crawfurd observed that in the 1820s the Chinese were clever in evading duties. Since the coasting trade was nearly free of duties, they would "intending in reality to proceed to Siam or Cochin China, for example, clear a junk out for the Island of Hainan, and thus avoid the payment of duties. When she returns, she will lie four or five days off and on, at the mouth of the port, until a regular bargain be made with the custom-house officers, for the reduction of duties. The threat held out in such cases is to proceed to another port, and thus deprive the public officers of their customary perquisites."[30]

In the early 1820s there were about 222 Chinese junks, averaging 200 tons each, from Fukien, Kwangtung, and Chekiang trading in the Eastern Seas, and 89 of these, or about 40 percent of the total force, involving over 2,000 crewmen, traded annually to Siam, making it the most important junk port of the period. The remaining junks traded elsewhere were: 8 to Singapore, 20 to Japan, 13 to the Philippines, 4 to Sulu Seas islands, 2 to the Celebes, 13 to Borneo, 7 to Java, 10 to Sumatra, 1 to Rhio, 6 to the east coast of the Malay peninsula, 20 to Annam, 9 to Cambodia, and 20 to Tongkin. In 1821, the total trade from China to Siam amounted to 168,500 piculs or 10,531 tons. Among the vessels, five junks of 3,000 piculs (400,000–567,000 lbs.) came from Chiang-men (Kiangmui) in Kwangtung, one of 5,000 piculs from Chang-lin, and two of 3,000 piculs each from Amoy. In addition, more than 50 smaller junks of 2,000 to 3,500 piculs (267,000 lbs.) each plied between Hainan and Siam under the Chinese flag. The number of Hainan junks trading to Siam may be attributed to the fact that coming from a location south of Siam, Hainan ships could leave port early in the northeast monsoon and reach Bangkok every year ahead of junks from any other part of China. They reached Bangkok in January, while others from Fukien and Chekiang usually arrived in late February or the beginning of April. G. William Skinner therefore sees the Bangkok trade as natural for the Hainanese. In addition, the sailing distance would permit them ample time to trade at Bangkok annually; the distance between Ch'iung-chou or Hai-k'ou and Bangkok required only eight or nine days of sailing.[31] Because of the comparatively shorter distance, Hainanese merchants could use smaller vessels, usually constructed of fir and other inferior woods, which they customarily furnished with masts, rudders, and wooden anchors, availing themselves of the abundance of material in Champa and Cambodia which lay on their route to Bangkok. Charles Gützlaff described how the Hainanese undertook this venture: "On their voyages to Siam, they cut timber along the coasts of Champa and Cambodia, and when they arrive at Bangkok, buy an additional quantity, with which they build junks. In two months or so the junk is finished ... These junks are then loaded with cargoes, saleable at Canton or their native island; and both junks and cargoes being sold, the profits are divided among the builders."[32]

Hainanese junks traditionally traded with neighboring places such as the upper parts of Indo-China, Macao, Canton, Ch'ao-chou, and so on. In the early part of the nineteenth century, 10 to 12 junks from Hainan also called annually at Koh Samui (an island off the coast from Surat Thani or Bandon), where they obtained primarily cotton and birds' nests.[33]

Ports

The Sino-Siamese trade at this time on the Siamese side was concentrated at Bangkok, with the exception of a few junks which traded to Songkla and Ligor. Chinese ports conducting the trade were mainly in Kwangtung (Canton, Kao-chou, Chiang-men, Chiang-lin and ports on Hainan, particularly Hai-k'ou), as well as Amoy, Ningpo, Shanghai, Sao-cheu (Soochow in Kiangnan) and as far north as Tientsin. Crawfurd alleged that he had been informed by the Praya Praklang that the most profitable part of the Sino-Siamese trade was carried on with Shanghai, Ningpo, Soochow, and the least lucrative was with Canton and Amoy. He attributed this to the fact that the latter two ports levied heavier duties, and the conduct of the officials there was more "vexatious than any other port of China."[34] Another plausible explanation may be that the role of Ch'ao-chou merchants in the Sino-Siamese trade was becoming more important.[35] For years prior to this, Ch'ao-chou merchants had been trading northward to Chekiang and Kiangnan. With trade developing on a phenomenal scale, particularly at Shanghai in the reign of Tao-kuang (1821–1850), Ch'ao-chou junks operating in the Sino-Siamese trade now also carried Siamese goods northward as well. The Chia-ch'ing edition (1814) of the *Shang-hai hsien-chih* stated that Siamese ships visited the port every year, and Crawfurd maintained that there were no Ningpo or Shanghai or Canton ships going to Siam at this time, since commerce was carried on mainly by the Ch'ao-chou traders from Siam. The ships left Bangkok in June or July when the southwest monsoon was at its full strength, and after arriving at Kwangtung, they made short voyages up the coast of China and back again before they had to catch the northeast monsoon to sail back to Bangkok.[36]

Imports from China to Siam at this time were numerous, comprising mainly "assorted cargoes" which included coarse earthenware and porcelain, tea, quicksilver, vermicelli, dried fruits, raw silk, crepes, nankeens, silk fabrics, fans, umbrellas, writing paper, josssticks, and other minor articles. Passengers were also important. Crawfurd said that a (Cantonese) junk could bring around 1,200 passengers to Bangkok at a time; the annual rate of immigration then was about 7,000.[37] In addition, from Rama I's reign on, many valuable articles were imported from Ningpo, such as satin, stone lions, and other figurines carved from rocks.[38] The ingenious Chinese often imitated native goods. From Rama I's reign on, the Siamese market was "invaded" with Chinese imitations of Siamese Swankaloke crockery ware. Originally produced in the eleventh century, the crockery was actually made by Chinese who used Chinese methods of production. However, in later periods, the polychrome painting was done by Siamese artists with original Siamese designs, and it was indigenously produced until the destruction of Ayudhya in 1766. Quantities of Chinese imitations began to flow in, some of them made to order and imported for the benefit of wealthy Chinese in order to make up for the scarcity of the old specimens.[39] The earthenware and porcelain industry was revived in the reign of K'ang-hsi and was fully developed in the Chia-ch'ing period.

The value of all Chinese external shipping at the time amounted to 6,918,240 Spanish dollars, of which 40 percent or roughly

3,000,000 dollars accounted for the shipping to Siam. The value of the Siamese shipping trade to China in 1821, was estimated by Crawfurd to have been 614,050 *baht* or 153,512.5 taels Siamese (£76,756), not including the Chinese vessels trading to Siam. One means by which we may judge the overall profitability of the Sino-Siamese trade at this time is the interest rate on money borrowed at Batavia for the junks in the China trade between Batavia and China—usually 40 percent. The net profit, then, cannot have been less than double this amount. On bulky articles (tea, porcelain), the advance price at Indian Archipelago ports was 150–200 percent; on wrought silks and cotton, it was 100 percent. These were not wholesale, but retail prices, for just as at the port of Bangkok, as soon as the junk arrived, shops (on board the vessels) were immediately opened and goods retailed by members of the vessel. The Crawfurd Mission to Siam around 1825 also reported that the trade with China was so profitable that it yielded at least a 300 percent profit. Large profits were realized even when only one out of two vessels returned, which may account for the involvement of the king, his court, and government officials.[40]

The Third Reign

In the Third Chakri Reign, with the aim of developing the country's economic resources as an objective, the Siamese government increasingly recognized and used the ability of the Chinese. Chinese were employed by the state for a variety of enterprises: junk trade, tax farming, and manual labor. Under the privileged status accorded them the Chinese were able to engage in entrepreneurial practices of their own, using wealth as their ultimate weapon in achieving mobility in the Siamese society, and many made their way into the governing class, or at least worked as part of the ruling machinery in one way or another.

Specific advantages of the Chinese over the Siamese included: exemption from corvée with payment of a small poll tax (1.5 to 3 *baht,* or 3.7–7.5 s., payable every three years), which enabled the Chinese to pursue any trade and not be bound by obligations. Chinese who became ennobled or officials were excused. In addition, the Chinese enjoyed high mobility, being permitted to go any place within the country, while the Siamese, obligated under the patronage and bondage systems, were immobilized.[41]

In Rama III's reign the country's foreign trade continued to be dominated by Chinese-style junks though toward the middle of this reign Western-style square-rigged vessels were introduced by the Siamese court. Trade continued to be conducted primarily with China, and also with neighboring places, Singapore in particular. Rama III or Pra Nangklao, came to the throne with considerable experience working in the Krom-ta where he acquired a knowledge of shipbuilding and direct participation in trade with China.[42] Rama III reappointed Dit Bunnag, the last Praya Praklang of Rama II, with whom he had worked in the same department, and together they endeavored to develop the China trade, to the profit of both official and personal accounts. (Dit also had working for him as a right-hand man, his son, Chuang Bunnag, who later became Praya Praklang himself in the same reign with the title of Praya Sisuriya-wongse.) Rama II also had Praya Choduk-ratchasetti, a descendant of Chinese immigrants in the Ayudhya dynasty, who was in charge of the Krom-ta; he had reportedly amassed a big fortune.[43] John Cady comments on Rama III's court system as "self-centered, interested in preserving its semidivine prerogatives, prestige, wealth, and power, and lacking concern for outside commercial [sic] opinion," concluding that such a system "was not destined to survive anywhere in Southeast Asia."[44] It was in such a milieu that the Sino-Siamese junk trade continued to thrive for one or two more decades, until the time when the commercial domain of the Eastern Seas was encroached upon by the more dominant Western maritime powers.

In the Third Reign, we have at least a partial list of junks delegated to these personages as shown in Table 9.

In addition to those listed in Table 9 Rama III's government is known to have possessed at least 9 royal junks, as well as 8 additional ones assigned to the various departments.[45] Altogether, some 30 to 40 such vessels were actively engaged in trade, primarily with China, contrary to the pledge that there would be free trade.

Table 9

A Partial List of Siamese Junks Trading Overseas
and Their Sponsors in the Third Reign

Name of vessel	Under whose sponsorship and responsibility
Nang-nok	Pra In
Nak-mai	Pra Sen
Lumpochiao	Luang Kaew-wayut
Tabtim	Prya Sipipat
Bun-li	Prya Cho-duk
Gim chun seng	Luang Apai-pinit
Ch'om-pu-nuj	Pra Cho-duk
Kaew kun muang	Praya Tun-ma
Gim hok lee	Praya Sipipat
Datfa-song-chan	Luang Suntorn
Daeng-pak-pla	Pra Sen
Hoo-song	Praya Kosa
Ngern	Praya Kosa
Sampao-nak	Khun Tong-chew
Jabanseng	Praya Sipipat

Source: Pongpun Supatrapun, "Karn-suksa tang prawatisart
kiew-duei ruang praklang-sin-ka," M.A. thesis,
Chulalongkorn University, Bangkok, 1968, p. 184.

British visitors, following on the heels of John Crawfurd, continued to observe the symbiotic trade relationships between the Siamese and Chinese. Commenting on the tariff, one of the advantageous aspects of such an arrangement, Captain Burney wrote in 1826: "The British merchant who pays an import duty of 8 percent and heavy export duties, cannot compete with the Chinese, who have brought up British cottons and merchandise from Singapore and the Eastern Islands, until the market at Bangkok is over-stocked and many articles of British manufacture are now selling here at much lower prices than what they bring at Singapore and other parts to the Eastward."[46]

The China trade, which had undergone a marked increase at the end of the eighteenth century, was still expanding under Rama III and was still considered the most valuable branch of the trade. This expansion was paralleled by a sharp increase in the number of tributary missions, to one for every other year, in addition to the annual dispatches to Canton for the purpose of trade. It was probable that presents were also taken on these occasions to local officials to expedite transactions. Prince Chula Chakrabongse said that, "Rama III sent tributary gifts to China every two years in order to maintain good trade relations which he considered more important than anything else." In addition to these gifts, various nobles and officials with a stake in the China trade also sent presents to the Chinese emperor and his officials on a regular basis. Considered outside of the regular tributary framework, these gifts were intended primarily to facilitate their trading ventures conducted through various Chinese merchants.[47]

The prevailing practice then was apparently to have a number of commercial ships tag along with the main tributary vessels to trade at Canton (as in the case of the 1780 Taksin mission). The commercial ships would then be likely to be granted tax privileges and would be better treated. In addition, they could acquire certain articles reserved normally for tributary vessels only, such as silks.[48] By 1844, the Chinese government had given in to the practice, while reasserting that only "legitimate" tributary ships would be duty-exempt, and not even those vessels coming to Canton for the express purpose of picking up the returning embassy from Peking would be given this privilege in accordance with precedence. They had also declared back in 1839 that "as a gesture of goodwill to Siam," the established rule of one tribute for every third year would thereafter be altered to one for every fourth year. According to the new tributary regulation, Vietnam was to present a tribute every two years at Canton and every fourth year at Peking while Korea and the Ryukyus were to present their tribute once every year at the capital.[49]

Burney observed in 1826 that the Siamese king and most of his courtiers participated in the China trade, which yielded them at least a 300 percent profit. They sold sapan wood, gamboge, and other goods at Chinese ports through Chinese merchants.[50] According to documents of the Third Reign, Siamese vessels trading to Canton, Shanghai, and Ningpo carried as their usual cargoes, such items as sapan wood, pepper, red wood, bee's wax, tin, cardamum, rudders, rhinoceros horns, and betel nuts. For 1844–1845, twenty ships were involved in the transport of such items to the above destinations. We also learn that the cost of outfitting a junk to trade there at least for that season was slightly over 1,380 taels Siamese (£690). Such a venture involved a number of junks from the Siamese side, including those vessels owned by resident merchants and chartered to the Siamese court.[51]

There were also many from the Chinese side which traded actively with Siam. Ships from the Hai-feng district of Ch'ao-chou under the nom de commerce of Chin (like Amoy ships) were active in this trade. In 1826, Captain Henry Burney observed that 36 to 50 junks from Canton, Eurin (Yu-lin), Ningpo, and other Kwangtung ports arrived annually at Bangkok; those from Hainan numbered between 20 and 45.[52] British commercial intelligence also reported that in 1826 Hainan vessels carried on a considerable foreign traffic with Macao, Cochin China, and Siam.[53]

D. E. Malloch, who accompanied the Burney mission to Bangkok in the mid-1820s, said that he witnessed in the beginning of the Third Reign for three successive years, "upwards of 150 junks at one time" in the Chaopraya river at the capital from Kwangtung, Hainan, and neighboring places, averaging more than 25,000 tons. Noting that the trade was increasing rapidly, he further commented that since teak and rice were then freely exportable (by Chinese), he expected that there would be room for at least 100,000 tons of shipping. Elsewhere, he commented on the quick discernment of Chinese merchants in discovering the "wants of the people."[54]

John Crawfurd estimated around 1830 that the total tonnage of the Chinese foreign trade with Siam was between 60,000 to 70,000 tons, exclusive of the small Hainan junks, which, estimated at 150 tons each, would make in all about 80,000 tons. By the early 1830s Chinese vessels trading to Cochin China, Siam, and

Singapore, as well as the Indian Archipelago, were mainly from
Ch'ao-chou and South Fukien, the former being most numerous
at Siam. Charles Gützlaff said at the time that there was no one
Southeast Asia port like Bangkok where so many red-prow Ch'ao-
chou traders were concentrated. A few junks, about 20 yearly,
were also leaving from Canton (annual trade was from 200,000 to
300,000 taels or £66,666 to 100,000). In addition, about two
dozen or so ships from Chekiang and Kiangnan (places noted for
their raw silks, teas, and nankeens) traded with Siam, as compared
to 16 for Cochin China, and 5 for the Philippines. Altogether ships
from the last two provinces amounted to 45, with a total tonnage
of over 17,000 tons, the vessels being of considerable size. Edmund
Roberts, first American envoy to the Siamese court, estimated in
1832 that the number of Chinese ships going to trade to Southeast
Asia from China annually was no less than a hundred, and one-
third of them were from Kwangtung. According to him, 6 to 8
went to Tongkin, 18–20 to Siam, Cochin China, and Cambodia,
4 or 5 to Singapore, Java, Sumatra, and Penang, and as many more
traded to Borneo, the Philippines, and the Celebes.[55] Many of the
vessels from Fukien and northern ports going south touched at
Canton on the outgoing and homeward journeys; but direct trade
to Southeast Asia by Canton merchants, according to Roberts, was
relatively small.

Mr. Abeel, a Protestant missionary at Bangkok, noted in 1832
that there were 80 Chinese junks visiting Bangkok that year.[56] Dr.
W. Ruschenberger, medical officer and historian attached to the
Roberts Mission, observed that a row of Chinese junks, numbering
from 30 to 70 with crews from 20 to 130 each, and averaging from
100 to 600 tons burden, was anchored in midstream at Bangkok,
extending for over two miles. They remained from February till
May or June. They were chiefly from Hainan, Kwangtung, and
Leang-Hae (Fukien?) but the crews all spoke the Ch'ao-chou dialect. The
number of Chinese junks trading with Southeast Asia around 1833–
1834 was quoted at one hundred, with one-third belonging to
Kwangtung (of which 18 to 20 traded to Siam). Another missionary

named Johnson wrote from Bangkok in 1836 that there were a great number of Chinese visiting Bangkok annually from different parts of China.[57]

A British report written around 1846 said that Kwangtung's foreign trade with Southeast Asia was in fact "quite considerable," though not comparable to the domestic commerce. This trade was mainly conducted in ships of a dead weight of 150 to 500 tons owned by men of Ch'ao-chou prefecture. Such vessels carried all kinds of produce, as well as several hundred immigrants. The report further noted that trade with Siam from this province was perhaps the largest in the area, employing about 20 to 30 junks.[58] The entire foreign trade of Kwangtung (in native junks, but exclusive of Hainan craft comprising 40 to 60 vessels of two to six hundred tons burden each) required a maximum capital of 5 million Spanish dollars, and was about one-sixth of the Canton city maritime trade to other provinces. Therefore the Siamese trading branch amounted to one-half of Kwangtung's junk force.[59] The report concluded that "these speculations turn out so advantageously that there are few engaged in them who do not amass considerable capital. They are in fact viewed as the most profitable branches of the whole maritime commerce. The vessels proceed to two ports only, viz: Chantaburi and Bangkok."[60]

Both Chinese and Siamese junks trading to China seem to have been engaged in the coasting trade. Goods were brought to China and traded up and down the coast from Hainan in the south to as far north as Shantung. For instance, Fukien ships trading to Siam usually called first at Kwangtung on the homeward journey and then proceeded north to Chekiang and Shanghai, where many Fukienese and Ningpo merchants were residing.[61] During the times of Chia-ch'ing and Tao-kuang (1796–1850), the coasting junks along China's coast were numerous. T'ien Ju-k'ang estimates that there were about 5,800 junks with a total capacity of 680,000 tons. The coasting trade along Chekiang and Kiangsu accounted for over 2,000 vessels with a tonnage of 300,000 to 500,000 tons, and that of Kwangtung, 1,200 vessels of 180,000 tons. The coasting trade

Table 10

Ships from Kwangtung Engaged in the
Coasting Trade for the Year 1831

Ships from Tseun-chow-foo (Ch'uan-chou fu):	80
Ships from Chang-chou fu:	150
Ships from Hui-chou and Ch'ao-chou:	300
Ships trading between Chiang-men and Fukien:	300
Ships from Canton to Tientsin and Liaotung:	16
Total	846

Source: T'ien Ju-k'ang "Tsai-lun shih-ch'i chih shih-chiu
shih-chi chung-yeh Chung-kuo fan-ch'uan-yen ti fa-
chan, *Li-shih yen-chiu,* no. 12:6 (1957).

to and from Kwangtung was carried on primarily by Ch'ao-chou
ships, but the largest ships in this trade belonged to Fukien. (See
Table 10 for the breakdown of the Kwangtung coasting trade of
1831.)

Phipps also gave an idea of the value of this trade: junks trading
from Shanghai to North China were worth ten million silver (Spanish)
dollars; those from Ningpo trading with North China were worth
400,000: and those from Ningpo trading with Fukien were worth
300,000; and so on. The total value of the entire coasting trade was
estimated at over 26 million Spanish dollars.[62]

The China coast was dotted with ports, mostly inland where
they were protected, and where shallow-draft junks had no problem
navigating. In Kwangtung, Hai-k'ou, P'u-ch'ien, and Ch'ing-lan, were
primary ports, and Yu-lin and Fu-t'ien secondary ports, on Hainan
island. In the Canton area, there were Canton city and Chiang-men
which were primary junk ports, while Macao, Hsiang-shan, and San-
sui were secondary ports. In the Ch'ao-chou area, Chang-lin was
now the main junk port, secondary ones included Huang-kang, Hai-
men, Shen-ch'uan,[63] J'ao-p'ing, Chieh-yang, and Nan-ao (Namoa).[64]

Fukienese ports maintaining connections with the Sino-Siamese
junk trade included Amoy,[65] Chang-chou, with Hai-ch'eng and T'ung-
an as secondary ones. The ports north of Fukien frequented by

Siamese junks were Ningpo, Soochow, and Shanghai. The foreign trade at Shanghai had become very important by the 1830s. The native trade there greatly exceeded that of Canton; for instance, in the early 1830s no less than 700 junks arrived in a week's time. During the reign of Tao-kuang as the restriction of foreign trade to Canton alone was breaking down and as the economy of the Kiangnan area developed, Shanghai's commercial relations with Southeast Asia, Korea, and Japan correspondingly expanded. As for Ningpo, foreign trade continued to flourish well into the 1840s because of its dense and industrious population, large town, excellent water communication, and rich merchants.[66] Table 11 gives some idea of junks from abroad having intercourse with Shanghai, Ningpo, and Soochow in a certain year of the early 1830s:

Table 11

Foreign Vessels from the Eastern Seas Trading to Shanghai,
Ningpo, and Soochow in a Certain Year in the 1830s

From	Number
Japan (10 junks, 2 voyages)	20
Philippines	13
Sulu Islands	4
Celebes	2
Borneo	13
Java	7
Sumatra	10
Singapore	8
Rhio	1
East Coast, Malay peninsula	6
Siam	89
Cambodia	9
Cochin China	20
Tongkin	20
Total	222

Source: John Phipps, *A Practical Treatise on the China and Eastern Trade* (Calcutta, 1835), p. 203.

Of all places in the Eastern Seas having commercial intercourse with the above coastal ports Bangkok remained the most important. George Earl, visiting the city in the early 1830s, gave a description of the Chaopraya at the capital, crowded with junks, boats, and floating houses, all "jumbled together in glorious confusion, and totally concealing the banks from view." Much of the trading was done aboard the junks moored in the river. The traders spread their wares in booths on the awning-covered decks and turned the place into a large floating bazaar, like the trading conducted by junks at Singapore.[67] Import and export commodities in this trade were, as usual, quite wide-ranging. One principal line of imports consisted of articles for the consumption of Chinese residents, such as tea, porcelain, nankeen, fans, umbrellas, rice, paper, incense sticks, and so on. A considerable amount of bullion was also imported by the Siamese court, because Siam's exports to China still far exceeded imports from there; the difference was made up by importing silver (back in the time of Rama II, silver ingots were already being imported by this means from China) for the purpose of minting specie. The increasing use of paid Chinese labor and greater demands for Western goods, including firearms, were among the important reasons necessitating a larger circulation of cash and money; the silver bullion was converted into silver lumps or "bullets" which was the main currency of the country. The third line of imports from China consisted of luxury items, such as fine porcelain and silks. Siam also imported brass and iron, articles considered strategic materials, and therefore mainly acquired through the tributary channel. In addition, delicate articles such as richly wrought silks and satins, carved ivory and feather fans, as well as preserves, were brought back from China for transhipment to Singapore, a venture that earned the Siamese a net profit of over 50 percent or about five million Spanish dollars annually in the late 1830s.[68]

Siam had much more to offer China on the export side. Vessels trading to China annually selected their export cargoes according to the various destinations. Those that sailed, for instance, for the northern Chinese regions took sapan wood (principally for use as dunnage of junks or as a dye wood; it was cheap and abundant in

Siam, and over 200,000 piculs [26,660,000 lbs.] were exported to China in 1832), betel nuts, and particularly, sugar. By the 1830s sugar had replaced rice in Siam as the country's principal export. J. R. Morrison said: "A few years ago [in the 1820s] above 100,000 piculs of raw sugar were annually shipped to China from Bombay, but in consequence of the competition of sugar from Manila and Siam, the quantity has greatly fallen off. This kind of sugar is the sort commonly used by the Chinese, its average price is about 5 Spanish dollars per picul.[69] In 1832, for instance, Siam exported some 96,000 piculs to China.[70]

In addition, pepper continued to be exported to the various China ports. The aggregate production of pepper in Southeast Asia in the early 1830s amounted to some 40.5 million pounds, half of which was taken to China in foreign bottoms, including Siamese junks. Siam at this time produced at least 65,000 piculs (8.7 m. lbs.), 40,000 of which was annually sold to the king in Bangkok and eventually exported to China. Also on the east coast of the Malay peninsula, Pattani and Kelantan produced some 16,000 piculs, and Tringganau 8,000. Much of the pepper was also taken to China.[71]

There were also the Siamese-built junks. Captain Burney had said in 1826 that "few places in the world could offer greater advantages for shipbuilding" than Bangkok, while he tried unsuccessfully to secure an agreement from the Siamese court to permit the British to engage in the activity.[72] Speaking in 1830, John Crawfurd pointed out to the Select Committee of the House of Commons that no less than 81 of the 89 large junks operating in the Eastern Seas were built in Siam and owned by Siamese, except for the small junks carrying on the Hainan trade which were built in China and owned by Chinese.[73] He estimated that the average size of the larger junks was about 300 tons.[74]

In 1832, Edmund Roberts described junk building as one of the few mechanical arts at Bangkok.[75] Another Western visitor to Bangkok, George Earl, described in 1833, what he saw in the lower part of Bangkok as follows: "Vast numbers of Chinese blacksmiths were busily employed in forging iron-work, probably for the junks which they were building on the banks."[76] Western merchants and visitors to Siam at the time did not fail to mention at least one aspect of the junk construction that was going on, an indication that it must have been rather extensive.[77]

The cost of junk construction in the 1820s and 1830s is reported to have been 25 *baht* (£3 2s. 6d.) a ton or 2.3 *baht* per picul. This cost was considered quite low, and hence a 400-ton vessel, with proper economical management, could be built for 20,000 *baht* or merely 4,000 taels at Siam.

Siam's Regional Trade

In addition to direct trade with China, Siam, in the reign of Rama II, maintained a vigorous trade with its neighboring areas; which was also exclusively managed by Chinese residents of Siam in the same manner as in the direct Sino-Siamese trade. There were in general three branches of this trade: 1) along the coast, from Bangkok to Siamese ports on the eastern and western sides of the Gulf of Siam, 2) with Cambodia and Cochin China, and 3) with the Indian Archipelago.

Coastal

The coasting trade in the Gulf of Siam included the ports of Chumporn, Bandon, Songkla, Ligor, Junkceylon (Phuket) on the Eastern and Western Sides of the Malay Peninsula, and Bangplasoi, Bangpra, Banglamung, Rayong, Chantaburi,[78] Tungyai and Koh Kong on the eastern side of the Gulf. All of these places characteristically had Chinese settlements. The main commercial activity was the collection of goods for the China trade, and to a lesser extent, for the regional trade in the Malay peninsula. Pepper seems to have been the main article collected, for it was grown in large quantities by Chinese commercial agriculturists at Chantaburi, (30–40,000 piculs or 4–5.2 million lbs. per annum), Tungyai (10–15,000 piculs or 1.3–2 million lbs. per annum), Songkla and Ligor. Other items collected were cardamum, gamboge, ivory, eagle wood, dyewoods, and bark. Much of the traffic in this category belonged to the Siamese king who secured the items both for trade and for tribute at the China market. For example, as we have mentioned, the Chakri monarchs consistently transported pepper from Chantaburi and Tungyai bought at concessional prices from the Chinese cultivators, and the places were barred to foreign traders. The king normally farmed out the privilege of transporting produce from these locales to Chinese merchants, a practice successfully put into effect from the time of King Taksin. They could sail their vessels to and from these ports all year round, because the topography of the area consisted of numerous islands and inlets which could provide shelters for junks from unseasonable winds and monsoons.[79]

Cambodia and Cochin China

The second branch of Siam's regional trade was conducted with Cambodia and Cochin China. Siamese junks traded with the ports of Hatien, Kampongsom (Sihanoukville), Teksia, Kamao in Cambodia, with goods of Chinese, Indian, and European manufacture, and returned with items mainly for the China trade (particularly gamboge, cardamum, and hides).[80] Siam's trade with Cochin China was conducted entirely in vessels from Bangkok which called at Saigon (where the biggest volume of trade for Cochin China was conducted), Faifo, and Hue.[81] Annually 40 to 50 small junks carried unwrought iron, iron pans, tobacco, and opium. They returned to Bangkok with mats for bags and sails, and wrought and unwrought silks.[82] In the 1830s and 1840s Siam's trade to Cochin China was also maintained with 20 to 50 smaller-model vessels. The trade, however, was not keeping up as well as it should; one reason was that Cochin China accorded preferential treatment (at least at Hatien) to Chinese junks, and, as a result Siamese junks as a rule had to pay higher duties.

The principal imports from Cochin China were again those articles destined mainly for the China trade, including mats for the junk's sails as well as for roofing, betel nuts, silk, coarse cotton, gamboge, cardamum, agulla wood, hides, elephant's teeth, and sticlac. Exports from Siam to Cochin China were iron, bark of trees for dyeing and other purposes, rice, and so forth. Ships from Cochin China also conducted trade to Siam. For example, goods from Cambodia were shipped to Bangkok at different times of the year in about 30 small coasting junks.

Indian Archipelago

The third branch of Siam's trade with neighboring countries was with the Indian Archipelago, including the Straits of Malacca. This trade was greatly extended, particularly after the establishment of Singapore in 1819; by 1821–1822, trade was conducted with Kelantan, Tringganau, Pahang on the Malaya Peninsula, Rhio, Singapore, Malacca, Penang, Batavia, Semarang, Cheribon, Palembang, and Potinak, which all had sizable Chinese commercial establishments and had been frequented by Chinese junks primarily from Amoy and South Fukien. Staple exports from Siam, included sugar, pepper, salt, oil, rice, and minor articles such as stic-lac, iron pans, coarse earthenware, and lard. Return items included those salable in the China market: local produce and European goods such as piece goods and opium. Crawfurd said, "Trade at Siam is at present carried on by certain Chinese residing there, who bring its produce to the European ports in the Straits of Malacca and receive European and Indian goods in return. At Ligor and Songkla, the local rulers, under the Bangkok court's auspices, hired Chinese to trade to the peninsula, especially at Penang and also to India in the reign of Rama II. The island of Penang was ceded to the British by the sultan of Kedah (Queda) in 1786. Almost unpopulated at the time it had 10,000 people in 1790. Trade developed vigorously in the 1810s with the participation of many Fukienese merchants. Penang exported opium and piece goods to Siam; its principal import was sugar. There was also a direct trade conducted between Penang and Bangkok."[83]

Since the beginning of the nineteenth century the Chinese had advised the Siamese king to trade with Java. After 1815 two 120-ton junks were sent to Batavia, navigated by Chinese but financed by the king himself. The Chinese were also responsible for taking Siamese produce (especially sugar, which was sold in volume at very cheap prices) in "considerable quantities" into different trading ports of the Straits of Malacca, from whence it found its way to Europe. When Singapore was opened (by Sir James Raffles whose idea was to realize a Singapore–Annam–China–Japan trade with reliance on Chinese junks),[84] Chinese junks immediately traded

there. Singapore came to take precedence over Penang in trade
with Siam, while Penang eventually developed trade with the
western side of the Malay peninsula, the part that belonged to Siam.
Crawfurd reported to George Swinton, Secretary of Government,
Fort Williams, in 1821–1822: "The commercial intercourse between
Singapore and Siam continued to increase in value and amount:
within the last six months twenty-one junks have arrived at this
place from the port of Bangkok and a large ship of the kind which
was in the habit of formerly proceeding to Calcutta or Bombay
stopped this year at Singapore where she disposed of a cargo of
considerable value consisting of tin, pepper, and sugar."[85]
   Singapore rose rapidly as a trading center when the Chinese
flocked there (in 1819, their number was 30, but by 1824, there
were 3,317 Chinese out of a total population of 10,683 on the
island). The Chinese apparently spread the news of Singapore as a
trade center so more Chinese came, and with them the junk trade.
The Chinese junk trade at Singapore was responsible for making
Singapore's external trade larger than that of Batavia by 1823.
Singapore, in fact, became the biggest East-West depot. The most
valuable, if not the largest, of the Chinese junks came from Amoy.
The largest came from Chang-lin, Canton, and Amoy; the smallest,
from Hainan.[86]
   In 1823, of the 136 Siamese junks engaged in the foreign trade
(38,856 tons), 35 junks traded with the Malay peninsula, and of
these 27 small ones (2,531 tons) traded with Singapore while only
5 (1,503 tons) called at Penang and Malacca, and so on. In 1824,
the following year, the number of Siamese junks trading with
Singapore increased to 44 of the seventy vessels from Cambodia,
Cochin, and Siam that called. By 1826, Singapore had definitely
emerged as the focal point for the Siamese junks trading with the
Indian island.[87]
   By the 1830s Siam's main import from Singapore, British
piece goods, was firmly in Chinese hands. For instance in the 1835–
1836 season, 18 percent of the total trade of Singapore was conducted with Siam, and rising, and Siam was the major purchaser of
the British cotton piece goods which accounted largely for this

percentage. At the same time, the Chinese also controlled Siam's export trade to Singapore, which included sugar, rice, sapan wood, coconut oil, and salt. For instance, in 1830, the Chinese in Siam exported goods totaling 771,057 sicca rupees. In addition, the rice exported was worth 79,095 and 72,633 rupees for sapan wood, while more than 15,600 piculs (2.1 m. lbs.) of salt was taken. All such commodities had a high value per unit of weight and made ideal items for trade at this time. But the principal export for that year was sugar, which was worth 353,067 rupees. The sugar for Singapore was eventually transhipped to Europe, while Western ships also went directly to Bangkok for it as in 1830 when they acquired some 6,000 piculs (800,000 lbs.). In the same year, Siam also exported 216,788 sicca rupees' worth of merchandise (rice: 76,685: 25,680; and sugar: 11,975) to the Prince of Wales Island and Malacca.[88]

The Siamese junks employed in this trade were considerably smaller than those of Canton and Amoy; they were from 100 to 350 tons, usually 150 to 200 tons, each carrying three to five thousand dollars worth of merchandise.[89] Table 12 shows the minimum numbers of Siamese vessels trading to Singapore in the Third Reign.

Besides the regular Siamese junks, 30 Malay ships traded between Malay states and Bangkok taking gold dust, birds' nests, dammer, tin, and so on, to the latter and returning to the Malay states with paddy (cargo rice), oil, sugar, salt, iron pots, stic-lac, gum benjamin, and so forth.[90]

Later in the reign of Rama III, about 50 small junks of 700 piculs (92,210 lbs.) traded from Queda, Pattani, Kelantan, and Tringganau (the first two were under direct Siamese rule while the last two states were Siam's tributary states) to Siam with goods suitable for the China market, which were sold to Chinese merchants at Bangkok. In return these junks also took on a considerable amount of Chinese merchandise.[91] Siam also traded to other places in the Indian Archipelago, though to a much lesser extent.

The comprehensiveness of the Sino-Siamese trade, including the regional trade handled by Chinese, during the Second and

Third Reigns may be seen in Tables 13 and 14 compiled by D. E. Malloch in the mid-nineteenth century.

Table 12

Siamese Ships Calling at Singapore, 1829–1851

Year	Number of junks
1829–30	31
1832–33	37
1835–36	23
1838–39	23
1841–42	28
1844–45	22
1847–48	20
1850–51	63

Source: Wong Lin Ken, "The Trade of Singapore, 1819–1869," *Journal of the Malayan Branch of Royal Asiatic Society,* 33.4: 148 (12.1960).

Table 13

Ships Frequenting Siam in the Second Reign

Port of origin	Number of junks	Total burden (approx. in lbs.)	Total value (in £)	Remarks
Kwangtung; junks arrived in Jan. and sailed from mid-May to mid-July	3	6. m.	15,000	Belonged to Siamese government
Kwangtung; junks arrived in Jan. and sailed from mid-May to mid-July	22 25	12. m. 8.3 m.	33,000 25,000	Belonged to Siamese government and Chinese in Siam
Kwangtung; junks arrived in Jan. and sailed from mid-May to mid-July	3 3	3.2 m. 4. m.	9,700 11,250	Belonged to Siamese government and Chinese in Siam

Fukien, Ningpo, Kiangnan, Shanghai arrived in Jan. and sailed from mid-May to mid-July	8 10	8.5 m. 8. m.	20,000 25,000	Owned by Chinese of the ports
Hainan, arrived in Jan. and sailed in May–June	45	15. m.	56,250	To Hainan
Cochin China, arrived in Jan. and sailed in May–June	36	3.7 m.	31,500	To Hainan and Cochin China
Malay coast, arrived and sailed at different times	35	3.3 m.	17,000	To Malaya and Siam
Singapore, arrived and sailed at different times	22 25 2	7.3 m. 6.7 m. 1.4 m.	55,000 10,000	
America	1	.5 m.	7,500	
Persian Gulf, arrived Sept. and sailed Dec.	1	.4 m.	3,750	
Overland trade from Singapore and Penang via Queda			25,000	
Total	241	88.3 m.	344,950	

Source: D. E. Malloch, *Siam: Some General Remarks on Its Productions* (Calcutta, 1852), p. 65. Adapted and modified from original.

Table 14

Ships Frequenting Siam in the Third Reign

Place of origin	(number of junks)						Average value cargo/junk (£)	Remarks
	1825	1826	1827	1836	1843	1850		
Kwangtung, arrived in Jan. and sailed mid-May to July	3	3	3	4	4	4	5,000	Owned by Siam government
Kwangtung, arrived in Jan. and sailed mid-May to July	22	18	21	25	26	27	1,500	Owned by Siam
	25	26	24	28	30	30	1,000	government and
	3	3	3	4	4	4	3,125	Chinese in
	3	3	4	4	4	4	3,750	Bangkok
Fukien, Ningpo, Kiangnan, Shanghai	12	8	13	14	13	15	2,500	Owned by
	14	12	11	13	13	14	2,500	the ports
Hainan	64	52	64	63	65	68	1,250	Hainanese
Hainan and Cochin China	38	40	43	47	50	51	875	To Hainan and Cochin China
Malay coast	30	27	34	38	40	45	500	Malay and Siam
Singapore	23	24	25	28	30	30		
Singapore	24	27	29	29	30	35	2,500	
Singapore (detained 3 mos.)	2	3	1	2	2	2		English
America	1	1		2	2	2		American
Persian Gulf	1	2		1	1	1		Mohammedan
Total	265	249	275	302	314	332		

Source: D. E. Malloch, *Siam: Some General Remarks of Its Productions* (Calcutta, 1852), p. 65. Adapted and modified from original.

Chapter X

CHINESE IMMIGRATION AND ITS ECONOMIC IMPACT
IN THE THIRD REIGN, 1824–1850

One of the most important contributions of the Sino-Siamese junk trade in Rama III's reign was the influx of Chinese into Siam and the subsequent growth in the importance of the Chinese minority. D. E. Malloch spoke of the Chinese immigration during this time: "The Chinamen are well pleased with the country, and their prospects; and the China junks which bring so many passengers carry very few away. A great many Chinamen arrive annually to see their friends, and on mercantile pursuits, but very few of them find their way back."[1]

Estimates of the Chinese population in Siam varied at times, but those appearing in Table 15 may be taken as a guideline.[2]

The annual rate of the flow of Chinese immigration to Siam was impressive. Burney estimated that in the mid-1820s it was about 2,000 to 3,000 a year. In the latter part of that decade, one contemporary observer put the figures at 2,000 to 12,000, and by the end of the reign in the late 1840s, the annual influx is said to have reached as high as 15,000 per year.[3] Walter Vella says of these

Table 15

Chinese Population in the Third Reign

Year	Chinese Population	Total Population
1822	440,000	2,790,500
1827	800,000	3,252,650
1835	500,000	3,620,000
1839	450,000	3,000,000
1849	1,110,000	3,653,150

Source: G. William Skinner, *Chinese Society in Thailand: An Analytical History* (Ithaca, N.Y., 1957), p. 72.

estimates: "If these estimates are at all accurate they would indicate that over 25,000 Chinese entered Siam during the Third Reign alone. Such estimates, are only guesses (*sic*), and all that can be said with accuracy is that the Chinese minority during the reign was large and grew rapidly."[4]

The Chinese minority grew in importance as it increased in size. The junk trade's development, so it seemed, was directly proportional to the rate of growth of the Chinese minority. And since the Chinese were generally industrious and enterprising, they soon worked in all fields of the internal trade as well. Tin mines in the south, notably at Junkceylon, were opened up by enterprising Fukienese, as Ch'ao-chou immigrants continued with their commercial agriculture in addition to establishing shops for commercial purposes.

Two other obvious results of the growth of the Chinese minority in the Third Reign were, first, the domination of Chinese in the field of mechanical arts, and, second, the breakdown of the traditional Siamese conception of wealth based on corvée labor and a move toward the development of a money economy. Western visitors to Siam at this time all noted that Chinese artisans were engaged in junk construction, the manufacture of iron pans and pots (preferred over cast iron vessels from Europe as they were cheaper and more sturdy), lockmaking, and carpentry. They also worked in gold, silver, and copper. These handicrafts were no doubt brought to Siam by the junk trade.[5] The rise of this group of professional craftsmen as an entrepreneurial class supplementing the classes of traders and commercial agriculturists in retrospect helped to prevent Siam from falling readily into the hands of Western imperialists. In a symbiotic relationship with the Siamese ruling class, they could stand up to the challenge of the growing Western economic encroachment, coming especially at this time from the British.

One common feature of these groups of dialect-specific professionals was that until the second half of the nineteenth century, they did not form any specialized guilds or associations. As we mentioned in chapter II, the activities of the Chinese in Siam (Bangkok included) centered around the temple. In the early

Bangkok dynasty, the Hakkas, for instance, met at their San-nai fu-jen temple at Thonburi. The Hainanese at Bangkok staged all their business meetings and social and religious activities at three or more temples in the Bangkok area (specifically at Samsen, Taladnoi, and Bangrak). Their main line of business in Bangkok was lumber.[6]

The mass of immigrants included a sizable portion of laborers and coolies. In Rama III's time, paid Chinese labor was preferred over the traditional corvée recruited from among Siamese common-ers since Chinese labor was more efficient and also readily available at any time and any place. Malloch observed that "the Chinese do nearly all the manual labour, and the Government are always too happy at the chance of getting them; because they know they can trust their going on regularly with their work, and having it well done, which they could not do with their own countrymen."[7]

Rama III made full use of paid Chinese labor for his extensive construction projects. This undermined the traditional social system which divided the society into essentially two classes of people: *nai* and *prai*. *Nai* was the privileged class which, in accordance with the *sakdina* ranking of its members, was entitled to the service of people from the *prai* class. Members of the *prai* class (which theoretically comprised all commoners) had to perform their duty usually by manual labor in private and public work for a prescribed period of time in a year, unless they had paid a sum of money or in kind in lieu of this obligatory service. The king himself owned many *prai-luang* or those who owed their services directly to the king (people in this category usually included foreigners who had been war cap-tives or recruited for the king by tributary states under Siam). Thus the role of *prai* became less and less important as more Chinese workers were used in their place, a change that contributed to the abolition of corvée labor in the Fifth Reign (1868–1910) in the direction of a money economy in which wealth came to be reckoned less as primarily based on *prai* labor, or the wealth of land; the revenues of the country were now more readily drawn from the expanded tax farming system as well as from the continual employ-ment of the junk trade. Akin Rabibhadana remarks: "With the economic changes manpower was no longer the sole source of

Table 16

Chinese Population in Bangkok in the Third Reign

Year	Chinese Population	Total Population
1822	(31,000)	(50,000)
1827	60,700	134,090
1828	36,000	77,300
1839	60,000	100,000
1840	70,000	350,000
1849	81,000	160,154

Source: G. William Skinner, *Chinese Society in Thailand: An Analytical History* (Ithaca, N.Y., 1957), p. 81.

wealth. Those nobles who were in a position to acquire wealth from new sources, e.g. minister of the *khlang klang,* became the heads of the informal hierarchies, instead of princes as in Ayudhya period."[8]

In the Third Reign Bangkok had a large commercial sector made up primarily of Chinese who were concentrated along the river banks in raft houses, which served both as shops and residences.[9] The majority of these Chinese were Ch'ao-chou who were engaged in supplying the junk trade as well as engaging in the mechanical arts. Table 16 gives an idea of the Chinese population in Bangkok during the Third Reign based on diverse sources (one cannot be certain about the absolute reliability of the figures, which can best be used as impressions; obviously while some must have been totally inaccurate or "exaggerated," others could have been close to the truth).

The freedom of movement enjoyed by the Chinese within Siam was responsible for the development of interregional trade. Chinese immigrants were prepared to move anywhere within the country where they could establish themselves economically, and, wherever they went, they took with them their native customs and improvements. For example, we have already pointed out that in the first decade of the nineteenth century, Ch'ao-chou commercial agriculturists developed sugar-cane plantations on a large scale at

Chantaburi, Machachai, and along the eastern coast of the Gulf of Siam, while also intensifying the cultivation of pepper at Chantaburi and Tungyai, as well as on the eastern side of Lower Siam. To the north, the Chinese also engaged in the exploitation of timber, material used essentially for house and junk construction. Skinner asserts that the pattern of Chinese settlement in Siam was one of occupational specialization.

Along the east coast of the Gulf, where junk construction and commercial argiculture predominated, Ch'ao-chou people congregated.[1] In the mid-1830s, at Chantaburi, they constructed annually some 50 odd vessels (one or two of 300 to 400-ton displacement, while the rest were smaller vessels).[11] The area from Bang-kacha (9 miles from Chantaburi, where an estimated 4,000 Chinese resided) to Tha-mai (about 400 to 500 Chinese and to the east), also not far from Chantaburi, was "highly civilized," almost exclusively occupied by Ch'ao-chou cultivating pepper, sugar cane, and tobacco, which were the chief crops.[12] In Lower Siam, the Chinese, mainly Fukienese,[13] with their aptitude for trade, acquired the most economic, as well as political, dominance. Fukienese immigrants became important merchants engaged in the junk trade; they also took up occupations as small traders going deep into the mountains to buy and sell with the natives. They were engaged in some aspects of home industry, such as shoemaking, dressmaking, carpentry, iron mongering, and, most often, tin mining.[14] Several Fukienese had been politically influential in Lower Siam since the reign of Taksin, ruling Songkla, Ranong, and Ligor, which were among the most vital spots in Lower Siam. These personalities often had rather modest beginnings, usually coming to the region as poor immigrants. Through their economic acumen, however, they established a crucial rapport with the Siamese court. We have already mentioned Wu Yang who became governor of Songkla through his post as a tax farmer of birds' nests. Burney also said in 1825 that the ruler of Ligor, a Chinese (a forebear of the na Nakorn family), owed his political influence to his economic enterprise. So the common factor shared by all such Fukienese attaining political power in the region may be said to have been the economic dominance of the

Fukienese in the area. Elsewhere in Lower Siam, local prosperity was contingent upon the Chinese presence. The governor of Junk-ceylon on the western side of the Malay peninsula encouraged the Chinese to settle there in great numbers. Chaiya, a port due north of Ligor, frequented by Fukien junks in the early decades of the eighteenth century, had in 1827 around 2,000 Chinese, and the chief traffic there had been rice.[15]

By Rama III's time Lower Siam did not participate much in direct trade with China, but it did contribute to this branch of trade in two ways: it produced sizable quantities of commodities destined for this trade (shipped mainly via Bangkok), and, it received a number of imports from China (including Fukienese immigrants).

By the time of Burney's visit to Ligor in 1826, the direct trade to Ligor from China had ceased, though the Chinese were in complete control of the transfer of goods to Bangkok for re-export to China. In Trang and Pattani, the Chinese also exported elephant's teeth, tin, and birds' nests to the capital for the junk trade.[16]

The phenomenal increase in the Chinese participation in Siam's economic activities is further seen in the monopoly of the Chinese immigrants over tax farming, to which Rama III consciously resorted for the first time as a means of enhancing the royal treasury (at a time when the Siamese court was discovering that the junk trade alone was unable to cope with spiraling state expenditures), and as a means of preserving the royal hold over the country's economic development.

What the king did was to delegate commercial functions more to the private sector and de-emphasize the royal trading system at a time when Siam was shifting toward a money economy.

Tax farming had formerly existed in the Ayudhya dynasty, when between 1688 and 1756, gambling was institutionalized and its taxes farmed out to Chinese.[17] By the Second Reign, the scope of tax farming had been further expanded so that it included the manufacture and sale of spirits, gambling, fishing, collection of birds' nests, and ship taxes. The highest bidders (Chinese) became tax farmers in their respective areas.[18] In the Third Reign, the system was seriously and consciously developed as an alternative to sole reliance on the royal trading monopoly system. With the help of his Praya Praklang, Dit Bunnag, Rama III turned what might have become a fiscal disadvantage created by free trade stipulations in the Burney Treaty into a system of farmed taxes and monopolies which worked to the advantage of the court.[19]

Rama III felt that tax farming would, indeed, generate much greater revenues since income collected this way was more certain. There was also more leeway in fixing the desired amounts each year: the state could set minimum sums in bids for various farms to be parceled out and only those going beyond the minimum would be granted the privilege. The king subsequently designated the Praklang sin-ka (Royal Warehouses Department) to centrally administer the farming system; the old taxes which were related to the acquisition of various goods for the junk trade now came to be handled by the Praklang maha-sombat (Royal Treasury).[20]

In the Third Reign, a total of thirty-eight kinds of taxes were farmed out; the most important ones were: gambling, lottery (huey), pepper (collected from prospective buyers for the junk trade), sapan wood, wood for shipbuilding, red wood (collected from buyers for the junk trade), and salt.[21] In return, the court received cash from the farm. This system in a way revolutionized the revenue structure of the government which hitherto had been based upon the collection of dues from the people in kind, a practice thus necessitating the direct involvement of the state in foreign trade so that the goods collected could be disposed of. Among the farmed taxes, aside from a few that were service-oriented and others dealing with relatively insignificant items of daily use and for local consumption, there were a variety of farms of various produce suitable for export. Hence it is justifiable to say that the tax farming under Rama III in actuality represented another side of foreign trade monopoly, which meant that Western merchants continued to be excluded from partaking in any part of the country's trade in spite of free trade pledges.

The expansion of the new system also meant the transfer of a large section of the king's private commercial interests to individual

Chinese, who had been a principal inspiration in the system's introduction in the first place.[22]

The normal procedure for farm acquisition was for the prospective farmer to propose to the king, through the sponsorship of various government departments (Mahattai, Kalahom Krom-ta, and so forth), which taxes they fancied. In the Third Reign, the king for example authorized one Praya Ratchamontri (Pu) to take charge of farms on gambling, lottery, and the manufacture of spirits throughout the realm. When approved (after the applicants had tendered the most satisfactory bids) the new farmers would first be ennobled, in the rank of *khun* or *luang* before assuming their duties, for, according to tradition, a person must have attained a *sakdina* grade equal to or above that assigned to the above rankings before he could be represented in a court of law, as the business of tax collection often involved litigation. Also in the feudal system, the king did business only with nobles. In Bangkok, the tax farmers were known as *khun-nang chao pasi-akon* (officials of taxation); in the provinces, they were called *krom ta chin* (of the Chinese port department).[23]

In the existing structure, the appointment of tax farmers naturally involved the patronage of high-ranking officials and nobles, for only the highest bidders with influential patrons behind them could be successful in obtaining the various farms and operating them. A few illustrations will prove the point.

At the end of Rama II's reign, a poor Chinese secured the patronage of the Praya Praklang and his brother Praya Sipipat; as a result, he was ennobled as Khun Pitac, farmer of sugar (at an annual fee of 30,400 *baht* or £3,800).[24] Captain Henry Burney was of the opinion that although the ostensible farmer was Khun Pitac, who contracted to supply sugar to the king at lower than the market price, the "real farmers" were the patrons themselves.[25]

Burney concluded that the patrons extracted as much profit from the farmer as they could, leaving the latter to fulfill the contract. Under the circumstances, Khun Pitac in turn milked the foreign buyers, or cheated them with inferior sugar, and in the process made a handsome 100 percent profit himself.[26] Similarly, in the 1840s, the Chinese sugar farmer was paying the king 2 *baht* (5 s.) plus another half a *baht* (1s. 3d.) as duty for each picul of sugar, while selling it to the British and other Westerners at 9 *baht* (1.2.6.); the regular price of sugar at the time stood only at 7 to 7.5 *baht*.[27]

The patronage system may further be seen in the instance involving the establishment of the lottery farm in 1835 at Bangkok. A Chinese spirit farmer submitted the proposal to the king through the same Praya Ratchamontri, director of the Praklang Maha-sombut or Royal Treasury. Rama III, then confronting a scarcity of money in circulation, appointed the Chinese Khun Banbloburirat (popularly known as Khun Ban for short). The fee was fixed at 20,000 *baht* (£2,500) a year.[28] Another Chinese gave his services to the eighth son of Rama III, while also posting his Siamese wife at the household of the king's third daughter. For this he was subsequently appointed by Rama III, through the recommendation of his son, as a tax farmer with the title of Khun Chaiyawari.[29]

Chinese in the provinces also became tax farmers through patronage. The best example in the Third Reign was that of Hsu Szu-chang (Kor-si-chiang, in Siamese transliteration). Originally a Penang immigrant from Fukien's Lung-ch'i district, Hsu conducted business in Lower Siam and eventually secured the patronage of the head of the Kalahom department (having jurisdiction over Lower Siam) in Bangkok. He was therefore appointed by Rama III as Luang Rattanasetti, farmer of tin taxes for the Ranong area. By 1854, he rose to the post of governor for that locale, a post later held by his own son.[30]

Because tax farmers paid their patrons well, a large number of nobles and courtiers, wishing to aid their Chinese clients, tried to persuade the king to establish farmers as his clients. There was a popular saying at the time that, *sib porka mai tao nung praya liang* ("Ten merchants are not equal to the patronage of one nobleman"),[31] signifying the lucrative nature of such a patron-client relationship in the system. The significance of this relationship also went beyond the immediate material gains for both sides, as Akin Rabibhadana states in his study of the patronage system of this time: "From the position of such tax farmers, many of them and their descendants became Thai nobles and worked as Thai officials in various positions. They often became officials in provincial towns, and were called *kromakanchin.* Some of them even became town governors and established important Thai noble families."[32]

Sometimes, however, farms were also given directly to nobles themselves, as in the case of the tax concession on teak given to one Praya Sisahatep for an annual fee of 8,000 taels Siamese (£4,000). This noble was a Chinese whose name was Tong-peng (Siamese transliteration for "Tung P'ing"?).[33]

H. G. Wales says that considerable extortion had to be practiced by the farmers to fulfill their obligations.[34]

The profitability of the tax farming system, as far as government revenues were concerned, may be seen in the fact that during the Second Reign, income from the gambling farm alone reportedly came to 260,000 *baht* (£36,500). By the Third Reign, this revenue had climbed up to 400,000 *baht* (£50,000) a year.[35] The government continued to benefit from foreign trade through indirect means with all the principal produce farmed out to Chinese individuals. Table 17 represents a partial list of the revenues due the government from farms given to Chinese for the year 1845:

Table 17

A Partial List of Farm Monopoly Fees Payable
to the Government for the Year 1845

Item	Duty payable
Sapan wood	60,000 *baht* (£7,525)
Pepper	33,600 *baht* (£4,200)
Refined cane sugar	52,800 *baht* (£6,600)
Birds' nests (Chumporn province)	12,800 *baht* (£1,600)
Cotton and tabacco	13,920 *baht* (£1,740)

Source: Prince Damrong Rajanubhab, *Tamnan pasi akon bangyang kab kam atibai* (Bangkok,1930), pp. 15-20.

The estimates by Edmund Roberts in 1832 on the annual
Siamese state revenues derived from farms are shown in Table 18.

Table 18

Estimates of Government Revenues from Selected
Monopoly Farms for the Year 1832

Item	Duty Payable
Teak	56,000 *baht* (£7,000)
Sapan wood	84,000 *baht* (£10,500)
Sugar	40,000 *baht* (£5,000)
Pepper	23,200 *baht* (£2,900)
Birds' nests	32,000 *baht* (£4,000)
Spirit shops (Bangkok)	104,900 *baht* (£13,112)

Source: Edmund Roberts, *Embassy to the Eastern courts of
Cochin China, Siam, and Muscat during the Years
1832-3-4* (New York, 1837), pp. 426–427.

There is no doubt that the institution of the farming system
ensured increased and predictable revenues for the royal coffers,
and, used to supplement the still lucrative junk trade, enriched
Rama III far more than any of his Chakri predecessors. He was now
able to pay out bonuses and grants to his court with greater ease,
which the monarchs since King Taksin had been unable to do.[36]

The development of tax farms in the Third Reign also stimulated the participation of Chinese secret societies in the economic
development of the country. The economic shift in the reign took
place at a time when the composition of the various Chinese dialect
groups in Siam, namely Ch'ao-chou, South Fukien, Cantonese,
Hakka, and Hainanese, was changing in numerical proportions.
This change created a situation in which horizontal unity was
lacking and where there were tendencies for interdialect rivalry in
the economic sphere.[37] During the times of Rama II and Rama III,
when royal trading monopolies and full government participation
in the China trade were most prevalent, the Ch'ao-chou group were

in a most favored position due to their connections with the Siamese court established in the Taksin era. The Ch'ao-chou junks were also the largest and most suitable in the country's overseas trade. As early as the Second Reign, Robert Morrison noted that virtually all the Chinese mercantile and financial officers in Bangkok were Ch'ao-chou. When a variety of monopoly farms were created, however, the different dialect groups competed for them intensely. And because of this competition, the secret societies came to participate in the economic activities of the Chinese residents.[38]

Wherever the Chinese went during the eighteenth century, their secret societies followed them. Triad societies (known variously as San-ho-hui, San-tien-hui, T'ien-ti-hui, Hung-men, and so on) dated back to at least the time the Cheng rebels were active around Fukien and Formosa. They eventually spread into Southeast Asia after the failure of the resistance movement. It is very possible that secret societies in Siam, known locally as the "Ang-yi" (transliteration of the Ch'ao-chou rendition of "Hung-tzu"), had existed before the Third Reign. As early as 1799 the Penang authorities were already reporting meetings by a local secret society, the T'ien-ti hui. In the 1810s, secret societies in Penang already had compatriots in nearby Junkceylon. T'ien Ju-k'ang is of the opinion that after the mid-eighteenth century, economic necessities compelled Overseas Chinese to band together for protection.[39]

Nevertheless, secret societies in Siam are said to have been visibly organized in the Third Reign; one reason was the role played by opium. Since the Siamese government had prohibited opium-smoking within the country as far back as 1813, secret societies flourished in coastal towns, such as Chachoengsao and Samutprakan, to collect opium from ships. The merchandise was consumed mainly among resident Chinese, but some also found its way to China. In Siam as in Malaya, the secret societies were divided along dialect lines. Hence the Ch'ao-chou and South Fukienese groups had a common name of Yi-hsing (Gee Hin), the Cantonese the Yueh-tung and Pa-chiao, the Hakkas the Ming-shun and Ch'un-ying, and Hainanese were also known as the Yi-hsing. Collectively, they all engaged in opium smuggling and collaborated with the government in running tax farms on gambling, lottery, the manufacture of liquor (which contributed as much as 40–50 percent of the government's annual revenues in the Third Reign).[40]

Nevertheless, in championing the cause of the Chinese peasants and urban working-class Chinese who had economic grievances against their employers and tax farmers, the secret societies also encountered legal difficulties. As their operations grew, they aroused the court's apprehension, for such organized groups with hundreds or thousands of members posed a possible threat to national security.[41] What was more disturbing was that the societies did not hesitate to resort to mob violence. The Rama III court, however, while resolute in curbing the violence generated by these bodies, never outlawed them. There were several instances in which the secret societies started trouble. In 1845–1846, some members joined up with pirates who went plundering ships between the ports of Pran and Langsuan on the Gulf of Siam, as well as seizing government grain ships and killing the officials in charge. In 1847, another uprising instigated by a secret society occurred at Nakorn Chaisi (a center of sugar plantations, and known to the Chinese as Lung-tzu-ch'u), resulting from the levying of a new tax on sugar refineries by the court. In the following year, another riot took place at Paet-riu.[42]

Secret societies were to become more powerful as the court moved further away from the junk trade toward tax farming in the Fourth Reign. This move contributed further to the economic rivalry among the dialect groups (and consequently factionalism in the secret societies) in areas in which no single group predominated, in spite of the fact that the Ch'ao-chou people were the most financially sound group. The increased reliance on revenues from such farms as lottery, gambling, and the manufacture and sale of spirits further enhanced the position of the secret societies. Furthermore, by the Fourth Reign, the opium that had been outlawed was legalized for Chinese residents in the form of opium farms which were given to Chinese farmers with the backing of the secret societies.

Chapter XI

DECLINING FORTUNES OF THE
SINO-SIAMESE JUNK TRADE

The junk trade, which had accelerated since the end of the eighteenth century, reached its peak by the early 1830s and, thereafter, began a slow but steady decline. The major reason for the decline was its failure to adapt to the fluid economic conditions in the Eastern Seas at this time. The West was beginning to pose strong economic and political alternatives that directly challenged the time-honored supremacy of the junk trade. Siam, for one thing, had come to accept, by the early 1830s, the superior Western-style brig in place of the Chinese junk. With this modification came a host of other changes in the traditional pattern of Sino-Siamese trade, which reduced its overall significance.

Furthermore, in the beginning of Rama III's reign, the intensification of tax farming as a main alternate source of state revenue and the forfeiture of the king's status as merchant-king in the royal trading monopoly system meant a de-emphasis on foreign trade, and a turning toward internal economic development. Foreign trade as engaged in by the Siamese court had been found to create management problems, and, besides, the revenues engendered could never be definitely ascertained owing to a variety of unforeseeable factors. Tax farming, on the other hand, afforded a fixed income for the government. By the time of the Second Reign the state was relatively secure; thus a stronger possibility existed for the exploitation of resources within the country. Also the British were pressuring for a semblance of free trade; Rama III feared that revenues from his junk trade would be directly threatened, and therefore felt a need to institute new internal taxes as a measure to compensate for any losses that might occur from the new arrangement. In time, tax farming came to rival and overshadow the junk trade.

Under Rama IV, the junk trade with China suffered a further setback. China, preoccupied with entanglements with the West, was becoming less of a focal point of Siam's economic activities, and the rapid dwindling of the court's interests in China is illustrated by the deterioration in tributary relations. Rama IV was compelled to open up his country to the Westerners in a real sense for the first time with the conclusion of the Bowring Treaty in 1855. As a result, the Chinese were faced with Western competition, and the government was obliged to rely on tax farming even more, at the expense of the junk trade.

Last, but not least, Siam was no longer an important entrepot in the Eastern Seas because with the opening of Hong Kong as an international free port, the British had a new access to the China market, thus voiding the erstwhile status of Siam as suppliers of Chinese goods. This development directly contributed to the diversion of Siamese commercial interests to other areas, particularly to the fast rising port of Singapore. Siam was no longer confined primarily to the China trade.

China's trade at this time also became increasingly Western-oriented, and the strong economic ties that had existed between southeastern Chinese ports and Southeast Asia started to loosen. The West, with its larger capital and ships, moved in to supplant the main overseas activities of the more weakly organized junk trade. Still it did not mean a complete collapse of this line of trade, which, in fact, continued to serve some crucial economic functions, such as conveying cargoes along the Chinese coast and waterways to places inaccessible to the larger Western-style vessels, or to areas where Western interests had yet to present themselves.

Change in the Third Reign

The catalytic cause responsible for the transformation of East Asia in the nineteenth century was of course the reassertion of Western political and economic power after over a century of dormancy. It has been pointed out that the Industrial Revolution which began in the West during the last part of the eighteenth century stimulated renewed European, particularly British, interests in the Eastern Seas in their quest for markets for raw materials and outlets for their manufactured goods.

Beginning with the last part of the reign of Rama II, Western economic influence began to be reasserted in and around Siam. A brief discussion as to its state at this junction is therefore warranted in comprehending the overall course of the Sino-Siamese junk trade. It may be said that starting at this time, the growth of Western influence inevitably became entangled with the development of this trade.

At the start of the nineteenth century, Siam's sole intercourse continued to be with China. Nevertheless, despite the fact that the bitter memory of the near fatal involvement with European adventurers in the seventeenth century remained very strong among the Siamese ruling clique, Rama II, given his temperament, did not completely avoid contacts with Westerners. For one thing, he had a tangible interest in the acquisition of Western firearms, though totally unprepared to modify the traditional monopolistic practices. The first European envoy to call at the Siamese court after a long hiatus was one Don Carlos Manoel Silviera, who headed a Portuguese mission from Macao in 1818. As Rama II's ships had been trading to Macao at this time (the outfitting of royal vessels to trade to Macao was under the charge of Praya Suriyawong-montri, an official of the Krom-ta; sailing operations were entrusted to Luang Surasakorn), the king granted the Portuguese a license to trade, and a Portuguese trader was also authorized to act as some kind of a shabandar (a trading agent) to ships of his own countrymen calling at Bangkok. In the same year, trade by the United States was also initiated with Siam. Two years later, the governor of Macao dispatched another embassy to request permission to construct a junk, as well as to acquire wood in Bangkok. Rama II allowed the Portuguese representatives to build ships in 1818 and later even bailed them out of financial trouble when they ran short of the necessary funds to complete the project.[1]

The European nation with which Siam was destined to have the most dealings in the years following was Britain, both for political and economic reasons. The physical expansion of Siam into the Malay peninsula meant a clash of interests with the British; many Malay sultanates had turned to Britain[2] to balance the growing power from Bangkok, with which they alone could not contend. Both Rama II and the Chinese merchants were determined to concede as little as possible regarding commercial matters in the peninsula to the British. In the time of Rama II, John Morgan led an unofficial mission in 1821 in the hope of making a commercial treaty with the Siamese court, but nothing came of the venture. He was followed by the mission of John Crawfurd sent by the governor of India with the objective of liberalizing trade. More specifically, the Crawfurd mission was to allay the suspicion the Siamese had toward British intentions in the peninsula so that the trade of Penang, India, and even England could benefit from it. The government of India wished, most of all, to have a fixed tariff schedule set up in order to prevent extortion, and "to expose the British traders to the least possible vexation."[3] Nevertheless, the attempt was again unsuccessful; part of the cause was interpreted by Crawfurd himself as misrepresentation of the "true" British intentions by jealous Chinese merchants to the Siamese court. He wrote in 1821 that these Chinese merchants said that "the English came now with smooth words, pretending to want trade only that in a little time they would ask for a factory, then for leave to build a wall round it, that on this wall they would soon plant cannons; and finally, that they would seize upon the country as they had done upon similar occasions."[4]

Notwithstanding any move by the Chinese merchants to play on the apprehension of the Siamese court, the failure of the Crawfurd mission was almost a foregone conclusion, because its demand ran contrary to the entire basis of the administered system of Siamese commercial intercourse in which the Siamese king himself had so big a stake. In traditional thinking, free trade was of course interpreted as a loss in direct revenues for the court, whereas royal monopolies were deemed as contributing directly to the royal coffers. Furthermore, the court, having been accustomed to dealing solely with Chinese merchants who "only thought in terms of huge profits and were willing to humble and conform to T'ai (Thai) customs" found the British unacceptable, since the latter "desired to preserve their dignity as well as deriving large profits in their trade."[5] Nevertheless, the failure of Crawfurd's mission reflected the entrenchment of Chinese economic influence within the Siamese government.

Rama II was thus successful in keeping out much of the Western influence, while continuing to develop closer economic ties with China by means of the junk trade. It should be observed that the Chinese had an important part in the preservation of the existing economic structure which in turn accounted for the unacceptability of Western demands for liberalized trade. Nevertheless, as time progressed, the Western, particularly British, pressure and encroachment developed, making it inevitable for Siam, with precedents established in other places throughout the Eastern Seas, to treat Westerners on an equal footing. When this occurred, it naturally meant a decline in the intensity of the existing Sino-Siamese trade. But for the moment, the ties remained stronger than ever.

By the early 1820s, Western economic influence had already permeated much of Southeast Asia. Fewer junks were now trading on the Malay peninsula and at Batavia. Chinese junks, in order to protect their economic independence, often had to concentrate their activities on areas where Dutch and British influences were still relatively weak, such as Kelamantan, Macassa, Amboya, Malacca, Tringganau, and Kelantan.[6]

After the failure of the Crawfurd mission, Lord Amherst, the governor of Bengal, deputed Captain Henry Burney to lead another mission to Siam (1825–1826) to settle the political issue over the sovereignty of Kedah in the Malay peninsula and also to obtain a commercial treaty which would allow Western merchants to pay fixed tariffs for the freedom to trade.[7] British pressure,[8] coupled with the growing needs for new revenues to meet the ever-increasing state expense, compelled Rama III to declare he would no longer monopolize the various articles of trade, which had been the custom in the Second Reign. In addition, he said he would no longer deal with foreign trade directly, thus giving up his status as merchant-king.[9]

Siam's direct trade with the West did not improve throughout the Third Reign despite commercial accords signed in the 1820s (with Captain Henry Burney in 1826) and the 1830s (with Edmund Roberts in 1833). As of 1832, the British still rarely visited Bangkok because of the heavy duties they had to pay in contrast to smaller Chinese junks which paid little or none. Only two or three cloth-laden vessels a year came from the Coromandel Coast in this branch of trade.[10] For the most part the West only indirectly affected the economic life of Siam—principally, as mentioned, through the trade at Singapore which was rapidly becoming an entrepôt in the East-West trade. George Earl said in the 1830s that the British normally acquired Siamese produce at Singapore, taken there by Sino-Siamese junks which paid no duty.[11] The prolific farming system was to nullify whatever advantages the Westerners received in the treaties with the British and Americans in 1826 and 1833 respectively. The system ensured the continued close, and closed, cooperation between the Siamese court and the Chinese in all economic spheres, including that dealing directly with the maritime trade, for the export trade now come to be entrenched in Chinese hands more than ever.

In the 1820s and 1830s very few British did business in Bangkok; the only merchants were Robert Hunter and J. Hayes. By 1843, there was only one Western firm conducting trade there— Messrs. Hunter, Hayes, and Company. Moreover, Rama III eventually reneged on his previous promise by going back to the royal monopoly system in the 1840s. The Burney Treaty provided that British traders could buy anything they wished without interference, with the exception of rice. By 1840, however, the king monopolized the production of sugar, then the most important export of the country and one much sought after by British merchants. The monopoly was fully reinstituted by 1842, and the price of sugar jumped by 40 percent. It meant that the government, once again, had the right of pre-emption on any quantity of sugar produced and at an arbitrary price. In addition, it demanded cash for sugar, instead of the usual barter.[12] Hence, the expanding tax farming system and the partial reversion to the former royal trade monopolies enhanced the symbiotic relationship of the Chinese and Siamese, at the expense of other traders. It may be noted here, too, that up to the end of his reign, Rama III refused to accept Western demands for equality in trade. He shunned both the Ballestier (American) mission in 1849 and the James Brooke (British) mission in 1850, which came to request treaty revisions. One reason for this was his determination to keep the farming system, because it had generated a great deal of income directly for the court.

The exclusion of Westerners from Siam's trade continued to be, as in Rama II's reign, partly due to the Chinese traders. According to Malloch, Chinese merchants in Siam told the court that all of Siam's needs could be supplied by Chinese junks trading to Singapore, Java, Penang, and China: this move was designed to keep out the British and other Westerners. His conclusion echoed the exasperation of John Crawfurd: "[The Chinese] have always been very jealous of the English encroaching too much on this very valuable part of their trade, and these crafty people take great pleasure in doing us [British] all the mischief they can by false and malicious representations to the King and Ministers [of Siam] to prejudice them against us, to induce them to keep us out of the country."[13]

Still it is to be noted that the importation of goods from the West in the Third Reign, though carried on indirectly through such intermediate ports as Singapore, at least shows that the West drew closer to the Siamese economy than it did in any period during the past one hundred and fifty years.[14]

In the middle of the Third Reign there were signs of the beginning of Western encroachment on both Siam and China. The Westerners, particularly the British, had long been dissatisfied with the position enjoyed by the Chinese junks in the Eastern Seas trade, and tried in every way to challenge it. In Siam this challenge came in an indirect fashion.

The most immediate Western triumph in the Third Reign was not in the form of treaties, but in the introduction of square-rigged vessels through Siamese initiative in the 1830s. Under the influence of the British and Portuguese, the Siamese court undertook the building of its first Western-style ship (brig) at Chantaburi in 1835 and christened it the *Kaew klang-samut* (the *Ariel* in English). Constructed under the supervision of the son of the Praya Praklang, Suang nai Sit (later, Chaopraya Sisuriyawong, close adviser to Rama IV and regent in the fifth Reign), the vessel was first used in the trade to Macao and Singapore. The *Ariel* proved to be so successful that in the following year, Suang Nai Sit was again put in charge of building two warships on the Western model, also at Chantaburi. By then the court had apparently become interested in Western-style vessels. The king's eldest son also joined in the venture, and soon Rama III himself decreed that no more junks were to be commissioned and that henceforth only European-style ships were to be constructed. Realizing further that the action would almost certainly mean the junk would eventually become a relic of the past, the king had a full-size model of the junk constructed for posterity. The model was to be erected in the compounds of a new monastery under construction, with a *chedi* or stupa built on top of it. Rama III, in naming the new monastery Wat Yanawa in obvious reference to the junk model, said, "so that those of the future generations who wish to know how the junk looks like can come and view it."[15]

This step heralded an era of square-rigged vessels which spelled the decline of the junks and the trade that was dependent on them. The introduction of the larger carriers inevitably led to the eclipse of the smaller ports both at the Siamese and Chinese ends which hitherto accounted significantly for the Sino-Siamese trade, and paved the way for the eventual rise of larger ports such as Swatow to replace them.[16]

The junk as a vessel was never totally abandoned by the Siamese government, for it still offered certain advantages in the China trade for example, lower port charges. In the 1840s and 1850s when Western-style ships were being built in Siam, attempts were made by the government to produce vessels which were a cross between the brig and the customary junk, and to try passing them off as *bona fide* junks at the Chinese ports. Praya Anumanrachaton described such efforts by the Siamese to disguise the ships so that they would continue to enjoy the comparatively lower tariffs at the Chinese ports of entry. He said that efforts at first were simply to cover the prow of the ship with bamboo boards shaped like the Chinese prow, with one eye painted on each side. Later a modified vessel was built so that the bow of the vessel resembled a junk and the stern a brig. The middle mast (main mast) and the rigging were also like an ordinary junk. This type of vessel was popularly referred to as *kampan buey,* meaning an "inferior brig."[17] Finally, Townsend Harris, the American envoy who visited Bangkok in 1856, also took note of the vessels at port, and wrote the following impression: "I have before noted the fine ships which the Siamese have built, and I now saw a new specimen. It was the complete fusion of the junk of China with the ship of the West. Her foremast was rigged as a ship, the main hoisted the enormous single sail of the junk, while the mizzen was bark rigged; the bow was open and had its two enormous goggling eyes of the junk, but out of the open space projected the bowsprit and jib booms of the ship of the West."[18]

In the meantime, Sino-Siamese tributary relations were languishing, apparently because of the de-emphasis by the Siamese court of the primacy of tributary trade as private and uncontrolled trade rose to take its place. The ritual of tribute presentation, hitherto regarded as an indispensable sanction for the vigorous trade, had by the 1830s lost much luster. A Western observer related the decrepit condition of the Siamese embassy in Canton in 1835: "wishing to see 'something of eastern splendor,' for which the Siamese are 'said to be' celebrated, I determined this afternoon to visit the residence of the ambassador of the king of Siam . . . The whole establishment is in ruins. One of the overseers, a Chinese, conducted me to the apartment of the chief ambassador, whom we found smoking opium, and so stupefied as to be almost incapable of conversation."[19]

The decline in the Siamese tributary trade became more apparent after 1844. Between then and 1851, Rama III sent only one mission to Peking—in 1848.

Disruption in the Fourth Reign

Rama IV (King Mongkut) who succeeded Rama III in 1851 is known in Siamese history as the first Chakri king to see the imperative of opening relations with the West. Dating back to the Chinese defeat in the Opium War of 1839–1842, most Siamese, including the late Rama III, believed the Chinese propaganda that the Nanking Treaty was no more than a means of controlling barbarians: to "pacify" the British in order to avoid further annoyances. According to Prince Damrong Rajanubhab, only three high-ranking personages at the time reportedly foresaw the repercussions of the event. The first was the future Rama IV who had acquired considerable knowledge about the West during his long stay (about 25 years) in a monastery; the others were, Pra Pinklao, Rama IV's half-brother, and Suang nai Sit the future confidante of Mongkut. One of the first things Rama IV decided upon his accession was that the king should no longer engage in trade following up on the decision of Rama III, a decision which was not, however, strictly adhered to. In spite of his announcement Mongkut did admit that when he first came to the throne, he used the little money he had as capital to purchase a cargo and entrust it to junks trading overseas. Bishop Jean Pallegoix, a contemporary Bangkok resident, also attested that at the beginning of the reign, the king annually sent some fifteen to twenty ships to Singapore, Java, and China. Nevertheless, it is likely that Rama IV's declaration was predicated on the consideration that the junk trade, or maritime trade for that matter, was no longer so remunerative, and other means of securing revenues had been resorted to. In a letter to Sir John Bowring (then governor of Hong Kong), the Praya Praklang also explained that the Sino-Siamese trade had suffered because China had of late been in a state of turmoil, making cargoes unsalable and the decline of trade was inevitable.[20]

Suang nai Sit advised a change from the former closed economy, so the king set out to liberalize trade with the West by initially proclaiming reductions in import duties, including measurement fees (from 1,700 *baht* £212.5 to 1,000 *baht* £125 per ship), freedom of opium imports for Chinese consumption (but sold only to authorized farmers), freedom of movement within the country's interior for Western residents (including religious freedom), and authorization of rice export (previously, even after the Burney Treaty, the Siamese king reserved the sole right on this question). The decision on rice came as a direct result of Western pressures, and although it may be viewed as the beginning of Western intrusion into a sphere formerly held exclusively by Chinese traders, one could also see it as the beginning of a further expansion of Siam's rice exportation. Because of growing demands abroad, and because the potential of rice cultivation within Siam was only half realized by 1850, there was considerable room for expansion. Indeed, starting from this period, rice production was to be greatly augmented and cultivation was to be extended almost to the exclusion of other produce, including sugar which was to reach its peak of production in the 1850s.[21]

The reasons for Rama IV's ready concessions were obvious. Back in the Third Reign, Rama III could still afford to turn away the James Brooke mission, but by the start of the Fourth Reign, the British threatened Bangkok from both Burma and Malaya, ready to back up renewed requests for treaty revision, though it must be admitted that the British were not to focus their attention on Siam until the mid-1850s.[22]

Therefore, despite the concessions the king declared he was willing to grant, in the first four years of the reign, very few Western ships traded at Siam, probably only a dozen or so a year.[23] European merchants, even though bolstered by the above privileges, could not compete with Chinese junk traders who continued to pay lower duties and enjoy other privileges. In addition, one principal obstacle was the "excessive" delay caused by officials' procrastinations for extortion. But most importantly Chinese influence over the country and the court was still so strong that any potential Western competition was kept out. In the early 1850s, the Chinese seem to have gained almost complete control of the regional market within the country, and native Siamese were apparently making no effort to challenge the dominance. Bishop Pallegoix spoke of the trade in the interior of the country and in particular of the exchange of Chinese goods for local rice and cotton.[24]

Furthermore, the Chinese, on good terms with officials, were in complete control of the tax farms, the main avenue of the state's income. Such a combination led to the situation described below by James Ingram: "When the monopolies were granted to the Chinese . . . the monopolists could make arrangements with each other for sharing and cooperating in the trade of different regions. Outsiders would find it extremely difficult to break into such friendly arrangements."[25]

One strong indication of Chinese influence was the repeated failure of the Siamese court to legislate against opium importation and smoking, principally by and for Chinese, leading to a concession in 1851 when Rama IV set up an opium farm for the exclusive benefit of the Chinese. This came about after certain Chinese petitioned the king to appoint them farmers to manage opium strictly among Chinese in Bangkok and provincial towns, for which they would pay an annual fee of 10,000 taels Siamese (£5,000). In addition to the right to import opium for local consumption, the farmers could also export it to China.[26]

Additional farms were further accorded the Chinese. In 1854, a Chinese requested the privilege of farming the production of beans and sesame seeds, fresh and dried shrimp, fish, and fish sauce, to which the king readily assented. Rama IV also revived the water tax (abolished by Rama III), parceling out farms in the various designated areas in Bangkok and thirty-seven other provincial towns to several Chinese at 7,400 taels Siamese (£3,700) a year.[27]

Export goods produced in Siam at this time were still largely sent to the China market. Sugar, a main export, still found its way in great quantities to China. Bishop Pallegoix noted that its production was prevalent in the beginning of the Fourth Reign; there were about thirty refineries in the town of Nakorn Pathom (southwest of Bangkok) and twenty more at Bangpakong (to the east of Bangkok and near the Gulf). In addition, pepper production also soared. In 1854, some 70,000 piculs or 4,200 tons were exported, with a dozen or more Chinese ships from China calling annually for this product. Trade on the whole continued to be controlled by Chinese under the patronage of the court or officials, and a few were also on their own. Chinese managed five ships trading to China, Singapore, and Japan on behalf of Rama IV's half-brother and Maha uparat, Pra Pinklao. There were also a score of ships owned by rich Chinese merchants and influential officials which traded to China. Annually fifty to sixty junks laden with merchandise and thousands of immigrants were calling at Siam from Hainan, Kwangtung, Fukien, and other ports.[28] Intercourse was also maintained with Singapore; in 1851 sixty-three junks and sixteen brigs traded there from Siam, while two years later, the composite number of vessels jumped to one hundred and twenty-two: eighty-five junks and thirty-seven brigs.[29]

In spite of continued Chinese dominance in Siamese economic life, events in the beginning of the Fourth Reign would soon prove that ties were loosening in the Sino-Siamese maritime trade. The first important sign was the suspension and eventual termination of tribute missions from Siam to China, which put an end to the tributary trade, and the rationale of sanction hitherto provided for other means of trade under the administered system. As customary, Rama IV, upon his accession in 1851, dispatched a formal mission (which sailed in two square-rigged vessels outfitted by Praya Sisuri-yawong, head of the Kalahom or Defense Department, and were accompanied by two Chinese serving as financial officers) to inform the Peking court of the death of Rama III and of his accession to the throne. But it so happened that Tao-kuang also died at this time, and the embassy was turned back by the Canton authorities on account of the elaborate mourning period then in effect, which would prevent the reception of the Siamese envoy in Peking.[30] Dutifully, Rama IV dispatched another embassy in the following year to request investiture. This mission also had a trading objective. Along with the king's letter, the Praklang sent a request to the Canton authorities for permission for the tribute ships to return to Siam for "reconditioning" immediately after the discharge of the envoy at port, and for the accompanying cargo (the ballast argument could no longer be valid in the case of a Western-style ship) to be sold without levies. Praya Praklang said in the letter that the Siamese ships needed to sail back in order to secure ropes and other equipment for reconditioning the masts and sails. The reply from the viceroy to the Siamese was that such ships would be allowed to return to Canton with a tax-free cargo.[31]

The mission was very well received and rewarded by the Chinese. For instance, members of the embassy received two thousand taels (£667 from the Peking court and other gifts of cash from Chinese officials along the way from Canton to the capital) which had been solicited from local merchants in the form of donations. To transport all this together with presents to the court of Rama IV by Hsien-feng, the Siamese required sixty bullock carts. Unfortunately, the returning party was raided by a maurauding band of Taiping rebels, which resulted in much loss of property as well as of face. When the Siamese embassy reached Hong Kong on its way back to Siam, the ambassador was advised by the governor, Sir John Bowring, to use the mishap as a pretext for discontinuing the practice of tribute, since Siam was supposedly an equal sovereign state.[32] Rama IV took Bowring's advice, and chose to suspend further missions to the Ch'ing court.

Rama IV stopped sending tribute to Peking after 1853 ostensibly because of the danger that existed in China due to the Taiping Rebellion. More plausibly the move represented a growing ambivalence toward existing tributary relations with China, especially in light of the advent of the West. As the West encroached on the sovereignty of China, Siam grew more and more dissatisfied with the existing pattern of intercourse between the two states, feeling that it needed a drastic readjustment. In reality the Siamese never openly objected to the sending of further tribute. They resorted instead to a delaying tactic: first putting off the issue by claiming that the political condition within China was such that it was inadvisable to dispatch any mission to Peking via the customary land route from Canton. When pressed again by the Chinese authorities to resume the dispatch of tribute embassies, the court proposed that missions be sent instead via Tientsin in order to avoid trouble spots in the interior of China. In the communication between the ministers of the Chinese court and Rama IV in 1863, the Siamese were ambivalent about any outright severance of tribute relations with China. This ambivalence was based not so much on the profit of the tribute trade—now actually becoming increasingly doubtful but more on the possible reaction from Chinese merchants resident in Siam who might deem the move injurious to their commercial dealings with China.[33] The tactic eventually agreed upon was for the Siamese to put off sending missions as long as possible, and business was left suspended more or less this way for the rest of the Fourth Reign.

Shortly after Prince Chulalongkorn, the son of King Mongkut, succeeded to the throne as Rama V (r. 1868–1910), however, the Siamese government, apparently realizing that a number of vessels were still engaged in trade with China, and "wishing to put them on the same footing as those of the Western countries," intimated to the Chinese government that the Siamese wished to send an embassy to Peking via Tientsin, provided that it be treated "somewhat in the same manner as those which have been sent by Western nations." The Ch'ing court, still regarding Siam as basically a tributary, rejected the proposal. In 1875, China again demanded tribute from Siam, but the latter again employed the evasive tactic and refused to act one way or another. Three years later, the Marquis Tseng Chi-tse, son of Tseng Kuo-fan, stopped by at Bangkok en route to take up his embassadorial post in London, and demanded tribute together with a new commercial treaty. Both requests were politely turned down by the Siamese court. The final note was struck when, in 1882, Siam formally renounced all its tribute obligations to China, and declared it recognized only the Western system of international relations. By severing her formal ties with China, Siam was merely confirming the increasingly close economic tie with Britain which it had carefully cultivated since the 1850s.[34]

The decision to discontinue sending tribute missions meant that official Siamese trade with China, formerly sanctioned by tribute presentation, would thereafter cease. Rama IV complained publicly that the Chinese government had all along hindered Siamese trade by imposing such demands as official letters and tribute as prerequisites.[35] The condition was further compounded by the dispatch of the Bowring Mission from the London government in 1855 with a view to opening Siam commercially. The mission received a favorable response from Rama IV who, after all, had wished to welcome Western trade to his country, as indicated by the measures he had adopted at his accession.[36] The Bowring Treaty was concluded, and did away with the age-old privileges enjoyed exclusively by the Sino-Siamese junk trade. The treaty contained the following clauses: 1) a uniform duty rate of 3 percent on goods actually unloaded, and permission to re-export and to receive a refund of the full amount of duty paid on unsalable articles (which had not been the case before); 2) one duty only on one kind of export goods; 3) the rescinding of the measurement fees; 4) equal privileges for junks and British vessels; 5) extraterritoriality for British subjects.[37] Within half a decade after this treaty, several other Western nations, including the United States, signed similar accords with the Siamese government.

Thus the trading monopoly arrangement worked out between the Siamese court and the Chinese in the form of the junk trade was finally breached, and the economic entrenchment of the Chinese was challenged. For the first time, the British were permitted a free hand in building ships in Siam, and thus partaking in the advantage of cheap materials long enjoyed exclusively by the Chinese merchants.[38]

One immediate effect of the new treaties was the rapid increase of Western ships in Bangkok, and the corresponding decline of junk traffic. W. A. Graham commented: "The years which fol followed the new treaties brought an expansion of foreign trade, at first not very conspicuous, but later becoming increasingly evident with every year that passed. The Chinese trade, however, never throve after the making of the treaties with European Powers, but, bereft of the support of the many corruptions by which it had formerly lived, and exposed to the comparatively honest [sic] and quite relentless competition of white men, it languished and declined."[39]

Apart from the suspension of the tribute missions, another obvious factor affecting junk trade fortunes after the 1850s was the continuing political decline of the Ch'ing dynasty, aggravated further by the Taiping Rebellion.[40] By 1863, all the shipping in foreign trade in the Ch'ao-chou area had been taken over by Western vessels which were concentrated at the new treaty port of Swatow.[41] The transportation of emigrants was now conducted by larger and faster Western ships, particularly in northeastern Kwangtung and southern Fukien.[42] Besides profiting immensely from this venture the Western ship also conveyed needed staples, such as rice from Siam, back to Southeast China.[43] In addition, junks came increasingly to be regarded as an unnecessary security risk now that better-equipped Western-style ships were available. Insurance firms preferred the Western ships which, in many instances, devised their own protective escorts against pirates.[44]

At Siam the once proud fleet of over 400 junks engaged in the Sino-Siamese trade was reduced by the competition of Western-owned brigs and steamers to less than a hundred. The last of the Siamese fleet, the *Buanheng* (Siamese transliteration for "Wan-hsing") which belonged to a Sino-Siamese nobleman named Praya Pisanponpanich, was wrecked at sea in 1874. Even the square-rigged vessels belonging to the king and other courtiers were eventually forced out by 1890, while Western ships trading to Bangkok increased to two hundred a year. In 1850, of some 332 foreign vessels that called at Siam, almost all were Chinese junks save for four British and American vessels. But by the 1880s the British had captured over 70 percent of the annual shipping of Siam, while the junk trade had declined to an average of 2 to 3 percent a year.

In the early pattern of British trade with Siam British ships would trade first to China before proceeding to Siam. They would use silver from China to purchase Siamese goods. As the Siamese mints then could not produce sufficient silver currency to meet the increasing demands of an enlarging market, the court accepted Chinese silver dollars (at an exchange rate of 5 *baht* 12.5 s. to every

3 Chinese dollars) and put them into local circulation as part of the national currency after the coins had been stamped with the Siamese royal emblems of the crown and the wheel. In essence, then, British ships were performing the function of the junks in the traditional Sino-Siamese maritime trade. In the shadow of Western competition, junks from China after the opening of treaty ports kept up trade with Southeast Asia (particularly with Siam), though the number of large junks steadily declined. The Ch'ao-chou red-prow traders from Kwangtung, for instance, which in 1858 stood at 400, dwindled to 300 a decade later. But the smaller junks, especially those from Hainan Island, remained a prominent feature of Bangkok until the First World War.[45]

Despite the apparent waning of the former expansive Sino-Siamese junk trade, Chinese influence in Siam continued to grow unabated. Foreign trading by resident Chinese did not stop. In 1859, aside from the brigs owned by the king, they also possessed a number of such ships which made two voyages a year, one to China and the other to Singapore, and even with the growing presence of steamers in the following decade, the brigs continued to trade.[46]

The area in which the Chinese proved most dominant was the internal farm monopolies, which the Fourth Reign carried over from the Third. After the treaties with various Western nations, the Chinese economic base became more entrenched than ever in the tax farming system. Because Western merchants were now permitted to trade freely at fixed tariff rates, income from the foreign trade of the court was dealt another blow, which meant a more intensified reliance on the farms for revenues. John Bowring had asked for the abolition of all the existing tax farms, but the Siamese court argued that if it did that, it would be deprived of proper income. The king reasoned too, that whereas in the royal trading monopolies the court practised pre-emption and exclusive rights over "restricted" articles and others did not have any opportunity to enjoy their benefits, in the farming system the court relinquished direct participation in commercial affairs, and ordinary people had a chance to participate without governmental interference. So the court once again turned to the enterprising Chinese and utilized their skills in carrying out the farming system, in one sense to block or counterbalance any serious inroad by Western capitalism. Thirty-eight farms, including the opium farm, were established in the beginning of the reign, supervised by various departmental heads, as was the case in the Third Reign.[47]

In addition to the expansion of the tax farming system, the Siamese court, in view of the open trade now allowable, was apprehensive of Westerners who, with their comparatively larger capital, might create economic crises within the country by buying up such essentials as rice and other staples. Therefore, another measure taken by Rama IV under the actual planning and leadership of Chaopraya Sisuriyawong, the king's close adviser, was the general development of the country. Canal-dredging projects, the building of roads and bridges, and so forth, were undertaken in order to facilitate communication and open up more land for agricultural development. In all such public projects, Chinese immigrants were employed in greater volume than ever before.[48] The government also built its first steamer in 1855, and by the early 1860s the country's merchant marine consisted of 23 steamships and 76 square-rigged vessels.[49]

In the midst of such developments, Chinese merchants in Siam continued to participate actively in the economic sphere. At least by 1860, they, too, were already operating steamships to China to trade.[50] The Chinese had proven themselves adroit businessmen who were quick to adapt to changing conditions, and this flexibility was a quality that enabled them to survive.

CONCLUSION

In the two hundred years before the Opium War, the Sino-Siamese junk trade had been an important branch of the overall Chinese maritime trade in the Eastern Seas. This trade was feasible in the context of an administered commercial structure on both sides which proved to be mutually exclusive and beneficial during the final phase of the East Asian premodern economy. On one end was Siam's royal trading monopoly system (which increasingly reflected a vested interest in the court for the trade with China as time went on); its energy was directed more and more at the China market after 1688. On the other end, the Chinese tributary framework, despite its restrictive posture, became flexible enough to accommodate the requirements of the Siamese system. The tributary orientation actually offered considerable opportunity for trade, and the Siamese court was adept at exploiting it. It has been argued that from the Siamese side the number of formal tribute missions was merely one means of determining the true dimensions of the trade. Besides formally admitting the regular embassies (which nonetheless came in an irregular pattern), the Chinese authorities (at Canton and Peking) in practice tolerated Siam's attempts at dispatching other types of semi-formal or informal missions whose primary object was trade.

The Siamese royal trade had also been permitted to do business beyond the regular tribute period (as seen in the conduct of the annual summer trade at Canton after the mid-eighteenth century), which was another vital component of the overall potential in the country's economic intercourse with China. From the second decade of the nineteenth century onward, the private junk trade from Siam to China accelerated to an unprecedented degree while formal missions continued to be sent to sanction it. This private trade was rapidly outstripping the tributary trade and maintaining its own independence—no doubt, also with help from local Chinese officials in Southeast China who had a stake in the venture in the form of "squeeze." Underneath it all, however, the administered framework

242

persisted, which meant that this trade was essentially controlled by the Siamese court in a system of patronage.

The regulated nature of the Sino-Siamese trade had been given a further impetus by other factors: geography, politics, and the employment of Chinese personnel to administer the trade. The position of Siam in the China trade was dictated both by the fact that Siam was situated close enough to the Southeast China market and the Indian Archipelago markets to play the role of an entrepôt, and that the country was endowed with the natural produce suitable for the Chinese junk trade. Politically, Siam was most of the time a strong and unified state ruled by pragmatic kings who were interested in enriching their court. Further, for a good century and a half, it was devoid of Western commercial and political interference. The *volte face* in Western commercial and political fortunes at the end of the seventeenth century (and, in this respect, one must also mention the similar fate suffered half a century earlier by the enterprising Japanese), forged a strong alliance between the Siamese court and Chinese individuals eager for profits and rewards (ennoblement, power, wealth, or recognition).

Over a long period of time, the Siamese court engaged Chinese and Mohammedan traders as mandarin merchants. By the seventeenth century, the Mohammedan merchants, who had traditionally concentrated on trade in the Indian Ocean and the Malay peninsula region, had declined as a strong commercial group, leaving their Chinese counterpart with superior commercial knowledge, organization, and royal sanction as the sole trading body in the country.

Thus a dependent relationship between the Chinese and the Siamese ruling class (the aristocracy, bureaucracy, and courtiers) existed owing to the pragmatism demonstrated by the Siamese king in seeking the services of the Chinese. Chinese-managed maritime trade became the one important *modus operandi* for the acquisition of state revenues throughout most of the period. Revenues were derived not only from profits from the direct sale of merchandise borne by royal junks, but also from revenue income and gains from related industries, such as shipbuilding. One "negative" effect, however, emerged from such an arrangement. In a way, exclusive Chinese

management presented no alternative model of dynamism and prevented the growth of a native enterprise. Since the Siamese ruler
traditionally discouraged his subjects from managing ships to trade
abroad because of security reasons, this Chinese monopoly was not
unwelcome. Although a number of Chinese and their descendants
came, in time, to be assimilated into Siamese society, it is noteworthy that as the assimilation process worked more deeply on
them, the more they were removed from activities related directly
to the junk trade. Hence, it seemed that those engaged in it were
mostly individuals who spoke more Chinese than Siamese, and
identified themselves more closely with Chinese civilization. Those
Chinese descendants who identified with Siamese culture often
sought their vocation in the regular bureaucracy, while those
clinging to their Chinese identity were predisposed to commercial
activities.

Hitherto the actual functions of the tributary trade have been
little studied, though the operation of tribute presentation has
been much discussed. In this respect, the Siamese case is exemplary
in illustrating the adroitness of a tributary in capitalizing on the
commercial aspect of such a ritual. Hence, the tax exemption of
ballast, the immediate cargo disposal upon the arrival of the tribute
ships at port, the pretext for four sailings in one mission, were
among the techniques employed by the Siamese to extract commercial gains. The Manchu authorities were frequently exasperated by
these techniques, but they nonetheless seemed exceedingly lenient
to the Siamese. Then, of course, the Siamese side had never shown
any pretense about its main motive behind the dispatch of embassies,
and fully appreciated the commercial opportunities as they arose
which in essence was the *raison d'être* of their *yu-shih chih kung,*
or "missions dispatched with an aim" principle.

The complementary nature of the Chinese and Siamese trading
orientations also bore a direct relationship to the Chinese influx
into Siam. Chinese immigrants were a handful in the seventeenth
century, increasing to several hundred thousand at the beginning of
the nineteenth century. If Chinese immigration was a follow-up of
the junk trade, it in turn helped develop the latter by being, first

of all, a crucial part of the cargo in the trade (especially after the Taksin period). Secondly, Chinese immigration helped to develop trade by creating an increase in the bulk and variety of the goods transacted—mainly by their subsequent development of commercial agriculture in Siam and the importation of commodities for their daily use. This activity contributed directly to an increase in the size of the junk fleets and in the number of hands available. Chinese immigration furthermore helped Siamese society to move closer to a money economy, since it contributed directly to the increased use of paid labor and less use of the traditional corvée labor. (No, doubt, corvée labor continued to be regarded as an important component of the overall economic assets of the society; it was still a means of reckoning wealth and determining status in the agrarian, feudal milieu.) All of this helped the indigenous Siamese society to prepare for changes to be brought about by the forced opening of the entire country by Westerners in the mid-nineteenth century.

A study of Sino-Siamese trade in the period under discussion must also take into consideration the private trade sector as well. As far as Siam was concerned, private trade existed within the protective framework of the tributary trade. The mandarin merchants who managed the Siamese king's trade conducted their own simultaneously. Thus the king's trade was a privileged form of private trade. Such individuals were permitted to send some of their own vessels with the tributary ships en route to Canton (as best evidenced by the 1781 mission sent by King Taksin), or to take cargoes belonging to them as well as to the king to trade to Kwangtung, Fukien, and Chekiang. Some merchants also had their vessels chartered by the Siamese court for trade to China, especially after the 1750s when the annual Canton summer trade was permitted. These various forms of private trade were meant as an incentive for Chinese individuals working for the royal court, but they actually benefited both the Chinese merchants and the courtiers and officials. Apart from its right to take part directly in the sale of cargoes carried by the ships, the ruling class also enjoyed the benefit of being patrons for all vessels constructed by Chinese traders within Siam.

Private trade conducted from the Chinese side fluctuated in accordance with a host of factors, but was particularly affected by measures taken by Chinese authorities. Although Canton served as the center for tributary trade and, to an extent, some private trade in the latter part of the seventeenth century, much of the Chinese private trade with Siam up to 1757 was conducted from the Amoy area. The South Fukienese had maintained a long tradition of trade with Siam and Southeast Asia, and in the thirty-year span between 1727 and 1757, they were foremost among the local merchants in spite of the fact that geographical (proximity and location in the junk traffic land) and structural (machinery and market adequacy) factors may have favored Canton more.

South Fukien merchants are also known to have gone to Kwangtung and Chekiang whence they traded with Southeast Asia, Japan, and the Western merchants. The eclipse of Amoy as a result of the Ch'ien-lung decree in 1757 shifted the focus of Chinese trade to Siam, not to Canton or Ningpo, but to Ch'ao-chou in northeastern Kwangtung. Owing partly to the accession of a Ch'ao-chou to the Siamese throne, the people from this region were to assume the position of eminence so long enjoyed by the South Fukienese in the Sino-Siamese trade. By the early decades of the nineteenth century, their ships dominated the Siamese trade and were transporting Siamese produce regularly up and down the southeastern China coasts as far north as Shanghai. Their commercial undertakings were greatly aided by Ch'ao-chou immigrants who developed commercial agriculture in Siam to feed the maritime trade. Ch'ao-chou merchants and navigators were also being joined by their Hainan counterparts after the turn of the century, though activities of the Hainanese could in no way match those of the Ch'ao-chou.

A word should also be said about Ningpo merchants who had a role in trade to Siam. These traders, at the close of the seventeenth century, joined with Fukien mariners in conducting the China–Japan–Siam triangular trade which was supplementary to the direct Sino-Siamese trade at the time. They usually frequented Lower Siam ports, and seemed mainly concentrated on acquiring cargoes for their trade with Nagasaki. Their role declined after the eighteenth century.

The Krom-ta in the Praklang department was the main body through which many Chinese individuals ascended in the Siamese bureaucratic hierarchy. In Southeast China, the offices of the governor-general, governor, customs superintendent, and provincial treasurer all played important roles in the transaction of trade—and also in malpractice and corruption. The actual conduct of business was left in the hands of organized merchant guilds. At Amoy, there were hong bodies, the *yang-hang,* which handled the Siamese trade at port and took part in the local merchants' trade to Siam through the system of mutual guarantees. Amoy merchant guilds seem to have dealt largely with the Southeast Asia trade. Guilds at Canton, on the other hand, seemed more varied and larger in size and number. In the eighteenth century we witnessed a metamorphosis in their organization toward an increasingly tight-knit and special-ized structure, within which there existed, alongside the main hong body dealing with Western trade, a collective group dealing with Sino-Siamese commercial intercourse. But because such regulated merchant establishments both at Amoy and Canton were at the constant mercy of extortionate officials and clandestine trade con-ducted by unauthorized persons, and because of their "expensive" habits, they commonly faced insolvency. In the seventeenth century, trade was characterized by dealings through regulated channels, but by the early nineteenth century, as the Ch'ing authority declined and hong bodies became moribund (those rele-vant to the Siamese-Chinese trade), private or less regulated trade seems to have flourished. At this time, however, the emphasis in this branch of trade had shifted toward the Siamese side, with Ch'ao-chou merchants based in Siam carrying out the bulk of trading activities.

If any one product can be singled out as the main contribution to the Sino-Siamese trade, it is Siamese rice. The rice trade that developed from the second decade of the eighteenth century on was significant for both Siam and China. The serious food shortage (due principally to the phenomenal increase of population coupled with crop failures and natural calamities) in Southeast China generated for the first time an interest by the Chinese government in large quantities of Siamese rice. Prior to that time the production of rice in Siam must have been limited primarily to local consumption, with occasional shipments abroad to the Indian Archipelago and Japan. The sudden increase in Chinese demands, creating high enough prices to make rice an attractive export article, spurred large-scale production, and in turn made rice a valuable object of foreign trade. Chinese merchants, whose dominance in Siam's external trade had become established by the early 1700s naturally handled the rice exportation to China exclusively though they themselves were never directly engaged in the cultivation of the staple, a venture traditionally in the domain of indigenous Siamese. From the 1720s through the 1750s, rice became the top foreign-exchange earner for Siam, and promoted the shipbuilding industry in the country as well. In time shipbuilding became a substantial industry responsible for further expansion of the Sino-Siamese junk trade in the nineteenth century.

The need for Siamese rice was a primary factor leading the Ch'ing court to eventually rescind the second maritime ban to Southeast Asia in the 1720s. This move by Ch'ing authorities and the subsequent encouragement of local merchants toward sizable Siamese rice imports ensured a period of vigorous trade. It was partly because of such incentive schemes instituted by the government that the Ch'eng-hai group emerged to assume the leadership of the rice trade after the South Fukienese group had relinquished the position in the 1760s. From that time on, the fortunes of the Ch'eng-hai merchants in the Sino-Siamese trade were established.

In deference to Siamese rice importation, the Ch'ing court had demonstrated unusual tolerance toward the Siamese practice of engaging Chinese personnel to manage their regular and tributary trade. It was not until the beginning of the nineteenth century, when the Siamese were thought to have carried this kind of "exploitation" too far (verging on impropriety), that the court finally ruled against it, though the effectiveness of such measures was doubtful.

The Siamese rice export to China also added an important dimension to the Sino-Siamese trade. Formerly the main objects of this trade had been the valuable "luxury" goods which were consumed only by the upper strata of Chinese society. Rice represented a commodity beneficial to the common people, and may be said to have opened up an avenue for the exchange of more items of popular use, which in time came to occupy a central position of the trade. Finally, because of this grain, the potential abundance of Siam attracted greater numbers of Chinese, and such action in turn laid the groundwork of the country's accelerated economic development in the nineteenth century, through commercial agriculture and other forms of internal development.

In terms of potential and real profitability in the Sino-Siamese trade, it is, of course, difficult to quantify without sufficient empirical data. However, in a descriptive approach, it is feasible to postulate that the Siamese side stood to benefit in the way of "turnover," that is, the number of times goods were bought and sold, and so forth. The possible risks, such as typhoons and piracy spoilage, seemed offset by potential gains through insured sales and purchases almost every time. Since Chinese merchants were quite skilled in determining specific market demands, shipments aboard royal ships were highly salable, and Chinese authorities seldom refused the Siamese the right to discharge whatever had been shipped for the tributary trade. Trade outside the tributary framework also seems to have enjoyed a certain amount of guarantee. The risk factor was lessened by the fact that, in a predominantly barter system, whatever the Siamese sold, they were able to receive full payment in kind as guaranteed by the authorities: hence, the possibility of default was small. In addition, tax privileges accounted for a good deal of the dramatic increase in junk traffic from Siam especially after Taksin's reign. Chinese goods were well received on the Siamese market, with shipments often fetching more than a 100 percent profit. Nevertheless, Siam seems to have maintained a favorable trade balance all along, shown by the fact that in the early part of the nineteenth century, the country's trade surplus was balanced off partially by the importation of silver bullion from China to be used for minting.

On the Chinese side, the gain from this branch of trade was not meager. We have noted the impact of rice relief especially in the early decades of the eighteenth century. An increasing number of local merchants became engaged in this trade, in spite of the fact that rice usually did not fetch as much profit (bulk for bulk) as some other commodities, especially exotic items such as birds' nests and rhinoceros horns. Indications seem to point to a greater possibility for good profits in rice especially for people of such coastal areas as Chang-chou and Ch'uan-chou whose livelihood depended mainly on maritime trade. But the interest group which stood to gain a certain and substantial share was perhaps the local officials at Kwangtung and Fukien directly responsible for the regulation of foreign trade. Controlling the machinery, they were often far from hesitant to resort to the time-honored practice of extortion. There was hardly any direct sanction against this kind of corruption from the Peking court, for the court itself received annual "pay-offs" from these officials. Local officials had to be reckoned with precisely because they supervised trading matters on behalf of the emperor who was far removed from the scene. Their advice on imperial decisions was therefore, crucial.

This power at work may clearly be seen in the case of the Taksin mission in 1780. Taksin's complaints about extortion by Canton authorities not only went unreported in the communication to the Peking court from the Liang-Kuang viceroy, Pa-yen-san, but the decision by Ch'ien-lung not to grant the Siamese requests on several matters was also apparently influenced by the way the viceroy's memorial had been drafted. This illustration points to the importance of securing cooperation from local officials; it was the sure way to success. On most occasions, though, the Siamese seem to have learned how the system worked, which in turn accounted for their ability to satisfy their commercial interests. It may be argued that overseas trade on the whole directly affected only urban areas, such as the agrarian-based city of Ayudhya and the indigenous commercial centers of Pattani, Bangkok, and so forth, and that in areas lying beyond external trade was insignificant. Nevertheless, it played an important role in enhancing the ruling class and those who shaped the destiny of the country. Besides, foreign trade, though small in proportion to the country's entire economic production, figured importantly in its total money transactions.

The impact of the Sino-Siamese trade on Siam may best be seen in the speedy recovery of the country after the fall of Ayudhya, and in its development under the first Chakri kings which was directly linked to the growing junk trade with China (making Bangkok the main junk port outside China proper). During the period after the Ayudhya dynasty the junk trade became the quick and convenient means of securing income for the state, and the profits derived were largely dispensed as grants to various government officials and grandees. The growing presence of Chinese in both the royal trade and in the government at large also serves to strengthen the assumption that if one equates the state economy to that of the king and the court, one could rightly say the impact was unquestionable. Although Rama IV was later to assert that the Siamese court had been placed at a disadvantage by all sorts of restrictions arbitrarily imposed by the Chinese government, the accusation was perhaps a justification for his decision to de-emphasize the Sino-Siamese trade and turn his attention to developing trade with the West.

One should also take into consideration the significance of the triangular trade between Siam, Japan, and China, which was conducted in the last part of the seventeenth century. The triangular trade served one important function of stimulating the Sino-Siamese trade at a time when it was still in a beginning stage marked by the vigorous application of the first maritime ban. The Chinese, acting in a private capacity for the Siamese court, took hides and other products to Nagasaki and returned with the much coveted copper, shells, lacquer wares, and screens. Trade was also conducted with Chinese ports en route. To a very important extent this branch of trade helped to develop direct intercourse between Siam and China. Pattani, Songkla, and Ligor in Lower Siam were visited by Ningpo and Amoy ships, and hence their status as international ports was in one way stimulated by this triangular trade. It also helps explain why Lower Siam came to be settled primarily by South Fukienese.

The development of the Sino-Siamese trade also led to commercial intercourse between Siam and her Southeast Asian neighbors in the nineteenth century. This branch of trade was handled exclusively by Chinese based in Siam.

The Sino-Siamese junk trade was a direct casualty of Western penetration into East Asia in the nineteenth century. Because this trade flourished under the "closed" system on both ends at Siam and China it became incompatible and anachronistic in the light of growing Western pressures for free and open trade under treaty obligations. Superior Western-style ships ensured the decline of the junk, and their presence led directly to the opening of larger ports along Southeast China coasts (which could service large vessels), and to the corresponding decline of smaller ports hitherto frequented by the smaller size junks. But it may be argued that the junk trade provided an impetus for the eventual penetration of Western maritime imperialism. It can further be said that Western economic activities, while introducing many benefits in the development of Southeast Asian economic resources, caused serious social and economic dislocations to the indigenous society (for instance, hurting native home industries by flooding the market with cheap and mass-produced items). The junk trade, on the other hand, was able to develop Southeast Asian markets without encouraging adverse effects and actually produced mutual benefits.

Nonetheless, the decline of the junk trade did not mean the corresponding decline of Chinese influence in the Siamese economy. It has been argued that owing to the entrepreneurial position of the Chinese in Siam (assured through the symbiotic relationship worked out with the court), the country was saved from being invaded economically and politically by the West. Indeed, in subsequent periods, the Western merchants, with their hard-won rights to free trade under the treaties, were still unable to supplant the Chinese economically, because the Chinese adapted themselves to the new economic realities and strove to benefit themselves as much as possible under the conditions of free trade.

The traditional rationale of the Siamese court about external trade was that free trade was not conducive to a healthy government treasury. The government felt that it had to engage directly in trade for the sake of revenue. In the same vein, government officials were encouraged to resort to trade to supplement their incomes, which varied from one year to another depending on the condition of the king's coffers.

In light of the growing uncertainties of the junk trade in the nineteenth century, due both to the Western pressure for free trade and the growing loss of revenue from royal trading monopolies, the Third Reign, and subsequently the Fourth Reign, resorted increasingly to the tax farming system as an alternate means of generating state income. It often proved to be a more predictable source of revenue. When Siam was forced to accept free trade provisions and open up the country to trade in the 1850s, the revenue derived from state-directed trade lessened considerably, making it necessary for Rama IV's government to increase the number of tax farms. Such an action augmented the power of individual Chinese as well as Chinese secret societies. Reliance on the tax farming system may be said to be a continuation of the traditional pattern predicated on the concept of state intervention in economic development, somewhat like the mercantilist orientation inherent in the former trading monopolies. The course of the Sino-Siamese junk trade ran parallel to the development of tributary relations between Siam and China. Trade officially commenced with Narai's first tribute presentation to the Ch'ing court in 1652. When missions were suspended after 1853, the decline of the junk trade was already manifest. In the two centuries during which tribute and trade remained complementary, the fortunes of the Sino-Siamese junk trade rose and fell, shaping the economic structure of Siam. The impact of this economic force is still felt in Siam today.

APPENDICES

NOTES

BIBLIOGRAPHY

GLOSSARY

ABBREVIATIONS

Chotmaihet 1	Chotmaihet krung Rattanakosin R.1
Chotmaihet 2	Chotmaihet krung Rattanakosin R.2
Chotmaihet 3	Chotmaihet krung Rattanakosin R.3
Chotmaihet 4	Chotmaihet Krung Rattanakosin R.4
CSK	*Ch'ing shih kao*
CTWCSL	*Ch'ing-tai wai-chiao shih-liao*
FCTC	Ch'en Shou-ch'i et al., comps. *Fu-chien t'ung-chih*
FCTCCSL	Liu Chien-shao, comp. *Fu-chien t'ung-chih cheng-shih lüeh*
HJAS	*Harvard Journal of Asiatic Studies*
HMC	Chou K'ai et al., comps. *Hsia-men chih*
HMC (TWH)	Chou K'ai et al., comps. *Hsia-men chih (T'ai-wan wen-hsien ts'ung-k'an)*
HTSL	*Hsuan-tsung shih-lu*
JSS	*Journal of the Siam Society*
JTSL	*Jen-tsung shih-lu*
KTSL	*Kao-tsung shih-lu*
KTCC	*Juan Yuan, ed. Kuang-tung t'ung-chih*
KTTC (chts)	*Juan Yuan, ed. Kuang-tung t'ung-chih (Chung-hua ts'ung-shu)*
LSYY	*Li-shih yü-yen yen-chiu so chi-k'an*
MCSL	*Ming-Ch'ing shih-liao*

SICTHL	*Shih-i ch'ao Tung-hua lu*
SLHK	*Shih-liao hsun-k'an*
STSL	*Shih-tsung shih-lu*
1STSL	*Sheng-tsu shih-lu*
TCHTSL	*(Ch'in-ting) Ta-Ch'ing hui-tien shih-li*
WHTP	*Wen-hsien ts'ung-p'ien*
YHKC	Liang T'ing-nan, comp. *Yueh-hai-kuan chih*
YCCP	*(Yung-cheng) Chu-p'i yü-chih*

APPENDIX A

A Chronological List of Siamese Ships Reported as Trading to Nagasaki

Source: Hayashi Harunobu, Hayashi Nobuatsu, comps., Ura Ren'ichi, anno., *Ka-i hentai* (Tokyo, 1958).

Year	Particulars	Reference
1679	One Siamese ship reported that four ships from Siam were bound for Japan that year.	I,196
1680	One Siamese ship reported that three more belonging to the Chinese residents (of Ayudhya), as well as three additional Amoy ships, were bound from Siam that year. It had called at Amoy enroute to load brown sugar. (Sugar cane was abundant in the prefectures of Changchou and Ch'üan-chou as well as Taiwan.)	I,309
1681	One Siamese ship reported that there were five ships due from Siam that season; only three actually arrived.	I,324–26.
1682	Two Siamese ships arrived.	I,348, 358.
1683	Five Siamese ships called, one having called at Canton to secure a cargo.	I,366, 368, 397–99.
1684	Four Siamese ships were bound for Nagasaki, two having stopped first at Canton.	I,403–05, 406.
1686	Four ships from Siam traded to Japan; the ship-masters of two of them were explicitly mentioned as Fukienese officials serving in the Siamese court; they reported no ships from Siam ventured to Japan in 1685. (The language used in the listing of titles of crew members with their *sakdina* grades on board Siamese ships calling at Nagasaki was that of Chang-chou. This only indicates the predominance of the South Fukienese in the triangular trade of Siam at the time. See Ishii, p. 167).	I,616–17, 633.

259

Year	Particulars	Reference
1687	One Siamese ship arrived with a crew of 114 Chinese, accompanied by 19 Siamese.	I,783.
1688	Two Siamese ships called, one reportedly with a shipment of deer hides and sugar (latter item being probably from the Amoy area).	I,783. II,990–91, II,987–89.
1689	Two Siamese ships traded at Nagasaki with over 100 Chinese crewmen aboard each ship.	II,1124–26.
1690	Three Siamese ships were reported in at Nagasaki. Nagasaki.	II,1273–75, II,1283–84.
1691	Three Siamese ships arrived, with two more reportedly on the way.	II,1387–88 1394–95.
1692	Four Siamese ships arrived.	II,1466–67, 1478–79.
1693	One Siamese ship called.	II,1588–90.
1694	Two Siamese junks arrived, one having visited Ch'ao-chou en route.	II,1655–56, 1674–75.
1695	One Siamese ship arrived from Amoy with a Chinese crew of forty-four.	II,1735–37.
1696	Two Siamese ships arrived; one had originally been a Ningpo ship which had traded to Siam in 1695 and apparently sold there; both reported that in that year three Chinese ships from Fukien, Kwangtung, and Chekiang traded to Siam.	II,1828–29, 1832–33, 1829.
1697	Three Siamese ships traded to Nagasaki; reported that two Chinese ships were en route from Siam after having traded there.	II,1932–33, 1935–36, 1947–48.
1698	One ship reported in at Nagasaki; mentioned that seven Chinese ships called at Siam that year.	II,1998.

Year	Particulars	Reference
1699	Two Siamese ships arrived; reported that six Chinese ships traded at Siam that year, with two planning to proceed to Nagasaki—while the rest returned to China; a Formosan and an Amoy ship reported that a third and fourth Siamese vessel bound for Nagasaki had been damaged en route and had to put in for repairs at Amoy. (The two damaged vessels eventually returned to Siam with a cargo acquired at Amoy.) In the same year, another Siamese ship en route back to Siam from Japan was also damaged and had to put in at Amoy for repairs. The ship, loaded with Japanese copper, managed to acquire another Amoy cargo to take back to Ayudhya.	II,1080-81, 2091-92, III,2126, 2127.
1700	A K'ao-chou junk reported that a Siamese ship en route to Japan put in at Canton in the fall of that year; it was one of the two Siamese ships which set sail for Japan that year; also another ship from Ningpo reported two additional Siamese ships traded at Amoy and Namoa.	III,2214, 2175, 2163.
1701	One Siamese ship arrived with a Chinese crew of 104; it had stopped at Namoa for repairs en route; a Nanking ship reported that two Siamese ships en route to visit Japan in the previous year had to put in at Canton due to storms; and one more Siamese ship was reported to have put in at the same port by another ship from Formosa in the same year.	III,2204-05, 2174, 2200.
1703	Three Siamese ships called; one reported that 10 Chinese ships had gone to trade at Siam in 1702; all the shipmasters of the ships from Siam were Fukienese, employed by the Siamese court.	III,2332-33, 2334-35, 2333-34.
1704	One Siamese ship with a Chinese crew of 76 and 3 Siamese officials traded at Nagasaki.	III,2409.
1707	Three ships from Siam arrived, their shipmasters being all Fukienese.	III,2496-97, III,2499.

Year	Particulars	Reference
1708	One Siamese arrived; it was part of the four-ship convoy bound for Nagasaki in 1707, but the rest had to put in for repairs at Kwangnam (Kuangnan, Annam); a Canton ship also reported that a Siamese ship which had visited Japan in the previous year stopped at Canton to procure a Canton cargo; the vessel had a crew of 82 Chinese.	III,2579, III,2563-64.
1709	One Siamese ship called; it had set sail for Japan in 1708 but had had to put in at Namoa for repairs; the shipmaster was a Fukienese under the Siamese king's employ.	III,2636-37.
1710	One Siamese ship captained by a Fukienese representative of the Siamese court arrived; a Nanking ship which also called at Nagasaki that year reported that there were 2 Siamese ships en route to Japan, and an Amoy ship visiting Nagasaki also reported that a Siamese ship to Amoy in 1710 had been damaged.	III,2665, 2667-68. *Hoi*, p. 3
1711	Three Siamese junks called; one had left from Ningpo with a crew of 43 Chinese; another reported that a Siamese ship had left from Siam to trade at Ningpo in 1710; the third had a crew of 89 Chinese plus three Siamese officials.	*Hoi*, 18-19, 22, 23.
1717	Two Siamese junks arrived; one reported that it had left Siam in the previous year, but met storms and had to stop at Namoa and at Tan-shan in Chekiang where it disposed of half of its original cargo; its shipmaster also reported that in 1716 there had been another Siamese ship bound for Japan but it eventually turned back.	III,2718-20, 2737-38.
1718	One Siamese ship arrived with 62 Chinese and 2 Siamese officials.	III,2805-06.
1719	One Siamese ship arrived with 98 Chinese crewmen and 3 Siamese officials.	III,2849-50.

Year	Particulars	Reference

1722   One Siamese ship with 57 Chinese crewmen called;   III,2927–29.
it arrived from Shanghai and led by a Fukienese
shipmaster who also reported that in 1721 a Siamese
ship en route to Japan ran into a storm and had to
put in at Wen-chou in Chekiang; he also said that
since the reimposition of the ban on travel and trade
to Southeast Asia by the Manchus in 1717, the junk
traffic of Siam had not suffered.

1723   One Siamese ship arrived; it had originally been a   III,2987–88.
Ningpo ship which had gone to trade at Siam in the
previous year—and had apparently been sold to the
Siamese; it had a crew of 47. (This shows that the
Manchu ban on trade with Southeast Asia imposed
for a second time in 1717 was not completely
successful).

A Chronological List of Pattani Ships Reported as Trading to Nagasaki

Source: Hayashi Harunobu, Hayashi Nobuatsu, comps., Ura Ren'ichi, anno., *Ka-i hentai* (Tokyo, 1958).

Year	Particulars	Reference
1675	One Pattani ship called.	I,118.
1683	One Pattani ship called.	I,379–81.
1684	One Pattani ship called; it left on the twenty-sixth day of the fifth moon and arrived at Nagasaki on the eighth taking over nine weeks of traveling time to reach Japan.	I,435–36.
1686	One Pattani ship traded at Nagasaki.	I,647–48.
1687	Two Pattani ships called; one had stopped at Ningpo en route; the other had proceeded from Amoy with a cargo of deer hides, sugar, and honey; one ship-master Ch'en T'ien-yun reported that there were 38 crewmen on his ship, and that ships from Amoy, Malacca, and other places traded to Pattani; the Chinese residents there, however, were down to 50 in number.	I,770–71. I,799–800.
1689	One Pattani ship with 36 Chinese crewmen called; it had orginally been a Canton ship trading at Pattani in the previous year. In that year three other vessels from Amoy are said to have called at Pattani.	II,1120–22.
1690	Two Pattani ships called; one had a crew of 68 and had also stopped at Amoy reported that several hundred Chinese lived in Pattani. In that year three ships from Amoy, one from Chang-chou, and one from Canton, visited Pattani.	II,1269–70.
1693	One Pattani ship with a crew of 66 called.	II,1606–07.

Year	Particulars	Reference
1694	Two Pattani ships visited Nagasaki; one had called at Wen-chou to secure an additional cargo; the other, with a crew of 37, had also called at P'u-t'o-shan for additional goods.	II,1683–84, 1685–86.
1695	One Pattani ship called; it had set off from Canton to Japan with a crew of 65. In that year two Amoy ships visited Pattani.	II,1735.
1696	One Pattani ship with a crew of 40 Chinese called; it had originally been a Ningpo ship which had traded to Pattani in 1695. In that year five to six Chinese ships traded to Pattani.	II,1838–39.
1697	Two Pattani ships called; one, originally a Ningpo ship, had gone to trade at Java and Pattani, and eventually sold to Pattani merchants, who loaded it with local produce for Nagasaki, stopping at Ningpo en route; the other, with a crew of 41—the first one had a crew of 56—had formerly been an Amoy ship. In that year five Chinese ships visited Pattani.	II,1940, 1944–45.
1700	*Ka-i hentai* (III,2214) states that according to a Kao-chou ship report, one Pattani ship stopped at Canton in the fall of that year.	
1701	One Pattani ship called; it reported that it had to put in for repairs at Canton; the shipmaster also mentioned two Siamese ships at Namoa: one traded there and returned to Siam, while the other was heading for Japan.	III,2203–04.
1709	One Pattani ship called; it had a crew of 37, having been originally a Ningpo ship.	III,2639–40.

A Chronological List of Songkla Ships Reported as Trading to Nagasaki

Source: Hayashi Harunobu, Hayashi Nobuatsu, comps., Ura Ren'ichi, anno.,
Ka-i hentai (Tokyo, 1958).

Year	Particulars	Reference
1686	One Songkla ship called; it had stopped at Amoy.	I,646–47.
1689	In that year one Amoy ship traded to Songkla.	
1693	One Songkla ship called at Nagasaki; it had originally been an Amoy ship which had traded to Songkla in 1693; it had a crew of 70 Chinese.	II,1573–74.
1694	Two Songkla ships visited Nagasaki; one was with a crew of 46 Chinese; the other had stopped at P'u-t'o-shan en route, and had a crew of 104.	II,1647–48, 1687–88.
1695	One Songkla ship called; it had originally been a Ningpo ship; with a crew of 38, it had also picked up a cargo of silk at P'u-t'o-shan en route.	II,1751–52.
1696	One Songkla ship called; it had originally been a ship from Namoa; it had a crew of 46. In that year one Amoy ship visited Songkla.	II,1831–32.
1697	One Songkla ship called; it had originally been an Amoy ship going to trade at Songkla; with a crew of 73 and a cargo of Songkla produce, it had also stopped at Amoy en route to Nagasaki.	III,1942–43.

APPENDIX D

A Chronological List of Ligor Ships Reported as Trading to Nagasaki

Source: Hayashi Harunobu, Hayashi Nobuatsu, comps., Ura Ren'ichi, anno., *Ka-i hentai* (Tokyo, 1958).

Year	Particulars	Reference
1684	One Ligor ship called for a shipment of copper.	I,433–35.
1689	One Ligor ship called; it had a crew of 62 Chinese, having stopped at Amoy en route. In that year one Amoy ship reportedly traded at Ligor.	II,116–17.
1690	One Ligor ship traded to Nagasaki; with a crew of 65 and one Siamese, it had called at Amoy en route. In that year one Amoy and one Ningpo ship went to Ligor.	II,1260–61.
1691	One Ligor ship arrived; it had a crew of 61 Chinese, having called at Amoy en route; it further reported that 5 Siamese ships were on their way to Japan.	II,1359–60.
1692	One Ligor ship with 39 Chinese crewmen traded at Nagasaki.	II,1474–75.
1693	One Ligor ship with 41 Chinese crewmen arrived.	II,1595–96.
1694	One Ligor ship with 41 Chinese crewmen traded at Nagasaki.	II,1668–69.
1696	Two Ligor ships arrived; both had originally been Ningpo ships which had sailed to Ligor in the previous year; their crews were 42 and 37 Chinese respectively.	II,1820–21, 1839–40.
1697	Two Ligor ships arrived; both, originally Ningpo ships, had been sold at Ligor to the Chinese merchants there who in turn loaded them with local merchandise for sale to Nagasaki; one had a crew of 55 Chinese, and its shipmaster reported that 3 or 4 Chinese ships were at Ligor that year; the other had a Chinese crew of 47, and its shipmaster reported that there were 5 ships from China trading at Ligor.	II,1949–50, 1948–49.

Dispatches of Royal Ships Trading to Kwangtung in the Second Reign

1. Report (from Un-tiew, Chinese navigator of the *Gim yok sun* dated the first moon of 1813 to [the ship's patron, the Crown Prince]: "The *Gim yok sun** passed Pulo Condore [tip of Vietnam] in the eighth moon [1812], but due to unfavorable weather, did not reach the Canton area until the ninth moon ... We hired ten fishing boats to tow the junk to an anchorage at the mouth of the Canton river in order to wait for favorable winds [to sail up the river to Canton city]. After several days ... we proceeded up the river together with six other junks of the Krom [probably, Krom-ta sai]: the *Gim yok seng, Gim yong lee, Gim sun huat, Yee sun gim, Inraksa, Hoo-song.* (A seventh ship, the *Song-praratchasarn,* caught fire; the fishing boats rescued two persons, and the rest of the crew presumably drowned.) In the same season, four more Siamese ships traded to Shanghai: the *Buk-gim, Gim sun seng, Yee buk gim, Yee sun gim, Gim sui lum.* In addition, seven other junks went to Ningpo: the *Gim sun seng, Gim sun an, Tai-lee, Yee pun gim, Yee ong heen, Gim bun seng, Tai-hong.* Five more called at Kao-chou [Kwangtung]: the *Siang-lee, Chun-gim,* and three others whose names are not known to us ..."

Source: Chotmaihet 2, J. S. 1175 or A.D. 1813, no. 2.

2. Report (from) Chin Gui the shipmaster of the *Gim yok sun* to His Majesty the King: "The junk *Gim yok sun* arrived at the Canton area ... In the tenth moon, shop was opened [on board ship for the sale of cargo]. Pepper was sold for 3 taels [Siamese] a picul, buffalo hides for 3 taels, 2 *salung,* 1 *fuang,* tin for 10 taels, elephant's teeth 45 taels, rattan 1 tael, 3 *baht,* 1 *salung,* deer skin 4 taels, 1 *baht,* 1 *fuang,* split betel nuts 2 taels, 460 *bia* ... It is not yet certain how well the cargo will sell. But regarding the shipment of wood, nothing has yet been sold, though there is an offer of 2,200 Spanish dollars for the wooden anchors and ebony. The junk *Gim yok sun* can possibly return [to Siam] by the second moon [1813], but the definite decision of its ship-master is not yet known. [In addition to those vessels trading to Shanghai, Ningpo, and Kao-chou which have been referred to in no. 1, three more called at Tientsin] which are: the *Bun-jui* and two others whose names are not known. Entering Tangleng [Tung-ning] were Boonruang's vessel and two other junks ...

Source: Chotmaihet 2, J.S. 1175 or A.D. 1813, no. 3.

*Note the designation of "Gim" (Chin) of most of the ships.

3. Shipmaster Chin Eng-chiu of the *Gim bok seng* requested his navigator to report to Rama II that in the tenth moon, the ship arrived at the mouth of the Amoy river [*sic*]. Owing to big waves, the ship's cargo was transferred to another vessel and taken to Amoy. However, because of projected enormous expenses [including exorbitant fees demanded by the officials], the cargo was shipped back to Canton. As many ships were present at port and cargoes were selling at low prices, it was not until the twelfth moon before shop was opened. Pepper was sold at 3 taels, 1 *baht* a picul, sapan wood 1 tael, 3 *baht,* 3 *salung,* 1 *fuang,* red wood 1 tael, 1 *baht,* 3 *salung,* buffalo hides 2 taels, 3 *baht,* 2 *salung,* 480 *bia,* cardamun 2 *chang,* 7 *tamlung,* 1 *baht,* tin 9 *tamlung,* 2 *baht,* 3 *salung,* betel nuts 2 taels, 1 *salung,* 232 *bia.* The ivory, rattan, water baskets, and refined sugar have not yet been sold . . ."

Source: Chotmaihet 2, J.S. 1175 or A.D. 1813, no. 4.

APPENDIX F

Letters from the King's Adviser to the Ruler of Songkla Concerning the Outfitting of Junks to Trade to Amoy

1. Letter from the [King's Adviser] to the [Ruler] of Songkla: "[We are in receipt of your letter] brought in by Muen Sen that the junk that had been ordered to be outfitted for trade to Amoy returned ... in the sixth moon. [It also said] the shipmaster had sold the tin at 11 *tamlung,* 1 *baht* a picul, sapan wood at 1 *tamlung,* 1 *baht,* 1 *fuang*... red wood at 3 *baht,* 2 *salung,* [etc.], and that the money from the transaction would be forwarded as soon as the account had been settled. [You also mentioned] the [crew], who said the vessel was leaky, was unable to sell it at Amoy, and so it was proposed that it be dismantled and the metal salvaged. This matter has been presented to His Majesty who ordered that instead of having the ship dismantled at Songkla, as it could no longer be serviceable for trade to China, that necessary repairs [temporary] be made and the disabled junk brought up to Bangkok for possible sale to the Chinese there."

The letter was dated the seventh moon of J.S. 1182.

Source: Chotmaihet 2, J.S. 1182 or A.D. 1820, no. 5.

2. Letter from the [King's Adviser] to the [Ruler] of Songkla: "In reference to [your] letter brought in by Kun In-montien together with the proceeds from the sale of a cargo at Amoy—the sum of [about] 5,153 taels [£2,576.5]—and [some glassware and cloths, which were donated by the people at Songkla], the [matter] was duly reported to His Majesty and all the items checked and accounted for ... A sum [equivalent to a quantity of the white cloths donated] is being entrusted with Kun In-montien for the Praya Songkla [Ruler of Songkla] to distribute to those who had donated the article. Let not even one *fuang* of the money be left unpaid."

The letter was dated the ninth moon of 1820.

Source: Chotmaihet 2, J.S. 1182 or A.D. 1820, no. 5.3.

NOTES

Introduction

1. Wang Tse-tsai, *Tradition and Change in China's Management of Foreign Affairs* (Taipei, 1972), p. 13.

2. John K. Fairbank, "A Preliminary Framework," in ibid., ed., *The Chinese World Order* (Cambridge, Mass., 1968), p. 2.

3. Charles Gützlaff, *Journal of Three Voyages along the Coast of China in 1831, 1832, 1833, with Notices of Siam, Corea, and the Loo-choo Islands* (London, 1834), p. 78.

4. An administered system in trade is defined by Mark Mancall as having the following features: no competition, prices preset, specific trading locales where any supply-demand mechanism was absent, and so forth. See his "The Ch'ing Tributary System: An Interpretative Essay," in John K. Fairbank, ed., *The Chinese World Order*, pp. 79–81.

5. Wang Gung-wu, "Early Ming Relations with Southeast Asia: Background Essay," in John K. Fairbank, ed., *The Chinese World Order*, p. 58.

6. Professor Fairbank in *Trade and Diplomacy on the China Coast* (Cambridge, Mass., 1953), I, 36 says, "The migration of the Chinese into southeastern Asia, which has been one of the significant phenomena of the nineteenth and twentieth centuries, is merely the later phase of a Chinese commercial expansion which had begun much earlier."

7. T'ien Ju-k'ang, "Tsai lun shih-ch'i chih shih-chiu shih-chi chung-yeh Chung-kuo fan-ch'uan-yeh ti fa-chan," *Li-shih yen-chiu*, no. 12:4 (1957). Actually, T'ien's reference here is specifically for the maritime ban imposed by the Ming dynasty between 1567–1644; the statement is, however, equally if not more applicable to the Ch'ing case, which continued to witness contradictions on this stand.

I. The International Context of the Sino-Siamese Trade

1. A word about the etymology of the term "junk." One theory is that it is the English derivation from the Malay approximation (*jong*) of the

271

Amoy pronunciation of the Chinese word *ch'uan,* i.e. *joon.* See David
Steinberg, Alexander Woodside, et al., *In Search of Southeast Asia* (New
York, 1971), p. 52. Another theory, advanced by Professor Pao Tsun-
p'eng in *Cheng Ho hsia hsi-yang chih pao-ch'uan k'ao* (Taipei, 1961), p.
9 asserts that *jong* was originally a Javanese word, meaning a large ship.
He also contends that the relationship which some Western scholars have
postulated between the Ming term *tsung* and the Javenese *jong* is doubtful, as the Chinese word should more accurately be defined as "a fleet
of ships" and not one single vessel. (See ibid., pp. 10–11.) On the other
hand, it could just as easily have been straight derivation from the Amoy
rendition. The Siamese equivalents for "junk" are *tapao* and *sampao.*
Tapao, a relatively recent term, is probably derived from the Chinese
word *poh* (denoting an ocean-going vessel) and Siamese term *ta* which
denotes the pair of "eyes" painted on the junk's prow. As for *sampao,*
Hsieh Yu-yung, a Thailand Chinese scholar, thinks it originated and is
associated with the popular name of Cheng Ho, the Grand Eunuch of
Ming who visited Siam, which is Sam Po Kong (San Pao Kung).

2.   Yu Chung-hsun, *Kakyō keizai no kenkyū* (Tokyo, 1969), p. 96. Siam as
a state did not come into being until the founding of the Sukothai
dynasty in A.D. 1238. Commercial contacts between China and the
territory Ch'ih-t'u, to which the Siamese were eventually to migrate and
on which the state of Siam was founded, must have dated back to the
seventh century, however. In A.D. 607, the Sui-yang ti (r. A.D. 605–
616) of the Sui dynasty (A.D. 589–618) dispatched an imperial mission
to the region with a hope for material gain and possible political domination. This was supposedly the first Chinese official mission by sea to
that region of Southeast Asia, which in turn opened up trade. See Chang
T'ien-tse, *Sino-Portuguese Trade from 1514 to 1644* (Leiden, 1969), p. 7.

3.   For details concerning Chinese junk routes and places of call, see Hsiang
Ta, *Liang-tsung hai-tao chen-ching* (Peking, 1961).

4.   The term *hsi-yang* was adopted in the Ming period to designate the
Southeast Asian mainland and the Indian Ocean region. See Pao Tsun-
p'eng, p. 19n.

5.   In the early 1600s, Persian merchants already noted that Siam was in a
favorable position, close to Indian ports and situated on the sea routes
to China and Japan. See John O'Kane, *The Ship of Suleimān* (New York,
Columbia University Press, 1972).

6.   Larry Sternstein, "Krung Kao, The Old Capital of Ayutthaya," *JSS* 53.1:112 (1965).

7.   Ibid., pp. 112–113.

8.   Spain, another European commercial power in the Eastern Seas, concentrated its principal resources in the Luzon-New World trade. After the trans-Pacific route was opened up between Luzon and Mexico in the 1560s Spanish galleons shipped silver from the New World mines to be exchanged for Chinese silks at Luzon brought in by Chinese junks. There was hardly any commercial intercourse between the Siamese and Spaniards during the seventeenth century.

9.   From the start, direct West-East trade, that is, the direct transportation of goods from Europe to the East, was an unprofitable venture, as J. C. van Leur comments: "Western trade with Asia was always a one-sided movement of goods in the sense that costly merchandise was received in exchange for coin and certain metals in ingot. The handicrafts of the Asian civilizations never left any important place for the sale of European craft goods. And European factory products found no admittance in Asia before the advent of steam and chemical techniques was able to bring about the beginning of a mass production of consumers' goods in Western Europe and convert the basis of economic life from wood to iron, before the disintegration of the old, tradition-bound patterns of European life in class, town, and state was able to open up markets for mass sales to an amazingly fast-growing population." See J. C. van Leur, "A History of the Netherlands East Indies: Three Reviews," in his *Indonesian Trade and Society* (The Hague, 1955), p. 281.

10.   C. P. Fitzgerald, *A Concise History of East Asia* (New York, 1966), p. 254. It is alleged that King Naresuan (r. 1590–1605) encouraged the Dutch to establish commercial ties with Siam. His successor, Ekatatsarote, r. 1606–1611, sent a mission to Holland in 1609, the first ever by a Southeast Asian king to Europe. See ibid., p. 255.

11.   Through most of the seventeenth century, the British considered Siam an intermediate point on the way to Japan. For instance, in 1682, the British East India Company even sent a letter to Narai requesting his help in establishing trade with Japan. See John Anderson, *English Intercourse with Siam in the Seventeenth Century* (London, 1890), p. 191. Regarding trade to China, since the British were unable to trade there

directly until 1699, and then only at Canton, they continued to see the advantages of Siam.

12. This policy was openly admitted by the Dutch representative in Siam during the 1630s, Joost Schouten. He had been sent to Ayudhya earlier to settle differences with the Siamese court concerning high-handed Dutch methods, which resulted in the closing down of the Dutch factory at the Siamese capital in the 1620s. See Francois Caron and Joost Schouten, *A True Description of the Mighty Kingdoms of Japan and Siam* (London, 1935), p. lxxxvi.

13. Anderson, pp. 99–100.

14. Suebsaeng Promboon, "Sino-Siamese Tributary Relations, 1282–1853," Ph.D. dissertation, University of Wisconsin, 1971, p. 255. Before the outbreak of the Revolt of the Three Feudatories in 1676, the Dutch, both the Company and the free merchants ("burghers") based in Batavia, had hoped to trade with China at Kwangtung and Fukien. See John Wills, Jr., *Pepper, Guns, and Parleys* (Cambridge, Mass., 1974), pp. 151–153.

15. France seemed a logical choice since this country and Holland were antagonists in Europe.

16. Anderson, p. 382.

17. W. A. R. Wood, *A History of Siam* (Bangkok, 1959), pp. 217–218.

18. Sternstein, p. 119 n.

19. Wood, p. 221. It should also be remembered that in the eighteenth century, France began to turn its attention away from Southeast Asia to India, where it became embroiled in a long rivalry with Britain for supremacy over the Mughal empire. See Fitzgerald, p. 255.

20. Gunji Ki'ichi, *Jūhichi seiki ni okeru Ni-Shin kandei* (Tokyo, 1934), p. 167.

21. The Dutch had found in Siam a vital source of cheap rice for Batavia, as exemplified by their large importation between 1627 and 1646. See Caron and Schouten, p. 136 n.

22. W. Blankwaardt, "Notes upon the Relations between Holland and Siam," *JSS* 20.3:256–257 (1929).

23. Ibid., p. 27.

24. John F. Cady, *Southeast Asia: Its Historical Development* (New York, 1964), p. 279.

25. Japanese shipbuilders improved their ships based on Chinese, Korean, and Portuguese models. They averaged 270 tons. The most important impetus for the development of the "red-seal trade" (*shuinsen bōeki*) by the Japanese seems to be the severance of the Japan-Ming trade in the mid-sixteenth century (as a result of the Chinese retaliation against rampant Japanese piracy along the China coast). Japanese, desiring Chinese silks, had now to seek elsewhere for them, and Southeast Asian markets were chosen as alternatives because Chinese merchants frequented there. See Iwao Sei-ichi, *Shuinsen bōekishi no kenkyū* (Tokyo, 1958), pp. 24–25.

26. Charles D. Sheldon, *The Rise of the Merchant Class in Tokugawa Japan* (New York, 1958), p. 19.

27. Luzon, with 54 ships, was third in terms of frequency of visits. See Iwao Sei'ichi, *Shuinsen to Nihon machi* (Tokyo, 1962), pp. 35–38.

28. For an expanded list of imports and exports in the "red-seal trade" with Siam, see Iwao Sei'ichi, *Shuinsen bōekishi no kenkyū,* pp. 240–249. In 1626, there were about 1,500 Japanese residents at Ayudhya; they were merchants, former Christian samurai (*rōnin,* including the famed Yamada Nagamasa [Tenjiku Tokubei] who arrived in 1614), and other Christian converts.

29. E. M. Satow asserts, in "Notes on the Intercourse between Japan and Siam in the Seventeenth Century," *Transactions of the Asiatic Society of Japan* 13:143–144 (1885), that the first Siamese ship permitted to trade to Japan was in 1606 while the first Japanese vessel to trade to Siam was in 1612. We know, however, that Siamese ships had been visiting Japan longer before that, though they might not have been formally recognized; besides, "red-seal ships" had traded at Ayudhya before 1612, according to the Japanese records cited.

30. The Japanese bought about 150,000 deer hides annually in addition to tin, teak, sugar, and lead. See Sa-nga Kanjanakapun, *Prawat karnka kong pratet Thai* (Bangkok, 1943), p. 206.

31. Satow, p. 185.

32. Prasart Thong tried to resume commercial intercourse with Japan by
    sending direct requests to the Shogunate and soliciting the assistance of
    Japanese who had previously fled Siam. See Satow, p. 178. The good
    offices of the Dutch were also sought. See Iwao Sei'ichi, "Taijin no tai
    Nikkoku bōeki hukkatsu undō," *Tōa ronsō* 4:85 (1941). Prasart Thong's
    successor, Narai, also tried to mend fences with Japan because he wanted
    its silver and copper. He attempted to send a mission to Edo in 1656,
    but it was declined: this stopped official communications between the
    two countries completely. However, the prohibition against trade from
    Siam was afterward relaxed, inasmuch as Chinese residents in Siam were
    permitted to trade at Nagasaki as members of the Chinese factory. This
    of course started the *tōsen* trade from Siam. See Satow, p. 179.

33. According to Ishii Yoneo in "Seventeenth-Century Japanese Documents
    about Siam," *JSS* 59.2:165 (1971), the Japanese authorities classified
    foreigners in a "tripartite" fashion: there were the Chinese (*tōjin*)
    Catholic Europeans (Spaniards and Portuguese; *namban jin*), and
    Protestant Dutchmen (*komoi jin*). Trade was predicated on the basis
    of who actually handled it.

II. The Siamese Trading Structure

1. Caron and Schouten, p. 109.

2. Matsuo Hiroshi, *Shinra kokumin keizai no tokuchō* (Taipei, 1938), p.
   152. David Steinberg (p. 52) on the other hand says that roughly one
   fourth of the Ayudhya court revenues were profits derived in this manner.

3. Damrong Rajanubhab, "Ruang Anglit kao-ma kor-tum sanya krang
   Ratchakarn ti song" in the *Prachoom pongsawadan chabab hor smut
   haeng chart,* installment 55 (Bangkok, 1971), XIII, 178–180.

4. Damrong Rajanubhab, *Tamnan pasi-akorn bangyang kap kam atibai*
   (Bangkok, 1930), p. 7.

5. G. William Skinner, *Leadership and Power in the Chinese Community
   of Thailand* (Ithaca, New York, 1958), p. 3.

6. Steinberg et al., p. 52.

7. Kanjanakapun, p. 105.

8. It is apparent that the Krom-ta sai was already in charge of outfitting junks for foreign trade and had been since the reign of King Trailokanat, because it was responsible for assigning *sakdina* grades to the various people in the ship's management. (The use of "dignity marks," was the Siamese feudal way of determining the degree of nobility and official recognition, or simply, one's ranking in the society, by designating a theoretical number of units of farmland on which basis the individual's standing was determined; hence, the higher one's station, the larger the *sakdina* units). For instance, the shipmaster was customarily assigned the *sakdina* grade of 400 *rai* (about 150 acres). See Pongpun Supatrapun, "Karn-suksa tang prawatisart kiewdeui ruang praklang sin-ka," M.A. thesis, Chulalongkorn University, Bangkok, 1968, p. 14.

9. Kanjanakapun, p. 104.

10. Luang Vichitwatakarn, *Karn-muang karn-pokkrong kong Siam* (Bangkok, 1932), pp. 44–45. The traditional Siamese nobility consisted essentially of five ranks, somewhat similar to the Chinese feudal ranking of the Chou dynasty: *chaopraya* (equivalent to the Chinese rank of *kung*); *praya* (equivalent to the Chinese rank of *hou*); *pra* (equivalent to the Chinese rank of *po*); *kun* (equivalent to the Chinese rank of *tzu*); and *muen* (equivalent to the Chinese rank of *nan*). Heads of the two super ministries were accorded the ranking of *chaopraya*. See Supatrapun, pp. 39–40. The volume of the junk trade with China was the most direct cause in the assumption of the Treasury department of the jurisdiction over foreign trade. See Kanjanakapun, pp. 102–103.

11. Ch'en Ching-ho, "Shih-ch'i shih-chi Hsien-lo tui wai mao-i yu Hua-ch'iao," in Ling Shun-sheng, ed., *Chung-T'ai wen-hua lun chi* (Taipei, 1958), pp. 174–176.

12. Simon de la Loubère, *The Kingdom of Siam* (Kuala Lumpur, 1969), 1, 94–95.

13. Damrong Rajanubhab, *Tamnan pasi-akorn,* p. 6.

14. Kanjanakapun, p. 229.

15. Caron and Schouten, p. 136 n.

16. Captain Henry Burney, *The Burney Papers* (Bangkok, 1911), vol. 2, pt. 4, p. 97.

17.   Prayud Sittipun, *Racha samnak Thai* (Bangkok, 1962), pp. 291, 293.

18.   Supatrapun, p. 173.

19.   Damrong Rajanubhab, *Tesapiban* (Bangkok, 1960), p. 10.

20.   De la Loubère, I, 112.

21.   Sittipun, *Racha samnak Thai,* p. 157.

22.   Damrong Rajanubhab, *Tamnan pasi-akorn,* pp. 1–2.

23.   Luang Vichitwatakarn, pp. 39–40.

24.   In the beginning, the measurement fee was one *baht* (2s. 6d.) per *wa* (6 ft. 6 in.). In Narai's time, it was increased to two *baht.* See ibid., p. 3.

25.   Jacques and Philemon-Louis Savary des Bruslons, *The Universal Dictionary of Trade and Commerce,* tr. Malachy Postlethwayt (London, 1751), II, 709.

26.   Damrong Rajanubhab, *Tamnan pasi-akorn,* pp. 2–3. Although exempt from measurement fees, the Chinese were required to pay this. See Savary, *Universal Dictionary,* II, 709.

27.   H. G. Wales, *Ancient Siamese Government and Administration* (New York, 1965), pp. 208–209.

28.   George White said in 1678 that the import duty was 10 percent. (See Anderson, p. 427.) But the Savary brothers said the Chinese paid 8 percent (*Universal Dictionary,* II, 709).

29.   Hosea Morse, *The Chronicles of the East India Company Trading to China, 1635–1834* (Oxford, 1926), I, 58. Morse, says that in 1685, a British ship, the *Delight,* which visited Amoy for trade, faced such an experience. In Siam the practice was terminated with the Bowring Treaty in 1855.

30.   Praya Anumanratchaton, *Tamnan sulakakorn* (Bangkok, 1939), p. 32.

31.   William Milburn, *Oriental Commerce* (London, 1813), 441.

32. An alliance between officials in a position of power and wealthy alien merchants was a common phenomenon which could be found from Persia to Japan. The Japanese example was the alliance between Chinese merchants and the governor of Nagasaki in the importation of Chinese silks. J. C. van Leur considers this form of bureaucratic regime to be "quite remarkable and progressive."

III: Initial Period, 1652–1720: Chinese Restrictions on Trade

1. The order to remove coastal inhabitants of Fukien and Kwangtung inland was made effective between 1662 and 1681. See Arthur Hummel, ed., *Eminent Chinese of the Ch'ing Period* (Washington, D.C., 1943), p. 109. For details concerning the Ch'ing *hai-chin* measures, see, for instance, Yano Jin'ichi "Shina no kaikoku ni tsuite," *Shigaku no zasshi* 33.5:1–28 (1922), and Tanaka Katsumi, "Shinsho no Shina enkai–senkai o chusin to shite mitaru," *Rekishi gaku* 6.1–2:73–81, 83–94 (1936).

2. Fu Lo-shu, comp. and tr., *A Documentary Chronicle of Sino-Western Relations, 1644–1820* (Tucson, 1966), II, 533 n.

3. Liang T'ing-nan, *Hsien-lo kuo,* in ibid., *Yueh tao kung-kuo shuo* (Taipei, 1968), pp. 8–9. Despite the stipulation in the Ch'ing statutes, the formal recognition of the ruler of a tributary state, in the form of investiture (*ts'e feng*), does not seem to have been an absolute prerequisite for the tributary trade. In fact, the Manchu formal recognition of the Siamese monarch came only eight years after tribute presentation and trade from Siam was authorized. And during the period between the 1600s and 1780s Siam received investiture only twice—the second occasion in 1786. But in between, official missions and trade went on unimpeded.

4. P'eng Tse-i, "Ch'ing-tai Kuang-tung yang-hang chih-tu ti ch'i-yuan," *Li-shih yen-chiu,* no. 1:5 (1957).

5. Yano Jin'ichi, p. 13.

6. *MCSL, keng* (7th. part), VI, 515b. Li Kuang-t'ao, in "Hua-i yu Hsien-lo," *Min-chu p'ing-lun* 2.9:440 (1957) says the three tribute ships were designated *cheng-kung, fu-kung,* and *t'an-kung.* It is, nevertheless, the assertion here (which will be argued) that *t'an-kung* vessels were a separate category of ships not included in the formal three-ship suite.

7. It is not known if the Ch'ing government at this point followed the example of its Ming counterpart in issuing permits to authorized ships as a method of control. In the case of Siam, the Ming authorities devised permits with the character *hsien* and *lo* (the combination of which constitutes the Chinese name for Siam) written on them. The halves bearing the character *hsien* were deposited with the Pu-cheng ssu at Canton, while the other halves with the character of *lo* were given to the Siamese side. The two halves had to be matched before a particular Siamese ship could engage in trade at Canton.

8. Shang K'o-hsi memorialized Peking that he had turned down presents the Siamese mission brought for him, and recommended that such a practice be imperially prohibited, to which the emperor consented. See Liang T'ing-nan, pp. 43–44.

9. *KTTC* 173:37a.

10. In that year a Siamese mission had been dispatched to Peking.

11. *ISTSL* 25:22a.

12. For regulations pertaining to the tribute presentation by Siam which were instituted in the K'ang-hsi reign, see the section entitled "Hsien-lo-kuo yu-kung i-chu shih-li" (Details governing the rituals of tribute presentation by Siam) in *KTTC, chuan* 170, *ching-cheng lueh* 13.

13. In the case of Liu-ch'iu, the *chieh-kung* ships also performed another function, that of rotating linguists stationed at the Ryukyuan residence at Foochow, so that there was always one different linguist there every year. See Ch'en Ta-tuan, *Yung-Ch'ien-Chia shih-tai ti Chung-Liu kuan-hsi* (Taipei, 1956), pp. 18–19.

14. Yin Kuang-yen and Chang Ju-lin, *Ao-men chi lueh* (Taipei, 1968), p. 24a.

15. *YHKC* 8:46.

16. Ch'u Ta-chun, comp., *Kuang-tung hsin-yu* (1700), 15:326–333a; Tseng Chien-ping, *T'ai-kuo Hua-ch'ao ching-chi* (Taipei, 1956), p. 8.

17. *TCHTSL* 510:42a–b.

18. *Ta-Ch'ing hui-tien* (1818), 30:4b.

19. Yi Ki-hon, "Yonhaeng ilgi" in *Yonhaengnok sonjip* (Seoul, 1962), pp. 771–772. Sometimes up to four months were required each way; for instance, the mission in 1823. See Li Kuang-T'ao, "Ming-Ch'ing liang-tai yu Hsien-lo," in Ling Shun-sheng, et al., *Chung-T'ai wen-hua lun chi* (Taipei, 1958), p. 69.

20. Liang T'ing-nan, pp. 55–56. In 1752, the principle was to be reconfirmed by the Chinese court, along with another that goods on board the regular tribute ships would be exempt from duty assessment.

21. *Kuang-chou fu chih* (comp. Shen T'ing-fang in 1758; 60:34a), a gazetteer of the prefecture of Canton, states that the Ayudhya–Canton voyage took one month. The Savary brothers, quoted by Negishi Tadashi, *Chūgoku no girudo* (Tokyo, 1953), p. 224, said it took from thirty to forty days.

22. *KTTC* 170:35.

23. Liang T'ing-nan, pp. 61–62.

24. Wang Hsi-ch'i, *Hsiao-fang-hu-chai yu-ti ts'ung-ch'ao* (Shanghai, 1877–1897), pt. 10, p. 254 n. However, the Siamese managed to secure some restricted items on this mission. See Li Kuang-t'ao, "Pa Ch'ien-lung san-shih-i nien chi Hsien-lo kuo-wang ch'ih-yu," *LSYY* 39:228 (1969).

25. Li Kuang-t'ao, "Ming-Ch'ing liang-tai," p. 71.

26. Ch'en Ta-tuan, "Yung-Ch'ien-Chai shih-tai," p. 32.

27. Li Kuang-t'ao, "Hua-i yu Hsien-lo," p. 440.

28. If we take the Siamese ships trading to Japan in the early 1700s, their carrying capacity was over 15,000 piculs (about 1.9.m.lbs.) and the ballast of one ship could be as much as 10,000 piculs. However, it appears that these ships would be larger than those trading to Canton as a whole, as they had to traverse greater distances. Nevertheless, Li Kuang-t'ao (in an interview at the Academia Sinica, Nankang, Taiwan, on December 6, 1973), said that the Ch'ing authorities traditionally permitted each crew member aboard the Siamese tribute ships up to 100 piculs (13,333 lbs.) of cargo. This means that for each mission, one ship carrying the maximum of one hundred crewmen as allowable by regulation could possess a cargo of up to 10,000 piculs, and therefore a three-vessel suite on one

tribute mission could carry a cargo of 30,000 piculs (3.8m.lbs.) on one trip.

29. Chang Te-ch'ang, "Ch'ing-tai ya-p'ien chan-cheng ch'ien chih Chung-Hsi yen-hai t'ung-shang," *Ts'ing-hua hsueh-pao* 10.1:96–145 (January 1935).

30. *Ta-Ch'ing hui-tien* 30:10b. Gifts would be given to envoys on the various occasions that required the presentation of an official mission to China. (See *MCSL, chia* 1st. part, p. 678.)

31. From a discussion at the Chinese University of Hongkong, Dec. 3, 1973.

32. Yu Chung-hsun, p. 243.

33. Kularb Krisananon, *Mahamukamattayanukunwong* (Bangkok, 1905), sec. 2, p. 182.

34. Anderson, p. 426.

35. On the other hand, the Manchus did not permit the Siamese to conduct tributary trade, just to conform to past practices; they were to a certain extent also counting on possible aid from the Siamese. According to Iwao Seiichi, the Ch'ing government could rely on the Siamese ships to carry such articles as foodstuffs for its war effort against the existing anti-Manchu forces; it also hoped to regulate or restrict the clandestine Siamese trade with the Cheng forces on Formosa.

36. P'eng Tse-i, p. 3.

37. One other important accomplishment by Narai was to get the Ch'ing court to declare a tax exemption on tribute-bearing-related ships of the *t'an kung* and *chieh kung* categories in 1685. It is also interesting to note that official leniency came after conditions along Southeast China had improved, and the authorities' fear of abuses had been allayed.

38. Canton historically had a Shih-po t'i-chu ssu (Maritime trade superin-tendency) in charge of foreign trade and taxation. The office was dis-continued in Ch'ing times, and in the beginning of the new dynasty, maritime trade duties were entrusted to the Yen-k'e t'i-chu ssu (Salt superintendency) until 1662. This perhaps accounts for the fact that richest merchants at Canton then were salt merchants. See Wada Sei, ed., *Shindai no Ajia,* vol. of *Tōyō bunkashi taikei,* Konuna Katsue, ed., (Tokyo, 1938–1939), p. 326.

39. P'eng Tse-i, p. 8. Shen Shang-ta was worth close to a million taels (over £325,000) in 1681 when his property was confiscated by the Ch'ing court.

40. Anderson, p. 426.

41. Liang Chia-pin, *Kuang-tung shih-san-hang k'ao* (Taipei, 1960), p. 51.

42. Laurence Thompson, "The Junk Passage Across the Taiwan Strait: Two Early Chinese Accounts," *HJAS* 18:170 (1968).

43. As a matter of fact, Amoy's hinterland prefectures were themselves not raw materials producing districts, and did not produce enough food to sustain the swelling population there. Nevertheless, Chang-chou did export such items as threads, cloths, tobacco, porcelain, umbrellas, and sweetmeats, while Ch'üan-chou produced paper, porcelain, and the like. See Huang Shu-ching, *T'ai-hai shih-ch'a lu* (Taipei, 1957), pp. 47–48. Amoy's economic foundation had always been precarious, though it had the special property of being the international port for South Fukien. Because of food conditions in the area, Amoy existed on the basis that it served as the departure point for those engaging in foreign trade and for those emigrating overseas, which in turn stimulated a flow of money in the form of profits from trade and remittances by emigrants to their relatives into an area that was otherwise rather poor. Prior to the founding of Amoy as an important trading center, Ch'üan-chou city, or Marco Polo's Zayton, was one of the most important ports of the world in the eleventh and twelfth centuries. In the Ming period, foreign trade at Ch'üan-chou was transferred to Chang-chou prefecture's Lung-ch'i district whose significance may be gauged from the fact that the compass routes (*chen-lu*) for both the "eastern ocean" and "western ocean" commenced here. See Negishi Tadashi *Gokō no kenkyū* (Tokyo, 1943), pp. 241–242. It remained a relatively important port for foreign trade even after the establishment of Amoy in 1684. For one thing, it was necessary to the existence of rich merchants engaged in trade with Southeast Asia. See Su Ch'ing-huai "Fu-ch'ien ts'ang-sang shih-hua" in *T'ai-kuo Fu-chien hui-kuan ch'eng-li wu-shih chou-nien shin-chih luo-ch'eng chi-nien t'e-k'an* (Bangkok, 1961), p. 97.

44. Frederic Wakeman, "The Canton Trade and the Opium War," a draft of chapter 4 in John K. Fairbank, ed., *The Cambridge History of China*, vol. 10, scheduled for publication in 1977 by the Cambridge University Press. Most of the residents of Chang-chou prefecture's An-p'ing district depended on foreign trade for a living. Wakeman says some families there,

the Ch'en, Yang, and Huang, produced shipwrights, sailors, maritime mercenaries, and merchants, generation after generation. See also Su Ch'ing-huai, p. 97.

45. Ch'en Ching-ho, "Shih-ch'i shih-chi chih Hsien-lo," p. 154. By the beginning of the eighteenth century, Chang-chou city, a flourishing trading center, was still carrying on an active trade with Siam. See Nishikawa Tadahide, *Ka-i tsūshō ko* (Tokyo, 1928), p. 300.

46. Hummel, p. 111.

47. Fu Lo-shu, p. 49.

48. Wang Chih-ch'un, *Kuo-ch'ao jou-yuan chi* (1895), 2:14a–b.

49. *FCTC* 87:1744.

50. George Hughes, *Amoy and the Surrounding Districts* (Hong Kong, 1872), pp. 111–112.

51. Tanaka Katsumi, p. 92.

52. Ts'ao Yung-ho, "Cheng Ch'eng-kung chih t'ung-shang mao-i" in *Cheng Ch'eng-kung fu T'ai san-pai chou-nien tsuan-chi* (Taipei, 1962), pp. 78–79.

53. Hummel, p. 111; Promboon, p. 253.

54. Kanjanakapun, p. 263.

55. Hsu Yun-ch'iao, "Chung-Hsien t'ung-shih k'ao," *Nan-yang hsueh-pao* 3:29 (September 1946); Cady, p. 178.

56. Hayakawa Jun'saburō, *Tsūkō ichiran* (Tokyo, 1912), pp. 167–527; *Ka-i hentai,* comp. Hayashi Harunobu, Hayashi Nobuatsu, anno. Ura Ren'ichi, Tōyō-bunko sō-kan, no. 15. (Tokyo, 1958), III, 2461.

57. Jacques and Philemon-Louis Savary des Bruslons, "Shinsho Kanton [Kōtō] bōeki kansuru ichi shiryō," tr. Miyazaki Ichisada, in *Tōa keizai kenkyū* 25.6:53 (1941).

58. W. A. Graham, *Siam* (London, 1924), 11, 95.

59. *Ka-i hentai,* 111, 2163; *Ibid., hoi,* p. 22.

60. Kanjanakapun, pp. 270–271.

61. See *SICTHL,* 18:25a–b. Actually the question of *hai-chin* was viewed differently among officials in Southeast China. For example, in Fukien, there were many at Foochow and Hsing-hua district who saw wisdom in the continued stoppage of overseas trade and travel, while at Chang-chou and Ch'uan the majority advocated its immediate repeal. See T'ien Ju-k'ang "Shih-wu chih shih-pa shih-chi Chung-kuo hai-wai mao-i fa-chan huan-man ti yuan-yin" *Hsin chien-she,* nos. 188–189:88 (1964).

62. Chang Te-ch'ang, "The Economic Role of the Imperial Household," *Journal of Asian Studies* 31.2:256 (February 1972).

63. Morse, I, 104.

64. The king's or emperor's merchants obviously referred to the mandarin merchant under the hoppo who received an imperial appointment.

65. Ibid., 1, 88, 100; Liang Chia-pin, pp. 28–29; Morse, I, 104; Wada Sei, p. 326.

66. Hirase Minokichi, *Kindai Shina keizai shi* (Tokyo, 1942), pp. 107–108.

67. See *YHKC* 17:9b; Wada Sei, p. 326.

68. Hummel, p. 777; *Ka-i hentai,* II, 1918, Sasamoto Shigemi, "Kanton no tetsunabe ni tsuite," *Tōyōshi kenkyū* 12.25:44 (1952).

69. Ibid., pp. 45, 35–36. Chinese iron pans were used primarily for cooking while other types of metal utensils played an important role in the opening up of land and for general construction work, and hence contributed directly to the course of Chinese immigration to Southeast Asia up to the nineteenth century. Such tools were manufactured exclusively at Fatshan, in the Namoi (Nan-hai) district near Canton city, since at least the Ming dynasty—though at Fukien there were in existence iron pan guilds, it is not known if they were involved in the actual manufacture, and if so, to what extent. In the early part of the Ch'ing dynasty, iron tools were commonly exported to Hainan Island, Manila, Japan, Indo-China, and Siam. Since they were heavy items, they were carried aboard as ballast or "bottom cargo" (see ibid., pp. 45, 45 n., 48). The bulk of iron tools were usually sold at very reasonable prices at Canton.

70. Savary des Bruslons, "Shinsho Kanton bōeki," p. 44.

71. Ibid., pp. 49–50, 51, 53. By the early part of the nineteenth century, the manufacture of iron pans and other tools became an established industry at Bangkok, a skill introduced and practiced solely by Chinese immigrants.

72. Ch'en Ching-ho, "Shih-ch'i shih-chi Hsien-lo," p. 177.

73. Three years prior to the formal abolition of the maritime ban in 1684, ships of 500 piculs (66,650 lbs.) burden from Chihli, Shantung, and Kiangsi were permitted to engage in coastal trading. See Tanaka Katsumi, p. 83.

74. *HMC(TWH)*, p. 194. According to George Hughes (pp. 104–105), the site of Amoy was chosen in spite of its lack of a firm economic base because "during the troublous times that were just finished (i.e. before 1683), the alluvial deposits brought down by the river Lung, had so shoaled its bed as to render its navigation by vessels of such a size, as had previously frequented it, impossible. Amoy, situated just at the mouth of the river, and possessing an admirable harbor accommodation was, notwithstanding its political insignificance, its paucity, in fact, almost absolute want of commercial intercourse, the spot fixed upon, and a customs house was opened there the same year."

75. Ibid., p. 106.

76. *HMC,* 5:27b.

77. Kato Shigeru, "Shindai Hukken Kōso no senko ni tsuite" *Shirin* 14.4:55–56 (1929).

78. J. C. van Leur ("The World of Southeast Asia: 1500–1650," in his *Indonesian Trade and Society,* p. 230) distinguishes between commenda and modern capitalistic partnership in the following way, "Commenda, with its separation of financiers and executors, gave a shipping enterprise the appearance of being a modern limited company. But that is of necessity quite out of the question in a situation where there was no continuous turnover of capital, no account of the return on sums invested, no account of profits from the capital account contemplated or set up . . . There was merely a balance made of the equipment and voyage accounts, and the remainder was paid out."

79. Su Ch'ing-huai, p. 97.

80. Hayakawa Junsaburō, 296:18.

81. Wang Hsiao-t'ung, *Chung-kuo shang-yeh shih* (Taipei, 1965), p. 191.

82. *Ka-i hentai,* I, 633; III, 2497.

83. Jacques and Philemon-Louis Savary des Bruslons, *The Universal Dictionary of Trade and Commerce,* tr. Malachy Postlethwayt, London, John and Paul Knapton, 1751, I, 492.

84. *FCTC* 270:5129.

85. Fu Lo-shu, I, 122.

86. *FCTC* 270:5129.

87. Lo Erh-kang "T'ai-p'ing t'ien-kuo ke-ming ch'ien ti jen-kou ya-po wen-t'i," *Chung-kuo she-hui ching-chi shih chi-k'an* 81:58 (1949). In 1712 K'ang-hsi had decreed that those Chinese who had gone abroad for long could legally return. As a result of the formal proclamation to that effect in 1716, three thousand or so returned. See Wang Ch'ing-yun comp., *Shih-ch'u yu chih* (1890), 15b.

88. T'ien Ju-k'ang, *Shih-ch'i shih-chiu shih-chi chung-yeh Chung-kuo fan-ch'uan tsai tung-nan Ya-chou* (Shanghai, 1957), p. 16, argues that the selling of such ships was not based on truth but rather on the apprehension of Hung Hua, the shipyard official who reported the matter to the emperor. Iron wood, for one thing, was abundant in Southeast Asia. The author says at this time the Chinese government built some ten junks which cost several "tens of thousands in gold."

89. Lu K'un and Ch'en Hung-ch'ih et al., comps., *Kuang-tung hai-fang hui-lan* (circa 1836) 35:13b. Later on in 1768, another provision was added meting out the penalty of one hundred strikes with the heavy bamboo and three months in the cangue for those who rented their junks to foreigners. See ibid., 35:14a.

90. Wang Chih-ch'un, 4:5a. However, in 1718, K'ang-hsi approved the petition from the viceroy of Liang-Kuang that Chinese vessels be permitted to trade to Annam, though it was technically part of Southeast

Asia. This was essentially to allow Chinese to continue obtaining copper there. See *ISTSL* 277:28b.

91. Yano Jin'ichi, p. 11. As almost all the trade with Southeast Asia was conducted from these three provinces, the ban was not applicable to the other coastal provinces, which in essence meant that the trade in the "eastern ocean" was still open. See *TCHTSL* 510:43a.

92. This recommendation was made by Ch'en An, commander of the military garrison at Chieh-chih (Kwangtung) and father of Ch'en Lung-ch'iung, author of *Hai-kuo wen-chien lu*. Ch'en An had been assigned to investigate remnants of the Cheng forces which had fled to Southeast Asia after the Formosa conquest. See ibid., 14b–15a.

93. Namoa, located near Ch'ao-chou and Chang-chou prefectures, received influences from both. Its strategic importance in commerce may be seen in the fact that in the past commercial intelligence could be gathered here from foreign ships by Chinese officials. Such vessels, proceeding north or south, were apt to call at the island en route. See *Nan-ao chih* 12:6 (1783), comp. Wu-yuan-chi-chung.

94. Wang Ch'ing-yun, 14a–b.

95. Yin Kuang-yen and Chang Ju-lin, p. 16a; Wang Ch'ing-yun, 14b; Mancall, p. 88.

96. Chang Te-ch'ang, "Ch'ing-tai yu-p'ien," p. 115.

IV. The Sino-Siamese-Japanese Triangular Trade

1. See also *Nagasakishi shi,* ed. Nagasakishi (Nagasaki, 1938), p. 1.

2. Ch'en Ching-ho, "Ch'ing-chu Hua-po chih Ch'ang-ch'i mao-i chi Jih-nan hang-yun," *Nan-yang hsueh-pao* 13.1:6 (June 1957).

3. Satow, p. 181.

4. Ishii Yoneo, p. 165.

5. Iwao Sei'ichi, *Taijin,* p. 119.

6.   Ch'en Ching-ho, "Ch'ing-ch'u Hua-po," pp. 179–180. As a point of comparison, between 1684 and 1685, at least two hundred junks visited Nagasaki, each with not less than fifty crewmen on board. See Savary des Bruslons, *Universal Dictionary,* II, 493.

7.   Ishii Yoneo, p. 173.

8.   *Nagasakishi shi,* p. 493.

9.   Copper mines in Japan, notably those at Sado, were the property of the Shogunate. Copper was sent to Osaka for eventual redistribution and export. See M. Paske-Smith, *Western Barbarians in Japan and Formosa in Tokugawa Days, 1603–1868* (Kobe, 1930), p. 198.

10. Ch'en Ching-ho, "Ch'ing-ch'u Hua-po," p. 4.

11. Miki Sakae, *Ni-Shin kōtsū shi* (Tokyo, 1934), p. 339.

12. Ishii Yoneo, p. 164.

13. Ch'en Ching-ho, "Ch'ing-ch'u Hua-po," pp. 9–10, 11–12. As Ch'en explains it, the Japanese authorities regarded these junks on the basis of their starting points, and not necessarily their real nationality. Hence, Chinese ships from China proper which sailed to Lower Siam and later headed for Japan with a Siamese cargo would normally be classified as being from Siam.

14. Ishii Yoneo, p. 166. The Toyo Bunko edition of *Ka-i hentai* (three bound volumes and one supplement) contains 1,465 reports of which 63 were from Siamese ships, and 18, 11, and 7 from Pattani, Ligor, and Songkla ships respectively. The time span covered is from 1644 to 1724. The *Ka-i hentai* is actually grouped under the larger collection of reports of Chinese ships entitled *Tōsen fusetsu sho* (Reports from the Chinese ships).

15. Before 1684, Siamese ships bound for Japan also called at Tung-ning on Formosa to trade with the Cheng forces. See *Ka-i hentai,* I, 307–308.

16. Miki Sakae, p. 340.

17. Ibid.

18. One exception was made, however. The Ch'ing authorized "experienced" Chinese at Foochow to serve as crew and attendants for each Ryukyuan investiture mission en route back to Liu-ch'iu from Peking. See John K. Fairbank, ed., *The Chinese World Order,* pp. 140–141.

19. On the other hand, as shall be noted, starting in the 1720s China had an increasing need for Siamese rice, which led the Yung-cheng Emperor (1723–1735) to declare that the practice of having Chinese manage Siamese ships was permissible. The justification used was ostensibly that such persons were long-time residents of Siam, and it was fitting to offer them a gesture of imperial magnanimity. This pronouncement came despite the 1717 ban designed to prevent Chinese trade to Southeast Asia.

20. Besides hides, Lower Siam offered the following articles which fetched good prices at Japanese and Chinese markets: pepper, tin, honey, birds' nests, dried shrimp, buffalo horn, and wax. See Nishikawa Tadahide, p. 331.

21. Sternstein, p. 113. Pattani had been a tributary of Siam since the thirteenth century; it concurrently sent tribute to China, for instance in 1634. See Hsu Yun-ch'iao, *Pei ta-nien shih* (Singapore, 1946), pp. 8–10. It was therefore classified by the Chinese authorities as a "li Hsien-lo chu-kung kuo" (supplementary tributary attached to Siam). See Ch'u Ta-chun, 15:32b–33a.

22. Li Chang-fu, *Chung-kuo chih-min shih* (Shanghai, 1937), p. 142.

23. Anderson, p. 53.

24. Kanazawa Kanemitsu, *Wa-Kan sen'yo shu* in Saigusa Hiroto, ed., *Nihon kagaku ko-ten zensho* (Tokyo, 1943), XII, 200.

25. Nishikawa Tadahide, p. 331.

26. See, for instance, the report given by the Pattani ship in 1699, in *Ka-i hentai,* III, 1944.

27. Ch'en Ching-ho in "Ch'ing-ch'u Hua-po," pp. 9–10, says that between 1648 and 1700 the number of Pattani ships calling at Nagasaki totaled 48.

28. Wei Yuan, *Hai-kuo t'u-chih* (1876), 6:5a. The best quality dried shrimp could be secured here.

29.   Anderson, p. 242. In 1680, King Narai, to undercut the Dutch influence in Lower Siam, even offered Songkla to the French as a base.

30.   See an instance in 1697, in *Ka-i hentai*, III, 1881.

31.   Ligor, as the most important religious and political center in Lower Siam historically, had a long history of trade with neighboring areas and China. Junks from China visited it as early as the T'ang dynasty (A.D. 615–905). At the time of Marco Polo's visit it was already a noted maritime port in the Eastern Seas. See Sawad Rattanasevi, "Prawatisart muang Nakorn Si Thammarat," in ibid., *Taman Pra Boromtat* (Nakorn Si Thammarat, 1973), pp. 1–2. One significant historical fact of Ligor's relations with Japan was that the famed Japanese mercenary, Yamada Nagamasa, who served the Siamese court in the 1620s was briefly made ruler of Ligor, which at that time had a Dutch settlement engaged primarily in trade to Japan. One could therefore notice the close relationship maintained between the Japanese and Dutch, which was undoubtedly one major factor accounting for the commercial well being of Ligor itself. See ibid., pp. 15–16.

32.   Hayakawa Jun'saburo 167:527.

33.   Nishikawa Tadahide, p. 331.

34.   *Ka-i hentai*, II, 1596.

35.   As was also the case with Pattani and Songkla ships, reports on activities of the Ligor ships were disclosed by the Chinese mariners managing them—when they could do so without getting themselves into any legal difficulty. Prior to 1684, their movements, considered clandestine by the Chinese authorities, would certainly have had to be kept secret.

36.   Negishi Tadashi, *Gōkō no kenkyū*, p. 492.

37.   Ch'en Ching-ho, "Ch'ing-ch'u Hua-po," p. 4, shows an upsurge of Chinese ships trading to Nagasaki: 73 in 1685, 84 in 1686, 115 in 1687, and 177 in 1688.

38.   Satow, p. 179.

39.   Ch'en Ching-ho, "Ch'ing-ch'u Hua-po," p. 4.

40.   John Hall, "Notes on the Early Ch'ing Copper Trade with Japan," *Harvard Journal of Asiatic Studies* 12.3–4, 445–461 (December 1949).

41. Allotments for the other Chinese ships were: 7 for Nanking, 1 for P'u-
    t'o-shan, 4 for Ningpo, with 200 *kan* each; 1 each for Nanking, and
    Batavia, with 300 *kan* each; 2 for Amoy, 4 for Formosa, with 130 *kan*
    each; 2 for Canton, with 125 *kan* each; and 1 each for Wen-chou,
    Foochow, Chang-chou, Tongkin, Cambodia, with 200 *kan* each. See
    Nagasakishi shi, pp. 338–340. Records on the Siamese ships in the *Ka-i
    hentai* cease after 1723. Thereafter the triangular trade became sporadic;
    Siamese ships traded to Nagasaki only in 1745, 1751, 1752, 1753, 1756,
    1758, 1759, 1760, and 1763. It is also apparent that the Japanese authori-
    ties had ceased to place a value on information-gathering from foreign
    vessels at Nagasaki.

42. Miki Sakae, p. 376.

43. Yamawaki Teijirō, *Nagasaki no Tōjin bōeki* (Tokyo, 1964), p. 165. By
    1732, only 29 ships were allowed and the number went down to 25 by
    1736. After 1790, only 10 Chinese ships a year were permitted, with
    an export value of less than 3,000 *kan* (2 m. lbs.). Fortunately for China,
    copper production within China rose dramatically after the first quarter
    of the eighteenth century, thus making it less dependent on Japanese
    copper.

44. Ch'en Chao-nan, *Yung-cheng Ch'ien-lung nien-chien ti yin-ch'ien pi-chia
    pien-tung* (Taipei, 1966), p. 42.

45. Savary des Bruslons, "Shinso Kanton bōeki," p. 56.

46. *MCSL, chi* (6th. part), VII, 626b–627b.

V. The Abrogation of the Second Maritime Ban

1. For instance, Fukien Governor Mao Wen-ch'uan memorialized in 1726
   that local merchants smuggled lead and tin from Siam into the province,
   using Macao as a reloading zone where smaller vessels were employed to
   transport the article into Ch'üan-chou prefecture. See *WHTP,* pp. 325–
   326.

2. Hughes, p. 106.

3. Ch'ing-shih kuan, ed., *Ch'ing-shih lieh-chuan* (Shanghai, 1928), p. 106.

4. The construction of junks alone required a sizable capital, with large vessels costing as much as 10,000 taels (£3,333) each. See *FCTC* 230:4191.

5. Besides jobs directly related to the junk business, Kao must have thought of those to be stimulated by it, such as the tea and sugar industries of interior Fukien.

6. Fu Lo-shu, 1, 157.

7. Hughes, p. 106.

8. *WHTP*, pp. 327–328.

9. *FCTCCSL* 14:22a; *STSL* 81:20b–21a; *MCSL, keng* (7th. part), 504a–b.

10. This viceroy, Na-su-t'u, also memorialized that in considering action against the Dutch as a result of their mistreatment of the Chinese in the East Indies, the court should ban trade with Batavia only, and not include all of Southeast Asia because of the existing intimate trade relationships. See *STSL,* 176:6a–b.

11. Wu Lien-hsun, comp., *Chang-chou fu chih* (Taipei, 1964) 33:64a–65a.

12. *Ka-i hentai,* III, 2988. For instance, one of the Chinese junks trading to Nagasaki in 1723 reported that rice was abundant in Siam in the previous year when it visited there.

13. Wang Ch'ing-yun, 6:12b.

14. *YCCP,* "Kao Ch'i-cho" 3, 126b–127a; *YCCP,* "Mao Wen-ch'uan" 5, 56b.

15. Lan Ting-yuan, *Lun Nan-yang shih-i shu* in his *Lu-chou ch'u-chi* (1732), 4b–5a.

16. Yeh Shao-shun, "Wuo-kuo i-min pei-ching chih t'an-t'ao" *Nan-yang yen-chiu* 6.5:21 (1936); Fukuda Shozo, *Kakyō keizai ron* (Tokyo, 1942), p. 14; Feng Liu-t'ang, *Shina shōku-ryō seisaku shi,* tr. Mori Gi'ichi (Tokyo, 1941), p. 252.

17. Dwight Perkins, Wang Yeh-chien et al., *Agricultural Development in*

China, 1368–1968 (Chicago, 1969), p. 144. The other grain-deficient spot was the Peking-Tientsin area.

18.   Louis Dermigny, *Le Commerce à Canton au XVIIIe siècle* (Paris, 1964), pp. 66–67.

19.   Lo Erh-kang, pp. 44–45.

20.   Narita Setsuo "Taikoku kakyō to kome," *Tōa-ronsō* 4:313 (1941).

21.   Abe Takeo, "Beboku jukyū no kenkyū: *Yōsei shi* no ishō to shite mita," *Tōyōshi kenkyū* 15.4:163 (1957); Nishikawa Tadahide, p. 299; Ch'üan Han-sheng and Wang Yeh-chien, "Ch'ing Yung-cheng nien chien mi-chia," *LSYY* 30a:181 (1959). Considering the level of technology and conditions at the time, 1.4 acres were below subsistence level. The national average then was 27.1 *mou* or 4.1 acres; *HMC(TWH)* p. 185; Takazaki Misako, "Jūhachi seiki ni okeru Shin-Tai kōshō shi," *Ochanomizu shigaku* 10:32 n. (1967).

22.   Abe Takeo, p. 173. As an illustration, between 1723 and 1735, prices of rice at Foochow ranged from 0.90 to 2 taels per picul (or about 6 to 14 shillings per 133.3 lbs.); those at Formosa were generally two maces lower and those at Chang-chou and Chüan-chou two mace to a tael (1.4–7 shillings) higher. This reflects the overall condition of rice supplies as they existed in Fukien at the time as well as later. Prices at the city of Amoy ranged from 1.4 to 2.3 taels per picul (about 10 to 16s. per 133.3 lbs.). See *YCCP,* "Kao Ch'i-cho" 3, 63a. By 1976, one picul of rice at Chang-chou cost from 2.8 to 3.3 taels (see Wu Lien-hsun 47:43b).

23.   Perkins, p. 163.

24.   23.7 *mou* or 3.6 acres (as compared to Fukien's 1.4 acres), though still below the national average of 4.1 acres. (cf. note 27). The population of Kwangtung in the early 1700s was at least 2.2 million, and by the 1720s it was around 2.5 million. See Ch'uan Han-sheng and Wang Yeh-chien, pp. 179–181.

25.   Abe Takeo, pp. 165, 162, 191.

26.   Ch'uan Han-sheng and Wang Yeh-chien, pp. 160, 164–165. The rice price at Ch'iung-chou prefecture around this time was about a tael a picul on the average.

27. Captain Alexander Hamilton, *A New Account of the East Indies* (London, 1744, II, 238. According to Hamilton, this rice was usually sold by the government locally at 5 mace (3.4s) a picul in accordance with the official control system, rather than actually being transported to Peking or elsewhere.

28. Perkins, p. 164. By diverting the tributary grain as classified, the government hoped to alleviate the rice problem within the province.

29. For instance, Shao-hsing had always been a rice-deficient area, dating back at least to 1710. See Wang Chih-ch'un, *Kuo-ch'ao t'ung-shang shih-mo* (1895), p. 4b.

30. Feng Liu-t'ang, *Chung-kuo li-tai min-shih cheng-ts'e* (Taipei, 1970), p. 233; *Ka-i hentai,* III, 2942, 2988, 2985, 2983, 2931, passim; *HMC (TWH),* p. 476.

31. Abe Takeo, p. 168.

32. Perkins, p. 164.

33. See Ch'uan Han-sheng and Wang Yeh-chien, p. 184; Ch'uan Han-sheng, "Ch'ing-ch'ao chung-yeh Su-chou ti mi-liang mao-i," *LSYY* 39b:74–75 (1969); Ch'uan Han-sheng, "Ch'ien-lung shih-san nien ti mi-kuei wen-t'i," in his *Chung-kuo ching-chi shih lun-ts'ung* (Hong Kong, 1972), II, 554–555; *YCCP,* "Mao Wen-ch'uan" 2.3:39.

34. *P'ing-tiao* was the traditional method of relief in times of adverse productivity on a so-called save-seven, sell-three principle, that is, the government undertook to sell 30 percent of the stock of rice it had on hand. Later on in the Ch'ien-lung period, up to 50 percent was allowed to be sold. This method mainly benefited urban dwellers because granaries were erected in populated administrative centers. As it turned out the system was vulnerable to abuse with merchants and officials in charge colluding.

35. *FCTC* 32 n.

36. Wang Shih-ch'ing, "Ch'ing-tai T'ai-wan ti mi-ts'an yü wai-hsiao, *T'ai-wan wen-hsien* 9.1:18, 26 (1958); Abe Takeo, p. 172; *HMC(TWH),* p. 27; see Wang Shih-ch'ing, p. 20; *HMC(TWH),* p. 27.

37. Feng Liu-t'ang, *Chung-kuo li-tai min-shih,* p. 234.

38. Perkins, pp. 148, 164; *YCCP,* "Mao Wen-ch'üan" 2, p. 39a; Abe Takeo, p. 194; *YCCP* "Yang Erh-te," p. 4b.

39. Perkins, p. 141.

40. Abe Takeo, pp. 164–165, 192, 172.

41. *YCCP,* "Huang Kuo-ts'ai" 2, 18a–28b, passim.

42. Feng Liu-t'ang, *Chung-kuo li-tai min-shih,* p. 233.

43. *Ka-i hentai,* III, 1887, 1892.

44. Cited in Fukuda Shōzō, p. 17 n.

45. Lan Ting-yuan, pp. 4a–5b. By the 1720s at least there was a rice dealers' guild among the Chinese in the Philippines. See Edgar Wickberg, "Early Chinese Economic Influence in the Philippines, 1850–1898," *Pacific Affairs* 35.3:282 (1962).

46. Ships from the various Chinese ports calling at Nagasaki that year all reported the high prices of rice in China. See *Ka-i hentai,* III, 2931, 2933 ff.

47. Wang Chih-ch'un, 2:14a.

48. Cited in James Ingram, *Economic Change in Thailand Since 1850* (Stanford, 1955), p. 23. As a rule, rice could only be exported from Siam after approval by the court, since the grain was the country's staple diet. See Sa-nga Kanjanakapun, p. 230.

49. Ishii Yoneo, p. 170.

50. Nishikawa Tadahide, pp. 332–333. According to the author, the rice shipped from Siam to Japan was polished rice.

51. *ISTSL,* quoted in Takazaki Misako, p. 19. Paddy, from the Malay word padi, applies to rice in husk. It is also known as "cargo rice," or *khao pluek* in Siamese. According to nineteenth-century estimates, a picul of paddy was equal to about 0.7 picul (93.1 lbs.) of polished rice. If this was also applicable to the 1722 case, then a picul of Siamese polished rice at that time would be 2.85 to 4.25 mace (1.2–2.9s.), and with the

cost of transportation added, one picul of polished rice would stand at 3 to 4.5 mace (2–3.2s.). Nevertheless, unhusked rice could keep longer than husked rice, and hence was more suitable for junk shipment. (Cf. n. 79).

52.   Liang T'ing-nan, *Hsien-lo kuo,* pp. 68–69.

53.   Takazaki Misako, p. 30 n. In addition, the emperor released two Siamese ships detained since 1717 as a result of the reimposition of the second maritime ban to the Siamese mission at Canton. See *TCHTSL* 511:52b–53a.

54.   Ingram, pp. 8–9. Ingram also estimates the annual per capita consumption of rice around 1850 which he put at 2.4 piculs to 3.4 piculs (about 320 to 455 lbs.) per paddy.

55.   This statement would put me at variance with Mark Mancall's assertion (p. 89) that "the emperor's [K'ang-hsi's] death at the end of 1722 marked the end of experimentation and encouragement in the field of foreign trade for well over a century," particularly when Mancall is referring here to K'ang-hsi's experimentation with importing cheap rice from Siam.

56.   Liang T'ing-nan, *Hsien-lo kuo,* p. 72. "The *hong,*" he said, "are not to raise or lower the set 5 mace per picul price memorialized so that they may buy when it is lower and sell when higher, i.e., so that merchants would not be able to manipulate prices at will, as the standard price had been fixed since 1722 for this would not represent my way of treating small nations with compassion. In addition, notices are to be sent to Chekiang and Fukien that the rice that has arrived and that which Siam is presently sending to follow up will be subjected to the same treatment as at Kwangtung."

57.   Ibid.

58.   Abe Takeo, p. 191.

59.   For instance, a rice shipment arrived at Amoy in 1728, whereupon the local customs attempted to extract a duty of the rice imported contrary to the officially declared exemption on Siamese rice at a rate of 2–4 *fen* or 20–40 percent per picul (in accordance with the tax schedule for the inland transport of rice whereby one picul of the grain was to be assessed

2-4 *fen,* and 11 percent or more for other kinds of staples). Liang T'ing-nan, *Hsien-lo kuo,* p. 72; Feng Liu-t'ang, *Chung-kuo li-tai min-shih,* p. 246.

60.   Liang T'ing-nan, *Hsien-lo kuo,* p. 73.

61.   Ibid., p. 74. The shipmaster of the Siamese tribute ship thanked the emperor for the latter's generosity through the Kwangtung viceroy (see *SLHK,* installment 7, *t'ien,* p. 246b).

62.   Ishii Yoneo, p. 170. *TCHTSL,* 510:44a. Apparently, the fact that China offered an ideal and potentially vast rice market made the Siamese court eager to export the grain.

63.   Ibid.

64.   *SLHK,* installment 7, *t'ien,* pp. 248b–249a. *HMC,* 7:3a; *KTSL,* 176:6a–8a.

65.   Takazaki Misako, p. 19.

66.   On the other hand, it is probable that the scribe might have erroneously substituted *chin* (catty) for *tan* or *shih* (picul).

67.   *TCHTSL,* 510:44b.

68.   Liang T'ing-nan, p. 76.

69.   Ibid. Actually this vessel was granted a waiver on its return ballast cargo (something that was contrary to the policy declared in the previous year that all articles except imported rice were subject to duty) only because it had met a storm on the way to Amoy. Hence the exemption might be taken as a gesture of kindness.

70.   Ibid., pp. 78–82.

71.   21:13b. Captain Alexander Hamilton (II, 160) also concurred with this observation.

72.   Ingram, p. 24, Wei Yuan, 5:13a.

73.   *SLHK,* installment 22, t'ien, 804a–b; *FCTCCSL,* 14:29b; see *YHKC,* 8:10a–11a.

74. Liang T'ing-nan, pp. 91–92. The *chuan-huo-shui* was taken to mean both export and import cargo duties, though Wang Hsi-ch'i in his *Hsiao-fang-hu-chai yu-ti ts'ung-ch'ao* (Shanghai, 1877–1897), dispatch no. 9, p. 4a, defined it as the "export cargo duty" only.

75. Feng Liu-t'ang, *Chung-kuo li-tai min-shih,* p. 234.

76. Takazaki Misako, p. 20. The emperor on the occasion also took note of the fact that the Siamese ships had been regularly supplying the grain to Fukien (see Wei Yuan, 5:7b).

77. *FTTC,* 27C:1513: *SLHK,* installment 14, *t'ien,* p. 271. Similarly, another shipment by one Hsueh Shih-lung (another Sino-Siamese merchant) in the 1740s, with less than a rice cargo of the prescribed five-thousand picul minimum, was granted special consideration by Peking.

78. Ibid. According to Wang Hsi-ch'i (p. 4a), it was in 1729 when the Chinese officially determined that foreign vessels transporting less than 5,000 piculs of rice, while not liable for import duties, must pay import taxes.

79. Takazaki Misako, who researched and wrote an article on the seventeenth century Sino-Siamese rice trade, argues this line.

80. Ch'uan Han-sheng, "Ch'ien-lung shih-san nien," II, 547–552, 566.

81. Takazaki Misako, p. 21.

82. Actually, Siam as a site for junk construction had been noted since the seventeenth century. Simon de la Loubère (I, 12) noted in 1687–1688 that the country had timber for building ships and masts in the Chinese style. According to a British East India Company representative in 1694, virtually all Siamese ships were constructed by Chinese (see Anderson, p. 22). In the early decades of the eighteenth century, Chinese officials commented that the cost of junk construction in Southeast Asia, Siam included, was five to ten times cheaper than it was in China. While an average-size junk in China would cost upwards of ten thousand taels, a large-size one cost merely two to three thousand to build in Southeast Asia. On top of this, the construction of vessels in Southeast Asia was better and subject to fewer restrictions than in China (see Negishi Tadashi, *Gōkō no kenkyū,* pp. 485–486). So what the Amoy merchants "discovered" in the 1740s in Siam was an industry which continued to present favorable prospects for the Sino-Siamese trade, and obviously many took advantage of it in the venture to transport rice to Fukien.

83. *KTSL* 285:6b–7a. T'ien Ju-k'ang (*Shih-ch'i shih-chiu shih-chi*, p. 24) gives two reasons for the choice of Siam as a shipbuilding center. First, it was abundant in the *tactona grandis* (*ma-lu-mu*) wood which was ideal for junk construction. Using the estimates of the early nineteenth century as guideline, T'ien stipulated that the cost of this wood was twice as much in Fukien as in Siam. Secondly, the symbiotic relationship between the Chinese and the Siamese court enabled the former to dominate the country's shipping industry, creating an ideal situation for the Chinese enterprise.

84. *KTSL* 285:6b–7a.

85. *SLHK*, installment 24, *t'ien*, p. 878a. In the following year, Fukien governor P'an Shih-chu reiterated that ships from Fukien returning from trade to Southeast Asia were certainly permitted, according to regulations, to ship back rice for sale. In the sixth and seventh moons of that year, sixteen Amoy ships returned to Amoy, each carrying 200 to 300 piculs (26,660–40 lbs.) of rice. (One Ho Ching-hsing, a merchant resident in Lung-ch'i district South Fukien, went to Siam and transported back 1,000 piculs 133,300 lbs. of rice). All the rice was sold at Amoy for popular consumption, which according to the memorializer, was extremely beneficial. He did not, however, mention whether the local merchants trading to Siam brought back any newly built ships.

86. Feng Liu-t'ang, *Chung-kuo li-tai min-shih*, p. 234.

87. Ibid.

88. Liang T'ing-nan, pp. 96–98.

89. *KTSL* 396:15a–16b.

90. Liang T'ing-nan, p. 99.

91. Takazaki Misako, p. 23. A local graduate (*sheng*) or a national academy student (*chien*) transporting 2,000 (266,600 lbs.) or more piculs would be given an honorary title (*hsien*) of a *li-mu* (Departmental Police and Jail Warden, 9b). An honorary title of the rank of *chu-po* (Assistant Magistrate, 9a) would be bestowed on those who brought back between 4,000 to 6,000 piculs (533,200–799,800 lbs.). Transporting between 6,001 to 10,000 piculs (799,933–1,333,300 lbs.) would earn one a title of the rank of *hsien-ch'eng* (Vice Magistrate, 8a). The governor-general

also devised a schedule for commoner-merchants as well. Hence, merchants carrying between 2,000 and 4,000 piculs (266,600-533,200 lbs.) would receive the button (*ting-tai*) of a ninth-rank mandarin; for a shipment between 4,001 and 6,000 piculs, they would receive the honorary button of an eighth-rank mandarin. Finally, those transporting between 6,001 and 10,000 piculs would be accorded the buttons of a seventh-rank mandarin.

92. *MCSL, keng* (7th. part), VI, 525. Among them a merchant named Chuang Wen-fei transported more than 3,900 piculs (519,870 lbs.) and was given the button of a ninth-rank mandarin, while another named Fang Hsueh-shan returned with more than 5,200 piculs (593,160 lbs.) and was awarded the button of an eighth-rank mandarin. He further reported that in 1759, local vessels returned to Amoy with 21,200 piculs (2,825,960 lbs.) of foreign rice. Among the carriers, one received a ninth-rank mandarin's button. The ship commanded by Yeh Shi-hui belonged to a shipowner whose nom-de-commerce was Chin Te-ch'un (see ibid., 528a). Chinese ships trading to Southeast Asia from the Amoy area carried the commercial designation of *Chin.*

93. Ibid., pp. 523b–528a. There were apparently also several shipments within 2,000 piculs which were duly awarded by the provincial authorities (see ibid., p. 525b).

94. Ibid., pp. 525–526a; 532b–533a.

95. Ibid.

96. Ibid., p. 533b.

97. Ibid.

98. Ibid.

99. Ibid.

100. *KTSL* 424:20b–21b.

101. F. H. Turpin, *History of the Kingdom of Siam,* tr. B. O. Cartwright (Bangkok, 1908), pp. 178, 176.

102. Damrong Rajanubhab, ed., *Pra-ratcha pongsawadan chabab pra-ratcha hatleka* (Bangkok, 1952), II, pt. 2, p. 2, ibid.

103. Sittipun, *Ratcha samnak Thai,* p. 169.

104. Jean Koenig, "Journal of a Voyage from India to Siam and Malacca in 1779," tr. from his mss. in the British Museum, *Journal of the Straits Branch of the Royal Asiatic Society* 26:161–162 (January 1894).

105. Ch'uan Han-sheng, "Ch'ing-tai ti jen-k'ou pien-tung," in *LSYY* 32:156 (July 1961).

106. *FCTCCSL,* 14:29b–30a.

107. *HMC(TWH),* p. 180; Negishi Tadashi, *Shina girudo no kenkyū* (Tokyo, 1942), pp. 60–61.

108. *JTSL,* 185:10a. Narita Setsuo (*Kakyō shi,* p. 227) comments that some of these Ch'eng-hai merchants were actually half-traders, half-pirates.

109. It also explains why the rice trade of Siam has continued to be dominated by the Ch'eng-hai group up to the present time.

110. In 1787 there was mention of Chinese vessels carrying rice to China from Siam. One such shipment was seized by Nguyen Anh, the future Gia Long Emperor of Vietnam, to aid his struggle for the Vietnamese throne. See Klaus Wenk, *The Restoration of Thailand under Rama I, 1782–1809,* tr. G. Stahl (Tucson, 1968), p. 113.

111. Chaopraya Thippakorawong, *Pra-ratcha pongsawadan krung Rattanakosin rachakarn ti nung rachakarn ti song chabab hor smut haeng chart* (Bangkok, 1962), pp. 176–177, 95.

112. Tseng Chien-ping, *T'ai-kuo Hua-ch'iao ching-chi* (Thailand's Overseas Chinese economy; Taipei, 1956), p. 8.

113. *YHKC,* 8:39a–40a. During these two decades, the decline of Ch'ing authority was increasingly apparent. In the 1790s, we witnessed the culmination of the popular consumption problem compounded further by social and popular unrest. Along with the White Lotus Rebellion, flooding of the Yangtze and Yellow rivers, the Chia-ch'ing Emperor was also concerned with rampant piracy along the southeastern coast. In the rice-deficient areas in Kwangtung, such as Ch'ao-chou prefecture, piracy was most serious. Noting that such places nevertheless depended on rice transported by sea, the emperor, instead of banning overseas movement

which would prove to be detrimental to the people's livelihood, opted for the alternative of strengthening the garrison on Namoa island, the outlet of Ch'ao-chou lying in the north-south traffic lane. This shows a modification in official policy designed to cope with the worsening food situation in Southeast China. See Lu K'un and Ch'en Hung-ch'ih, 34:15a–b.

114. *KTTC,* 8:40a; Wei Yuan, 8:3b. Cf. similar action in the beginning of Yung-cheng's reign.

115. "Intelligence Report on the Import of Rice," *Asiatic Journal* 21:242–243 (1826).

116. Morse, *Chronicles,* III, 37–38; IV, 27.

117. From this instance, another hazard of foreign rice import may be discerned: that of sharp fluctuations in rice price between the time of order and the arrival of the shipment. In this case, when the order was placed by Chinese officials and merchants in 1806 the price agreed upon was four Spanish dollars per bag of 164½ pounds; however, when the shipment reached Canton the price had fallen below the cost to the importers. It was only after considerable dispute and continued insistence that the Chinese finally yielded. See Morse, *Chronicles,* III, 38.

118. Lo Erh-kang, p. 33.

119. In 1825, American ships also imported close to 50,000 piculs (6.7 m. lbs.) of rice, worth about 100,000 Spanish dollars, into Canton. See Morse, *Chronicles,* IV, 118.

120. *Dai Nam thúc luc chin-binh,* Tô Châu et al., comps. (Tokyo, 1970), 16:13b. In 1820–1822, rice was also reportedly scarce and expensive in the country.

121. *Chinese Repository,* XI, 1 (January 1942), pp. 17–18.

122. John Crawfurd, *History of the Indian Archipelago* (Edinburgh, 1820), III, 348.

123; Ibid. The junks mentioned in Crawfurd's statement were probably mostly owned by the Siamese king, his court, and Chinese residents of Siam. Many Ch'eng-hai merchants, restricted by the prohibition imposed in the 1800s by the Chinese authorities against licenses to transport rice from Siam, emigrated to Siam in order to continue participating in the rice trade to China.

124. Wong Lin Ken, p. 144.

125. *CTWCSL*, pp. 117-118; Wang Hsi-ch'i, pt. 9, *ts'e* 77, p. 3b.

126. Wei Yuan, 8:4a; William Hunter, *The Fan Kwae at Canton before Treaty Days, 1825-1844.* (London, 1911), p. 100; Wang Hsi-ch'i, pt. 9, *ts'e* 77, p. 3b.

127. Morse, *Chronicles,* IV, 107.

128. *Chinese Repository* (April 1836), IV, 544-545.

129. Phipps, pp. 143-144.

130. John R. Morrison, *A Chinese Commercial Guide* (Canton, 1848), pp. 23-24.

131. *Chinese Repository* (January 1842), XI, 17-19.

132. *Chinese Repository* (September 1834), VIII, 234; Wang Hsi-ch'i, supplementary, pt. 2, *ts'e* 77, p. 2b; Morrison, p. 162. In the 1830s foreign rice prices were reportedly quite good: 1.75 to 2.25 Spanish dollars and rising in a season of scarcity to 2.75 to 3.00 dollars.

133. Wales, p. 207; Pongpun Supatrapun, p. 177.

134. O. Frankfurter, "The Mission of Sir James Brooke," *JSS* 8:29-30 (May 1912).

135. Ingram, p. 24.

136. Edmund Roberts, *Embassy to the Eastern Courts of Cochin-China, Siam, and Muscat during the years 1832-1834* (New York, 1837), p. 251. In 1831, however, as a result of drought and flooding, outside rice had to be sought, and the people were paid rice in lieu of money for their services. See Damrong Rajanubhab, *Tamnan karn lurk bon-bia lae karn lurk huey,* in *Prachoom pongsawadan chabab hor smut haeng chart* (Collected chronicles and annals of the various reigns, National Library Edition; Bangkok, 1964), installment 17, V, 455.

137. "Chotmaihet mit-channari American" in *Prachoom pongsawadan chabab hor smut haeng chart* (Bangkok, 1964), installment 31, VII, 580.

138. Gützlaff, p. 85. Eighteen thirty-six was apparently a very abundant year. The rice produced in that year was an estimated amount of 1,696,423 *koyan* or the equivalent of 215,589.5 taels Siamese (£107,794.75).

139. *Chou-pan i-wu shih-mo,* 26:36b–37a (I, 511–512); Wei Yuan, 6:15b–16a. Singapore's rice came mainly from Siam (see Wong Lin Ken, p. 144); Hsu Chi-yü, *Ying huan chih lueh* (1873), p. 29a; Wang Shih-ch'ing, p. 23; Feng Liu-t'ang, *Chung-kuo li-tai min-shih,* p. 253; Akin Rabinbhadana, *The Organization of Thai Society in the Early Bangkok Period, 1782–1873* (Ithaca, N.Y., 1969), p. 9; Wong Lin Ken, p. 144.

140. D. E. Malloch, *Siam: Some General Remarks on Its Production* (Calcutta, 1852), p. 43. Malloch also said that the yield of rice was about forty times the quantity of the seed.

141. Ingram, p. 72.

142. Feng Liu-t'ang, *Chung-kuo li-tai min-shih,* p. 228; George Bacon, *Siam: The Land of the White Elephant* (New York, 1881), pp. 89, 317; Feng Liu-t'ang, *Chung-kuo li-tai min-shih,* p. 231; Yang Han-cheng "Chin pai-nien lai Hsien-lo mi-yeh kai shu" in *Hsien-ching mi-shang kung-so san-shih chou nien chi-nien k'an* (Bangkok, 1949), p. 59.

VI. Southeast China's Trade Organizations

1. *HMC* 5:29a–b; *YCCP,* "Kao Ch'i-cho" 3, pp. 100a–b; *STSL* 74:2a–3a.

2. *YCCP,* "Kao Ch'i-cho" 4, p. 31.

3. *HMC* 15:5b.

4. *SLHK,* installment 22, *t'ien,* pp. 802a–b; *Fu-chien sheng-li* (Taipei, 1964), p. 625.

5. Wu Lien-hsun, comp., *Chang-chou fu chih* (preface, 1877), 1964 ed. 33:64a–65a; Ch'en Ju-chien, comp., *Chang-p'u hsien chih* (1876) 22:28a–b. The prosperity of the Chinese trade with Southeast Asia at this time is contrasted sharply with the frustrations faced by Western

merchants at Canton and Amoy. For instance in 1733, only five British, three French, and four Dutch ships traded at Canton. Besides, British ships never succeeded in trading at Amoy.

6. T'ien Ju-k'ang, *Shih-ch'i shih-chiu shih-chi,* p. 27; T'ien Ju-k'ang, "Shih-wu chih shih-pa shih-chi Chung-kuo hai-wai mao-i huan-man ti yuan-in, p. 87.

7. John Crawfurd, in *Journal of An Embassy from the Governor-General of India to the Courts of Siam and Co-chin China* (London, 1830), II, 160–161, gathered some first-hand information concerning the remuneration of the crew aboard a Chinese junk trading to Siam:

   a. Shipmaster: no fixed salary, but received 100 piculs of tonnage both ways and bad cabin accommodations for passengers at his disposal which were worth between 150–200 Spanish dollars, and got 10 percent commission on the net profit of sales.
   b. Pilot: 200 Spanish dollars per voyage plus 50 piculs of tonnage.
   c. Accountant: 100 dollars plus 50 piculs of tonnage.
   d. Steerage captain: 15 piculs of tonnage.
   e. Anchor and hold captains: 9 piculs of tonnage each.
   f. Seamen: 7 piculs each.

   According to Crawfurd, "These proportions apply to a junk of 6,000 piculs 700,000 lbs., but vary a little as the vessel is large or small."

8. "A Dissertation upon the Commerce of China," in Rhoads Murphey, ed., *Nineteenth-Century China: Five Imperialist Perspectives* (Ann Arbor, Michigan, 1972), pp. 36–37.

9. Negishi Tadashi, *Chūgoku no girudo,* p. 231; D. J. MacGowan, "Chinese Guilds or Chambers of Commerce and Trade Unions," *Journal of the China Branch of the Royal Asiatic Society* 21.3:136 (1887); Naosaku Uchida, *The Overseas Chinese: A Bibliographical Essay* (Stanford, 1960), p. 37; Norman Jacobs, *The Origins of Modern Capitalism and Eastern Asia* (Hong Kong, 1958), pp. 38–39; "T'ai-kuo Fu-chien hui-kuan chien-shih" (A brief history of the Fukien Association in Thailand), in *T'ai-kuo Fu-chien hui-kuan ch'eng-li wu-shih chou-nien hsin-chih lo-ch'eng chi-nien t'e-k'an* (Bangkok, 1961), p. 44. The first Fukienese guild in Siam was established in Bangkok in 1869; it was probably the earliest Chinese guild in Siam; Negishi Tadashi, *Chūgoku no girudo,* p. 235; Liang Chi-fan, "Kuan shih" in *T'ai-kuo Hai-nan hui-kuan hsin hsia lo-ch'eng chi-nien t'e-k'an* (Bangkok, 1958), p. 1.

10. Hirase Minokichi, *Kindai Shina keizai shi* (Tokyo, 1942), pp. 116–117; Morse, *Chronicles,* 1, 56, 125, 128, 135.

11. South Fukienese as a rule were wealthier merchants than their northern counterparts or the Hokchiu (Foochow) traders. See Naosaku Uchida, p. 7.

12. Negishi Tadashi, *Shina girudo no kenkyū* (Tokyo, 1942), p. 51.

13. *HMC* 5:29b.

14. *YCCP,* "Kao Ch'i-cho" 3, no. 14, pp. 86b–87b; William Schurz, *The Manila Galleon* (New York, 1939), p. 71.

15. Negishi Tadashi, *Gōkō no kenkyū,* p. 494.

16. Su Ch'ing-huai, p. 97. This situation merits a comparison with what transpired in the Chinese trade at Bantam at the end of the sixteenth century, described in the following words of J. C. van Leur: "The merchants who are wealthy in general stay home, then when some ships are ready to leave they give those going with them a sum of money to be paid doubly, more or less according to the length of the voyages, of which they make an obligation, and if the voyage is prosperously completed then the giver is paid according to the contract, and if the drawer cannot pay the money because of some misfortune then he must give his wife and children in pledge for the whole time until the debt is paid. Unless the ship be wrecked—then the former loses the money he lent." See J. C. van Leur, p. 104.

17. Wakeman, pp. 11–12.

18. Chinese merchants usually employed noms de commerce as designations for commercial firms and for themselves throughout the eighteenth century; ships with the "Chin" designation frequented Siam, indicating the extent of the participation by the Amoy *chiao* in the Sino-Siamese trade. See Negishi Tadashi, *Chūgoku no girudo,* p. 226.

19. Wu T'ang and Pa-ho-pu, comps., *T'ung-an hsien chih* (1798) 5:27a–29b.

20. Negishi Tadashi, *Shina girudo no kenkyū,* pp. 60–61.

21. The British, on the other hand, found the Amoy market a great dis-

appointment. In 1735, the British ship *Houghton* found neither merchants of standing nor those with sizable stocks. In addition, merchandise was expensive and its acquisition required five to six months (as compared to the customary three or four at Canton) at a time. This revelation perhaps affirms the exclusive status of the Amoy *yang-hang* in relation to the Southeast Asia trade. See Morse, *Chronicles,* I, 232.

22.   *HMC(TWH),* p. 180.

23.   See Hou-p'ei, "Wu-k'ou t'ung-shang i-ch'ien wuo-kuo kuo-chi mao-i chih kai-k'uang" (General conditions of our country's foreign trade prior to the opening of the Five Treaty Ports), *Ts'ing-hua hsueh-pao* 4.1:1248 (1972); Morse, *Chronicles,* I, 297; Earl Pritchard, *The Crucial Years of Early Anglo-Chinese Relations, 1750–1800* (Pullman, Washington, 1936).

24.   *HMC(TWH)* pp. 180–181.

25.   In 1813, the sole surviving *yang-hang* firm petitioned the Amoy authorities that all lighters, which had been used extensively to make clandestine cargo runs along the coasts between Fukien and Kwangtung, be placed under its supervision. Four years later, with smuggling rampant, the viceroy finally made a move to curb it, but it is not known how successful he was.

26.   Morse, *Chronicles,* III, 171–172, noted the peculiar attitude of the Chinese authorities toward the restriction of various articles in export trade, which may serve to underline the policy pursued above regarding the exportation of tea from Amoy: "The Chinese indeed, carry the principle of the mercantile system to an extreme. They are peculiarly prepossessed in favour of that foreign trade, which appears to bring in the largest share of money; and they prohibit its exportation. They prohibit also the exportation of all articles in use, and some to which the absurd nationality of the people attach a fictitious value . . . Notwithstanding these restrictions, it is by no means to be supposed that the prohibited articles are not traded in. By force of corruption, all-powerful in China, the articles deemed by law contraband are freely imported and exported, and a thorough understanding to evade the law exists between the magistrate and the merchant. The only bad effect, therefore, of this clandestine system is that the bribery which is indispensable, enhances the price of the goods, and, on that account, restricts consumption."

27.   *HMC(TWH),* p. 179.

28.   MacGowan, p. 145; Wang Chih-ch'un 4:4b–5a.

29.   Along this line, it is interesting to note that even though Amoy is said
      to have been the most important port in China for the Southeast Asia
      trade during the first half of the eighteenth century, the little informa-
      tion that is available about it comes essentially from one single source,
      the *Hsia-men chih.*

30.   Wakeman, p. 29.

31.   Morse, *Chronicles,* I, 163. The actual date of the formation of the
      cohong has been subject to much debate. Western scholars have generally
      chosen the year 1720, while Chinese and Japanese scholars have insisted
      on other dates. Inaba Iwakichi, in his article "Shindai no Kanton
      bōeki," has opted for 1760, while Liang Chia-pin in his book on the co-
      hong has argued 1685, with Wu Han ("Kuang-tung shih-san-hang k'ao
      shu-p'ing") settling for 1682. P'eng Tse-i, in his article "Ch'ing-tai Kuang-
      tung yang-hang chih-tu ti ch'i-yuan," postulates that it was founded in
      1686, after the establishment of the Canton maritime customs superin-
      tendency. According to him, the viceroy and hoppo felt the necessity
      of establishing a new trading monopoly in the face of the rapid growth
      of foreign commerce at Canton. Formerly, there was no distinction
      between local merchant organizations engaged in local and foreign trade;
      thereafter, they became classified as *chin-szu hang* and *yang-huo hang,*
      specializing in local and foreign trade respectively. A sixth theory,
      advanced by Wang Chu-an in his "Shih-san hang yu Ch'u Ta-chun Kuang-
      chou chu-chih tz'u" asserts that the co-hong was already in existence in
      1684.
          In 1724, there was an attempt by one Bouqua, a "governor" *(fuyen)*
      merchant, to secure a monopoly on all of Canton's Western trade for
      that year, in return for an £8,000 contribution to the governor's coffer.
      He was, however, successfully resisted by the British and other Chinese
      merchants (see Liang Chia-pin, p. 65). Also in 1726, Kwangtung Gover-
      nor Yang Wen-chien backed two firms in an attempt to monopolize
      foreign trade. See Sasaki Masaya "Etsu kaikan no roki (Illegal tariff of
      the Canton customs during the Ch'ing dynasty)" *Tōyōgaku hō* 34.1–4:
      143 (1952).

32.   Pritchard, p. 140.

33.   Morse, *Chronicles,* II, 1; Liang Chia-pin, p. 66. After 1720, as much as
      90 percent of the influential merchants at Canton were Fukienese. See
      Wu Yu-kan, *Chung-kuo kuo-chi mao-i shih* (Shanghai, 1928), pp. 63–64.

34. *KTTC*(chts), III, 3313; *MCSL, keng* (7th. part), VI, 577; Ch'u Ta-chün, 15:34a.

35. P'eng Tse-i, "Ch'ing-tai Kuang-tung yang-hang chih-tu ti ch'i-yuan," *Li-shih-yen-chiu* 1:16–17 (January 1957).

36. Wakeman, pp. 67 n., 43.

37. Louis Dermigny, *Le commerce à Canton au XVIIIe siècle, 1719–1833* (Paris, 1964), 1, 339–340. Following an old practice, in existence since 1685, foreigners were allowed to trade only with specified licensed merchants. In 1745, Canton authorities selected for the Wai-yang hang a few merchants who, by virtue of their wealth and status, would be required to guarantee the payment of taxes in the foreign trade at the port in addition to supervising the conduct of foreign vessels' crews and the well-being of their cargoes. These *pao-shang* or "security merchants" were responsible directly to the hoppo. The system may be regarded as "a near perfect instrument of extortion, tax collection, and control over the foreigners." (See Wakeman, p. 35.)

38. See Hirase Minokichi, p. 185; Jao Tsung-i, comp., "Ch'ao-chou chih kao," in ibid., *Ch'ao-chou chih hui-p'ien* (Hong Kong, 1965), pp. 28b–29a. *YHKC* 25:10a; 10b–13a.

39. *KTTC* 180:22.

40. Hsiao I-shan, *Ch'ing-tai t'ung-shih* (Taipei, 1962), II, 834; see *KTSL* 704:13b–14a.

41. Liang Chia-pin, p. 105.

42. Morse (*Chronicles,* I, 301) says that it was entirely the effort of Puankhequa who paid the Canton viceroy £100,000 that he had received in turn from the British East India Company. Li in his tenure as the Liang-Kuang viceroy profited immensely from bribes from local merchants.

43. In 1775, an association of ten merchants was rumored to be re-established at Canton under the viceroy's protection, but it did not materialize partly due to the protests from the British and Puankhequa. See Morse, *Chronicles,* II, 13–22.

44. Ibid., II, 82.

45. Consoo funds were established in 1780 to alleviate the constant problem of insolvency through the stipulation of collective responsibility by all hong members in sharing the payment of debts by individual members. In other words, when one firm became bankrupt, other firms collectively paid for its debt with funds drawn from an extra *ad valorem* of 3 percent of purchase by foreign merchants.

46. Ibid., II, 53–54. Causes of indebtedness usually included: official extortions, merchants' conspicuous consumption, loaning of money at high interest and high risk.

47. *YHKC* 25:10b–13a; Hirase Minokichi, p. 185.

48. Negishi Tadashi, *Shina girudo no kenkyū*, p. 391; Liang Chia-pin, pp. 118–119. Puankhequa alone was asked to donate 500,000 taels (£183,000); Negishi Tadashi, *Shina girudo no kenkyū*, p. 391.

49. *YHKC* 25:10b–13a. At this time, then, both the tributary trade and other forms of the Sino-Siamese trade came under the management of the same group at Canton.

50. According to British accounts, Chi-shan was "most rapacious," looking constantly for new sources of revenue. The control of the co-hong and the selection of individual hong merchants were in his hands. See Morse, *Chronicles*, II, 360, 421.

51. *YHKC* 25:10b–13a; 13b–14a.

52. See Li Kuang-t'ao, "Hua-i yu Hsien-lo," p. 436, Chao Praya Thippakora-wang, comp., *The Dynastic Chronicles, Bangkok Era: The Fourth Reign*, tr. Chadin Folood (Tokyo, 1965), II, 281.

53. Dermigny, I, 339–340.

VII. The Sino-Siamese Tributary Trade: From Late Ayudhya to Early Bangkok Period

1. Hsu Yun-ch'iao, "Chung-Hsien t'ung-shih k'ao," pp. 26–30.

2. One in 1723 which was cast on the shores of Chekiang by a storm (see *TCHTSL* 510: n.p.); one in 1747 which bore a tribute of animals for the

emperor (see *TCHTSL* 502: n.p.); one that came in 1749, the year the Siamese court also dispatched a normal embassy (see *TCHTSL* 510: n.p.); and one in 1760 which was rejected (see ibid.)

3.   *MCST, keng* (7th. part), VI, 515b–516b.

4.   Shu Yun-ch'iao, "Chung-Hsien t'ung-shih k'ao," p. 26; John K. Fairbank and Teng Ssu-yü, "On the Ch'ing Tributary System," in ibid., *Ch'ing Administration: Three Studies* (Cambridge, Mass., 1968), p. 144; Ch'u Ta-chun, 15:32b–33a.

5.   *TCHTSL* 510:45b–46a.

6.   The question of the *t'an-kung* mission and its commercial nuances for the period may perhaps be best illustrated by the following report filed by the Board of Rites around 1762:

The governor-general (Su Ch'ang of Liang-Kuang) discovered that the Siamese king had dispatched ship merchant Ts'ai Hsi-wang to take a *t'an-kung* ship to Kwangtung. In 1761 the said king had sent one *cheng* and one *fu* tribute ship to present tributes. The *fu-kung* vessel loaded cargoes under the supervision of local officials who escorted them out to the ocean in 1762. Now the Siamese king has instructed Praya Prak-lang to send Ts'ai Hsi-wang to visit the Siamese mission in China with a letter (The Namoi district officials) found that the ballast of the *t'an-kung* ship was quite sizable. It was (subsequently) stored up at the T'ai-shun hang (Canton hong firm) ... In 1757 the Siamese had sent a ship merchant named Wu Shih-chin to visit the Siamese embassy at Canton ... The vessel's ballast was given duty exemption and the crew provided with a daily ration (as in the case of a formal mission). Now Ts'ai ... has asked local authorities to memorialize on his behalf for imperial kindness in permitting him to sell his ballast without delay (since long storage would cause spoilage to the merchandise) and without duty. He also has asked that the crew be given a daily ration from the date of the ship's arrival at Canton until the time of the Siamese party's return from Peking ... The ship's Chinese crewmen are said to have grown up in Siam and have families there. They should therefore be permitted to return to Siam. *MCSL, keng* (7th. part), VI, 529b–530a.

7.   Takazaki Misako, pp. 19–20.

8.   Fairbank and Teng, p. 144. The Ch'ien-lung edition of the *Ta-Ch'ing hui-tien* (1764) included the following items as prohibitive for export: iron, iron pans, weapons, gold, copper, and copper cash (see *HMC,* 7:7b–10a).

9. *TCHTSL* 511: n.p.; Hsu Yun-ch'iao, "Chung-Hsien t'ung-shih k'ao," p. 27.

10. *MCSL, keng* (7th. part), VI, 516a.

11. Ch'en Chao-nan, pp. 42–43.

12. Wu Ti, "T'un-wu-li huang-ch'ao shih," tr. Ch'en Li-sung, *Chung-yuan yueh-k'an* 1.8:43 (1941). Howard Malcom, *Travels in Southeast Asia,* II, pt. 2, pp. 3–4.

13. Chotmaihet 4, no. 82 (J.S. 1215 or A.D. 1853). In general, Siamese records tended to neglect the mention of trade in Taksin's reign because they seemed more concerned with the political and military developments that went on, in the fight against the Burmese and other rebellious factions within Siam. In such a situation, economic considerations were regarded as secondary. See Sittipun, *Racha samnak Thai* p. 168.

14. Throughout his reign, Taksin had attempted to seek recognition from the Ch'ing court several times. As early as 1767, he sent a Chinese merchant, Ch'en Mei-sheng, with a Siamese embassy to request investiture from Peking, informing Ch'ien-lung that he had become founder of a new dynasty. The mission was, however, turned away by Li Shih-yao who was of the opinion that the last Ayudhyan king, then thought still to be alive, ought to be found and reinstated (see *SLHK,* installment 30, *ti,* p. 105b). Four years later, Taksin dispatched another embassy headed by two natives of his father's home district in Ch'ao-chou, Ch'en Chun-ch'ing and Liang Shang-hsuan, to present tribute. This embassy, too, failed to win Chinese recognition for the new Siamese king. Taksin, nevertheless, did not give up. In 1775, he asked another Ch'ao-chou merchant, Ch'en Wan-sheng, to take a letter to the Ch'ing government to press the issue. The effort again proved fruitless, with another trial in the following year suffering a similar fate. In 1777, yet another embassy was sent under a Chinese merchant named Yang Ching-su. It was not until 1781, the last year of his reign, that Peking was finally prepared to recognize Taksin. See *Kao-tsung shun huang-ti sheng hsun* in *Ta-Ch'ing sheng-hsun* (Taipei, 1965), 293:3b–4a.

15. Hsieh Yu-yung, *Hsin-p'ien Hsien-lo kuo chih* (Bangkok, 1953), p. 77.

16. *KTSL* 1036:16b; King Chulachomklao (Rama V), ed. and anno., *Pra rachavijarn* (Bangkok, 1908), p. 135; "Chotmaihet rai-wan tup smai krung Thonburi" in *Prachoom pongsawadan,* installments 65–66 (Bangkok, 1969), 80–81 n, 117 n; *KTSL* 1036:16b–18b.

17. Li Kuang-t'ao, "Ming-Ch'ing liang-tai," p. 71. The *hou-wang po-lai* was a principle invoked by the Chinese side to indicate the considerable trouble the tributary went through to present tributes. Therefore it was always proper to, first of all, give in return valuable gifts and take good care of the visiting mission; secondly, to allow the mission to sell its ballast cargoes completely duty-free; thirdly, to accord other generous treatment. All this was reflected in Ch'ien-lung's edict in response to Taksin's mission.

18. *KTSL* 1137:16a–19b.

19. *KTSL* 1137:19b. According to the viceroy of Liang–Kuang, in the suite were only two bona fide Siamese ships, the rest being Kwangtung junks which frequently traded to Siam and had tagged along for the purpose of trade.

20. Hsu Yun-ch'iao, "Cheng-chao ju kung Ch'ing-t'ing k'ao," *Nanyang hsueh-pao* 6:15 (June 1957), pp. 12–14.

21. King Chulachomklao, p. 134. The Siamese record stated that Taksin requested the hand of a Chinese princess, but there was no mention to this effect in the Chinese documents. Recent scholars of Taksin have tended to doubt its credibility, though none has produced any concrete evidence to disprove it.

22. Hsu Yun-ch'iao, "Cheng-chao ju kung," p. 12; Li Kuang-t'ao, "Hua-i yu Hsien-lo," p. 438; *KTSL* 1137:16a–19b.

23. King Chulachomklao, pp. 134, 130.

24. *KTSL* 1137:19b.

25. See, for example, the case of 1752. *KTSL* 433:12b–13a; *KTSL* 1137: 17a; The emperor kept only the elephants which formed part of the "supplementary tributes"; Hsu Yun-ch'iao, "Cheng-chao ju kung," p. 15.

26. *KTSL* 1137:18a.

27. See Hsieh Ch'ing-kao, *Hai-lu* (1842), pp. 5b–15b; Mancall, p. 84.

28. See precedent in 1736.

29. *KTSL* 1137:18a.

30. For instance, the 1780 mission was richly rewarded. See Hsu Yun-ch'iao, "Chung-Hsien t'ung-shih k'ao," p. 26; Hsu yun-ch'iao, "Cheng-chao ju kung," p. 15

31. *Ta-Ch'ing hui-tien* 30:18a.

32. Hsu Yun-ch'iao, "Cheng-chao ju kung," p. 15; King Chulachomklao, p. 136.

33. Ibid., p. 135.

34. *TCHTSL* 510: n.p.

35. Western trade continued to be dormant, particularly at this moment when the Napoleonic War was engrosing everybody's attention. Originally the Macartney Mission which visited China in 1793 was also aimed at opening Japan, Cochin China, Siam, and the Eastern Archipelago to British trade by means of a treaty. The outbreak of the Napoleonic War, however, prevented Lord Macartney from going elsewhere after he left China.

36. His father, Praya Akson Suntonsad, was the descendant of a rich Chinese family of Ayudhya; his mother, Yok (Siamese transliteration of "Yu"), was the daughter of a rich Cantonese merchant.

37. Chotmaihet 4 (J.S. 1215 or A.D. 1853), no. 82.

38. Thippakorawong, *Pra-ratcha pongsawadan krung Rattanakosin,* p. 222.

39. Ibid., p. 260.

40. Chang Te-Ch'ang, "Ch'ing-tai ya-p'ien," p. 115.

41. Fairbank and Teng, pp. 167–168; Wei Yuan 5:12a.

42. Li Kuang-t'ao, "Ming-Ch'ing liang-tai," p. 67; Hsu Yun-ch'iao, "Chung-Hsien t'ung-shih k'ao," p. 34; Liang T'ing-nan, *Hsien-lo kuo,* pp. 111–112; Li Kuang-t'ao, "Chi Ch'ing-tai ti Hsien-lo kuo-piao," *LSYY* 30b:553 (October 1959).

43. Rama I maintained for tribute presentation and trading purposes two principal vessels christened the *Hu-song* and *Song-praratchasarn.*

44. "Praratchasarn pai muang Chin, J.S. 1148, in the Damrong Rajanubhab Files, Department of Hand-Written Documents, National Library, Bangkok, p. 4; Hsieh Yu-yung, p. 80.

45. Ch'en Chao-nan, pp. 42–43.

46. See also Li Kuang-t'ao, "Chi Ch'ing-tai," p. 521; *YHKC* 21:30a.

47. Li Kuang-t'ao, "Chi Ch'ing-tai," pp. 530–531.

48. *MCSL, keng* (7th. part), VI, 542b.

49. Li Kuang-t'ao, "Hua-i yu Hsien-lo," pp. 437–438. The Chinese crew was further permitted to return to Siam with the ship.

50. Liang T'ing-nan, *Hsien-lo kuo,* pp. 109–110, 111.

51. In 1789 the Liang-Kuang viceroy, Fu-k'ang-an, memorialized that Siam had had no commercial intercourse with eastern Kwangtung ports, obviously a piece of misinformation (see *YHKC* 17:5b–6a). On the other hand Fu might have been in collusion with the Siamese to conceal the truth from Peking. A collaborator of the notorious eunuch Ho Shen, Fu-k'ang-an served as the Kwangtung viceroy from 1789, a very lucrative post because of the flourishing stage of foreign trade at Canton. Arthur Hummel in his *Eminent Chinese of the Ch'ing Period* (p. 254) says, "His use of public office to further his own political and financial fortunes gave him a reputation for unscrupulousness second only to that to Ho Shen."

52. Gützlaff, p. 184.

53. *MCSL, keng* (7th. part), VI, 561b–562a.

54. Fairbank, *Trade and Diplomacy,* I, 38.

55. Ibid., I, 35.

VIII. Chinese in the Siamese Economic Life
of the Eighteenth and Nineteenth Centuries

1. Chang T-ch'ang, "Ch'ing-tai ya-p'ien," p. 142.

2. Krisananon, sec. 2, pp. 287–288. Ong was originally the operator of a junk that traded in bricks to Ayudhya from South Fukien.

3. Wang Chih-ch'un 4:1b; Takazaki Misako, p. 20.

4. Liang T'ing-non, p. 67.

5. *TCHTSL* 511: n.p.

6. Ch'en Ta, *Nan-yang Hua-ch'iao yu Min–Yueh she-hui* (Changsha, 1938), pp. 36–37; Li Kuang-t'ao, "Ming-Ch'ing liang-tai," p. 435; *MCSL, keng* (7th. part), VI, 513–514a; Li Kuang-t'ao, 'Ming-Ch'ing liang-tai," p. 435.

7. Harley MacNair, *The Chinese Abroad: Their Position and Protection* (Shanghai, 1926).

8. Decreed in either late 1740s or early 1750s, but rescinded in 1754, the court nevertheless expected the Chinese merchants to return to their homeland eventually.

9. Lo Erh-kang, p. 59; *SLHK,* installment 10, *t'ien,* pp. 360–361.

10. Liu-ch'iu seemed to be the only state which the Chinese authorities made an exception: in the case of an investiture mission, Chinese navigators were permitted to help the Liu-ch'iu accomplish the mission.

11. See Ch'en Yu-sung, "Ch'en I-lao an yu Ch'ing-tai ch'ien-min cheng-ts'e chih kai-pien," *Nan-yang hsueh-pao* 12.1:17–19 (June 1956).

12. Wang Chih-ch'un 4:1b.

13. Krisananon, sec. 2, pp. 275–278; Sittipun, *Ratcha samnak Thai,* p. 151; Krisananon, sec. 2, pp. 296–297. The income of one such Chinese mandarin merchant who was permitted to take two vessels of his own along with the king's royal fleet to trade at China every year in Taksin's reign shows how much wealth could be acquired in this way. In six short years, the merchant amassed a fortune of 400,000 Siamese taels (approx.

£213,333), all from the sale of cargoes and the two junks he was authorized to construct annually with the exemption of the normal *Ka-pak-rua* fees. See Sittipun, *Racha samnak Thai,* p. 157.

14.   Krisananon, sec. 2, pp. 283–286.

15.   *KTSL,* pp. 185–420.

16.   *CTWCSL,* I, 419–420.

17.   See Morse, *Chronicles,* II, 422–423. Wen Hsiung-fei, *Nan-yang Hua-ch'iao t'ung-shih* (Shanghai, 1929), p. 145.

18.   Of the five main customs posts along the Kwangtung coast, four were located in the prefecture of Ch'ao-chou. This may be taken as one indication of the district's role in foreign trade.

19.   Liang T'ing-nan, p. 129.

20.   *CTWCSL,* I, 288, 285–286.

21.   Ibid, III, 290–291.

22.   *MCSL, keng* (7th. part), VI, 565a–b.

23.   *CTWCSL,* II, 417–418.

24.   *TCHTSL,* 513:43b–44a.

25.   Crawfurd, *Journal of an Embassy,* II, 160; *TCHTSL,* 512:9a–b.

26.   There had been a great influx of Chinese into Java in the 1730s; out of about 100,000, 80 percent were concentrated around Batavia. When this caused unemployment, the Dutch authorities in 1740 decided to deport many of them to Ceylon (then held by the Dutch), causing a revolt to break out in which thousands of Chinese were massacred.

27.   John Furnivall, *Netherlands India: A Study of Plural Economy* (Cambridge, Eng., 1939), p. 46.

28.   Schurz, p. 97. Because the Chinese had completely monopolized the trade and retail business of the colony, the Spaniards wanted them out.

Between the 1750s and 1850s, the colonial government made it a policy to limit the number of Chinese residing in the Philippines to a total of four or five thousand. After that, however, when the Spanish government realized the desirability of promoting economic development in the colony, unlimited Chinese immigration was again permitted. See Edgar Wickberg, "Early Chinese Economic Influence in the Philippines, 1850-1898," *Pacific Affairs* 35.3:277-278 (Fall 1962).

29. Only at Borneo where the Chinese on the whole were probably better off in this period. See Miyazaki Ichisada, "Chūgoku-Nanyō kankei shi gaisetsu," ibid., *Ajia shi kenkyū* (Kyoto, 1959), II, 526-528.

30. Furnivall, pp. 46-47; Schurz, p. 98.

31. Damrong Rajanubhab, *Pra-ratcha pongsawadan,* II, 398. Taksin's father, Cheng Yung, was a native of Ch'eng-hai district, Ch'ao-chou prefecture. He earned a commission from the Siamese court as a gambling tax farmer in the Reign of King Baromakot.

32. Thippakorawong, *Pra-ratcha pongsawadan krung Rattanakosin,* vol. 2, pt. 2, p. 1.

33. Adrien Launay, *Histoire de la mission de Siam, 1622-1811* (Paris, 1920), p. 187.

36. Rama IV, "The Establishment of the Kingdom," tr. "S.J.S.," *Siam Repository,* vol. 1, art. 32, p. 67 (1869).

37. Koenig, p. 161.

38. Tseng Chien-ping, p. 6. Another area adjacent to Sampeng, Taladnoi, was also given to a Chinese merchant by Rama I in 1789; it is still an important part of the major Chinese settlement in Bangkok today. See Krisananon, sec. 3, pp. 313-315.

39. David Wyatt characterizes the strength of the early Bangkok monarchy as lying in among other things, its "receptiveness to the outside world through involvement in Overseas trade." See Steinberg, et al., p. 111.

40. Krisananon, sec. 2, pp. 322; sec. 3, pp. 445-456. Gun's younger sister was Taksin's concubine and he himself had been close to Rama I when the latter was still serving under Taksin. When Rama I came to power,

Gun was entrusted with duties in the royal warehouses, including the outfitting of royal junks to trade to China.

41.   Ibid., sec. 2, pp. 317–318.

42.   Prayud Sittipun, *Ton trakoon kun-nang Thai* (Bangkok, 1962), pp. 172–173.

43.   Wang Gung-wu, *Nan-yang Hua-jen,* p. 100.

44.   *Siam Repository* 1:67 (1869).

45.   Chula Chakrabongse, *Lords of Life* (London, 1968), p. 97; Thippakora-wong, *Pra-ratcha pongsawadan krung Rattanakosin,* pp. 67–68; Damrong Rajanubhab, *Pra-ratcha pongsawadan,* vol. 2, pt. 2, p. 139.

46.   Such as Wu Yang and his descendants at Songkla. Up to the time of Rama V (1868–1911), the Siamese court pursued the decentralized system for its provincial government. Known as the *ghin-muang* (literally, "eat state"), the system permitted governors to retain full autonomous local power, while requiring them to send annual tributes to Bangkok. See Damrong Rajanubhab, *Tesapiban,* pp. 24–25.

47.   Siam's tin mining, which ultimately became most important on the western shores of Lower Siam, notably at Junkceylon (Phuket), from the time of Rama IV, was basically concentrated in the eastern coastal region at this time. Nevertheless, in the late eighteenth century Junkcey-lon already had tin mining, which according to a British account in 1784, was farmed out by the Siamese court to Chinese. Annually about 500 tons were exported. See G. E. Gerini, "Historical Retrospect of the Junk Ceylon Island," *JSS* 2.2:55 (1905). The activities of Captain Francis Light in the 1770s and 1780s on the island also attracted a number of Chinese immigrants. See L. F. Comber, *Chinese Secret Societies in Malaya* (New York, 1959), pp. 33–34.

48.   This was according to Hsieh Ch'ing-k'ao (pp. 3b–4a) who spent some fourteen years at sea and frequented Pattani at the turn of the century. He also mentioned that Songkla was trading with China.

49.   As we shall see in the next section, Ligor was the southern base of Rama II's junk trade with China; I am not certain that it assumed such a func-tion during Rama I's time. Chaiya, north of Ligor, which was a port

frequented by Chinese merchants at Yung-cheng's time, was, however, destroyed by the invading Burmese in 1787 and ceased to be a vital port in the Sino-Siamese trade.

50. Visiting Chantaburi in the 1780s Swedish botanist Jean Koenig (pp. 177, 181–182) said that no foreign trade was allowed there and all produce must be sent to the capital, particularly pepper.

51. Hatien made a quick recovery after its second destruction at Siamese hands in 1771, when Cambodia, which claimed control over it, refused to recognize Taksin (see Thippakorawong, *Pra-ratcha pongsawadan krung Rattanakosin,* p. 33). Siam did not formally relinquish Hatien to Vietnam until 1810 when the latter dispatched an embassy to discuss its transfer with the Siamese court. See Tôńg Phúc Ngoan and Dủóng Văn Châu, *Xiêm-la-quôć lô-trình tâp-luc* (Hong Kong, 1966), p. 3. After the 1780s the city was already under *de facto* Vietnamese administration, the Siamese having withdrawn their forces not long after the conquest. See *Khâm-dhinh-Dai-Nam hôi diêń sủ lê* (Tokyo, 1962), 48:38a.

52. Skinner, *Chinese Society in Thailand: An Analytical History* (Ithaca, Cornell University Press, 1957), p. 40.

53. *KTSL,* 1382:18a–b; W. Winterbotham, *View of the Chinese Empire* (London, 1795), p. 71; Yu Wen-i, comp., *Hsu-hsiu T'ai-wan fu chih* (Taipei, 1962), p. 452.

54. Skinner, *Chinese Society,* p. 87.

55. Morse, *Chronicles,* II, 427.

56. According to John Crawfurd (*Journal of an Embassy,* II, 161–162) passengers, who formed the most valuable importation from China to Siam, paid six and eight Spanish dollars in ready money for passages from Chang-lin and Amoy respectively in the early 1820s.

57. See *MCSL, keng* (7th. part), VII, 693b–694a.

58. The administrative structure of Siam from Rama I to Rama IV's reigns was as follows: immediately below the king was the Maha uprat or "Second King" who ruled a separate palace known as Wang-na or "Front Palace" with considerable autonomy. Immediately below him were two "super" ministers, the Akaramahasenabodi, in charge of the Kalahom

and Mahattai ministries. The bottom rung or the central administration comprised four departments, Praklang (Treasury), Wang (Palace), Muang (Capital), and Na (Agriculture). The Praklang had considerable importance since it was in charge of foreign affairs, foreign trade, and the administration of certain coastal territories; it had under its charge, the Krom-ta and Krom praklang sin-ka. For more details see Damrong Rajanubhab, "Pu-boriharn rachakarn paendin nai adit," in King Chulalongkorn (Rama V), Damrong Rajanubhab et al., *Ruang tiao ti tang-tang* (Bangkok, 1962), II, 65–66.

59.   Thippakorawong, *Pra-ratcha pongsawadan krung Rattanakosin,* p. 678. Rama IV, "The Establishment of the Kingdom," vol. 3. Since Ayudhya, Chinese had traditionally been in charge of gambling farms. From 1760 on, the operators began using counters (*pi*) in lieu of actual currency. Made of porcelain glass or lead in the various shapes, colors, and denominators, these counters in time came to be used as regular currency outside the gambling hall because they filled a long-felt need for small coins so well. It also shows the extent of the economic influence wielded by Chinese. See Joseph Haas, "Siamese Coinage," *Journal of the North China Branch of the Royal Asiatic Society,* new series 14:53–54 (1879).

61.   In 1794 Ch'ao-chou faced such a bad famine that people were forced to eat tree bark (see Jao Tsung-i, "Ch'ao-chou chih kao," p. 30a); and two years later floods at Chang-chou and Ch'üan-chou forced many to emigrate overseas (see *KTSL* 1:20b).

62.   Skinner, *Chinese Society,* pp. 45–46.

63.   Ibid., pp. 83–84.

64.   Ide Kiwata, *Kakyō* (Tokyo, 1943), p. 79; Skinner, *Chinese Society,* p. 112.

65.   In the early 1820s the total output per year from Siam was 60,000 piculs (about 8m, lbs.); the king engrossed 40,000 for monopoly sale. See John Crawfurd, *The Crawfurd Papers* (Bangkok, Vajinanana National Library, 1915), pp. 111–112.

66.   Yu Chung-hsun, p. 100.

67.   George White of the British East India Company had reported from Ayudhya in 1678 that sugar, produced in great quantities, was annually

exported to Japan and Malacca. See "Chotmaihet nai paendin Somdej Pra Narai Maharat" in installment 18, vol. 5 of *Prachoom pongsawadan chabab hor smut haeng chart* (Bangkok, 1965), installment 18, p. 502. Chinese crewmen on a Siamese ship at Nagasaki around that time also gave us an idea of sugar production in Narai's time, "Siam is also a great producer of raw sugar . . . Our ship has brought several hundred thousand catties of sugar each year." See Ishii Yoneo, p. 170.

68.   Koenig, p. 175; Crawfurd, *Journal of an Embassy,* II, 177–178.

69.   Yu Chung-shun, pp. 100–101; Burney, vol. 2, pt. 4, p. 103.

IX. The Height of The Sino-Siamese Trade

1.   Chinese shippers had a better knowledge of conditions at local ports: the kinds of commodities, prices, dealings with authorities, and so on. Furthermore, Chinese shippers dealt in goods of traditional character which were in demand.

2.   T'ien Ju-k'ang, *Shih-ch'i shih-chiu shih-chi,* p. 36.

3.   Crawfurd, *History of the Indian Archipelago,* III, 173–174.

4.   John Phipps, *A Practical Treatise on the China and Eastern Trade* (Calcutta, 1835), p. 205; T'ien Ju-k'ang, *Shih-ch'i shih-chiu shih-chi,* pp. 31–32.

5.   In the first decades of the eighteenth century, Siam was already building large junks capable of carrying a 10,000 picul (670 tons) cargo. See Ch'en Lung-ch'iung, *Hai-kuo wen-chien lu* (1793), 1:24b–25a.

6.   Crawfurd, *Journal of an Embassy,* II, 165.

7.   The oldest son of Rama I, Rama II married his own cousin, daughter of his father's second sister whose husband was a wealthy Chinese merchant. Known then as Prince Issarasuntorn, Rama II was made Rama I's Maha uparat. In 1807 he succeeded his uncle who died that year. See Chula Chakrabongse, p. 82.

8.   Luang Vichitwatakarn, "Pasi-akorn," in *Nang-su Vichit anusorn,* pp. 108–109.

9. Thippakorawong, *Pra-ratcha pongsawadan krung Ratanakosin,* pp. 720–721. Known then as Prince Issarasuntorn, Rama II was made Rama I's Maha uparat in 1807, succeeding his uncle who died that year. See Chula Chakrabongse, p. 82.

10. Thippakowarong, *Pra-ratcha pongsawadan krung Rattanakosin,* pp. 436–437; "Letter to the Chinese Emperor, A.D. 1812," in the Prince Damrong Rajanubhab Files (Bangkok, Department of Hand-Written Documents), p. 12.

11. Supatrapun, pp. 167–168.

12. Burney, I, pt. 1, p. 180.

13. Quoted in Supatrapun, pp. 164–165.

14. Akin Rabibhadana, *The Organization of Thai Society in the Early Bangkok Period, 1782–1873* (Ithaca, New York, 1969), p. 142; Crawfurd, *Journal of an Embassy,* II, 111–113.

15. Ibid. The king received 27,000 taels Siamese (£13,500) from the sale of 4,000 piculs (533,200 lbs.) of tin a year. Half of this amount may be considered as expenses (advances to miners, junk transport, etc.), and the rest was a net revenue. The king also sold 400 piculs of elephants' teeth annually (given to him as tribute) on which he made 10,000 taels Siamese (or about £5,000). The 100 piculs of eagle wood for the king annually fetched him 11,250 taels Siamese. Rama II received as tribute 400 piculs of gamboge, for whose sale he netted 6,000 taels Siamese. Revenues generated by the sale of swallows' nests and turtle eggs amounted to 25,000 taels and 1,250 taels respectively a year. 4,000 piculs of pepper was acquired by the king, for which the king paid 8 *baht* per picul to the cultivators plus transport charges, but sold for the junk trade at Bangkok for 20 *baht* a picul. Thus 100,000 taels Siamese could be generated. Finally the king got 35,000 piculs of cane sugar a year. He paid the manufacturers 7 *baht* while selling it at 10 per picul. He thus made 26,250 taels (£13,125).

16. Thippakorawong, *Pra-ratcha pongsawadan krung Rattanakosin,* p. 695; ibid., pp. 559–560; Crawfurd, *The Crawfurd Papers,* pp. 131–132.

17. Crawfurd, *History of the Indian Archipelago,* III, 182–183.

18. Chotmaihet 2 (J.S. 1176 or A.D. 1814), no. 16.

19. Crawfurd, *The Crawfurd Papers,* p. 117. The *Malapranakorn,* commanded by Luang Surasakorn (apparently an ennobled Chinese), also traded to Macao on a regular basis after 1819. See Thippakorawong, *Pra-ratcha pongsawadan krung Rattanakosin,* pp. 592–598.

20. Damrong Rajanubhab, *Tamnan pasi-akon,* p. 10; Chotmaihet 2 (J.S. 1182 or A.D. 1820), p. 52; Thippakorawong, *Pra-ratcha pongsawadan krung Rattanakosin,* p. 666.

21. Crawfurd, *Journal of an Embassy,* II, 166–167.

22. Ide Kiwata, p. 67; Damrong Rajanubhab, "Pu-borihan paendin," p. 78; Thippakorawong, *Pra-ratcha pongsawadan krung Rattanakosin,* pp. 379–380.

23. Gerini, pp. 82–83. The population of Junkceylon at this time was about 15,000–20,000 including about 800 to 1,000 Chinese.

24. Crawfurd, *Journal of an Embassy,* I, 269. Opium—both sales and consumption—was officially banned by Rama II in 1821. See Thippakorawong, *Pra-ratcha pongsawadan krung Rattanakosin,* pp. 391–393. But dating back to the 1810s, Chinese merchants had been steadily shipping the drug into the country, apparently in collusion with Siamese officials. See O. Frankfurter, "Unofficial Mission of John Morgan," *JSS* 11.1:5 (1914).

25. Burney, vol. 2 pt. 4, p. 80.

26. Supatrapun, p. 160; T'ien Ju-k'ang, *Shih-ch'i shih-chiu shih-chi,* p. 33. Several written reports are available on the royal trade to China conducted by Rama II; they are at present kept at the Department of Hand-Written Documents, the National Library, Bangkok. See Appendixes for samples.

27. See Appendices for some communications between the Bangkok court and the ruler of Songkla regarding the outfitting of junks by the latter for trade to China.

28. See Sa-nga Kanjanakapun, *Pab-prawatisart krung Rattanakosin* (Bangkok, 1962), I, n.p.

29. Crawfurd, *Journal of an Embassy,* II, 166; T'ien Ju-k'ang, *Shih-ch'i shih-chiu shih-chi,* p. 33; Crawfurd, *The Crawfurd Papers,* pp. 120–121.

30.   Phipps, pp. 206–207.

31.   Crawfurd, *Journal of an Embassy*, II, 109–110, 159; Skinner, *Chinese Society*, p. 44; See Li Tseng-chieh *Hai-wai chi-yao*, in Ch'en K'un, ed., *Ts'ung-cheng hsu-yü-lu* (1881), 7:20b.

32.   Gützlaff, pp. 82–83.

33.   Crawfurd, *Journal of an Embassy*, II, 212–213.

34.   Ibid., II, 162–163. As a rule, all properly constructed junks paid neither measurement fee nor the accumulation of fees and percentage known as *kumsha* (originally paid to different officers, but gradually transferred to the custom's superintendency's account as part of the imperial revenue). Duties paid on goods exported or imported differed from one part to another: the highest was at Amoy and the lowest at Hainan. (See Phipps, p. 206). A Siamese ship reported to the king in 1813 that Amoy collected such high "customary fees" that it was more profitable for junks to trade at smaller ports along the coast where assessments were so favorable as to offset the lower prices the cargo could fetch at the lesser ports. See Chotmaihet 2, J.S. 1175 or A.D. 1813, no. 15, pp. 4–5.

35.   The role of the Fukienese at Siam had been overshadowed by that of the Ch'ao-chou. Nevertheless, the Fukienese at this time conducted the greatest portion of the trade with the Indian archipelago, where the most numerous, largest, and richest junks sailed from Fukien loaded with black tea. See Crawfurd, *History of the Indian Archipelago*, III, 172.

36.   Huang Wei, *Shang-hai k'ai-fu ch'u-ch'i tui-wai mao-i yen-chiu* (A study of Shanghai's external trade in its initial operning period, 1842–1863); (Shanghai, 1961), pp. 6–7; Crawfurd, *Journal of an Embassy*, II, 159, 155. Many Chinese junks trading with foreign ports west of China (Siam included) frequently went on voyages to the north in the same season. About 20 large junks and many small ones went annually from Kwang-tung to Sao-cheu (Soochow) where they sold opium at an advance of 50 percent beyond the Canton prices. Some also went as far north as Ch'in-chou (Shantung). From this, one could surmise the lucrative trade that could be conducted by junks acquiring goods from Siam. See Phipps, p. 207.

37.   Ibid., II, 162. Harley MacNair (p. 32 n.) says that an 800–900 ton Amoy junk could carry at least 1,600 passengers.

38. Sa-nga Kanjanakapun, *Pab-prawatisart krung Rattanakosin* I, n.p. Among Chinese articles exported to the Indian Archipelago in the late 1810s, black tea, coarse porcelain, wrought iron, and cotton cloths constituted the most important items. See Crawfurd, *History of the Indian Archipelago,* III, 181.

39. See G. E. Gerini, *"Siam's Intercourse with China,"* *Asiatic Quarterly Review* 14.28:393 (October 1902).

40. T'ien Ju-k'ang, *Shih-ch'i shih-chiu shih-chi,* p. 37; Crawfurd, *Journal of an Embassy,* II, 159; Crawfurd, *History of the Indian Archipelago,* II, 178–179; Burney, vol. 2, pt. 4, p. 81. A description of the trade conducted by the Chinese junks upon arrival at Bangkok may be of some interest. The following account by C. B. Buckley, author of *An Anecdotal History of Old Times in Singapore,* about Chinese junks calling at Singapore in the 1820s was probably typical also of Bangkok:

   "The commercial activity of the Chinese is seen to the greatest extent during the annual visit of the junks from China. These remain in the harbour from December until June, and throughout the whole period boats filled with Chinese are continually passing and repassing among the shipping, giving it the appearance of a floating fair.

   "The first junk, which arrives generally a little before Christmas, is most anxiously looked for, and when its approach is notified by the crew of a Malay sampan which has been on the lookout to the eastward, the greatest bustle pervades the Chinese community ... Many hasten off to the vessel to learn the news from China ... The first reaches the junk when she is still several miles distant, and as she nears the town she gains an accession of bulk at every fathom, until at last the unwieldy mass slowly trails into the roads, surrounded by a dense mass of boats, having an appearance of a locust which has inadvertently crossed an ant's nest, and is dragging after it countless myriads of the enraged inhabitants, attached to its legs and feelers. As the decks of the junk are always crowded with immigrants, the greater proportion of the visitors are obliged to remain in the boats, and those endeavour to gain as much information as they can by shouting out questions to the people on board.

   "Other junks arrive, and although these do not excite quite as much interest as the first, the same scene is enacted over each. For a day or two after their arrival, there is little business transacted, as the crews are all engaged in building roofs over the vessels to shelter the wares which are to be exposed for sale on the decks. When these arrangements are completed, the fair commences, and the junks are surrounded from

morning till night by the boats of the Chinese traders from the shore."
Quoted in Song Ong Siang, *One Hundred Years of History of the Chinese
in Singapore* (Singapore, 1967), pp. 41–42.

41. Wales, p. 201. The influence of the Chinese at Bangkok by this time had
     become so pervasive that Bangkok's palaces and other large edifices bore
     a heavy Chinese influence. The main palaces with their enclosures
     resembled the Forbidden City at Peking. See Ch'en Hsu-ching, *Hsien-lo
     yu Chung-kuo* (Ch'ang-sha, 1941), p. 51.

42. Rama III was the half-brother of the future Rama IV. Though a concu-
     bine's son—as against the future Rama IV who was the queen's offspring
     —Rama III gained the throne over his more legitimate brother because
     the former was considered to have possessed more administrative experi-
     ence and political backing. See Steinberg, p. 111.

43. Damrong Rajanbuhab, *Prawat Somdet Chaopraya Borom-maha Sisuriya-
     wong* (Bangkok, 1929), pp. 2–3; Burney, vol. 2, pt. 4, p. 82.

44. Cady, p. 341.

45. Ibid., p. 185.

46. Burney, I, 177.

47. Chula Chakrabongse, p. 162; Sa-nga Kanjanakapun, *Prawat karnka,* pp.
     106–107.

48. Silks were much prized by Siamese officials and the nobility. D. E.
     Malloch (p. 11) said that, "The Siamese dress gaudily in silks, satins,
     and velvets, to attend manages and festivals, and these articles of dress
     are mostly imported from China."

49. *TCHTSL* 511:16a–b; *HTSL* 320:37a–b.

50. Ibid., vol. 2 pt. 4, p. 80.

51. Again from available commercial dispatches in Rama III's reign we
     obtain a partial list of Siamese junks trading to China for the 1844–
     1845 season (some owned, some chartered), namely the *Kuntong* (Chin
     Kao was shipmaster), carrying a cargo of pepper, sapan wood, red wood,
     bee's wax, and so forth; the *Chun-ha* (outfitted by Prince Tinnakorn

with Chin Sin as shipmaster), carrying a cargo of sapan wood, red wood, pepper, tin bee's wax, rudders, wooden boards and planks, red sugar, and so forth; the *Ngek-chai* (outfitted by Pra Swadwari); the *Li-chai;* the *Li-heng;* the *Hong-chai;* the *Li-hon;* the *Li-sun;* the *Hong-chai;* the *Li-hon;* the *Li-sun;* the *Ek-si;* the *Chun-li* (outfitted by Pra Sombat-wanit); the *Eng-tai;* the *Eng-sun;* the *Eng-euy* (outiftted by Luang Maitri-wanit); the *Huat-seng* (outiftted by Luang Po-karat); the *Gi-nguan* (outfitted by Luang Prasert-wanit); the *Man-sun* (outfitted by Khun Pakdi-akon); the *Eng-Li* (outfitted by Khun Wattana-pirom). These vessels, apparently commissioned by Rama III to carry official cargoes, were assigned to trade at Canton, Ningpo, and Shanghai. Ibid., pp. 183–184.

52. See *MCSL, keng* (7th. part), VI, 577; Burney, vol. 2, pt. 4, p. 80.

53. "The Island of Hainan," *The Asiatic Journal* 21.1:15–16 (1826). These Hainan ports were rarely visited by Western ships, because they were considered to be in the "western route" (*hsi-lu*) of the Kwangtung maritime traffic. Instead, Western ships of course concentrated at Canton, which was considered to be in the "middle route" (*chung-lu*). Chieh-shih and Namoa to the northeast were regarded as lying in the "eastern route" (*tung-lu*). See *Chou-pan i-wu shih-mo* 3:28b–29a (IV, 64).

54. Malloch, pp. 28, 8.

55. Phipps, p. 204; cited in Wang Gung-wu, *Nan-yang Hua-jen,* p. 80; Phipps, pp. 204, 203; Roberts, pp. 121–122.

56. *Chinese Repository* (March 1833), I, 469.

57. W. S. Ruschenberger, *A Voyage Round the World* (Philadelphia, 1838), pp. 278–280; *Chinese Repository* (1834), II, 64; Ibid. (September 1836), I, 235. Also in the late 1830s Howard Malcom, a visitor to the Siamese capital, estimated that there were no fewer than 200 junks from China visiting Siam a year, many of them of five or six hundred tons, while some were over a thousand tons. Seventy to eighty junks sometimes were in the river at Bangkok at a time. He further concurred with John Crawfurd that "Bangkok has certainly the largest commerce, next to Canton, of any place in the world, not inhabited by White men." See Howard Malcom, *Travels in Southeast Asia* (Boston, 1839), II, 127–128.

58. "A Dissertation upon the Commerce of China," p. 36.

59. Ibid., pp. 35–36. One reason why the trade conducted by the Ch'ao-chou people was so large may have been the overpopulation and unemployment in northeastern Kwangtung, which compelled the local government to grant liberal allowances for foreigh trade. Furthermore, the local people were permitted to emigrate to avoid rebellion, and they sent back large remittances; junks had been known to carry 60,000 Spanish dollars on one run for such purposes. See Gützlaff, pp. 165–166.

60. "A Dissertation upon the Commerce of China," p. 36.

61. T'ien Ju-k'ang, "Tsai-lun shih-ch'i chih shih-chiu shih-chi chung-yeh Chung-kuo fan-ch'uan-yeh ti fa-chan," *Li-shih yen-chiu,* no. 12:6 (1957). Shanghai, the principal port for the trade of the Yangtze river basin, was rapidly becoming a major entrepôt of the Chinese coastal trade. By 1769, there were enough Ningpo merchants there for a guild. See Susan Mann Jones, "Finance in Ningpo: The 'Ch'ien Chuang; 1750–1880," in W. E. Willmott, ed., *Economic Organization in Chinese Society* (Stanford, 1972), p. 57.

62. Ibid., p. 7.

63. Skinner, *Chinese Society,* p. 41.

64. Gützlaff, p. 84. Gützlaff said that Namoa was where Siamese junks without proper permits to call at mainland Ch'ao-chou had to anchor, and from there small boats came out from the mainland to fetch the ship's crew (see ibid., p. 85).

65. Gützlaff (ibid., p. 178) in the early 1830s described Amoy as "one of the greatest emporiums of the empire, and one of the most important markets of Asia. "The people there were enterprising merchants who also settled in Formosa, Indo-China, Siam, and the East Indies. He also noted that officials there would not permit foreigners to trade at the port.

66. Skinner, *Chinese Society,* p. 42; Phipps, p. 204; Huang Wei, p. 6; Robert Fortune, *Three Years' Wanderings in the Northern Provinces of China* (London, 1847), p. 90.

67. George Earl, *The Eastern Seas or Voyages and Adventures in the Indian Archipelago in 1832-33-34* (London, 1837), p. 160. See also C. B. Buckley, *An Anecdotal History of Old Times in Singapore* (Singapore, 1902) for a description of Chinese junks calling at Singapore in the 1820s, a scene which was probably typical also of Bangkok. Cf. n. 40.

68. Walter Vella, *Siam under Rama III, 1824–1851* (New York, 1957), pp. 19–20; Malcom, II, 128.

69. Gützlaff, p. 53; Phipps, p. 285; Morrison, p. 181.

70. Roberts, p. 316. Siamese sugar exports reached their peak year in 1859. In the 1850s, several thousand laborers were employed on plantations and in factories at Nakorn Pathom (near Bangkok) which also had upwards of thirty sugar-refining centers, each employing two to three hundred Chinese (see Yu Ching-hsun, pp. 100–101). Unlike the manufacture of sugar, rice cultivation was the exclusive domain of native Siamese; the Chinese acted as middlemen, processors, and shippers.

71. Morrison, p. 161; Phipps, p. 329.

72. Burney, II, pt. 4, p. 104.

73. Gützlaff correctly observed (p. 72) that every vessel built in Siam had a Siamese noble for its patron or sponsor.

74. Phipps, p. 204.

75. Roberts, pp. 272, 311.

76. Earl, p. 159.

77. Ibid., p. 206.

78. A visitor to Chantaburi in the early 1820s, George Finlayson, described the place (pp. 255–257) as one of the richest provinces of Siam; it had a good harbor and abundant timber for shipbuilding. The population was composed mostly of Chinese who dominated the economy of the area.

79. Crawfurd, *Journal of an Embassy,* I, 290; II, 206, 162–163.

80. Ibid., II, 164. The 1818 edition of the *Ta-Ch'ing hui-tien* (30:15a) also mentioned dried fish, dried shrimp, betel nuts, and bee's wax, among the articles acquired for the China trade.

81. Crawfurd, *Journal of an Embassy,* II, 320. But according to the *Khâm dinh Dai-Nam hôi diên sù lê* (48:8a), there were also Siamese ships based at Hatien trading to the towns in Vietnam's Gia-dinh province by the turn of the century.

82. Crawfurd, *Journal of an Embassy,* II, 164. The *Khâm-dinh Ðai-Nam hôi
     diên sử lê* (48:3a–4a) said that Canton, Shanghai, Macao, and Southeast
     Asian vessels paid the highest duties at Vietnamese ports; those of Ch'ao-
     chou less, and Hainan ships paid the least.

83. Crawfurd, *History of the Indian Archipelago,* III, 182–183; Crawfurd, *The
     Crawfurd Papers,* p. 191; see Chotmaihet 2 (J.S. 1175 or A.D. 1813), no.
     12, and (J.S. 1179 or A.D. 1817), no. 2; see L. Mills, "British Malaya,
     1824–67," *Journal of the Malayan Branch of Royal Asiatic Society*
     33.3:115 (1960).

84. Crawfurd, *History of the Indian Archipelago,* III, 186; T'ien Ju-k'ang,
     Shih-ch'i shih-chiu shih-chi, p. 39.

85. Crawfurd, *The Crawfurd Papers,* p. 186.

86. Comber, pp. 49–50; T'ien Ju-k'ang, *Shih-ch'i shih-chi,* p. 39; Crawfurd,
     Journal of an Embassy, II, 361.

87. Wong Lin Ken, "The Trade of Singapore, 1819–1869," *Journal of the
     Malayan Branch, Royal Asistic Society* 33.4:34, 138 (December 1960).

88. Ibid., p. 152; Phipps, p. 286; Burney, vol. 3, pt. I, pp. 188–189; Wong
     Lin Ken, p. 151.

89. Burney, vol. 3, pt. 1, p. 189.

90. Ibid., vol. 2, pt. 4, p. 80.

91. Malloch, p. 31.

X. Chinese Immigration and Its Economic Impact

1. Malloch, p. 8.

2. Skinner, *Chinese Society,* p. 72, considers the figures for the Chinese
    population in 1822 and 1827 (supplied by Crawfurd and Malloch respec-
    tively) exaggerated; they were probably based on impressions of principal
    trading places in Lower Siam and along the Gulf and Bangkok where
    Chinese congregated, and hence did not represent a true picture for the
    whole country, to which the observers applied the above figures. Skinner's

own estimate for 1822 is that it was closer to 200,000 and no higher than 250,000. (See ibid., p. 71.) He also finds fault with the figure for the Chinese population given for 1849, and thinks (ibid., p. 72) that it should be no more than 325,000.

3. Again, Skinner thinks (ibid., p. 58) that the estimate of 15,000 per annum was too high; he gives his own at 6,000 to 8,000.

4. Vella, p. 26.

5. Earl, pp. 169–170; Roberts, pp. 173–174; Joseph Jiang, "The Chinese in Thailand," *Journal of Southeast Asian History,* 7.1:45 (1966).

6. Yu Chung-hsun, p. 103; Hsiao Ji-i, "Pen-hui hui-shih," in *T'ai-kuo Hua-ch'iao K'e-shu tsung-hui san-shih chou-nien chi-nien t'e-k'an* (Bangkok, 1958), p. 4.

7. Liang Chi-fan, p. 1.

8. Malloch, p. 10.

9. Rabibhadana, p. 153.

10. One contemporary French visitor, M. Bruguière in "Notices of the Religion, Manners, and Customs of the Siamese," English trans., in *Chinese Repository* (April 1844), VIII, 196, described these numerous raft houses along the Bangkok river, "Chinese merchants, to save expense, build their houses on the river; they construct a bamboo raft, which is secured on two sides to posts, and as the cords are loose, the raft rises and falls with the tide. Houses and shops are built upon these rafts, which at need can be loosened from the post, and floated off to a new spot."

11. Gützlaff, p. 71.

12. As reported by Dr. Dan Bradley in 1835, and cited in Bacon, pp. 209–210.

13. Ibid., pp. 211, 216.

14. Most Fukienese coming to Lower Siam at this time were from Ch'üan-chou and Chang-chou. They left from the ports of these two prefectures,

and transferred via Kwangtung, Formosa, or Chekiang. It was not until after the Opium War that most left directly from Amoy. See Chuang Wei-chi, Lin Chin-chih et al., "Fu-chien Chin-chiang tsuan-ch'u Hua-ch'iao shih t'iao-ch'a pao-kao," *Hsia-men ta-hsueh hsueh-pao* 1:114–115 (1958).

15. Burney, vol. 2, pt. 1, p. 18; Okamoto Ryūzō, p. 137; H. Warrington Smyth, *Five Years in Siam* (London, 1898), II, 76.

16. Burney, vol. 3, pt. 1, pp. 5–6.

17. Damrong Rajanubhab, *Tamnan karn lurk bon-bia,* pp. 4–12 *passim.* Chula Chakrabongse, p. 150.

18. Rabibhadana, p. 142. For instance, edible birds' nests in the vicinity of Chaiya and Smui island were farmed out to one Luang Chamnan of Chaiya (see Chotmaihet 2, J.S. 1176 or A.D. 1814, no. 19).

19. Dit Bunnag was an adroit adviser to Rama III. David Wyatt in "Family Politics in Nineteenth-Century Thailand," *Journal of Southeast Asian History* 9.2:220 (1968) speaks of him as follows: "He carefully built up his economic base both domestically in the Western provinces and through external trade, and he seems to have contracted an alliance of convenience with the growing Chinese community which was under his jurisdiction as Praya Praklang."

20. Supatrapun, pp. 185–186.

21. Damrong Rajanubhab, *Tamnan psai-akorn,* pp. 11–13. Rama III in the process also abolished some of the farms maintained in the previous reign.

22. Damrong (ibid., p. 14) said the Siamese system was probably based on the Chinese conception of quotas. The Siamese term for the farm tax, *pa-si,* was derived from the Ch'ao-chou appelation of the term *wu-ssu* (*boo-si,* in Siamese transliteration), which designated an office in charge of revenue collection.

23. Rabibhadana, pp. 142–143; Sittipun, *Ton trakoon kun-nang Thai,* p. 177; Rabibhadana, p. 135; Damrong Rajanubhab, *Tesapiban,* p. 30. In certain provinces, such as Songkla, the governor was himself a tax farmer. See Praya Anumanrachaton, *Tamnan sulakakorn* (Bangkok, 1939), p. 44.

24.   Burney, vol. 2, pt. 4, p. 102. The farm of refined cane sugar in the Third
        Reign was given to one Chin Tong-kao (a Chinese) in 1834. See Sittipun,
        Ton trakoon kun-nang Thai, p. 182.

25.   Burney, vol. 1 pt. 1, p. 180.

26.   Ibid., vol. 2, pt. 4, pp. 101–102.

27.   Sittipun, *Ton trakoon kun-nang Thai,* pp. 183–184.

28.   B. O. Cartwright, "The Huey Lottery," *JSS,* 18.3:222 (1924). The
        lottery farm proved to be so successful that it lasted 81 years, only to
        be abolished in 1916.

29.   Sittipun, *Ton trakoon kun-nang Thai,* pp. 179–182.

30.   Damrong Rajanubhab, comp., "Tamnan muang Ranong," in *Prachoom
        pongsawadan chabab hor smut haeng chart* (Bangkok, 1970), install-
        ment 50, XII, 386–392.

31.   Damrong Rajanubhab, "Pu-boriharn paendin," p. 69.

32.   Rabibhadana, pp. 162–163. Such as Hsu Szu-chang who became the
        founder of the na Ranong family.

33.   Sittipun, *Ton tradoon kun-nang Thai,* pp. 141–142.

34.   Wales, pp. 219–222. "The taxes were only to be levied according to a
        fixed rate (usually 10%) and the farmers were prohibited from oppressing
        the people, though the conditions under which they had to work, apart
        from the temperament of the individual farmer, often obliged them to
        exercise oppression. The tax farmer, who was usually Chinese, was respon-
        sible to an official of the Gland Singa Klang Sin-ka or any other *kram*
        department to which he had to pay the amount of tax money he agreed to
        deliver during the course of the year. This sum was arrived at by putting
        up for auction each particular tax each year, the bidders being guided in
        the amount of their bids by preliminary inquiries and inspection of the
        places where the particular trade was carried on. The farmer paid the
        money to the treasury as follows: "three months' payment in advance for
        the first month (the two-months' installment being in the nature of a
        guarantee, and so on at the rate of one twelfth of the total sum per
        month until the tenth month, the guarantee . . . will be readily appreciated

that to obtain these lucrative monopolies the would-be farmers sometimes bid sums that meant considerable extortion had to be practised by
them to fulfill their obligations."

35. Damrong Rajanubhab, "Tamnan karn lurk bon-bia," p. 414, 415. By
     Rama IV's time, it had increased to 500,000 *baht* (£62,500) a year.

36. Chotmaihet 4 (J.S. 1215 or A.D. 1853), no. 82.

37. Skinner, *Leadership,* p. 6. Skinner postulates that there was less sense of
     community among the Chinese then than during the previous Ayudhyan
     period when Fukienese were the single most dominant group.

38. Hsieh Yu-yung, p. 276; Okamoto Ryūzō, pp. 110–111.

39. Wen Hsiung-fei, pp. 110–111; Comber, p. 38; Yu Chung-hsun, p. 243,
     quoting from T'ien Ju-k'ang's "Chin-tai Hua-ch'iao shih."

40. Chotmaihet 2 (J.S. 1175 or A.D. 1813), no. 17; Damrong Rajanubhab,
     Nitarn boran-kadi (Bangkok, 1968), pp. 160–161; P'an Hsing-nung, p.
     30; Okamoto Ryūzō, p. 111; Chotmaihet 4 (J.S. 1226 or A.D. 1864),
     no. 94.

41. The growth of secret societies in Siam coincided with the proliferation
     of the San-ho hui on Formosa, at Kwangtung and Kwangsi, Chiangsi,
     and the Indian archipelago. See Hirayama Amane, *Chūgoku himitsu
     shakai shi* (Shanghai, 1932).

42. Preecha Niyomwong, "Man-ku huang-ch'ao shih chi: La-ma ti erh shih-
     huang shih-tai" (Rama II period), tr. "T'ang-hua," *Chung-yuan yueh-
     k'an* 1.6:62 (1941). Interestingly enough, Nakorn Chaisi remains today
     populated by lower-class Chinese. Between 1844 and 1848, Rama III
     tried unsuccessfully to stamp out Chinese opium smuggling along the
     coast. See Vella, p. 18.

XI. Declining Fortunes of the Sino-Siamese Junk Trade

1.   Sor Prainoi, *Chao-tangpratet nai prawatisart Thai* (Bangkok, 1973), p.
     218; Chakrabongse, p. 133; Cady, p. 326; Frankfurter, "The Mission of
     Sir James Brooke," p. 6; Thippakorawong, *Pra-ratcha pongsawadan
     krung Rattanakosin,* p. 607.

2. Britain emerged from the Napoleonic War (1793–1813) as the leading sea power, and attempted to find new markets in the East for its Lancashire textiles. In addition to a search for markets, the Industrial Revolution had increased British demands for tropical materials.

3. Anumanratchaton, pp. 18–19; Mills, pp. 156–157.

4. Crawfurd, *Journal of an Embassy,* II, 138–139.

5. Chakrabongse, p. 136. Nevertheless, the mission did register some positive achievements. It collected valuable information on the geography, resources, population, government, and trade of the country. It also received assurances from the Siamese court that there would be no further increase in duties and charges on British ships calling at Siamese ports, and that trade would be facilitated.

6. T'ien Ju-k'ang, *Shih-ch'i shih-chiu shih-chi,* p. 35.

7. Siamese Legation, Paris, comps., *State Papers of the Kingdom of Siam, 1664–1886* (London, 1886), pp. 76–80.

8. Not only had the British been entrenched in Penang, Singapore, and parts of mainland Malaya, they were also conducting campaigns against the Burmese, which culminated in the signing of the Treaty of Candabo in 1826 in Britain's favor. See Cady, p. 335.

9. Burney, I, 50–51.

10. Cady, p. 338.

11. Earl, p. 177.

12. Wong Lin Ken, p. 140; Frankfurter, "The Mission of Sir James Brooke," pp. 21–22; Supatrapun, p. 180.

13. Malloch, pp. 28–29.

14. Vella, p. 19.

15. *Chinese Repository* (September 1836), V, 235–236; Anumanrachaton, p. 26.

16. Jao Tsung-i, "Ch'ao-chou chih kao," *Shih-yeh chih,* p. 1b.

17. Anumanrachaton, pp. 27–28.

18. Townsend Harris, *The Complete Journal of Townsend Harris* (New York, 1930), pp. 101–102.

19. *Chinese Repository* (August 1835), IV, 190–191.

20. Damrong Rajanubhab, "Introduction of Western Culture in Siam," *JSS* 20.2:96 (1926); S. Bateman, "Letter, March 10, 1870," *Siam Repository* (1870), II, 299; Vichitwatakarn, "Pasi-akon," pp. 105–106; Bishop Jean Baptiste Pallegoix, *Lao-ruang muang Thai*, tr. Sunt Komolabut (Bangkok, 1963), p. 306; Supatrapun, pp. 263–264.

21. Wong Lin Ken, p. 147; Malloch, p. 27; Wales, p. 207.

22. Opart Sevikun, *Praracha bida haeng karn patiroop* (Bangkok, 1970), pp. 152–154.

23. W. A. Graham, *Siam* (London, 1924), II, 121; Ingram, pp. 19–20.

24. Pallegoix, *Description du royaume Thai ou Siam* (London, 1969), I, 324–325.

25. Ingram, pp. 19–20.

26. Sir John Bowring, *The Kingdom and People of Siam* (London, 1969), I, 255; Damrong Rajanubhab, *Tamnan pasi-akon*, pp. 43–51.

27. Ibid., pp. 58–67, 17.

28. Pallegoix, *Description,* I, 72–73; Bowring, I, 277–281; Pallegoix, *Lao-ruang,* p. 325.

29. Wong Lin Ken, p. 148. By the end of the 1860s the number of junks trading to Singapore from Siam had dwindled so fast that in 1865–1866, only one junk is said to have called.

30. Pra Intramontri, "T'ai-kuo tsui-hou i-ch'ih ju-kung Chung-kuo chi-lu-shu," tr. "T'ang-hua," *Chung-yuan yueh-k'an* 1:16 (1941).

31. "Supa-aksorn chong-tok moo-i tung Chaopraya Praklang klang-ti si," in Damrong Rajanubhab Files, Department of Hand-Written Documents.

32.   Intramontri, pp. 17, 26.

33.   Thippakorawong, *Chronicles,* II, 284. According to Rama IV himself, the junks trading between Siam and China were still sailing every month in the year 1862.

34.   Hsu Yun-ch'iao, "Chung-Hsien t'ung-shih k'ao," p. 33; Tseng Chien-ping, p. 39; Promboon, pp. 294–295.

35.   Narong Traiwat, "Mua Ror Si song tat kwam maitri kab Pak-king," in ibid., *Keb-tok* (1961), pp. 311–313.

36.   Abbot Low Moffat, *Mongkut, the King of Siam* (Ithaca, New York, 1961), p. 25.

37.   Siamese Legation, Paris, comps., *State Papers of the Kingdom of Siam, 1664–1886* (London, 1886), pp. 81–85. Treaty with the United States was signed in 1856.

38.   Fukuda Shōzō, p. 327.

39.   Graham, II, 98–99.

40.   But the Ch'ing efforts in the suppression of the rebels led to increasing demands for Siamese timber for the construction of warships. In T'ung-chih's reign, the Fukien governor sent officers to buy timber at Bangkok. See *Siamese Repository* (April 1870), II, 298–299.

41.   T'ien Ju-k'ang, "Tsai-lun," p. 7.

42.   Han Ch'ao, *Ch'ao-chou feng-wu* (Hong Kong, 1970), p. 5.

43.   Jao Tsung-i, "Ch'ao-chou chih kao," *chiao-t'ung,* p. 7b. Regular steamship services between Swatow and Bangkok (via Hong Kong) were initiated in 1876, and direct services in 1892.

44.   T'ien Ju-k'ang, "Tsai-lun," pp. 7–8. Chinese junks came now to be restricted primarily to certain routes and/or the transportation of certain articles. In China for instance, junks were still relied on to carry soybeans from Manchuria to the south. They also carried cargoes from larger Western-style ships at the main ports for distribution to other lesser ports along the coast and inland waterways. See ibid., pp. 10–11.

45. Graham, II, 98–99; Anumanrachaton, p. 28; Damrong Rajanubhab, *Tamnan ngern-tra* (Bangkok, 1933), p. 4; T'ien Ju-k'ang, *Shih-ch'i shih-chiu shih-chi,* p. 41; Smyth, II, 268, Damrong Rajanubhab, *Tamnan ngern-tra,* pp. 5–6; Jao Tsung-i, "Ch'ao-chou chih k'ao," *chiao-tung,* p. 3b; Skinner, *Chinese Society,* p. 45.

46. Wong Lin Ken, p. 149.

47. Damrong Rajanubhab, *Tamnan pasi-akon,* p. 21; Damrong Rajanubhab, *Prawat Somdet,* p. 22; Supatrapun, pp. 264–265; Ide Kiwata, p. 67; Vichitwatakarn, "Pasi-akon," p. 88.

48. Damrong Rajanubhab, *Prawat Somdet,* pp. 22, 25–26. This fell in with the 30-year period from 1847 to 1874 during which some 250,000 to 500,000 Chinese emigrated overseas, mainly to Southeast Asia.

49. Skinner, *Chinese Society,* p. 43.

50. Thippakorawong, *Chronicles,* II, 30.

Chinese and Siamese Dynasty and Reign Names
from the Seventeenth to the Late Nineteenth Centuries

Ming dynasty

Wan-li 萬曆 (1573–1619)

T'ai-ch'ang 泰昌 (1620)

T'ien-ch'i 天啓 (1620–1627)

Ch'ung-ch'en 崇禎 (1627–1643)

Ch'ing dynasty

Shun-chih 順治 (1644–1661)

K'ang-hsi 康熙 (1662–1722)

Yung-cheng 雍正 (1723–1735)

Ch'ien-lung 乾隆 (1736–1795)

Chia-ch'ing 嘉慶 (1796–1820)

Tao-kuang 道光 (1821–1850)

Hsien-feng 咸豐 (1851–1861)

T'ung-chih 同治 (1862–1874)

Ayudhya dynasty

Naresuen หเรศวร (1590–1605)

Ekatotsarote เอกาทศรถ (1605–1611)

Songtam ทรงธรรม (1611–1628)

Jettatirat เชษฐาธิราช (1628–1629)

Atityawong อาทิตยวงศ์ (1629)

Prasart Tong ประสาททอง (1630–1655)

Chaofah Jai เจ้าฟ้าชัย (1655–1656)

Srisutammaraja ศรีสุธรรมราชา (1656)

Narai หารายณ์ (1656–1688)

Petracha เพทราชา (1689–1703)

Prachao Sua พระเจ้าเสือ (1703–1709)

Taisra ท้ายสระ (1709–1733)

Boromakot บรมโกษ (1733–1758)

Utumporn อุทุมพร (1758)

Ekatat เอกทัต (1758–1766)

Thonburi dynasty

Taksin ตากสิน (1767–1781)

Chakri dynasty

Rama I ร.๑ (1782–1809)

Rama II ร.๒ (1809–1825)

Rama III ร.๓ (1825–1851)

Rama IV ร.๔ (1851–1868)

BIBLIOGRAPHICAL NOTE

This study covers a period of two centuries and range of issues with emphasis on economic relations between China and Siam. But Sino-Siamese trade is a little-studied subject and, as in any pioneer work, the substantive reference material required for a definitive exposition is inadequate. First, although there was an active trade between Siam and China in the seventeenth, eighteenth, and nineteenth centuries, it was not subject to extensive documentation. Merchants, seamen, and others who were engaged in such an enterprise were hardly inclined to keep written accounts. This was not merely a problem of literacy (as most of them could neither read nor write) nor of inclination (as they were not scholars but individuals dealing with the practical aspects of livelihood); it also stemmed from, as in the case of China, the negative official policy toward overseas maritime commerce. Furthermore, since much of the officially sanctioned trade of Siam with China was conducted in the politically oriented tributary framework, any official record kept by participants would invariably stress the political and ceremonial aspects, leaving little room for economic matters. In the perception of Chinese officialdom, foreign trade was assigned a secondary role in the agrarian and self-sufficient Chinese society. Trade with China affected the Siamese court more directly, and no doubt some accounts were kept by royal scribes, but this trade was mainly entrusted to resident Chinese merchants, which partially explains the dearth of written records. In addition, the humidity of the tropical climate, the relatively late introduction of printing (the first printing press was set up in Bangkok in the 1830s by a Western missionary), and the physical destruction of Ayudhya, Siam's former capital, in 1776, may all have contributed to the scarcity of documents.

There is also a lack of extensive Western accounts. The period between the close of the seventeenth and the beginning of the nineteenth centuries was a watershed in the history of Western involvement in the Eastern Seas; it divides the first phase of Western expansionism in the East, which started and ended with the rise and fall of the Portuguese and Spanish sea power, and the second phase, which saw the emergence of British maritime supremacy. During this time, the Eastern Seas were for the most part devoid of substantial Western political and economic influence, while the Chinese and other indigenous junk traders prospered. Few Western traders and adventurers paid attention to the region. The situation was drastically altered in the wake of the Industrial Revolution toward the end of the eighteenth century when Britain, in the forefront of other Western nations, began to reassert itself in the economic and political life of the Eastern Seas.

342

By far the most important references in this study are official and semi-official records pertaining to governmental, political, and economic institutions. On the Chinese side, the copious collection of edicts, memorials, rescripts, and so forth, for the successive reigns of the Ch'ing dynasty, namely, *Ta-Ch'ing li-ch'ao shih-lu* is an indispensable primary source. Although it is the most extensive collection, it is by no means exhaustive. There are other court records available, grouped according to a specific period or subject matter. For instance, *Ming-Ch'ing shih-liao* is an important collection of documents for the late Ming and early Ch'ing periods; Part 7 of this work contains a good selection of documents relating to Sino-Siamese affairs. In 1930 the National Palace Museum in Peking published a series of historical papers from its archives known as *Shih-liao hsun-k'an*. Finally, *Wen-hsien ts'ung-p'ien* published by the Historical Records Office in Taiwan is another collection of official documents belonging to the early nineteenth-century era.

In the reign of the Yung-cheng Emperor (1723–1735), the court paid considerable attention to economic conditions; the emperor instructed officials throughout the realm to submit to him periodic assessments of the local situation. *Yung-cheng chu-p'i yu-chih* consists of memorials of this nature and the emperor's comments on them. Such information provides an important basis for understanding an eighteenth-century Southeast China which was beginning to feel the Malthusian squeeze of rising population and falling economic productivity. This source is also important for figures on grain production and prices at various localities.

This study profits from documents concerning Ch'ing China's foreign relations in general. A notable collection of documents of the late eighteenth and early nineteenth centuries is entitled *Ch'ing-tai wai-chiao shih-liao*. Published by the National Palace Museum in Taipei, this volume contains records of the Chia-ch'ing and Tao-kuang periods. Particularly noteworthy are those official communications that throw light on the extent to which the Siamese side had managed to "abuse" the tributary system by the early nineteenth century. For documents on foreign relations between Ayudhya Siam and the early Ch'ing dynasty, it is useful to consult Wang Chih-ch'un's *Kuo-ch'ao jou-yuan chi* (known alternately as *Kuo-ch'ao t'ung-shang shih-mo*), in which trade is a main theme.

Not long ago, Li Kuang-t'ao, a senior researcher at the Institute of History and Philology of the Academia Sinica in Taiwan, published several primary documents on eighteenth-century Sino-Siamese state relations which he had come upon in the Institute's archives. Published in the Institute's journal under the heading of "Chi Ch'ing-tai ti Hsien-lo kuo-piao," these state papers are translations of original Siamese court communications to the Peking court which were borne by Siamese envoys on occasions of tribute presentation and so forth.

Ch'ing official regulations and statutes governing tributary relations with Siam are to be found in *Ta-Ch'ing hui-tien* and its companion volume which contains cases affected by such regulations: *Ta-Ch'ing hui-tien shih-li.*

Fang-chih or local gazetteers which were compiled by individuals or communities at the provincial or county level under official sanction or encouragement constitute an important source of information for Sino-Thai relations and the Chinese junk trade. Foremost is *Hsia-men chih* by Chou K'ai et al., which provides details on ships and shipping as well as on Chinese oceanic trade from Amoy during the first decades of the eighteenth century. A brief survey of foreign trade from South Fukien after the second maritime trade ban was lifted in the 1720s can also be found in a work on provincial administrative affairs entitled *Fu-chien t'ung-chih cheng-shih lueh. Fu-chien t'ung-chih* further provides a list of foreign trading countries with which Fukien maintained contact as well as official regulations pertaining to maritime trade.

Information on foreign trade in Kwangtung province and regulations governing tributary missions from Siam may be found in *Kuang-tung t'ung-chih* which was compiled by Liang-Kuang Governor-General Juan Yuan. Relevant information on tributary trade and relations, local economic conditions, emigration, and so on, may also be gleaned from other provincial gazetters such as *Ao-men chi-lueh* by Ying Kuang-yen and Chang Ju-lin, *Kuang-tung hai-fang hui-lan* by Lu K'un and Ch'en Hung-ch'ih, and Sheng T'ing-fang's *Kuang-chou fu chih.* (Similarly, such South Fukien local gazetteers as Wu Lien-hsun's *Chang-chou fu chih,* Ch'en Ju-chien's *Chang-p'u hsien-chih,* and *Fu-chien sheng-li* may be examined for mention of the area's trade and economic organizations.)

Liang T'ing-nan, a Canton official in the nineteenth century, compiled and edited two works dealing with tributary states that sent tributes to Peking via Canton, and the Canton customs superintendency which was in charge of foreign trade at Canton. In his *Yueh-tao kung-kuo shuo,* Liang hand-copied several official documents pertaining to relations between Siam and China, particularly those which involved the Canton authorities. *Yueh-hai kuan chih* was Liang's more copious and general work containing a collection of archival sources. (Chapters 21 to 24 describe China's tributary trade with various countries including Siam.)

Like Chinese official documents, Siamese official materials comprise mainly the recording of events and other information pertaining to the court and government, the main concern being the conduct of government and civil functions. They are essentially descriptive in form and are arranged to provide some historical continuity.

Siamese writings that are available on the subject are far fewer than Chinese, and most of the extant sources date only from the nineteenth century. A substantial number of documents pertaining to the Siamese court's dealings with China are in the *Damrong Rajanubhab Files* which are kept in the Thai National Library. (Prince Damrong Rajanubhab, a son of Rama V, is dubbed the "Father of Thai History" for his great contribution to modern Thai history and historiography.) This set of documents describes various Siamese missions to the Ch'ing court during the period from the end of the eighteenth century through the 1800s; they essentially detail the ritual of tribute presentation.

Over the last few years, the Department of Hand-Written Documents of the Thai National Library has been making public court records of the Chakri dynasty, especially of the post-Rama I era. Documents belonging to the reigns of Rama I through Rama IV are classified and grouped under the general heading of *Chotmaihet krung Rattanakosin.* Together they constitute the single most complete source of official papers on the role of the Siamese court in the Sino-Siamese relationship. A good illustration of the kind of documents to be found in this collection is a missive from the Kwangtung viceroy to the Siamese minister of foreign affairs, the Praya Praklang, in the reign of Rama IV, querying about the delay by Siam in sending a tributary mission to Peking. This Chinese official letter is found in Siamese translation and entitled "Supa-aksorn chong-tok moo-i tung Chaopraya Praklang klang-ti si."

In the Chakri dynasty, private official records and court-sanctioned semi-official histories came into being and have been made available to scholars. Under Ramas IV and V, serious efforts toward the compilation of historical evidence were undertaken. Rama IV was interested in documents of all kinds, including religion, government, and history. He himself wrote about the court-conducted trade with China in "The Establishment of the Kingdom." His son, Rama V, annotated *Pra rachavijarn,* a record kept by a courtier named Princess Narindr Thevi between 1767 and 1820. In this rare manuscript, which describes events in the reigns of King Taksin, Rama I, and Rama II, is a rather detailed account of the Siamese tributary mission to the Ch'ing court in 1780.

A high-ranking courtier who served Rama III, Rama IV, and Rama V was responsible for chronicling state events in the first four reigns of the Chakri dynasty. At the behest of Rama V, Chaopraya Thippakorawong published records of court ceremonies, diplomacy, war, and other royal activities, employing essentially the Chinese chronology style with the monarchy as the main focus. His compilation of events during the reigns of Rama I and Rama II is published as *Praratcha pongsawadan krung Rattanakosin rachakarn ti nung rachakarn ti song,* while that for the reign of Rama IV has been translated into English by Chadin and Thaddeus Flood and is entitled *The Dynastic Chronicles, Bangkok Era, the Fourth Reign.* Relations with China is one notable subject in these chronicles or *pongsawadan.*

If Thippakorawong's chronicles represent in content and style traditional Siamese historiography with perhaps some Chinese influence, subsequent works by Prince Damrong Rajanubhab in the early part of the twentieth century bear the signs of Western impact. His shorter and more general chronicle of the Ayudhya dynasty, *Praratcha pongsawadan chabab pra ratcha hatleka,* represents a departure from the traditional *pongsawadan* which emphasized events and rituals. Under his influence, other chronicles have been compiled and some translated from works of observation by Westerners; they may be found in the collection of *Prachoom pongsawadan chabab hor smut haeng chart.* Another important documentary source particularly related to Siam's intercourse with Western countries between the seventeenth and nineteenth centuries is *State Papers of the Kingdom of Siam, 1644–1886,* compiled by the Siamese legation in Paris from archives in Western nations.

The local history of Siam is not adequately documented. But *Chotmaihet krung Rattanakosin* does contain a few documents on Lower Siam, particularly reports of performance by the overseas junk trade to China and other parts of Southeast Asia which was entrusted to local authorities. Chronicles by later scholars on the various provinces are available, but they tell little about the subject under study.

Official documents of Japan and Vietnam are also important. *Ka-i hentai* is a Toyo Bunko publication of shipping reports collected at Nagasaki mainly in the latter half of the seventeenth century. One finds here a large collection of written reports submitted to the Japanese authorities by foreigners (largely Chinese) who traded to the Japanese port. They were in essence intelligence reports about the situation in the Eastern Seas including the movement of Chinese shipping in the region. A few official Vietnamese records of the first half of the nineteenth century also throw light on the coastal trade conducted by junks in the South China Sea particularly in the 1820s and 1830s. From *Dai Nam thuc luc chin-binh* we find that Siam played a part in the rice export to Vietnam in the 1820s. Some information concerning the existing trade between Siam and southern Vietnam, including that on shipping regulations instituted by Vietnamese authorities, is derived from *Kham-dhinh Dai-Nam hoi dien su le* of the Gia Long and Minh Mang reigns.

This study profits considerably from a number of dictionaries, periodicals, and geographical references. *The Universal Dictionary of Trade and Commerce* by the Savary brothers of France is an informative commercial guide written during the first part of the eighteenth century. The information is arranged by country, and there is a detailed section on trade to China. In the following century, William Milburn published his *Oriental Commerce,* a commercial guide for the Eastern Seas with a similar encyclopedic format.

In the mid-nineteenth century, Westerners were publishing all sorts of information on China and Siam. *The Chinese Repository* was a regular periodical dealing with political, economic, and social features about China.

Foreign trade at Canton was a major area of attention. A similar magazine venture, *Siam Repository,* was started some time later in Bangkok by Samuel Smith, a foreign adviser to Rama V, but this venture was comparatively short-lived.

Writings on navigation, shipping, and geography provide additional insights into the study of Sino-Siamese relations. Hsiang Ta in the early 1960s compiled and annotated a collection of descriptions of navigational routes between Southeast China and Southeast Asia which were apparently used by sailors of Chinese junks in the seventeenth and eighteenth centuries. *Liang-tsung hai-tao chen-ching,* containing original names (and their modern equivalents) of promontories lying along the various junk routes, was used as a guide by sailors. In addition, a few works deal with the subjects of Chinese ships and shipping. Pao Tsun-p'eng's *Cheng Ho hsia hsi-yang chih pao-ch'uan k'ao* is an attempt to examine the kind of ships employed by the Chinese in overseas travel in the early Ming period. It may be supplemented by Kanazawa Kanemitsu's *Wa-Kan sen'yo shu* which describes Chinese ships deployed in the Eastern Seas in the seventeenth century. One would expect to find relatively little change in the types of vessels used by Cheng Ho's expeditions in the fourteenth century and those in service a few centuries later—except in size.

Chinese interest in geographical study in the Western sense did not emerge until the mid-nineteenth century. Hsieh Ch'ing-k'ao's *Hai-lu,* and particularly Wei Yuan's *Hai-kuo t'u-chih* represent a mixture of the traditional and Western approaches, while a representative of the traditional orientation may be found in the eighteenth-century work of *Hai-kuo wen-chien lu* by Ch'en Lun-ch'iung. A nineteenth-century work with a distinctive Western influence is Wang Hsi-ch'i's *Hsiao-fang-hu-chai yu-ti ts'ung ch'ao* which provides details of the economic geography of the various countries, with China no longer the center of the universe.

General works on East Asia as a whole provide a useful background for this study. The standard ones employed are: John K. Fairbank and Edwin O. Reischauer, *East Asia: The Great Tradition* for China; E. M. Satow, *Japan and the West* for Japan; John F. Cady, *Southeast Asia: Its Historical Development,* and David Steinberg, Alexander Woodside, et al., eds., *In Search of Southeast Asia: A Modern History,* for Southeast Asia.

A few bibliographies are helpful in identifying available materials on the various topics under study. John K. Fairbank's *Ch'ing Documents: An Introductory Syllabus,* his *Japanese Studies of Modern China,* in collaboration with Banno Masataka in the 1950s, and the recent supplement: *Japanese Studies of Modern China since 1953* by Noriko Kamachi, John K. Fairbank, and Chūzō Ichiko, published in 1975, are examples. Naosaku Uchida's *The Overseas Chinese: A Bibliographical Essay* contains various writings on the Overseas Chinese up to the 1960s.

The tributary system naturally formed the backdrop for China's foreign relations and economic intercourse with other countries. The theoretical and operational mode of this time-honored system is portrayed in John K. Fairbank's *The Chinese World Order,* the product of a symposium on Chinese foreign relations held at Harvard University in 1968. How the system actually operated in the Ch'ing period is described in Mark Mancall's article, "The Ch'ing Tributary System: An Interpretative Essay," in this volume, and also in another study written some time ago by John K. Fairbank and Teng Ssu-yü, entitled "On the Ch'ing Tributary System."

In the Ch'ing period, Korea and the Ryūkyūs (Liu-ch'iu) were two of the most intimate tributary states of China. *Yonhaengnok sonjip* is a collection of writings about Korea's tributary relations with Ch'ing China, including accounts kept by Korean tributary missions to the Peking court such as Yi Ki-hon's "Yonhaeng ilgi." The history of Sino-Ryukyuan relations in the eighteenth and early nineteenth centuries is treated in Ch'en Ta-tuan's *Yung-Ch'ien-Chia shih-tai ti Chung-Liu kuan-hsi.*

A handful of works exists concerning China's relations with Siam. Hsu Yun-ch'iao of Singapore has written a long article surveying over five hundred years of this tributary intercourse between the two countries in *Nanyang hsueh-pao* under the title of "Chung-Hsien t'ung-shih k'ao." This approach was recently imitated by Suebsaeng Promboon in his Ph.D. dissertation called "Sino-Siamese Tributary Relations, 1282–1853." The article "Ming-Ch'ing liang-tai yu Hsien-lo" by Li Kuang-t'ao of the Academia Sinica, a more specific treatment of relations during the Ch'ing period, describes the commercial motive behind the tributary relationship. In "Lun Ming-Ch'ing Kuang-tung kuo-chi mao-i yu chin-tai Chung-T'ai chih kuan-hsi," Liang Chia-pin also examines the operation of trade in the guise of tribute presentation.

Certain incidents in the Sino-Siamese tributary relationship receive enough documentation to form some sort of tentative picture. The celebrated case of King Taksin's attempt in 1780 to dispatch a tributary mission to the Ch'ien-lung court is the subject for Hsu Yun-ch'iao's article, "Cheng-chao ju-kung Ch'ing-t'ing k'ao." A first-hand account, written in the style of a traveling poem, was also kept by a member of the mission and is now published as *Niras pai muang Jeen.* An annotation and explanation for this account have been furnished by Hsu in another article entitled "Cheng-chao kung-shih ju ch'ao Chung-kuo chi-hsing-shih shih-chu." Events leading up to the severance of tributary ties with China by Rama IV in the 1850s were recorded by Pra Intramontri, the last Siamese tributary envoy to the Ch'ing court. His accounts have been translated into Chinese in a magazine article appearing for the first time in 1941 as "T'ai-kuo chui-hou i ch'ih ju-kung Chung-kuo chi-lu shu." Narong Traiwat in his article, "Mua Ror Si song tat kwarm maitri kab Pakking," also dwells on the circumstances behind the Siamese decision to end the apparently unequal relationship and to demand an equitable substitute from the declining Ch'ing court.

That Siam maintained the tributary relationship with China for centuries primarily for commercial reasons shows the extent of Chinese economic influence in the region in the pre-Industrial Revolution days. During the first two centuries of the Ch'ing dynasty, junks were crisscrossing the Eastern Seas and dominating the commercial scene. The best short treatment of the rise and fall of the junk trade is by Mainland historian T'ien Ju-k'ang. In his *Shih-ch'i shih-chiu shih-chi chung-yeh Chung-kuo fan-ch'uan tsai tung-nan Ya-chou,* and "Tsai-lun shih-ch'i chih shih-chiu shih-chi chung-yeh Chung-kuo fan-ch'uan-yeh ti fa-chan," employing both Chinese and Western sources, T'ien Ju-k'ang tells of an unchallenged Chinese maritime enterprise which actually surpassed in numbers of ships and ship tonnage the Western shipping of the time. In another study a few years later, optimism gave way to pessimism when T'ien described the decline of this once-expansive maritime venture and discussed causes for the failure of the Chinese junk trade to develop after the beginning of the nineteenth century. In "Shih-wu chih shih-pa shih-chi Chung-kuo hai-wai mao-i huan-man ti yuan-in," the author gave faulty organization as the single most important reason for the decline.

Nevertheless, during the first decades of the nineteenth century, a time when the West was only beginning to re-establish its presence in the East, the Chinese junk trade was still a force in its own right. This may be seen in John Crawfurd's portrayal in his *History of the Indian Archipelago* at the start of the 1820s, or in John Phipps's *A Practical Treatise on the China and Eastern Trade* in the following decade. Crawfurd and Phipps both saw the position of the Chinese junk trade in the Eastern Seas as "enviable."

Before the Second World War, under the shadow of Western imperialism, scholarship on the subject of trade in the Eastern Seas generally assigned the junk trade to a secondary role, and, as a result, much more attention was paid to Western maritime penetration and eventual dominance. The writings by J. C. van Leur, the Dutch historian, were an exception. Chang Teh-ch'ang's 1935 article, "Ch'ing-tai ya-p'ien chan-cheng ch'ien chih Chung-Hsi yen-hai t'ung-shang," attributes the main cause of the decline of the Chinese junk trade to the increase in Western maritime penetration. Hou Hou-p'ei makes a similar argument in an article a few years earlier entitled "Wu-k'ou t'ung-shang i-ch'ien wuo-kuo kuo-chi mao-i chich kai-k'uang." Nevertheless, perhaps from a different motive, contemporary Japanese scholars who were interested in this subject of Eastern trade were paying greater attention to indigenous roles in the maritime trade development in the region of an earlier period. Hence one finds discussions of trade relations between Eastern countries during the seventeenth and eighteenth centuries. The works of Miyazaki Ichisada, the noted sinologist at Kyoto University, fall into this category, as we see in his "Shinsho Kanton [Kōtō] bōeki ni kansuru ishi-ryō" (which is a translation of a part from the Savary brothers' eighteenth-century commercial encyclopedia), as well as his "Chūgoku-Nanyō kankei shi gaisetsu" (which describes the Sino-barbarian—i.e. Southeast Asian—trade at the turn of the eighteenth century). Interest in the development of indigenous trade is also expressed in a work called *Ka-i tsūshō ko* which is part of a sizable collection of works dealing with trade and economy published in 1928.

The single Chinese junk activity of the seventeenth and eighteenth centuries on which there is satisfactory documentation has to do with the so-called "China–Japan–Southeast Asia triangular trade" of the day. It shows that the Chinese junk network was extensive as well as economically influential in the Eastern Seas.

The sudden involvement of Japanese in overseas maritime trade in the Eastern Seas during the second half of the sixteenth century, well described in Iwao Sei'ichi's *Shūinsen bōeki no kenkyū* and *Shūinsen to Nihon machi,* is a significant historical event which could have altered the course of the history of the region, and particularly, that of Southeast Asia. But just as overseas expansion had the active support of various high-ranking Japanese lords who encouraged the construction of ships and the conduct of overseas trade and settlement, self-imposed isolation was also swiftly instituted after the beginning of the seventeenth century, thus bringing to an abrupt halt the development of Japanese influence that was quickly forming in the Eastern Seas. In the final analysis, the Chinese gained from this *volte face.*

After Japanese withdrawal from commercial activities in the 1630s, Chinese junks became the main conveyors of trade between China, Japan, and Southeast Asia. The *Ka-i hentai* collection testifies to this, and Ch'en Ching-ho of New Asia College, Hong Kong, points out the role played by Chinese vessels in the trade between the port of Nagasaki, China proper, and Southeast Asia in his "Ch'ing-ch'u Hua-po chich Ch'ang-ch'i mao-i chi Jih-nan hang yun." The Chinese influence on the Eastern trade which also involved Nagasaki is further confirmed in other studies such as Hayakawa Jun'-saburō's *Tsūkō ichiran,* and Yamawaki Teijirō's *Nagasaki no Tōjin bōeki,* as well as *Nagasakishi shi* published by the city of Nagasaki.

The triangular trade which dealt with Siam is also well documented. Aside from many intelligence reports in the *Ka-i hentai,* which also indicate the extent of Chinese control of this branch of commerce, further documentation may be obtained from sources cited by Ishii Yoneo in his "Seventeenth Century Japanese Documents About Siam." In the latter part of the nineteenth century, E. M. Satow was already pointing out the involvement of Chinese in the court-to-court transactions between Ayudhya Siam and Tokugawa Japan in his article, "Notes on the Intercourse between Japan and Siam in the Seventeenth Century." The Siamese court's attempts to resume trade to Nagasaki in the mid-seventeenth century under the guise of Chinese shipping is further noted by Iwao Sei'ichi in his "Taijin no tai Nikkoku bōeki hatsukatsu undō." Mention of the Chinese role in the promotion of bilateral trade between Siam and Japan can be found in Miki Sakae's *Ni-Shin kōtsū shi,* and Gunji Ki'ichi's *Jūhichi seiki ni okeru Ni-Shin kankei.*

Finally, the possibility that the triangular junk trade in the seventeenth and eighteenth centuries may have at one point involved or in some fashion connected with the shipping enterprise of the forces of Koxinga and his son which controlled parts of the Southeast China coast and the island of Formosa can be detected from Ts'ao Yung's article, "Cheng Ch'eng-kung chih t'ung shang mao-i."

The foreign maritime trade of China was traditionally conducted from locales on the coast of Southeast China. Although Amoy and its environs may have been at one time the most important junk center for the Southeast Asia trade, as is portrayed by George Hughes in his *Amoy and the Surrounding Districts* and other works cited above, and Ningpo was the most important port for trade with Japan in the seventeenth century, it was Canton that figured most prominently in the Chinese external trade up till the middle of the nineteenth century. Louis Dermigny's *Le commerce à Canton au XVIIIe siècle, 1719-1833* gives a lucid and detailed treatment of Sino-Western trade at this southern port, based primarily on Western sources. It gives a good picture of how the Canton trade (i.e. foreign trade conducted at Canton) was actually handled, with references to individual Chinese officials and merchants who were engaged in activities traditionally deemed somewhat undignified according to Confucian mores. Another source often cited on the subject of the Canton trade is H. B. Morse's *The Chronicles of the East India Company Trading to China, 1635-1834.* The work is both a record of the activities of the British East India Company in China and a portrayal of the Canton system. Together the last two works form a background to the study of the significance of Canton between the seventeenth and the nineteenth centuries.

Information on the economic situation at Canton in the seventeenth century is rather limited, but one may wish to consult Ch'u Ta-chun's *Kuang-tung hsin-yu.* To form at least a partial picture of foreign trade at this locale in the same period, Professor Miyazaki Ichisada's translation of the exposition on Canton trade by the Savary brothers, "Shinsho [Kanton] Kōtō bōeki kansuru ishi-ryō," and Sasmoto Shigemi's "Kōtō [Kanton] no tekka ni tsuite" are available. These two pieces mention particularly the foreign trade with Southeast Asia from Canton.

The growth of British influence at Canton after the eighteenth century resulted in the dissemination of more knowledge about Canton's economic and trade conditions through reports and observations. John R. Morrison's *A Chinese Commercial Guide* presents details of facts and figures on the Canton trade in the 1840s, while "A Dissertation upon the Commerce of China," written also in the 1840s by an anonymous Englishman, endeavors to present certain views on the state of this trade.

As a matter of fact, most views of the Canton system through the centuries centered on the problem of restriction and corruption. The history of China's trade with Southeast Asia in the Ch'ing period was marked by a tendency on the part of China to impose restrictions on itself for security and moral-ethical reasons. Liang Ting-nan, one of the handful of Ch'ing officials in the early part of the eighteenth century who argued for the liberalization of trade with Southeast Asia, presented the view that continued contact would be preferable to closure from the standpoint of the people's livelihood in his *Lun Nan-yang shih-i shu*. This line was actively pursued by Fukien Viceroy Kao Ch'i-cho who, in the light of the grain shortage in the province in the 1720s, managed to win approval from the Ch'ing court for a temporary re-opening of Amoy to trade from and with Southeast Asia.

Much has been written on the corruptive practices of the Canton customs service, a very powerful official arm for the conduct of foreign trade at Canton. Because of its connection with the Ch'ing court (Chang Te-ch'ang in his "The Economic Role of the Imperial Household" establishes the link between the Canton maritime superintendency and the Imperial Household or Nei-wu fu) the customs service was in a position to dictate terms for foreign trade. Sasaki Masaya gives an overall picture of the type of power this body wielded in "Etsu kaikan no roki." In the nineteenth century, on the eve of the fateful change in the Canton system, the complaint by the Western traders against the malpractices of this organization is reflected in James Matheson's *The Present Position and Prospects of the British Trade with China.*

The picture of trade at Canton after the conclusion of the Nanking Treaty in 1842 is summed up in John K. Fairbank's *Trade and Diplomacy on the China Coast.* The argument therein is that the traditional Canton system did not totally disappear in fact, and many questions remained unresolved well into the 1850s. On the contrary, in Chinese thinking, Canton was to remain the center for tributary trade unaffected by new treaties and agreements worked out with the various Western nations.

An understanding of the Chinese trading structure or commercial guilds helps to define the picture of China's maritime trade. A few works on the general aspects of such business associations are available. H. B. Morse's *The Gild of China,* and D. J. MacGowan's "Chinese Guilds or Chambers of Commerce and Trade Unions" are two pioneer studies which give a general description of the structure and role of Chinese guilds during the last century. However, through the efforts of Japanese scholar Negishi Tadashi we obtain a deeper insight into the functions of these organizations. His *Shina girudo no kenkyū, Chūgoku no girudo,* and *Gōkō no kenkyū* provide a historical perspective for commercial guilds as they developed in Canton, Ningpo, Shanghai, and so forth.

The foreign trade guilds at Canton, known popularly as *hong,* were perhaps the best known to foreign traders and have been well researched. A well-documented study which represents the most complete work in Chinese on Canton to date is *Kuang-tung shih-san hang k'ao* by Liang Chia-pin. Another study which contains information not cited in Liang's work and presents some different angles of interpretation as to the origin of the Canton foreign trade guilds is P'eng Tse-i's "Ch'ing-tai Kuang-tung yang-hang chih-tu ti ch'i-yuan." A more recent discussion on the subject with more interpretative emphasis is Frederic Wakeman's draft essay, "The Canton Trade and the Opium War," to be published in 1977 as part of the forthcoming *Cambridge History of China,* vol. 10.

Little is known about similar foreign trade guilds in South Fukien that played a role in the Chinese junk trade with Southeast Asia prior to the nineteenth century; only a few details may be gleaned from local gazetteers. Susan Mann Jones discusses the role of the Ningpo merchants in overseas trade during the eighteenth century in her article, "Finance in Ningpo: The 'Ch'ien Chuang, 1750–1880.'"

In spite of a lack of written records about Siam before the twentieth century, there are a few studies of the country's government and political institutions, including the Siamese society in history, which are informative. H. G. Quaritch Wales's *Ancient Siamese Government and Administration* remains an important source for the study of the country's premodern government structure and administration in spite of its age (it was written a few decades ago) and the lack of a historical perspective about the evolution of various institutions cited. Luang Vichitwatakarn's *Karn-muang karn-pokkrong kong Siam,* also written in the 1930s, presents a summary of the development of Siamese government institutions since the days of Ayudhya, and Prince Damrong Rajanubhab gives a discourse on regional administration in Siamese history after the eighteenth century in his article entitled, "Pu-boriharn rachakarn paendin nai adit." A pioneer analysis of Siamese society in the period of the first century of the Chakri dynasty is Akin Rabibhadana's *The Organization of Thai Society in the Early Bangkok Period, 1782–1813.* It still stands as the only substantial study of the composition of early Bangkok society in English.

Klaus Wenk's *The Restoration of Thailand under Rama I, 1782–1809,* and Walter Vella's *Siam Under Rama III, 1824–1851* examine Siam in certain periods of the Chakri reign through the role played by the court. Since much of the traditional historiography centers around the court or, more precisely, the king and the royal family, as well as the high-ranking nobility, one would expect to find relatively more studies about this group of people. Prince Chula

Chakrabongse's *Lords of Life: A History of the Kings of Thailand* is a survey of the House of Chakri from the time of its founding in 1782. Opart Sevikun's *Pra racha bida haeng karn patiroop,* and Abbot Low Moffat's *Mongkut, the King of Siam* are works of biography about Rama IV in particular. Biographies of courtiers and nobles provide clues to various happenings—including conditions and events of overseas trade and economic development. Prayud Sittipun's *Racha samnak Thai* and *Ton trakoon kun-nang Thai* provide information on the genealogy of various members of the Siamese nobility with Chinese ancestry. Kularb Krisananon was a prominent publisher and controversial historian in the reign of Rama V. With his access to the royal archives, he produced at the turn of the twentieth century a genealogical study tracing the origins of various courtiers who were then serving under Rama V. He demonstrated in his *Mahamukamattayanukunwong* that many members of the Siamese nobility had risen through the rank and file and had amassed great fortunes from their connection with the junk trade with China in one way or another. The life history of one of the courtiers, Chaopraya Si Suriyawong, who presided over Siam's modernization in the reigns of Rama IV and Rama V is told by Prince Damrong Rajanubhab in his *Prawat Somdet Chaopraya Borom Maha Si Suriyawong.* One significant event that he presided over was the introduction of steamships and the subsequent decline of the junk trade with China.

The Siamese court had historically been directly engaged in foreign and domestic trade through royal trading and had had a monopoly over the major revenue-generating activities through the exercise of royal monopoly and tax farming. Pongpun Supatrapun's thesis, "Karn-suksa tang prawatisart kiew-duei ruang praklang sin-ka," describes the agencies under the Siamese court that were in charge of handling all activities related to foreign and domestic trade. *Tamnan sulakakorn* by Praya Anumanrachaton traces the history and development of government revenue-acquisition and royal trading. Both Prince Damron Ranjanubhab's "Tamnan pasi-akorn bangyang kap kam atibai" and Luang Vichitwatakarn's "Pasi-akorn" examine the evolution of certain taxes which dealt with foreign trade or which were related to the establishment of tax farming under royal sanction. In effect, these studies indicate the extent of Chinese influence over the economic life of Siam and the financial well-being of the court and nobility.

Chinese involvement in Siam's foreign trade, including the Sino-Siamese trade before the twentieth century, is pointed out in Sa-nga Kanjanakapun's *Prawat karnka kong pratet Thai.* The dependence of the court and nobility (until well into the nineteenth century) noted therein was clearly acknowledged dating back to the seventeenth century. The Dutch East India Company agent in Ayudhya, Joost Schouten, was also commenting on the arrangement between the Siamese king and Chinese merchants in trade to China which was having an effect on the Dutch effort to establish an economic foothold in

Siam in the 1620s and 1630s. Francois Caron and Joost Schouten's *A True Description of the Mighty Kingdoms of Japan and Siam* describes the Siamese king as actively involved in foreign trade. In John Anderson's *English Intercourse with Siam in the Seventeenth Century,* British East India Company agent at Ayudhya George White was reporting in the mid-seventeenth century about the role of the Siamese king in the royal monopolies, which included trading to China and other parts of the Eastern Seas. (George White's dispatches have been translated into the Thai language and may be found in *Chotmaihet nai paendin Somdej Pra Narai Maharat.*) Simon de la Loubère, French envoy to the court of King Narai, confirmed the widespread presence of the royal monopolies and the revenues they generated for the court in his *The Kingdom of Siam.* A general discussion of the symbiotic relationship between the Siamese system of royal monopolies and the mode of foreign trade as conducted by Chinese individuals on the Siamese court's behalf is to be found in "Shih-ch'i shih-chi Hsien-lo tui-wai mao-i yu hua-ch'iao" by Ch'en Ching-ho.

With the exception of a few sources containing observations by Western voyagers and writers (such as the account by Swedish botanist Jean Koenig on Siam based on his visit there in the 1770s, "Journal of a Voyage from India to Siam and Malacca in 1779," and F. H. Turpin's work based on Catholic priests' reports about Siam in the reign of King Taksin entitled *History of the Kingdom of Siam*), mention of the role of the Siamese court in overseas trade—that is, tributary trade with China—in the eighteenth century is found mainly in official Chinese documents cited earlier. Following the first decades of the nineteenth century when Chinese officials were paying more and more attention to the growing presence of the West in the Eastern Seas, and fewer references to the relationship with Siam (and, in fact, with other tributary states as well) appeared in official Chinese records, Westerners were once again taking an active interest in Siam and other parts of the Southeast Asian peninsula. In 1821, John Crawfurd was appointed by the governor-general of India to head a good will visit to the court of Rama II. *Journal of An Embassy from the Governor-General to the Courts of Siam and Co-chin China* (portions were subsequently translated into Thai by Prince Damrong as "Ruang Anglit kaoma kor-tum sanya krang Ratchakarn ti Song") is based on his observations while in Bangkok of life and customs among the Siamese. In his other official papers and correspondence, published together as *The Crawfurd Papers,* Crawfurd detailed trade conditions at the end of the Rama II reign, noting the extent of the junk trade from Bangkok.

Following the Crawfurd mission, another Englishman named Captain Henry Burney was dispatched to Bangkok by the governor of Bengal to conclude a commercial treaty. *The Burney Papers* comprises his notes and letters, including the inevitable comment on the dominance of the junk trade and the Siamese court's involvement in it.

In the 1830s, more accounts were published by Western visitors to Siam, all indicating in one way or another the dominance of Chinese in the commercial scene at Bangkok and the apparent involvement of the Siamese court in Chinese-run enterprises such as trade and tax farming—an institution that became popularized in the reign of Rama III. Edmund Roberts, the American envoy who signed the first Western treaty in East Asia with Siam in 1832, together with the physician in his mission, Dr. W. S. Ruschenberger, described the busy commercial scene at the capital with the notable presence of Chinese traders in their *Embassy to the Eastern Courts of Cochin-China, Siam and Muscat during the Years 1832, 1833, 1834* and *A Voyage Round the World*, respectively. Other visitors' observations during this period, for instance George Earl's *The Eastern Seas* or Howard Malcom's *Travels in Southeast Asia*, were similar.

Starting with the reign of Rama III, Western missionaries began to arrive in the country in good numbers, and their written observations provide a further insight into socioeconomic conditions which prevailed then. Charles Gützlaff, a Protestant missionary who arrived in Siam in the late 1820s, wrote about his association with Chinese crewmen from ships plying between China and Siam and of his subsequent voyages on board Chinese junks in his *Journal of Three Voyages along the Coast of China in 1831, 1832, 1833, with Notices of Siam, Corea and the Loo-Choo Islands*. Monseigneur Jean-Baptiste Pallegoix, a French Catholic priest, came to Siam in the Third Reign, and subsequently became one of the most observant of visitors. His *Description du royaume Thai ou Siam* (translated into Thai by Sunt Komonbutr as *Lao ruang muang Thai*) features facts and events during the 1840s and early 1850s, including a discourse on state trade and revenues with mention of Chinese influence. This work later provided a basis of information for Sir John Bowring in his *Kingdom and People of Siam* published in the 1850s.

In the long history of economic intercourse between Siam and China, Chinese individuals played the role of carriers and intermediaries. Mention has already been made of the link some of them maintained with the Siamese court and nobility. G. William Skinner's two early works, *Chinese Society in Thailand: An Analytical History*, and *Leadership and Power in the Chinese Community of Thailand*, contain sections on the historical background for the rise of Chinese influence in Thai society. Several other works pertaining to the prominence of the Chinese in Siamese economic life over the years are available, such as Tseng Chien-ping's *T'ai-kuo hua-ch'iao ching-chi*, and Joseph Jiang's "The Chinese in Thailand." The handling of the Siamese junk trade to China in the Ch'ing period is well described in Li Kuang-t'ao's article, "Hua-i yü Hsien-lo." The role played by these Chinese seafarers and merchants, particularly in the conveying of rice from Siam to China in the eighteenth century and thereafter, is described in Narita Setsuo's "Taikoku kakyō to kome," as a historical basis for understanding the dominance of the Chinese in the Siamese rice trade in more recent times.

Narita's work was part of an effort by the Japanese before and during the Second World War to learn as much as possible about the pervasive influence of the Overseas Chinese in the economy of Southeast Asia. Ide Kiwata's *Kakyō,* and Fukuda Shozo's *Kakyō keizai ron* are further examples of this kind of research. In recent years, there has been a renewed interest in the Overseas Chinese question among Japanese scholars, and many more publications on the subject have appeared. Among them, Yu Chung-hsun's *Kakyō keizai kenkyū,* a study of the economic role of the Overseas Chinese with a historical perspective, is worthy of note.

The symbiotic relationship between enterprising Chinese traders and the Siamese court nobility shows the influence of the Chinese in Siamese history. Several genealogical records of the nobility, such as the above-mentioned *Mahamukamattayanukunwong* by Kularb Krisananon, attest to this fact. The Chinese influence in the country's economic life became more apparent after tax farming became the main source of revenue for the court (replacing the junk trade) in the nineteenth century, and more Chinese became involved in the economic infrastructure of the indigenous society. Prince Damrong's "Tamnan karn lurk bon-bia," and B. O. Cartwright's "The Huey Lottery" explain one area of tax farming in the nineteenth century where Chinese influence was strongly felt, while Praya Anumanrachaton's *Tamnan sunlakakorn* and *The Burney Papers* present a list of taxes Chinese individuals were permitted by the court to administer.

As Chinese economic influence began to spread to a wider spectrum in the society and as Chinese immigration increased in the nineteenth century, one social phenomenon that followed was the emergence of secret societies. Hirayama Amane describes the history of the Chinese societies in his *Chūgoku himitsu shakai shi,* citing their religious, social, and political roots. Prince Damrong's *Nitarn boran-kadi* describes the Chinese secret societies in Siam from the reign of Rama III, particularly after the introduction of opium into the country by English traders. As far as legitimate Chinese socioeconomic organizations were concerned, available documentation, that is, publications by Chinese clan associations or professional organizations in Thailand, gives an impression that they did not come into existence until the latter part of the nineteenth century.

The Ch'ing government's attitude and policy toward Chinese emigration is clearly pointed out in Harley MacNair's *The Chinese Abroad: Their Position and Protection.* Since the early days, the Manchu court viewed this matter with great apprehension. C. R. Boxer's article, "Notes on Chinese Abroad in the Late Ming and Early Manchu Periods, Compiled from Contemporary European Sources (1500–1750)," discusses the heavy penalties imposed by the Ch'ing authorities on Chinese going overseas, citing security as the primary motive. The case in the eighteenth century of a Chinese named Ch'en I-lao who traveled abroad was subsequently employed by a tributary state in Southeast Asia, and who was punished by the Ch'ing authorities, is presented in Ch'en Yu-sung's "Ch'en I-lao an yu Ch'ing-tai ch'ien-min cheng-ts'e chih kai-pien."

Although emigration policy may have remained stern throughout the Ch'ing dynasty, population pressure and economic difficulty in Southeast China had at least by the nineteenth century led local Chinese authorities to turn a blind eye to the movement of Chinese overseas. Charles Gützlaff observed in the 1830s that Chinese crewmen on the vessel on which he was traveling freely disembarked and embarked at several ports in Southeast China without official interference. He further noticed that the crewmen all brought rice and other items from Siam to present to their relatives or friends in China. (See his *Journal of Three Voyages.*) In actual fact, Cheng Lin K'uan in his "Fu-chien hua-ch'iao hui-k'uan" discusses the importance of Overseas Chinese remittances to South Fukien's economic welfare. This contribution made it impractical for the authorities to restrict the overseas movement of Chinese citizens.

On the other hand, even though the expressed official policy was to discourage emigration and prohibit Chinese individuals from coming into the employ of foreigners, the Siamese court, in the guise of tributary dealings, managed to continue using Chinese individuals to operate its vessels and trade to the very end. In spite of official admonitions by the Ch'ing authorities (found in such official documents as the *Shih-lu* and *Ch'ing-tai wai-chiao shih-liao*) in the eighteenth and nineteenth centuries, the practice went on unobstructed.

The socioeconomic background of Chinese emigrants to Southeast Asia from Kwangtung and Fukien is the subject of Ch'en Ta's *Nanyang hua-ch'iao yu Min-Yueh she-hui.* Although it deals with the situation in the twentieth century, particularly in the 1920s and 1930s, the picture of the living conditions of emigrants helps one to understand the situation in the eighteenth and nineteenth centuries. Investigations into an area in Fukien known to have had many emigrants to Southeast Asia were conducted by a team from Amoy University in the 1950s. Preliminary findings published by Chuang Wei-chi and other faculty and student members of the University entitled, "Fu-chien Chin-chiang tsuan-ch'u hua-ch'iao shih t'iao-ch'a pao-k'ao," dwell on the history of emigration as well as statistical data of the number of persons, places of immigration, and the time of emigration. It is not known if the field research was continued and more facts published in accordance with the expressed intention of the researchers.

The rice trade from Siam to China constitutes the single most important economic factor in the eighteenth century. The phenomenal demographic changes are discussed in Ch'uan Han-sheng's "Ch'ing-tai ti jen-k'ou pien-tung" and Lo Erh-kang's "T'ai-p'ing t'ien-kuo ke-ming ch'ien ti jen-k'ou ya-po wen-t'i." Food shortages in China in the eighteenth century and governmental efforts at relief are treated in Feng Liu-t'ang's *Chung-kuo li-tai min-shih cheng-ts'e shih* (translated into Japanese as *Shina shōku-ryō seisaku shi*). Faced with the problem of famine, rice importation from abroad was officially commenced in the 1720s, to supplement local production.

Rice cultivation and supply within China in the mid-Ch'ing period is outlined in *Agricultural Development in China, 1368–1968,* by Dwight Perkins, Wang Yeh-chien, et al. More specific treatment of the distribution pattern of rice in the mid-Ch'ing period is found in Ch'uan Han-sheng's studies. In his "Ch'ing-ch'ao chung-yeh Su-chou ti mi-liang mao-i," Ch'uan discusses the role of Soochow as a distribution point for rice from the Szechwan, Hukuang, and Chiangsi areas destined for points in Chekiang and Fukien provinces. His "Ch'ien-lung shih-san nien ti mi-kuei wen-t'i" is an attempt to show the significance of the fluctuation in rice prices during the Ch'ien-lung reign, particularly after 1748 owing to the scarcity of supply.

Data on rice prices, production, and importation seem most complete for the reigns of Yung-cheng and Ch'ien-lung. The two emperors were beset with mounting economic problems and naturally encouraged sober reporting from the provinces. In "Bekoku jukyū no kenkyū *Yosei shi* no ishō to shite mita," Abe Takeo comments on the supply and demand of rice in the Yung-cheng period based on a substantial use of official Chinese documents including memorials, edicts, and so on. (It remains to date the most important piece of research on the subject.) Ch'uan Han-sheng and Wang Yeh-chien in their "Ch'ing Yung-cheng nien-chien mi-chia" assemble statistics from official sources to formulate a picture of the unstable nature of rice supply in Southeast China; they further discuss the inter- and intra-provincial transportation of rice for relief and price stabilization purposes.

Siam has traditionally been noted for an abundance of rice, but not much has been recorded about its cultivation and distribution prior to the twentieth century. James Ingram's *Economic Change in Thailand Since 1850* and Yang Han-cheng's "Chin pai-nien lai Hsien-lo mi-yeh kai-shu" discuss rice production in the country since the nineteenth century. Recently, from research on official documents, Pornapa Prudhinarakorn and Suebwatana Taveesilp have written their "Kao nai prai Ayudhya" which dwells on the rice situation toward the end of the Ayudhya dynasty in the eighteenth century. Other references, such as *Ka-i hentai*, Matsuo Hiroshi's *Shinra kokumin keizai no tokuchō,* and D. E. Malloch's *Siam: Some General Remarks on Its Productions,* show the dominance of rice in the Siamese economy. Furthermore, Malloch also provides figures for the country's annual production and export.

Information on Siam's rice trade to China can be found in the various official Ch'ing records, notably the *Shih-lu*. The role of the Overseas Chinese in handling Siamese rice exports to China is discussed in Narita Setsuo's "Taikoku kakyō to kome," but by far the most comprehensive treatment of this topic for the eighteenth century is Takazaki Misako's "Jūhachi seki ni okeru Shin-Tai kōshō shi." Using mainly Ch'ing documents for reference, the author argues that rice transaction was at the core of the eighteenth-century Sino-Siamese relationship.

BIBLIOGRAPHY

Abe Takeo 安部建夫. "Bekoku jukyū no kenkyū: *Yōsei shi no ishō to shite mita*" 米穀需給の研究—「雍正史」の一章としてみた (The supply and demand of rice in the reign of the Yung-cheng Emperor), *Tōyōshi kenkyū* 東洋史研究 (Journal of Oriental research) 15.4:120–213 (March 1957).

Anderson, John. *English Intercourse with Siam in the Seventeenth Century.* London, Keagan Paul, Trench, Trubner, 1890.

Anumanrachaton, Praya อนุมานราชธน, พระยา (Yong Satienkoset ยง เสฐียรโกเศศ). *Tamnan sulakakorn* ตำนานศุลกากร (Government revenue and royal trading in ancient times). Issued at the funeral of Prince Prompong Atiraj พระองค์เจ้า พร้อมพงศ์อธิราช Mar. 27, 1939. Bangkok, 1939.

Bacon, George. *Siam: The Land of the White Elephant.* New York, 1881.

Blankwaardt, W. "Notes upon the Relations between Holland and Siam," *Journal of the Siam Society,* vol. 20, no. 3 (1929).

Bowring, Sir John. *The Kingdom and People of Siam.* Oxford in Asia History Reprints. 2 vols. London, Oxford University Press, 1969.

Bruguière, M., "Notices of the Religion, Manners, and Customs of the Siamese," English trans., in *Chinese Repository* 8:196 (April 1844).

Brunnert, H. S., and V. V. Hagelstrom. *Present-Day Political Organization of China*, tr. A. Beltchenko and E. E. Moran. Taipei, n.d.

Buckley, C. B., *An Anecdotal History of Old Times in Singapore.* Singapore, Fraser & Neave, Ltd., 1902.

Burney, Captain Henry. *The Burney Papers.* 5 vols. Bangkok, Vajiranana National Library, 1911.

Cady, John F. *Southeast Asia: Its Historical Development.* New York, McGraw-Hill, 1964.

Caron, Francois, and Joost Schouten. *A True Description of the Mighty Kingdoms of Japan and Siam.* London, 1935.

Chakrabongse, Prince Chula. *Lords of Life: A History of the Kings of Thailand.* 2nd ed. London, Alvin Redman, 1967.

Chang Te-ch'ang 張德昌 . "Ch'ing-tai ya-p'ien chan-cheng ch'ien chih Chung-Hsi yen-hai t'ung-shang" 清代鴉片戰爭前之中西沿海通商 (The Sino-Western maritime trade before the Opium War), *Ts'ing-hua hsueh-pao* 清華学報 (Ch'ing-hua journal) 10.1:96–145 (January 1935).

——— "The Economic Role of the Imperial Household in the Ch'ing Dynasty," *Journal of Asian Studies* 31.2:243–273 (February 1972).

Chang T'ien-tse. *Sino-Portuguese Trade, from 1514 to 1644.* Leiden, E. J. Brill, 1969.

Ch'en Chao-nan 陳昭南 . *Yung-cheng Ch'ien-lung nien-chien ti yin-ch'ien pi-chia pien-tung.* 雍正乾隆年間的銀錢比價变動 (Monetary fluctuations in the reigns of Yung-cheng and Ch'ien-lung) Taipei, 1966.

Ch'en Ching-ho 陳荆和 . "Ch'ing ch'u Hua-po chih Ch'ang-ch'i (Nagasaki) mao-i chi Jih-nan hang-yun" 清初華舶之長崎貿易及日南行運 (The role of Chinese vessels in the Nagasaki trade and Japan-South [southeast Asia] navigation of the early Ch'ing period), *Nan-yang hsueh-pao* 南洋学報 (Journal of the South Seas Society) 13.1:1–52 (June 1957).

——— "Shih-ch'i shih-chi Hsien-lo tui wai mao-i yu Hua-ch'iao"

十七世紀暹羅對外貿易與華僑 (The role of the Overseas Chinese and Siam's external trade in the seventeenth century), in Ling Shun-sheng 凌純聲 ed., *Chung-T'ai wen-hua lun-chi* 中泰文化論集 (Collection of essays on Sino-Thai relations). Taipei, 1958.

Ch'en Hsu-ching 陳序經 . *Hsien-lo yu Chung-kuo* 暹羅與中國 (Siam and China). Ch'ang-sha, 1941.

Ch'en Ju-chien 陳汝咸 , comp. *Chang-p'u hsieh chih* 漳浦縣志 (Gazetteer of Chang p'u district). 1876.

Ch'en Lun-ch'iung 陳倫烱 . *Hai-kuo wen-chien lu* 海國聞見錄 (A record of things seen and heard among the maritime nations). Author's preface, 1730; wood-block reprint, 1793.

Ch'en Shou-ch'i 陳壽祺 et al., comps. *Fu-chien t'ung-chih* 福建通志 (Gazetteer of Fukien province), *Chung-kuo sheng-chih hui-p'ien* 中國省志彙編 (Collection of Chinese provincial gazetteers), no. 9. Taipei, 1968.

Ch'en Ta 陳達 . *Nan-yang Hua-ch'iao yu Min-Yueh she-hui* 南洋華僑與閩粵社會 (Southeast Asia's Overseas Chinese and the Fukien and Kwangtung societies). Changsha, 1938.

Ch'en Ta-tuan 陳大端 . *Yung-Ch'ien-Chia shih-tai ti Chung-Liu kuan-hsi* 雍乾嘉時代的中琉關係 (Sino-Ryukyuan relations in the reigns of Yung-cheng, Ch'ien-lung, and Chia-ch'ing). Taipei, 1956.

Ch'en Yu-sung 陳育崧 . "Ch'en I-lao an yu Ch'ing-tai ch'ien-min cheng-ts'e chih kai-pien" 陳怡老案與清代遷民政策之改變 (The case of Ch'en I-lao and the Ch'ing policy on emigration), *Nan-yang hsueh-pao* 12.1:17–19 (June 1956).

Cheng Lin-k'uan 陳林寬 . *Fu-chien Hua-ch'iao hui-k'uan* 福建華僑匯款 (Remittances of the Fukien Overseas

364

Chinese). *Fu-chien t'iao-ch'a t'ung-chi ts'ung-shu* 福建調查統計叢書 (Investigative reports on Fukien). Fukien, 1940.

The Chinese Repository, vols. 1–20, Reprinted. Tokyo, Maruzen, 1968.

Ch'ing shih 清史 . (History of the Ch'ing dynasty), comp. Chao Erh-hsun 趙爾巽 . Taipei, 1960.

Ch'ing shih kao 清史稿 . (Draft history of the Ch'ing). Shanghai, 1942.

Ch'ing-shih kuan 清史館 , ed. *Ch'ing-shih lieh-chuan* 清史列傳 (Biographies from the history of the Ch'ing dynasty). Shanghai, 1928.

Ch'ing-tai wai-chiao shih-liao 清代外交史料 . (Materials on Ch'ing foreign relations), ed. National Palace Museum. Taipei, 1968.

Chotmaihet krung Rattanakosin R.1 จดหมายเหตุกรุงรัตหโกสิททร์ รัชกาลที่หนึ่ง (Documents of the First Reign of the Rattanakosin Dynasty). Bangkok, Department of Hand-Written Documents, National Library.

Chotmaihet krung Rattanakosin R.2 จดหมายเหตุกรุงรัตหโกสิททร์ รัชกาลที่สอง (Documents of the Second Reign of the Rattanakosin Dynasty). Bangkok, Department of Hand-Written Documents, National Library.

Chotmaihet krung Rattanakosin R.3 จดหมายเหตุกรุงรัตหโกสิททร์ รัชกาลที่สาม (Documents of the Third Reign of the Rattanakosin Dynasty). Bangkok, Department of Hand-Written Documents, National Library.

Chotmaihet krung Rattanakosin R.4 จดหมายเหตุกรุงรัตหโกสิททร์ รัชกาลที่สี่ (Documents of the Fourth Reign of the Rattanakosin Dynasty). Bangkok, Department of Hand-Written Documents, National Library.

Chotmaihet mit-channari American จดหมายเหตุมิชชันนารีอเมริกัน
(Documents of the American missionaries), in *Prachoom
pongsawadan chabab hor smut haeng chart* ประชุมพงศาวดาร
ฉบับหอสมุดแห่งชาติ (Collected chronicles and annals
of the various reigns, National Library ed.), installment 31,
vol. 7. Bangkok, 1964.

Chotmaihet nai paendin Somdej Pra Narai Maharat จดหมายเหตุ
แผ่นดินสมเด็จพระนารายณ์มหาราช (Documents
of the reign of King Narai), installment 18, vol. 5 of the
Prachoom pongsawadan chabab hor smut haeng chart.

"Chotmaihet rai-wan tup smai krung Thonburi" จดหมายเหตุรายวัน
ทัพสมัยกรุงธนบุรี (Military dispatches of the Thonburi reign), in *Prachoom pongsawadan chabab hor smut haeng
chart,* installments 65–66. Bangkok, 1969.

Chou K'ai 周凱 et al., comps. *Hsia-men chih* 廈門志 (Gazetteer of Amoy). First preface, 1832; last preface, 1839.

——— *Hsia-men chih* (Gazetteer of Amoy). *T'ai-wan wen-hsien
ts'ung-k'an.* (Collection of sources on Taiwan), no. 59. Taipei,
1962.

Chou-pan i-wu shih-mo 籌辦夷務始末 (A complete account
of the management of barbarian affairs). Peking, 1930.

(Yung-cheng) Chu-p'i yü-chih.(雍正)硃批諭旨 (Vermillion
endorsements, edicts, and rescripts in Yung-cheng's reign).
Compiled 1738.

Ch'u Ta-chun 屈大均 comp. *Kuang-tung hsin-yu* 廣東新語
(New treatise on Kwangtung province). Published, 1700.

Ch'uan Han-sheng 全漢昇 "Ch'ing-tai ti jen-k'ou pien-tung"
清代的人口變動 (Demographic fluctuations in the
Ch'ing dynasty), *Li-shih yü-yen yen-chiu-so chi-k'an* 历史
語言研究所集刊 (Journal of the Institute of History
and Philology, Academia Sinica), 32:139–180 (July 1961).

——— "Ching-ch'ao chung-yeh Su-chou ti mi-liang mao-i"

366

清朝中葉蘇州的米糧貿易 (The grain trade at Soochow
in the mid-Ch'ing period), *Li-shih yü-yen yen-chiu-so chi-k'an*
39b: 71–86 (October 1969).

――― "Ch'ien-lung shih-san nien ti mi-kuei wen-t'i" 乾隆十三年
的米貴問題 (The question of the dearness of rice
price of the thirteenth year of the Ch'ien-lung era), in his
Chung-kuo ching-chi shih lun-ts'ung 中國經濟史論叢
(Collected articles on Chinese economic history). 2 vols.
Hong Kong, 1972.

――― and Wang Yeh-chien 王業鍵 . "Ch'ing Yung-cheng nien
chien mi-chia 清雍正年間米價 (Rice prices in the
Yung-cheng reign) *Li-shih yü-yen yen-chiu-so chi-k'an* 28b:17–
550 (1957).

Chuang Wei-chi 庄為璣 , Lin Chin-chih, 林金枝 et al.
"Fu-chien Chin-chiang tsuan-ch'u Hua-ch'iao shih t'iao-ch'a
pao-kao" 福建晉江專區華僑史調查報告
(Investigation into the history of the Overseas Chinese of
Ch'uan-chou), *Hsia-men ta-hsueh hsueh-pao* 厦門大学学
報 (Journal of Amoy University) 1:93–127 (1958).

Chulachomklao จุฬาจอมเกล้า . King (Rama V or King Chulalongkorn), ed. "Pra rachavijarn" พระราชวิจารณ์ (The record kept
by Princess Narindr Thevi นรินทรเทวี from 1767–1820; a
ms.). Bangkok, 1908; second printing 1916 (issued at the
funeral of Prince Nakornchaisi Suradej กรมหลวงนครไชยศรี
สุรเดช 1916).

Comber, L. F. *Chinese Secret Societies in Malaya.* Monographs of
the Association for Asian Studies, no. 6. New York, J. J.
Augustin, 1959.

Crawfurd, John. *History of the Indian Archipelago.* 3 vols. Edinburgh, Archibald Constable and Co., 1820.

――― *Journal of An Embassy from the Governor-General of India* to the Courts of Siam and Co-chin China. 2nd ed. London, Henry Colburn and Richard Bentley, 1830.

——— The Crawfurd Papers. Bangkok, Vajiranana National Library, 1915.

Dai Nam thúc luc chin-binh 大南寔錄正編 (Proper edition of the Veritable Records of Vietnam) Tô Châu 苏珍 et al., comps. Tokyo, 1970.

De la Loubère, Simon. The Kingdom of Siam. Oxford in Asia History Reprints. 2 vols. Kuala Lumpur, Oxford University Press, 1969.

Dermigny, Louis. Le commerce à Canton au XVIIIᵉ siècle, 1719–1833. 4 vols. Paris, S.E.V.P.E.N., 1964.

"A Dissertation upon the Commerce of China" (written circa 1846), in Rhoads Murphey, ed., Nineteenth-Century China: Five Imperialist Perspectives. Michigan Papers in Chinese Studies, no. 13. Ann Arbor, University of Michigan, 1972.

Earl, George. The Eastern Seas or Voyages and Adventures in the Indian Archipelago, London, 1837.

Fairbank, John K. Trade and Diplomacy on the China Coast. 2 vols. Cambridge, Mass., Harvard University Press, 1953.

——— ed. The Chinese World Order. Cambridge, Mass., Harvard University Press, 1968.

Fairbank, John K. and Ssu-yü Teng. "On the Ch'ing Tributary System," in John K. Fairbank and Teng Ssu-yü, Ch'ing Administration: Three Studies. Cambridge, Mass., Harvard University Press, 1968.

Feng Liu-t'ang 馮柳堂 Shina shōku-ryō seisaku shi 支那食糧政策史 (A history of China's general policies on the question of popular consumption), tr. Mori Gi'ichi 森儀一 . Tokyo, 1941.

——— *Chung-kuo li-tai min-shih cheng-ts'e shih* 支那历代民食政策史 (A history of China's general policies on the question of popular consumption). Taipei, 1970.

Fitzgerald, C. P. *A Concise History of East Asia.* New York, 1966.

Frankfurter, O. "The Mission of James Brooke," *Journal of the Siam Society* 8:29–30 (May 1912).

Fu-chien sheng-li 福建省例(Regulations of Fukien Province). Taipei, 1964.

Fu Lo-shu, comp. and tr. *A Documentary Chronicle of Sino-Western Relations, 1644–1820.* Association for Asian Studies, Monographs and Papers, no. 22. 2 vols. Tucson, University of Arizona Press, 1966.

Fukuda Shozo 福田省三 . *Kakyō keizai ron* 華僑経済論 (The Overseas Chinese economy). Tokyo. 1942.

Furnivall, John. *Netherlands India: A Study of Plural Economy.* Cambridge, England, 1939.

Gerini, G. E. "Siam's Intercourse with China," *Asiatic Quarterly Review* 14.28:391–408 (October 1902).

Graham, W. A. *Siam.* 2 vols. London, Alexander Moring Ltd., The De La More Press, 1924.

Gunji Ki'ichi 郡司喜一 . *Jūhichi seiki ni okeru Ni-Shin kankei* 十七世紀における日暹関係 (Japanese-Siamese Relations in the seventeenth century). Tokyo, 1934.

Gützlaff, Charles. *Journal of Three Voyages along the Coast of China in 1831, 1832, 1833, with Notices of Siam, Corea and the Loo-choo Islands.* London, R. Westley and A. H. Davis, 1834.

Haas, Joseph, "Siamese Coinage," *Journal of the North China*

Branch of the Royal Asiatic Society, new series 14:53–54
(1879).

Hall, John, "Notes on the Early Ch'ing Copper Trade with Japan,"
Harvard Journal of Asiatic Studies 12.3–4, 445–461 (December 1949).

Han Ch'ao 韓潮 *Ch'ao-chou feng-wu* 潮州風物 (Customs
and peculiarities of Chao-chou prefecture). Hong Kong, 1970.

Hayakawa Jun'zaburō 早川純三郎 . *Tsū-kō ichiran* 通
航一覽 (Views on navigation). Tokyo, 1912.

Hayashi Harunobu 林春勝 and Hayashi Nobuatsu 林信篤 ,
comps., Ura Ren'ichi 浦廉一 , anno. *Ka-i hentai* 華夷
變態 (The barbarization of China). Tōyō-bunko sō-kan
東洋文庫叢刊 (Publication of the Oriental Research
Library), no. 15. Tokyo, 1958.

Hirase Minokichi 平瀬改吉 . *Kindai Shina keizai shi* 近代支那
經濟史 (Modern Chinese economic history). Tokyo, 1942.

Hirayama Amane 平山周 . *Chūgoku himitsu shakai shi* 中国
祕密社会史 (A history of the Chinese secret societies).
Shanghai, 1932.

Hou Hou-p'ei 侯厚培 . "Wu-k'ou t'ung-shang i-ch'ien wuo-kuo
kuo-chi mao-i chih kai-k'uang" 五國通商以前我國
國際貿易之概況 (General conditions of our
country's foreign trade prior to the opening of the Five Treaty
Ports). *Ts'ing-hua hsueh-pao* 4.1:1248 (1927).

Hsia-men chih 廈門志 (Gazetteer of Amoy). T'ai-wan wen-
hsien ts'ung-k'an 台灣文献叢刊 (Collection of sources
on Taiwan) 1962.

Hsiang Ta 向達 . *Liang-tsung hai-tao chen-ching* 雨种海道針
經 (Two kinds of navigational directions) Peking, 1961.

Hsiao I-shan 蕭一山 . *Ch'ing-tai t'ung-shih* 清代通史 (A
comprehensive history of the Ch'ing dynasty). Taipei, 1962.

Hsiao Ji-i 蕭戟儒 . "Pen-hui hui-shih" 本會會史 (The

history of this association) in *T'ai-kuo Hua-ch'iao K'e-shu tsung-hui san-shih chou-nien chi-nien t'e-k'an* 泰国華僑客屬總會廿週年紀念特刊 (Special issue commemorating the thirtieth year of the founding of the Hukka association of Thailand). Bangkok, 1958.

Hsieh Ch'ing-kao 謝清高 . *Hai-lu* 海錄 (A record of the seas). 1842.

Hsieh Yu-yung 謝猶榮 . *Hsin-p'ien Hsien-lo kuo chih* 新編暹羅国志 (A new edition of the annals of Siam). Bangkok, 1953.

Hsu Chi-yü 徐繼畬 . *Ying huan chih-lueh.* 瀛環志略 1873.

Hsu Yun-ch'iao 許雲樵 . "Cheng-chao kung-shih ju ch'ao Chung-kuo chi-hsing-shih shih-chu" 鄭昭貢使入朝中国記行詩譯注 (Translation and annotation of a traveling poem by Taksin's ambassador to China), *Nan-yang hsueh-pao* 1:33–47 (December 1940).

——— *Pei ta-nien shih* 北大年史 (A history of Pattani). Singapore, 1946.

——— "Chung-Hsien t'ung-shih k'ao" 中暹通史考 (A study of the diplomatic intercourse between China and Siam), *Nan-yang hsueh-pao* 3:3–35 (September 1946).

——— "Cheng-chao ju kung Ch'ing-t'ing k'ao" 鄭昭入貢清廷考 (A study of Taksin's embassies to the Ch'ing court), *Nan-yang hsueh-pao* 6:1–17 (June 1951).

Hsuan-tsung shih-lu 宣宗實錄 (Veritable records of the Tao-kuang Emperor), in *Ta-Ch'ing li-ch'ao shih-lu* 大清歷朝實錄 (Veritable records of successive reigns of the Ch'ing dynasty). Tokyo, 1937.

Huang Shu-ching 黃叔敬 . *T'ai-hai shih-ch'a lu* 台海便槎錄 (A raft journey in the Taiwan Strait). Taipei, 1957.

Huang Wei 黄葦 . *Shang-hai k'ai-fu ch'u-ch'i tui-wai mao-i yen-chiu* 上海開埠初期對外貿易研究 (A study of Shanghai's external trade in its initial opening period, 1842–1863). Shanghai, 1961.

Hughes, George. *Amoy and the Surrounding Districts.* Hong Kong, 1872.

Hummel, Arthur, ed. *Eminent Chinese of the Ch'ing Period.* Washington, D.C., U.S. Government Printing Office, 1943.

Hunter, William. *The Fan Kwae at Canton before Treaty Days, 1825–1844.* London, 1911.

Ide Kiwata 井出季和太 . *Kakyō* 華僑 (Overseas Chinese). Tokyo, 1943.

Ingram, James. *Economic Change in Thailand Since 1850.* Stanford, Calif. Stanford University Press, 1955.

"Intelligence on the Import of Rice," *Asiatic Journal* 21:242–243 (1826).

Intramontri, Pra อินทรมนตรี, พระ . "T'ai-kuo chui-hou i ch'ih ju-kung Chung-kuo chi-lu shu" 泰国最後一次入貢中国紀録書 (Record of Siam's last tributary mission to China), tr. "T'ang-hua," 棠花 *Chung-yuan yueh-k'an* 中原月刊 (Chung-yuan monthly magazine) 1.1:15–26 (January 1941).

Ishii Yoneo. "Seventeenth-Century Japanese Documents about Siam," *Journal of the Siam Society* 59.2:161–174 (July 1971).

"The Island of Hainan." *The Asiatic Journal* 21.1–6:15–16 (1826).

Iwao Sei'ichi 岩生成一 . "Taijin no tai Nikkoku bōeki hukkatsu undō" 泰人の對日国貿易復活運動 (Restoration of the Siamese trade to Japan), *Tōa ronsō* 東亞論叢 Collected studies of East Asia) 4:77–122 (April 1941).

——— *Shūinsen bōeki shi no kenkyū* 朱印船貿易史の研究 (A study of the red-seal ship trade). Tokyo, 1958.

——— *Shūinsen to Nihon machi* 朱印船と日本町 (Red-seal ships and the Japanese overseas settlements). Tokyo, 1962.

Jao Tsung-i 饒宗頤 , comp. "Ch'ao-chou chih kao" 潮州志藁 (Draft of the gazetteer of Ch'ao-chou) in ibid. *Ch'ao-chou chih hui-p'ien* 潮州志匯編 (Collected works of Ch'ao-chou). Hong Kong, 1965.

Jen-tsung shih-lu 仁宗實錄 (Veritable records of the Chia-ch'ing Emperor), in *Ta-Ch'ing li-ch'ao shih-lu* 大清历朝實錄 (Veritable records of successive reigns of the Ch'ing dynasty).

Jones, Susan Mann. "Finance in Ningpo: The Ch'ien Chuang; 1750–1880," in W. E. Willmott, ed. *Economic Organization in Chinese Society.* Stanford, 1972.

Juan Yuan 阮元 , ed. *Kuang-tung t'ung-chih* 廣東通志 , (Gazetteer of Kwangtung province). 1864.

———, ed. *Kuang-tung t'ung-chih* 廣東通志 (Gazetteer of Kwangtung province). *Chung-hua ts'ung-shu* 中華叢書 (Collected works on China). Taipei, 1959.

Kanazawa Kanemitsu 金澤兼先 *Wa-Kan sen'yo shu* 華漢船用集 (Sino-Japanese vessels), in Saigusa Hiroto 三枝博音 , ed. *Nihon kagaku ko-ten zensho* 日本科学古典全書 (Complete work of classics of Japanese science), Tokyo, 1943.

Kanjanakapun, Sa-nga การญาหาคพันธ์, สง่า *Prawat karnka kong pratet Thai* ประวัติการค้า ของประเทศไทย (History of Thailand's foreign trade), Bangkok, 1943.

——— *Pab-prawatisart krung Rattanakosin* ภาพประวัติศาสตร์กรุง รัตนโกสินทร์ (A pictorial history of the Bangkok dynasty). Bangkok, 1962.

Kao-tsung shih-lu 高宗實錄 (Veritable records of the Ch'ien-lung Emperor), in *Ta-ch'ing li-ch'ao shih-lu.* Tokyo, 1937.

Kao-tsung shun huang-ti sheng-hsun 高宗純皇帝聖訓 (Sacred instructions of Kao-tsung), in *Ta-Ch'ing sheng-hsun*

大清聖訓 (Sacred instructions of the Ch'ing dynasty) Taipei, 1965.

Kato Shigeru 加藤繁 "Shindai Hukken Kōso no senko ni tsuite" 清代福建江苏の船行に就いて (On navigation in Fukien and Kiangsu during the Ching period). *Shirin* 史林 vol. 14, no. 4 (1929).

Khâm-dhinh-Dai-Nam hôi diên s'u lê 欽定大南會典事例 (The Vietnam administrative statures and precedent cases). Tokyo, 1962.

Koenig, Jean, "Journal of a Voyage from India to Siam and Malacca in 1779," tr. from his ms. in the British Museum. *Journal of the Straits Branch of the Royal Asiatic Society,* vol. 26 (January 1894).

Krisananon, Kularb กฤตศักดาหกหก, กุหลาบ *Mahamukamatta-yanukunwong* มหามุขมาตยานุกุลวงศ์ (Genealogies of the various Siamese nobles). Bangkok, 1905.

Kuang-chou fu chih 廣州府志 (Gazetteer of Kwangchow prefecture), comp. Shen T'ing-fang. 1758

Lan Ting-yuan 藍鼎元. *Lun Nan-yang shih-i shu* 論南洋事宜書 (A discussion of a proper policy regarding the Southern Ocean) in his *Lu-chou ch'u-chi* 廣州初集 (First collection from Lu-chou). 1732.

Launay, Adrien. *Histoire de la mission de Siam, 1622–1811.* 4 vols. Paris, P. Tegui, 1920.

Li Chang-fu 李長傅. *Chung-kuo chih-min shih.* 中国殖民史 (A history of Chinese immigration) Shanghai, 1937.

Li Kuang-t'ao 李光濤, "Hua-i yu Hsien-lo" 華裔与暹羅 (Overseas Chinese and Siam), *Min-chu p'ing-lun* 民主評論 (Democratic review) 8.18:434–440 (Sept. 16, 1957).

——— "Ming-Ch'ing liang-tai yu Hsien-lo" 明清兩代与暹羅 (Sino-Siamese relations during the Ming and Ch'ing dynasties), in Ling Shun-sheng 凌純声, ed., *Chung-T'ai wen-hua lun-chi* 中泰文化論集 (Collection of essays on Sino-Thai relations). Taipei, 1958.

——— "Chi Ch'ing-tai ti Hsien-lo kuo-piao" 記清代暹羅国表 (Notes on the Siamese state letters to the Ch'ing court), *Li-shih yü-yen yen-chiu-so chi-k'an* 30b:511–566 (October 1959).

Li Tseng-chieh 李增階. *Hai-wai chi-yao* 海外紀要 (A record of essentials concerning the outer seas), in Ch'en K'un 陳坤, ed., *Ts'ung-cheng hsu-yü-lu* 從政緒餘錄 (Remnant notes of government service). 1881.

Liang Chi-fan 梁寄凡, "Kuan shih" 館史 (Club history), in *T'ai-kuo Hai-nan hui-kuan hsin hsia lo-ch'eng chi-nien t'e-k'an* 泰國海南會館新廈落成紀念特刊 (Special issue commemorating the new headquarters of the Hainanese Association in Thailand). Bangkok, 1958.

Liang Chia-pin 梁嘉彬, "Lun Ming-Ch'ing Kuang-tung kuo-chi mao-i yu chin-tai Chung-T'ai chih kuan-hsi" 論明清廣東国際貿易與近代中泰之關係 (Discussion of foreign trade at Canton during the Ming and Ch'ing dynasties and recent Sino-Siamese relations), in Ling Shun-sheng 凌純声, ed., *Chung-Tai wen-hua lun-chi* 中泰文化論集 (Collection of essays on Sino-Thai relations). Taipei, 1958.

——— *Kuang-tung shih-san-hang k'ao* 廣東十三行考 (Hong merchants of Canton). Taipei, 1960.

Liang T'ing-nan 梁廷枏 *Yueh-hai-kuan chih* 粤海關志 (The Canton maritime superintendency). 1839.

——— *Hsien-lo-kuo* 暹羅国 (Documents on Siam). First part of his *Yueh-tao kung-kuo shuo* 粤道貢国説 (Discourse on tributaries using the Canton route), *Chung-hua wen-shih ts'ung-shu* 中華文史叢書 (Collected works on Chinese history), no. 58. Taipei, 1968.

Light, Francis, "A Letter from Captain Light to Lord Cornwallis, dated 20th June 1788." *Journal of the Royal Asiatic Society, Malayan Branch* 16.1:115–126. (July 1938).

Liu Chien-shao 劉建韶 , comp. *Fu-chien t'ung-chih cheng-shih lueh* 福建通志政事略 (A survey of administrative affairs for the gazetteer of Fukien province). N.d.

Lo Erh-kang 羅爾綱, "T'ai-p'ing t'ien-kuo ke-ming ch'ien ti jen-kuo ya-po wen-t'i" 太平天国革命前的人口壓迫問題 (Problem of population pressure in the pre-Taiping days), in *Chung-kuo she-hui ching-chi shih chi-k'an* 中国社会經済史集刊 (Collection on Chinese social and economic history), vol. 81. 1949.

Lu K'un 盧坤 and Ch'en Hung-ch'ih 陳鴻墀 et al., comps. *Kuang-tung hai-fang hui-lan* 廣東海防彙覽 (A compendium of Kwangtung maritime defense.) ca. 1836.

MacGowan, D. J. "Chinese Guilds or Chambers of Commerce and Trade Unions," *Journal of the China Branch of the Royal Asiatic Society,* vol. 21, no. 3 (1887).

MacNair, Harley. *The Chinese Abroad: Their Position and Protection.* Shanghai, The Commercial Press, 1926.

Malcom, Howard. *Travels in Southeast Asia.* 2 vols. Boston, Gould Kendall and Lincoln, 1839.

Malloch, D. E. *Siam: Some General Remarks on Its Productions.* Calcutta, Baptist Mission Press, 1852.

Mancall, Mark, "The Ch'ing Tributary System: An Interpretative Essay," in John K. Fairbank, ed., *The Chinese World Order.* Cambridge, Mass., Harvard University Press, 1968.

Matheson, James. *The Present Position and Prospects of the British Trade with China.* London, Smith, Elder and Co., 1836.

Matsuo Hiroshi 松尾弘 *Shinra kokumin keizai no tokucho* 暹羅国民経済の特徴 Taipei, 1938.

Miki Sakae 三木榮 . *Ni-Shin kōtsū shi* 日暹交通史 (A history of Siamese-Japanese intercourse) Tokyo, 1934.

Ming-Ch'ing shih-liao 明清史料 (Historical materials relating to the Ming and Ch'ing dynasties), ed. Academia Sinica. Taipei, 1960.

Miyazaki Ichisada 宮崎市定 "Chūgoku-Nanyō kankei shi gaisetsu" 中国南洋関係史概説 (An outline of the history of China-Southeast Asia relations) in Miyazaki Ichisada, ed., Ajia shi no kenkyū アジア史の研究 (Asiatica: Studies in Oriental history), vol. 2. *Tōyōshi kenkyū sōkan* 東洋史研究叢刊 (Oriental research), no. 1, pt. 2. Kyoto, 1959.

Moffat, Abbot Low, *Mongkut, The King of Siam* (Ithaca, New York, 1961).

Morrison, John R. *A Chinese Commercial Guide.* 3rd ed. Canton, Chinese Repository, 1848.

Morse, Hosea. *The Chronicles of the East India Company Trading to China, 1635–1834.* 5 vols. Oxford University Press, 1926.

Nagasakishi shi 長崎市史 (A history of Nagasaki), ed. Nagasakishi. Nagasaki, 1938.

Nan-ao chih 南澳志 (Gazetteer of Namoa Island), comp. Wu-yuan-chi-chung 婺源齊中 1783.

Narita Setsuo 成田節男 . "Taikoku Kakyō to kome" 泰国華僑と米 (Thailand's Overseas Chinese and rice), *Tōa ronsō* 東亞論叢 (Collected studies on East Asia) 4:307–320 (April 1941).

Negishi Takashi 根岸佶 *Shina girudo no kenkyū* 支那ギルドの研究 (A study of the guilds of China) Tokyo, 1942.

——— *Gōkō no kenkyū* 合股の研究 (Study of joint investment or partnership). Tokyo, 1943.

——— *Chūgoku no girudo* 中国のギルド (The guilds of China). Tokyo, 1953.

Nishikawa Tadahide 西川求林斎 . *Ka-i tsushō ko* 華夷通商考 (An examination of the Sino-barbarian trade), vol. 4 of the *Nihon keizai daiten* 日本経済大典 (An encyclopedia of Japanese economy), ed. Takimoto Sei'ichi 瀧本誠一 . Tokyo, 1928.

Niyomwong, Preecha ณิยมวงศ์, ปรีชา . "Man-ku huang-ch'ao shih-chi La-ma ti erh shih-huang shih-tai" 曼谷皇朝史記拉馬第二世皇時代 (Notes on Bangkok dynasty Rama II period), tr. T'ang-hua 棠花 *Chung-yuan yueh-k'an* 中原月刊 (Chung-yuan monthly) 1.6 (1941).

O'Kane, John, tr. *The Ships of Suleimān.* New York, Columbia University Press, 1972.

Pallegoix, Mgr. Jean-Baptiste. *Lao ruang muang Thai* เล่าเรื่อง เมืองไทย (Description du royaume Thai ou Siam), tr. Sunt Komolabut. Bangkok, 1963.

Pao Tsun-p'eng 包遵彭 *Cheng Ho hsia hsi-yang chih pao-ch'uan k'ao* 鄭和下西洋之寳船考 (A study of Grand Eunuch Cheng Ho's ships in the Western Ocean). Taipei, 1961.

P'eng Tse-i 彭澤益. "Ch'ing-tai Kuang-tung yang-hang chih-tu ti ch'i-yuan" 清代廣東洋行制度的起源 (The rise of co-hongs in Canton during the Ch'ing dynasty), *Li-shih yen-chiu* 历史研究 (Historical studies), no. 1:1–24 (January 1957).

Perkins, Dwight, Wang Yeh-chien, et al. *Agricultural Development in China, 1368–1968.* Chicago, Aldine Publishing Co., 1969.

Phipps, John. *A Practical Treatise on the China and Eastern Trade.* Calcutta, The Baptist Mission Press, 1835.

Prainoi, Sor. พรายห้อย, ส. . *Chao-tangpratet nai prawatisart Thai* ชาวต่างประเทศในประวัติศาสตร์ไทย (Foreigners in Thai history). Bangkok, 1973.

Pritchard, Earl. *The Crucial Years of Early Anglo-Chinese Relations, 1750–1800.* Research Studies of the State College of Washington, vol. 4, nos. 3–4. Pullman, Washington, 1936.

Promboon, Suebsaeng, "Sino-Siamese Tributary Relations, 1282–1853." Ph.D. dissertation, University of Wisconsin, 1971.

Prudhinarakorn, Pornipa พฤมินารากร, พรนิภา and Suebwatana Thaweesilp สืบวัฒนะ ทวีศิลป์ "Kao nai prai Ayudhya" ข้าวในปลายอยุธยา (Rice in Late Ayudhya), *Varasarn Thammasart* วารสารธรรมศาสตร์ (Thammasart journal) 4.3:40–60 (February–May 1975).

Rabibhadana, Akin. *The Organization of Thai Society in the Early Bangkok Period, 1782–1873.* Southeast Asia Program Data Paper, no. 74. Ithaca, Cornell University, 1969.

Rajanubhab, Damrong Files, Department of Hand-Written Documents, National Library, Bangkok.

Rajanubhab, Prince Damrong ราชานุภาพ, กรมพระยาดำรง . *Prawat Somdej Chaopraya Borom Maha Si Suriyawong,* ประวัติสมเด็จ เจ้าพระยามหาศรีสุริยวงศ์ (Biography of Si Suriyawong). Issued at the funeral of Prince Mahidol Adulyadej มหิดลอดุลยเดช . December 30, 1929. Bangkok, 1929.

——— *Tamnan pasi-akorn bangyang kab kam atibai* ตำหาหภาษีอากร บางอย่างกับคำอธิบาย (Stories on certain taxes and their commentaries). *Latti tam-niem tang-tang* series ลัทธิ ธรรมเนียมต่างๆ (Customs and ideologies) no. 16. Issued at the funeral of Luang Raksa Nittisart หลวงรักษานิติศาสตร์ (Perm Chawanon เพิ่ม วาหหท์), 1930. Bangkok, 1930.

——— *Tamnan ngern-tra* ตำหานเงินตรา (Stories of Thai currencies). Bangkok, 1933.

——— *Tesapiban* เทศาภิบาล (Regional administration) Bangkok, 1960.

——— "Pu-boriharn rachakarn paendin nai adit" ผู้บริหารราชการ แผ่นดินในอดีต (Rulers and administrators of the realm in the past), in King Chulalongkorn (Rama V), Prince Damrong Rajanubhab กรมพระยาดำรงราชานุภาพ , et al., *Ruang ti tiao ti tang-tang* เรื่อง เที่ยวที่ต่าง ๆ (Travelogues), vol. 2. Issued at the funeral of Luen Saisnan na Ayudhya เลื่อน สายสนั่น ณ อยุธยา , Oct. 29, 1962.

——— *Tamnan karn lurk bon-bia lae karn lurk huey* ตำหานการเลิก บ่อหเบี้ยและการเลิกหวย (Story on the abolition of the gambling and lottery tax farms), in *Prachoom pongsawadan chabab hor smut haeng chart*. Bangkok, 1964.

——— *Nitarn boran-kadi* หิทาหโบราณคดี (Classical stories). Issued at the funeral of Nien Lapanukrom เหียน ลาพหุกรม 1968. Bangkok, 1968.

——— "Ruang Anglit kao-ma kor-tum sanya krang Ratchakarn ti song" เรื่องอังกฤษเข้ามาขอทำสัญญากลางรัชกาลที่สอง (On the British request for a treaty in the middle of the Second Chakri reign) in *Prachoom pongsawadan chabab hor smut haeng chart,* installment 55. Bangkok, 1971, XII, 178–180.

———, ed. *Pra-ratcha pongsawadan chabab pra ratcha hatleka* พระราชพงศาวดารฉบับพระราชหัตถเลขา (Royal chronicles, Pra-ratcha hatleka ed.). 2 vols. Bangkok, 1952.

———, comp. "Tamnan muang Ranong" ตำหานเมืองระหอง (Story of Ranong province), in *Prachoom pongsawadan chabab hor smut haeng chart*. Bangkok, 1920.

Rama IV. "The Establishment of the Kingdom" tr. "S.J.S.," *Siam Repository*. 1869.

Rattanasevi, Sawad รัถหเสวี, สวัสดิ์ . "Prawatisart muang

Nakorn Si Thammarat ประวัติศาสตร์เมือง นครศรีธรรมราช (History of Ligor), in *Tamnan Pra Boromtat* ตำหาน พระบรมธาตุ (Stories of the Pra Boromtat temple at Ligor). Nakorn Si Thammarat, 1973.

Roberts, Edmund. *Embassy to the Eastern Courts of Cochin-China, Siam and Muscat during the Years 1832, 1833, 1834.* New York, 1834.

Sasaki Masaya 佐久木正哉 "Etsu kaikan no roki" 粤海関の陋規 (Illegal tariff of the Canton customs during the Ch'ing dynasty), *Tōyōgaku hō* 東洋学報 (Reports of the Oriental Society) 34.1–4:143 (1952).

Sevikun, Opart เสวีกุล, โอภาส . *Pracha bida haeng karn patiroop* พระราชบิดาแห่งการปฏิรูป (The father of reform, Rama IV). Bangkok, 1970.

Sasamoto Shigemi 笹本重巳 , "Kanton no tetsunabe ni tsuite" 廣東の鐵鍋に就いて (Market for the Canton-made iron pan after the fifteenth century), *Tōyōshi kenkyū* 12.2:35–48 (December 1952).

Satow, E. M. "Notes on the Intercourse between Japan and Siam in the Seventeenth Century," *Transactions of the Asiatic Society of Japan* 13:139–210 (1885).

Savary des Bruslons, Jacques and Philemon-Louis, "Shinsho Kanton [Kōtō] bōeki ni kansuro ichi shiryō" 清初貿易に関する一資料 (Un matèrial sur le commerce de Kuangtung au commencement de la dynastie Tsing), tr. Miyazaki Ichisada. *Tōa keizai kenkyū* (Revue d'economic politique d l'Extrême-Orient) 25.6:42–62 (November–December 1941).

——— *The Universal Dictionary of Trade and Commerce,* tr. Malachy Postlethwayt. London, John and Paul Knapton, 1751.

Schurz, William. *The Manila Galleon.* New York, 1939.

Sheldon, Charles D., *The Rise of the Merchant Class in Tokugawa Japan.* New York, Locust Valley, 1958.

Sheng-tsu shih-lu 聖祖實錄 (Veritable records of the K'ang-hsi Emperor), in *Ta-ch'ing li-ch'ao shih-lu* 大清歷朝實錄. Tokyo, 1937.

Shih-i ch'ao Tung-hua lu 十一朝東華錄 (Records from the Tung-hua Hall, eleventh reign ed. Wang Hsien-chi, 1911.

Shih-liao hsun-k'an 史料旬刊 eds. (Historical materials, published every ten days). National Palace Museum. Peking, 1930–1931.

Shih-tsung shih-lu 世宗實錄 (Veritable records of the Yung-cheng Emperor), in *Ta-Ch'ing li-ch'ao shih-lu* 大清歷朝實錄. Tokyo, 1937.

Siam Repository, ed. Samuel Smith. 2 vols. Bangkok, n.d.

Siamese Legation, Paris, comps. *State Papers of the Kingdom of Siam, 1664–1886.* London, 1886.

Sittipun, Prayud สิทธิพันธ์, ประยุทธ. *Ton trakoon kun-nang Thai* ต้นตระกูลขุนนางไทย (Genealogy of the Siamese nobility). Bangkok, 1962

——— *Racha samnak Thai* ราชสำนักไทย (The Siamese royal court). Bangkok, 1968.

Skinner, G. William. *Chinese Society in Thailand: An Analytical History.* Ithaca, Cornell University Press, 1957.

——— *Leadership and Power in the Chinese Community of Thailand.* Ithaca, New York, 1958.

Smyth, H. Warrington. *Five Years in Siam.* London, 1898.

Song Ong Siang. *One Hundred Years of History of the Chinese in Singapore.* Singapore, University of Malaya Press, 1967.

Steinberg, David, Alexander Woodside, David Wyatt, William Roff, John Smail, and David Chandler. *In Search of Southeast Asia: A Modern History.* New York, Praeger, 1971.

Sternstein, Larry. "Krung Kao: The Old Capital of Ayutthaya,"
  Journal of the Siam Society 53.1:83–122 (January 1965).

Su Ch'ing-huai 蘇清淮. "Fu-ch'ien ts'ang-sang shih-hua" 福
  建滄桑史話 (A history of great changes in Fukien), in
  *T'ai-kuo Fu-chien hui-kuan ch'eng-li wu shih chou-nien shin-
  chih lo-ch'eng chi-nien t'e-k'an* 泰国福建會館成
  立五十週年新址落成記念特刊 (Special
  edition commemorating the fiftieth anniversary and establishment of a new headquarters of the Fukien Association in
  Thailand). Bangkok, 1961.

"Supa-aksorn chong-tŏk moo-i tung Chaopraya Praklang klang-ti si"
  ศกอักษรวงตึกมูอีถึงเจ้าพระยาพระคลังครั้งที่สี่
  (Fourth missive from the Kwangtung viceroy to the Praya
  Praklang), in *Damrong Rajanubhab Files*.

Supatrapun, Pongpun สุภัทรพันธุ์, พ่องพัน . "Karn-suksa tang
  prawatisart kiew-duei ruang praklang sin-ka" การศึกษาทาง
  ประวัติศาสตร์เกี่ยวด้วยเรื่องพระคลังสินค้า (A historical study of the system of royal monopolies in Siam). M.A.
  thesis, Chulalongkorn University, Bangkok, 1968.

Ta-Ch'ing hui-tien 大清會典 (Collected statutes of the Ch'ing
  dynasty). Chia-ch'ing 嘉慶 ed., 1818.

(Ch'in-ting) Ta-Ch'ing hui-tien shih-li 欽定大清會典事例
  (Imperial edition of the collected statutes of the Ch'ing dynasty,
  with precedents). Kuang-hsu ed., 1899.

Ta-Ch'ing li-ch'ao shih-lu 大清历朝实錄 (Veritable records
  of successive reigns of the Ch'ing dynasty). Tokyo, 1937–1938.

*T'ai-kuo Fu-chien hui-kuan ch'eng-li wu-shih chou-nien hsin-chih
  lo-ch'eng chi-nien t'e-k'an* 泰国福建會館成立五十
  週年新址落成記念週刊 (Special edition com-
  memorating the sixtieth anniversary of the Fukien Association,
  Thailand). Bangkok, 1961.

Takazaki Misako 高崎美佐子. "Jūhachi seiki ni okeru Shin-Tai kōshō shi" 十八世紀における清泰交渉史 (Sino-Thai relations in the eighteenth century), *Ochanomizu shigaku* お茶の水史学(Study of history), Ochanomizu University 10:18–32 (1967).

Tanaka Katsumi 田中克巳. "Shinsho no Shina enkai-senkai o chusin to shite mitaru" 清初の支那沿海:遷界を中心とに見る (The coastline of China in the early Ch'ing dynasty: The question of forced evacuation) *Rekishi gaku kenkyū* (Historical research), vol. 6, nos. 1, 2 (1936).

Thippakorawong, Chaopraya ทิพกรวงศ์, เจ้าพระยา. *Pra-ratcha pongsawadan krung Rattanakosin rachakarn ti nung rachakarn ti song chabab hor smut haeng chart* ,พระราชพงศาวดาร กรุงรัตนโกสินทร์รัชกาลที่หนึ่งรัชกาลที่สอง ฉบับหอสมุด แห่งชาติ (Royal chronicles of the First and Second Reigns of the Rattanakosin Bangkok dynasty, National Library ed.). Bangkok, 1962.

——— comp. *The Dynastic Chronicles, Bangkok Era. The Fourth Reign* (B.E. 2394–2411), tr. Chadin Flood. 3 vols. Tokyo, Center for East Asian Cultural Studies, 1965.

T'ien Ju-k'ang 田汝康. "Tsai-lun shih-ch'i chih shih-chiu shih-chi chung-yeh Chung-kuo fan-ch'uan-yeh ti fa-chan," 再論十七至十九世紀中葉中国帆船業的發展 (A further study of the development of the Chinese junk trade between the seventeenth and mid-nineteenth centuries), *Li-shih yen-chiu,* no. 12 (1957).

——— *Shih-ch'i shih-chiu shih-chi chung-yeh Chung-kuo fan-ch'uan tsai tung-nan Ya-chou* 十七十九世紀中葉中国帆船在東南亞洲 (Chinese-style vessels in Southeast Asia during the seventeenth and mid-nineteenth centuries). Shanghai, 1957.

——— "Shih-wu chih shih-pa shih-chi Chung-kuo hai-wai mao-i huan-

384

man ti yuan-in" 十五至十八世紀中國海外貿易緩慢的原因 (Reasons for the retarded development of China's maritime trade between the fifteenth and eighteenth centuries). *Hsin chien-she* 新建設 (New construction), nos. 188–189 (1964).

Tông Phúc Ngoan 宋福元 and Dúo'ng Văn Châu 楊文珠 *Xiem-la-quoc lo-trinh tap-luc* 暹羅國路程集錄 (Collected records of the routes to the Kingdom of Siam). Hong Kong, 1966.

Traiwat, Narong ไตรวัฒน์ , ณรงค์ . "Mua Ror Si song tat kwarm maitri kab Pakking" เมื่อ ร.๔ ทรงตัดความไมตรีกับปักกิ่ง (When Rama IV severed relations with Peking), in ibid. *Keb-tok* เก็บตก (Miscellany). 1961.

Ts'ao Yung-ho 曹永和. "Cheng Ch'eng-kung chih t'ung-shang mao-i" 鄭成功之通商貿易 (Trade conducted by Koxinga), in *Cheng Ch'eng-kung fu T'ai san-pai chou-nien tsuan-chi* 鄭成功復台三百週年專輯 (Special edition marking the three hundredth anniversary of the restoration of Taiwan by Koxinga). Taipei, 1962.

Tseng Chien-ping 曹建屏. *T'ai-kuo Hua-ch'iao ching-chi* 泰国華僑經濟 . (Economy of the Overseas Chinese in Thailand). Taipei, 1956.

Turpin, F. H. *History of the Kingdom of Siam,* tr. B. O. Cartwright. Bangkok, 1908.

Uchida, Naosaku. *The Overseas Chinese: A Bibliographical Essay.* Stanford, 1960.

Van Leur, J. C. *Indonesian Trade and Society.* The Hague, 1955.

Vella, Walter. *Siam under Rama III, 1824–1851.* New York, 1957.

Vichitwatakarn, Luang หลวงวิจิตรวาทการ . *Karn-muang karn-pokkrong kong Siam* การเมืองการปกครองของสยาม

(Government and politics of Siam) Bangkok, 1932.

——— "Pasi-akon" ภาษีอากร (On taxes), in *Nang-su Vichit anusorn* หนังสือวิจิตรอนุสรณ์ (Publication in memory of Luang Vichitwatakarn). Bangkok, 1962.

Wada Sei 和田清 ed. *Shindai no Ajia* 清代のアジア (Asia during the Ch'ing dynasty) vol. of *Tōyō bunkashi taikei* 東洋文化史大系 (A compendium of Oriental cultural history). Konuna Katsue 小沼勝衛 , ed. Tokyo, 1938–1939.

Wakeman, Frederic. "The Canton Trade and the Opium War," a draft of chapter 4 in John K. Fairbank, ed., *The Cambridge History of China,* vol. 10, scheduled for publication in 1977.

Wales, H. G. Quaritch. *Ancient Siamese Government and Administration.* New York, Paragon Book Reprint, 1965.

Wang Chih-ch'un 王之春 . *Kuo-ch'ao jou-yuan chi* 国朝柔遠記 (Record of the ruling dynasty's kindness to strangers), or *Kuo-ch'ao t'ung-shang shih-mo* 国朝通商始末 (Trade of the ruling dynasty, from beginning to end). 1895.

Wang Ch'ing-yun 王慶雲 , comp. *Shih-ch'u yu chi* 石渠餘紀 (Remnant notes from Shih-ch'u). 1890.

Wang Chu-an 汪杼庵 "Shih-san hang yu Ch'u Ta-chun Kuang-chou chu-chih tz'u" 十三行與屈大均廣州竹枝詞 (The co-hong and Ch'u Ta-chun's poem) in P'eng Tse-i, "Ching-tai Kuang-tung yang-hang chih-tu ti ch'i-yuan,"*Li-shih yen-chiu,* no. 1:1–24 (January 1957).

Wang Gung-wu. "Early Ming Relations with Southeast Asia: Background Essay," in John K. Fairbank, ed. *The Chinese World Order.* Cambridge, Mass., Harvard University Press, 1968.

——— 王賡武 . *Nan-yang Hua-jen* 南洋華人 (Chinese in Nanyang). Taipei, n.d.

Wang Hsi-ch'i 王錫祺 , ed. *Hsiao-fang-hu-chai yu-ti ts'ung-ch'ao*

小方壺齋輿地叢鈔 (Collected copies of works on geography, from the Hsiao-fang-hu study). Shanghai, 1877–1897.

Wang Hsiao-t'ung 王孝通 . *Chung-kuo shang-yeh shih* 中国 商業史 (A commercial history of China) Taipei, 1965.

Wang Shih-ch'ing 王世慶 "Ch'ing-tai T'ai-wan ti mi-ts'an yü wai-hsiao" 清代台湾的米産與外銷 (Rice cultivation and export in Ch'ing dynasty Formosa), *T'ai-wan wen-hsien* 台湾文献 (Taiwan literary collectanea), vol. 9, no. 1 (1958).

Wang Tse-tsai. *Tradition and Change in China's Management of Foreign Affairs.* Taipei, 1972.

Wei Yuan 魏源 *Hai-kuo t'u-chih* 海国图志 , (An illustrated gazetteer of the maritime countries). Completed, 1842; 1876 ed.

Wen-hsien ts'ung-p'ien 文献叢編 (Collectanea from the Historical Records Office). 1964.

Wen Hsiung-fei 温雄飛. *Nan-yang Hua-ch'iao t'ung-shih* 南洋 華僑通史 (A comprehensive history of the Overseas Chinese in Southeast Asia). Shanghai, 1929.

Wenk, Klaus. *The Restoration of Thailand under Rama I, 1782–1809,* tr. G. Stahl. Tucson, 1968.

White, George. *Ruang chotmaihet nai paendin Somdet Pra Narai Maharat* เรื่องจดหมายเหตุในแผ่นดินสมเด็จพระนารายณ์ มหาราช (On the dispatches in the reign of King Narai), tr. Prince Damrong Rajanubhab. Installment 18, vol. 5 of the *Prachoom pongsawadan chabab hor smut haeng chart,* National Library ed. Bangkok, 1964.

Wickberg, Edgar. "Early Chinese Economic Influence in the Philippines, 1850–1898," *Pacific Affairs* 35.3 (1962).

Wills, Jr., John. *Pepper, Guns, and Parleys.* Cambridge, Mass., Harvard University Press, 1974.

Winterbotham, W. *View of the Chinese Empire* (London, 1795).

Wong Lin Ken, "The Trade of Singapore, 1819–1869," *Journal of the Malayan Branch, Royal Asiatic Society* 33.4:5–315 (December 1960).

Wood, W. A. R. *A History of Siam.* Bangkok, 1959.

Wu Han 吳晗 "Kuang-tung shih-san-hang k'ao shu-p'ing" 廣東十三行考述評 (A short note on the co-hong of Canton), in P'eng Tse-i, "Ch'ing-tai Kuang-tung yang-hang chih-tu ti ch'i-yuan," *Li-shih yen-chiu,* no. 1:1–24 (January 1957).

Wu Lien-hsun 吳聯薰 , comp. *Chang-chou fu chih* 漳州府志 (Gazetteer of Chang-chou prefecture). Taipei, 1964.

Wu T'ang 吳堂 and Pa-ho-pu 巴合布 , comps. *T'ung-an hsien chih* 同安縣志 (Gazetteer of T'ung-an District). 1798.

Wu Ti 吳迪 . "T'un-wu-li huang-ch'ao shih" 吞武里皇朝史 (History of the Thonburi Court) tr. Ch'en Li-sung 陳禮頌 , *Chung-yuan yueh-k'an* 1.8:43 (1941).

Wu Yu-kan 武育幹 . *Chung-kuo kuo-chi mao-i shih* 中國国際貿易 (The development of China's foreign trade). Shanghai, 1928.

Wyatt, David. "Family Politics in Nineteenth-Century Thailand," *Journal of Southeast Asian History* 9.2 (1968).

Yamawaki Teijiro 山脇悌二郎 *Nagasaki no Tōjin bōeki* 長崎の唐人貿易 (Chinese trade at Nagasaki). Tokyo, 1964.

Yang Han-cheng 楊漢錚 "Chin pai-nien lai Hsien-lo mi-yeh kai shu" 近百年來暹羅米業概述 (Sketch of the development of the rice trade in Siam in the past century), in *Hsien-ching mi-shang kung-so san-shih chou nien chi-nien k'an* 暹京米商公所三十週年紀念刊 (Commemorative issue, the thirteenth year of the Thailand Rice Dealers' Association). Bangkok, 1949.

Yano Jin'ichi 矢野仁一 . "Shina no kaikoku no tsuite" 支那の開

国に就いて(On the opening of China) *Shigaku no zasshi* 史学 の雑誌 33.5:1–28 (1922).

Yeh Shao-shun 葉紹純. "Wuo-kuo i-min pei-ching chih t'an-t'ao" 我国移民背景之探討 (Investigation into the background of Chinese imigrants). *Nan-yang yen-chiu* 南洋研究 (South Sea research) 6.5:21 (1936).

Yi Ki-hon 李基憲 "Yonhaeng ilgi" 燕行日記 (Diary of a journey to Peking), in *Yonhaengnok sonjip* 燕行錄選集 (Collection of notes on Journey to Peking). Seoul, 1962.

Yin Kuang-yen 印光任 and Chang Ju-lin 張汝霖. *Ao-men chi lueh* 澳門記略 (Brief notes on Macao). Taipei, 1968.

Yu Chung-hsun 游仲勳. *Kakyō keizai no kenkyū* 華僑経済の研究 (A study of the Overseas Chinese economy). *Ajia keizai chōsa kenkyū sosho* アジア経済調査研究双書 Economic Research Office series, no. 164. Tokyo, 1969.

Yu Wen-i 余文儀, comp. *Hsu hsiu T'ai-wan fu chih* 續修台湾府志 (A continued compilation of the gazetteer of Taiwan prefecture). Taipei, 1962.

GLOSSARY

(Names and terms referred to in the notes, except those appearing in the bibliography, are included.)

A-k'e-tun 阿克敦
A-li-k'un 阿里袞
Ai-i 哀夷
Akaramahasenabodi อัครมหา
เสนาบดี
akon (akorn) อากร
Akson Suntonsad, Praya พระยา
อักษรสุนทรศาสตร์
An-p'ing 安平
Anumanrachaton, Praya พระยา
อนุมานราชธน
Apaipanit, Luang หลวงอภัย
พาณิชย์

Banbokburirat, Kun ขุนบาล
บอกบุรีรัตห์
Bandon บ้านดอน
Bankradae บ้านกระแด
Bang-kok (Ban-kok) บางกอก
(บ้านกอก)
Banglamung บางละมุง
Bangpakong บางปะกง
Bangplasoi บางปลาสร้อย
Bangpra บางพระ
Bangrak บางรัก

Bodhisatva-Chakravatin โพธิ
สัตว์ จักรวาทิน
Boromakot บรมโกษ
boo-si บู๊ซี
Buan-heng บ้วนเฮง
Bunli (Wan-li) บันลิ

Chachoengsao ฉะเชิงเทรา
Chaiya, Praya พระยาไชยา
Chakri จักรี
chang ช้ง
Chang-chou 漳州
Chang-lin (Changlim) 樟林
Chang Ts'uan 張專
changkob จังกอบ
changkob rua จังกอบเรือ
changkob sin-ka จังกอบสินค้า

Ch'ang-lai 常賚
Chantaburi (Chantaboon) จันทบุรี
(จันทบุน)
Chao-an 詔安
Chao-Kuang 肇廣
Chaopraya เจ้าพระยา
Chao-ta เจ้าท่า

389

Ch'ao-chou 潮州

ch'ao-kung mao-i 朝貢貿易

Ch'ao-yang 潮陽

Chatu-sadom จตุสดมภ์

che-sua (cho-shan) เจ๊สัว 庢山

chen-lu 針路

Chen-tsung 真宗

Ch'en 陳

Ch'en Ang 陳昂

Ch'en Ch'ang-hsu 陳長緒

Ch'en Chao-k'ua 陳昭誇

Ch'en Ch'eng-fa 陳澄發

Ch'en Ch'eng-wen 陳成文

Ch'en Chin 陳金

Ch'en Chün-ch'ing 陳俊卿

Ch'en Fen-jen 陳懋仁

Ch'en Hung-mou 陳宏謀

Ch'en Kuan-ch'eng 陳觀成

Ch'en K'un-wan 陳坤萬

Ch'en Mei-sheng 陳美声

Ch'en Ta-shou 陳大受

Ch'en T'ien-yün 陳天運

Ch'en Wan-sheng 陳萬勝

Ch'en Yüan-yu 陳元裕

Cheng 鄭

Cheng Chao 鄭昭

Cheng Ch'eng-kung 鄭成功

Cheng Ching 鄭經

cheng-erh 正額

Cheng Fo 鄭佛

Cheng Fu 鄭福

Cheng Hua 鄭華

cheng-kung ch'uan 正貢船

Cheng Ming 鄭明

Cheng Yung 鄭鏞

Ch'eng-hai 澄海

Ch'eng-hai pu 澄海布

Chetsada-bodin, Prince กรมหมื่น เจษฎาบดินทร์

chi 己

Chi-i hang 集義行

chi-mi 羈縻

Chi-shan 佶山

Chi Tseng-chün 稽曾筠

chia 甲

Chiang-men 江門

Chiang Wang-t'ing 江王廷

Chiang-yu 江右

Chiangsi (Kiangsi) 江西

chiao (kao) 郊

chiao-sung-yin 繳送銀

chieh-kung 接貢

Chieh-shih 碣石

Chieh-yang 揭陽

chien 監

Chien-chu-wen 犬竹汶

Chien-ning 建寧

ch'ien-che wei huan er hou-che chi hsun-huan lo-i wu-yu hsiu-hsi 前者未還而後者繼 循環絡繹無有消息

Ch'ien-lung 乾隆

Chih Kang 紫崗
ch'ih 尺
ch'ih shu 勅書
Ch'ih-t'u 坺土
Chim Cho-cho จิมโกโก
Chin 金
Chin Chiam จีนเจียม
chin-chih pu-chin 禁之不禁
Chin ch'ü shun 金聚順
Chin hsieh shun 金協順
Chin kuang shun 金廣順
Chin Gun จีนกุน
Chin Kak จีนกัก
Chin Kao จีนเกา
chin-luang จีนหลวง
Chin nai Gai จีนทายก่าย
Chin Ruang จีนเรือง
chin-szu hang 金絲行
Chin Sin จีนสิน
Chin te-ch'un 金得春
Chin yuan feng 金源豐
Ch'in-chou 欽州
Ching-te chen 景德鎮
Ch'ing-fu 慶復
Ch'ing-lan 清瀾
ch'iu-kung 秋貢
Ch'iu Shou-yuan 邱壽元
Ch'iung-chou 瓊州
cho-shan 座山
Choduk, Pra พระโจทก
Choduk-ratchasetti, Pra พระ
โจทการเศรษฐี

Chom-pu-nuj ชมพูนุ
Chou Hsiang 周享
Chou Hsüeh-chien 周學健
chou-p'an 州判
chu-kung 助貢
chu-po 主簿
chu-shang 主商
ch'u-chih-che 出資者
Ch'ü Yü-t'ang 邱毓堂
ch'uan 船
ch'uan-chang 船長
ch'uan-ch'ao 船鈔
ch'uan-chu 船主
ch'uan-hu 船戶
ch'uan-huo-shui 船貨稅
ch'uan-kuei 船規
ch'uan-t'ou 船頭
Ch'üan-Chang 泉漳
Ch'üan-chou 泉州
Ch'üan-nan pi-chi 泉南筆記

Chuang Bunnag ช่วง บุนนาค
Chuang Ch'ing-hsing 莊慶興
Chuang Wen-fei 莊文輝
Chumporn ชุมพร
Chun-ha ชุนฮะ
Chun-li ชุนลี
ch'un-kung 春貢
Ch'ün-ying 群英
Chung-hsiang 中祥

chung-lu 中路

Daeng-pak-pla แดงปากปลา

Damrong Rajanubhab ดำรง ราชานุภาพ

Dao-rueng ดาวเรือง

Datfa-song-chan ดาษฟ้า ส่องจันทร์

Ek-si เอกสิ
Eng-euy เองอวย
Eng-li เองลิ
Eng-sun เองซุน
Eng-tai เองท่าย

fan-shao 番梢
Fan-yü 番禺
Fang Hsien 方賢
Fang Hsueh-shan 方学山
Fang shih pu-kan fang, chin yu
    chin pu-liao, kuan yeh kuan
    pu-hao
    放是不敢放禁又禁不了,
    管也管不好
Fang Yung-li 方永利
fen 分
fen-t'ou 分頭
Feng-chin hang 豐進行
Fo-shan (Fatshan) 佛山
Fu-Ch'ao hang 福潮行
Fu-chou 福州
Fu-k'ang-an 福康安

fu-kung 副貢
Fu-le-hun (Furgun) 富勒渾
Fu sung szu 福送幸
Fu-t'ien 福田
Fu Yuan-ch'u 傅元初
fu-yen (fu-yuan) 撫院

ghin-muang กินเมือง
Gi-nguan กินหงวน
Gim-chai (Chin-ts'ai) กิมทาย 金財

Gim chun seng (Chin ch'un-
    sheng) กิมชุนเส้ง (金春盛)
Gim hok lee (Chin fu li) กิมหกลิ
    (金福利)

Hai-ch'eng 海澄
hai-chin 海禁
Hai-feng 海丰
Hai-k'ou 海口
hai-shen 海參
Hai-men 海門
Hai-nan hang 海南行
hang (hong) 行
hang-pao-jen 行保人
hang-shang 行商
heh-ch'ien 黑鉛
Heh-ch'ing 赫慶
Herakamsamut เหราข้ามสมุทร

Ho-ch'eng yang-hang
    合成洋行

Ho Ching-hsing 何景興
ho-ku 合股
Ho Shen 何珅
hoi 補遺
Hoo-song 凇
hou 候
hou-wang po-lai 厚往薄来
Hsi-kuan 西關
hsi-lu 西路
hsi-yang 西洋
Hsia-fang t'ing 廈防廳
Hsiang-shan 香山
Hsieh Wen-pin 謝文彬
hsien 銜
hsien-ch'eng 縣丞
Hsien-lo kuo kung-kuan 暹羅国公館
Hsin-an 新安
Hsin-chu 新柱
Hsin-ning (T'ai-shan) 新寧
Hsin Shih-tuan 辛時端
hsing-che ju-hai chu-che fu-chih 行者入海 住者出資

Hsing-hua 興化
Hsu K'uan 徐寬
Hsu Mou 徐茂
Hsu Shih-mei 徐世美
Hsu Szu-chang 許泗漳
Hsueh Shih-lung 薛士隆
Hsueh Yuan-ch'un 薛元春
Hu-chou 胡州

hu-kung 護貢
hu-shih chu-kuo 互市諸国
Huai-yuan i-kuan 懷遠譯館
Huang 黃
Huang-kang 黃岡
huang-shang 皇商
Huang Tung 黃棟
Huat-seng นายเส็ง
huey หวย
Hui-ch'eng 會城
Hui-chou 惠州
hui-kuan 會館
Hui-lung hang 會隆行
huo ch'uan 貨船
huo-shui 貨稅
Hung Hua 玄燁
hung-t'ou ch'uan 紅頭船
Hung-tzu 洪字
huo-hao 火耗
huo-pi ching-chi 貨幣経済

I-ch'eng hang 義成行
I-ho hang 怡和行
i shih t'ung jen wu chien hsia erh 一視同仁無間 遐迩
I-shun hang 怡順行
Issarasuntorn อิศรสุนทร
I Wen-hung 倪文宏

Jabanseng จับหเส็ง

Jao-p'ing 饒平

jen-k'e (nangkhe) 人客

jo (chang) 丈

jou-yuan 柔遠

Ju-shun hang 如順行

Juan Yuan 阮元

ka-lim-tong ค่าลิ่มทอง

ka-pak-rua ค่าภาคเรือ

K'a-erh-chi-shan 嗻爾吉善

Kaewklang-samut แก้วกลาง สมุทร

Kaew kun-muang แก้วกึ้นเมือง

Kaew-wayat, Luang หลวง แก้ววายัด

Kalahom กลาโหม

kampan buey กำปั่นบ๊วย

kan 貫

K'ang-hsi 康熙

Kao Ch'i-cho 高其倬

Kao-chou 高州

keng 庚

khao pluek ข้าวเปลือก

khun-nang chao-pasi-akon ขุนนางเจ้าภาษีอากร

Khun-tong-wari ขุนทองวารี

klang sin-ka คลังสิทค้า

Koh Kong เกาะกง

Koh ha เกาะห้า

Koh si เกาะสี

kōmōi jin 紅毛人

Kor-si-chiang คอซีเจียง

Kosa, Praya พระยาโกษา

Krom kan chin กรมการจีน

Krom praklang sin-ka กรม พระคลังสิทค้า

Krom-ta กรมท่า

Krom-ta chin กรมท่าจีน

Krom-ta klang กรมท่ากลาง

Krom-ta kwa กรมท่าขวา

Krom-ta sai กรมท่าซ้าย

Kuan-in-fen 觀青粉

kuan-li t'ung-shang 管理通商

Kuang-nan (Kwangnam) 廣南

kuan-yün 官運

Kuang-Chao 廣肇

Kuang-li hang 廣利行

kuchibune 口船

Kun-tong ขุนทอง

K'un-shuang-mo (Khun-samut) (ขุนสมุทร)

kung 公

kung-hang 公行

kung-kuo 貢国

kung-so (consoo) 公所

kung-wai chih kung 貢外之貢

Kung Yü-hsun 孔毓珣

kung-yün 公運

Kuo Chun-ying 郭俊英

Kuo I-kung 郭意公

Kwaeng-muang Nakorn แขวงเมืองนคร

Lai-hu ไล่ฮู่
Lang-chin-chu-li-shuang-mo po-li
   (Luang Chinchuli-samut
   pakdi) 郎金朱里双末
      博里
   (หลวงจีนจุลี สมุทรภักดี)
Li-chai ลิชาย
Li Ch'u 李楚
Li-ch'üan hang 麗泉行
Li-heng ลิเฮง
li-Hsien-lo chu-kung kuo
   隸暹羅助貢国
li-mu 吏目
Li-sun (Li shun) ลิซุน (利順)
Li Shih-yao 李侍堯
Li Tsou 李奏
Li Wei 李衛
Liang-Kuang 兩廣
Liang Shang-hsuan 梁上選
Lien-chou 廉州
lien-huan-pao 联環保
Lim Hoi ลิมหอย
Lin Ho-wan 林合萬
Lin Kuang-ch'ao 林孔超
Lin Ngou ลิ๋โหงา
Lin Tao-ch'ien 林道乾
Lin Tse-hsu 林則徐
Lin Yen 林然
Lin yung fa 林泳發

Liu Ho-hsin 劉和新
Liu-k'un (Ligor) 六坤
Liu Kuo-hsien 劉国軒
Lu Tsan 陸贊
lu-t'ou-ch'uan 綠頭船
lu-ying 綠營
luang หลวง
lucha ลูชา
Lui-chou 雷州
Lumpochiao ลำโปเจียว
Lung 瀧
Lung-ch'i 龍溪
Lung-tu 隆都
Lung-tzu-ch'u 龍仔厝

Ma-hsiang 馬巷
Ma Kuo-pao 馬国宝
ma-lu-mu 麻栗木
Mac (Mo) 莫
Mahachai มหาชัย
Mahattai มหาดไทย
Maha uparat มหาอุปราช
Maitri-wanit, Luang หลวง
   ไมตรีวาณิช
Malapranakorn มาลาพระนคร

Man-sun (Wan shun) มันซุน (萬順)

Mao Wen-ch'üan 毛文銓
Min-Che 閩浙
Min-lao 閩佬
Min-nan 閩南

Ming-shun 明順
Mu-t'eng-o 穆騰額
Mua-seng ม้าเส็ง
muang เมือง
muen หมื่น

Na นา
Nakayama Hachirō 中山八郎
na Nakorn ณ นคร
Na-su-t'u 那蘇圖
nai-hang นายห้าง
Nak-mai นากไม้
naka okubune 中奥船
Nakorn Chaisi นครไชยศรี
Nakorn Pathom นครปฐม
nambanjin 南蠻人
nan 男
Nan-hai (Namoi) 南海
Nang-nok นางนก
Narai นารายณ์
Naresuen นเรศวร
Nei-wu-fu 內務府
Ngek-chai เง็กฉาย
Ngern เงิน
Nien-hsi-yao 年希堯
Ningpo 寧波

okubune 奥船
okuminato 奥湊
Ong (Wang) อ๋อง (王)
Ong Heng-chuan (Wang Hsing-

ch'üan) 王興全
อ๋องเฮงฉ่วน

Pa-chiao 八角
pa-si ภาษี
pa-tsung 巴總
Pa-yen-san 巴延三
Paetriu แปดริ้ว
Pai-ling 百齡
pai-t'ou-ch'uan 白頭船
Pakdi-akon, Khun ขุน
ภักดีอากร
P'an Chen-ch'eng 潘振成
P'an Chih-hsiang 潘致祥
P'an Shih-chü 潘思榘
pang 邦
pao-chia 保甲
pao-shang 保商
Pei-ta-nien 北大年
Pen-chiang-hang 本港行
Petracha เพทราชา
Phuket ภูเก็ต
pi (pi) ปี้ (幣)
Pichaiwari, Pra พระพิชัยวารี
p'ing-t'iao 平糶
Pipat-kosa, Praya
พระยาพิพัฒน์โกษา
Pipit, Praya พระยาพิพิธ
P'i-ya-shih-hua-li 丕雅史滑釐
Pinklao, Pra พระปิ่นเกล้า

Pisanponpanich, Praya พระยาพิศาลผลพาหิชย์

Pitac, Khun ขทพิทักษ์

Pitsanuloke พิษณุโลก

po 伯

poh (boh) 舶

Po-karat, Luang หลวงโกคาราช

pra พระ

prai ไพร่

prai-luang ไพร่หลวง

prai-suei ไพร่ส่วย

Praklang พระคลัง

Praklang mahasombat พระคลังมหาสมบัติ

Praklang sin-ka พระคลังสิหค้า

Prasart Tong ปราสาททอง

Prasert-wanit, Luang หลวงปราะเสริจ้าาพิช

praya พระยา

Pu-cheng shih (ssu) 布政使(司)

pu-kung 補貢

P'u-ch'ien 鋪前

P'u-t'o-shan 普陀山

Punkang ปุทกัง

Rachasetti, Praya พระยาราชเศรษฐี

Ratakosa-tibodi รัฐโกษาธิบดี

Ratcha-kapitan, Luang หลวงกปิตัน

Ratchamontri, Praya พระยาราชมหตรี

Rattanakosin รัตหโกสิทท์

Rattanatibet, Chaopraya เจ้าพระยารัตหฺิเบศ

Rayong ระยอง

sakdina ศักดิหา

sakoku 鎮国

sam สาม , ส้า

sampao สำเภา

Sampaonak สำเภาหาด

Sampeng สำเพ็ง

Samsen สามเสห

Samuhanayok สมุหหายก

Samutprakan สมุทปรากาห

San-hsing 三星

San-kuo chih 三國誌

San-nai fu-jen 三奶夫人

San-sui 三水

San-tien 三點

San-ho hui 三合會

Sen, Pra พระเสห

Sawadiwari, Praya พระยาสวัสดิวารี

seng-lee hor mai hor kor por-jai kar-kai kan เซ็งลี่ฮ้อไม่ฮ้อก็พอใจค้าขายกัห

Setti-kar-sampao เศรษรีค้าสำเภา

Setti Tanon-tarn เศรษรีกททตาล

Shan-t'ou (Swatow) 汕頭

Shang 尚

Shang Chih-hsin 尚之信

shang-ch'uan 商船

Shang K'o-hsi 尚可喜

shang-p'in sheng-ts'an ching-chi
商品生產經済

shang-ssu 賞賜

Shao-hsing 紹興

Shao-wu 邵武

Shen-ch'üan 神泉

Shen Shang-ta 沈上達

sheng 生

shih 市

shih-huo 市伙

Shih-lang 施琅

Shih-ming-chou (Amoy)
思明州

Shih-po ssu 市舶司

Shih-po t'i-chü ssu
市舶提舉司

Shih-san hang 十三行

Shih-wan-ta-shan 十萬大山

shimpai 信牌

Shinra tōsen fūsetsu
暹羅唐船風説

Shotoku shinritsu 正德新例

shu-kuo 屬国

shu-in 朱印

shui 税

Shuin-sen 朱印船

Shun 順

Shun-chih 順治

Si ซี

sib porka mai tao nung pra-ya, liang สิบพ่อค้าไม่เท่าหนึ่งพระยาเลี้ยง

Sipipat, Praya พระยาศรีพิพัฒน์

Sisuriyawongse, Praya พระยาศรีสุริยวงศ์

Sivipott, Okphra ออกพระศรีวิพงษ์

Sombat-wanit, Pra พระสมบัติวาณิช

Song-praratchasarn ทรงพระราชสาส์น

Songtam ทรงธรรม

Su-ch'ang 蘇昌

Su-chou 蘇州

Su-teng 蘇等

Sua, Prachao พระเจ้าเสือ

Suang nai Sit สร้วงนายสิทธิ

suei ส่วย

sui-kung 歲貢

Sui-yang 隋煬

Sukotai สุโขทัย

Sun Shih-i 孫士毅

Sung-k'a 宋卡

Suntorn, Luang หลวงสุนทร

Surasakorn, Luang หลวงสุรสาคร

Surin, Krom muen กรมหมื่นสุรินทร์

Suriyawong-montri, Praya พระยาสุริยวงศ์มนตรี

Swadwari, Pra พระสวัสดิวารี
Swankaloke สวรรคโลก

Ta-ch'eng hang 達成行
Ta-feng hang 達豐行
ta-k'u-ssu 大庫司
ta-t'ou 大頭
tai-shih 代駕
T'ai-shan 台山
Taisra ท้ายสระ
Taksin ตากสิน
Taladnoi ตลาดน้อย
Tan ตัน
Tan-shan 舟山
tan-t'ou 担頭
t'an-kung 探貢
t'ang-i-pu 唐一部
t'ang-liu-pu 唐六部
t'ang-wu-pu 唐五部
Tanon Bantanao
กททบ้านตะนาว
Tao-ch'ien-kang 道乾港
tapao ตาเภา
Teng Chang-chieh 鄧彰傑
Thonburi ธนบุรี
ti 地
ti-yu 迪尤
t'ieh-kuo 鐵鍋
t'ieh-li-tao 鐵梨笏
t'ien 天
t'ien-chuang ching-chi
田莊經濟

T'ien-ti hui 天地會
Ting-chou 汀洲
ting-tai 頂帶
Tipkosa, Pra พระทิพย์โกษา
Tōjin 唐人
tōjinkan 唐人館
Tongchew, Khun ขุนทองจิ๋ว
Tong-peng ทองเพ็ง
tor-long chin-chai
ต้อหลงฉินไฉ้
tōsen 唐船
tou 斗
Trad ตราด
trakien ตระเกียห
Trailokanat ไตรโลกนารถ
Tred-noi เกร็ดน้อย
tsai-kuan chiao-i 在館交易
Ts'ai Ch'i-ho 蔡啓合
Ts'ai Chia 蔡嘉
Ts'ai Chih-kuei 蔡志貴
Ts'ai Hsin 蔡新
Ts'ai Hsi-wang 蔡錫望
ts'ai-tung 財東
Ts'ai Wen 蔡文
Ts'ai Wen-hao 蔡文浩
Ts'ai Yuan-ma 蔡元媽
ts'ao-mi 糟米
ts'e-feng 册封
Tseng Chi-tse 曹紀澤
Tseng Kuo-fan 曹国藩
Tseng Tzu-sheng 曹子声

tsung 艅宗

tsung-shang 總商

Tubtim ทับทิม

Tung-ch'uan 東川

tung-lu 東路

Tung-lung 東瀧

Tung-ning 東寧

Tung-pen-tao 東本島

Tung-sheng hang 東生行

Tungyai ทุ่งใหญ่

tung-yang 東洋

T'ung-an 同安

T'ung-ch'eng 桐城

t'ung-shih 通事

T'ung-wen hang 同文行

Tunma, Praya พระยาตรวมา

tzu 子

wai-huan nei-luan 外患內亂

Wan-ch'ü hang 萬聚行

Wan-hsing 萬興

Wang 王

Wang Chih-ch'un 王之春

wang-lai mao-i 往來貿易

Wang-na วังหน้า

Wang P'i-lieh 王丕烈

wang-shih mao-i 王室貿易

Wang Yuan 王元

Wang Yuan-cheng 王元正

Wang-yun chi 王雲記

Wat Sampluem วัดสามปลื้ม

Wattana-pirom, Khun
ขุนวัฒนาภิรมย์

wen 文

Wen-chou 溫州

Wen-te hang 文德行

Weng Jih-sheng 翁日陛

Wijayen, Praya
พระยาวิชเยนท

wu-chien nei-wai chun-shih i-t'i
無間內外均視一体

Wu Ching 吳竟

Wu Han 吳晗

Wu Shih-chin 吳仕錦

Wu Hsing-tso 吳興祚

Wu Hsiung-kuang 吳熊光

wu-ssu 賦司

Wu Yang 吳讓

ya-ch'ang huo-wu
壓艙貨物

Yamada Nagamasa
山田長政

Yang 楊

Yang Ching-su 楊景素

yang-ch'uan 洋船

yang-hang 洋行

Yang-huo hang 洋貨行

yang-huo hang-jen
洋貨行人

Yang Kuei 楊奎

yang-kuei 洋規

Yang Li-ts'ai 楊利彩

Yang Lin 楊琳

yang-mi 洋米

yang-po 洋駁

Yang Ta-ch'eng 楊大成

Yang T'ing-chang 楊廷璋

Yang-tze 楊子

Yang Wen-ch'ien 楊文乾

Yang Ying-chü 楊應琚

Yang Yu 楊由

Yao Chün-ho 姚峻合

yao-p'ai 腰牌

Yeh Chien-ch'en 葉間臣

Yeh Min-shen 葉民琛

Yeh Hsi-hui 葉錫會

Yeh Shun-te 葉舜德

Yen-k'e t'i-chü ssu

盐課提舉司

Yen-p'ing 延平

yen-ts'ai 燕菜

Yi-hsing 義興

yiab-hua-tapao

เหยียบหัวตาเกา

ying-yü 盈餘

Yok (Yu) หยก (玉)

yu-shih chih kung 有事之貢

yu-shih chih shih 有事之使

Yü-lin (Eurin) 榆林

Yueh Chün 岳濬

Yueh-tung 粤東

Yung-cheng 雍正

Yung-ting 永定

INDEX

A-li-kun, 106

Abeel, David, 196

Achin (Sumatra), 51, 52

Agriculture: Chinese faith in primacy of, 1; by Chinese in Siam, 178–179, 211, 245, 246, 249

Akin Rabibhadana, 212, 218

akon (duty assessed as payment for concessions), 24

Amboy, 65

Amboya, 227

American Steam Rice Milling Co., 120

American traders: rice brought to China by; in 19th-century Siam, 225

Amherst, Lord, 227

Amoy: place of in S. E. Asian trade, xii, 43, 189, 246; trade described, 44; Siamese ships at, 47; second in foreign trade, 52; commenda system in, 53; in triangular trade, 61, 252; sugar from, 63; sample cargoes and profits, 68–69; reopening of trade to, 70–71; in rice trade, 72–73, 90, 92, 95; junks built abroad by merchants of, 96; port for rice junks, 102, 117; closed to trade by foreigners, 109, 167; in 18th century, 121–122; hongs of, 125, 134; foreign trade discouraged at, 128–129; specialist in S. E. Asian trade, 135; Siamese tributary trade at, 142, 148; cost of junks at, 181; trade with Lower Siam, 186–187; junks from, 188, 198

Amoy Defense Bureau (Hsia-fang t'ing), 129, 130

Ampo, 205

Ang-yi (secret societies in Siam), 221

Anhwei, 83

Annam: on route of junk trade, 7; Japanese trade with, 15, 66; Fukienese trade with, 43, 44; in rice trade, 72, 105; Chinese junks to, 188

Anqua, 131

Arabia, Dutch posts closed, 14

Augsberg, League of, 14

Australia, 120

Auydhya, 250, crossroads in junk trade,

7–8; Portuguese traders at, 9; Dutch in, 9, 13; British in, 10, 13; Japanese trade with, 15; royal warehouses in, 35; clandestine trade at, 42; Chinese population of, 46, 160; Amoy trade with, 52; Ningpo trade with, 53; fall of, 107, 143, 171, 251; crockery-making at, 190

Ayudhya dynasty, xii, 24, 140, 147; tax farming under, 215

Ballast cargo (*ya-ch'ang huo-wu*), 34–40, 148, 155–156, 244; trading system explained, 36–37; size of, 38; commercial worth of, 39; of rice, 87; inoperative in Western-style ship, 236

Ballestier mission, 229

Bandon, 202

Bang-kacha, 214

Bangkok: as main junk port, 4, 7, 185, 189, 190, 197, 250, 251; clandestine trade at, 42; Ch'eng-hai merchants in, 109; construction of new capital at, 110, 172, 173; chief port in coasting trade, 200; Chinese population of, 213; British merchants in, 228; increase of Western ships at, 238, 239

Banglamung, 202

Bangpakong, 178, 234

Bangplasoi, 178, 179, 202

Bangpra, 202

Batavia: founded, 10; obstacles to Chinese trade at, 11; Canton trade with, 51; Amoy trade with, 52, 122, 129; smuggling of rice to, 55, 78; piracy in, 56; ships to Japan from, 65; in rice trade, 73, 116; massacre of Chinese in, 91, 170; Pen-Chiang hang trade to, 135; Ch'ing attitude toward trade of Chinese residents in, 163; Siamese trade with, 187, 204; money borrowed in, 191; decline of junk trade to, 227

Bengal, rice to Canton from, 111, 112

Betel nuts: trade in, 59, 195, 203; Siamese export, 201

Birds' nests: trade in, 48, 206, 215, 250;

at Songkla, 63, 164; royal monopoly, 183

Boca Tigris, 37

Bombay, 205; export of sugar from, 201

Boonchoo, 172

Borneo, 120, 188, 196

Boromakot, King, 160

Bowring, Sir John, 232, 236; Mission of, 238; Treaty of (1855), 118, 224, 238

Brass, Siamese import of, 200

Bricks, Siamese import of, 146, 149, 171

Brig, Western, substituted for junk, 223

British East India Company, 10, 176; lack of success of, 13; in S. E. Asian trade from Amoy, 125; tonnage of, 180

British traders: in Siam, 9; East India Co., 10; intra-Asian trade of, 10–11; at Amoy, 53; in rice trade, 116; and Flint episode, 129; in 19th-century Siam, 193, 228, 238, 239–240; significance of Hong Kong for, 224; see also Great Britain

Brooke, James, mission of, 229, 233

Buanheng (Wan-hsing), the, 239

Buffalo: horns traded, 10; hides traded, 59, 73

Burma, 40, 107; Siamese struggles against, 144–145, 170, 177, 186; British in, 233

Burney, Captain Henry, 182, 186, 193, 194, 195; on junk-building, 201; on Chinese population in Siam, 210, 214, 215, 217; mission of, 227; treaty of, 216, 228, 233

Cady, John, 14, 192

Calcutta, 205

Cambodia, 182; on route of junk trade, 7, 44; ships to Japan from, 65; in rice trade, 73, 105; Pen-chiang hang trade to, 135; laborers from, 173; Chinese junks to, 188, 189, 196; Siam's regional trade with, 203

Camphor, trade in, 59

Canton: importance of in Sino-Siamese trade, xi, xii, 189; Portuguese forbidden to trade at, 10; in Siamese tributary trade, 30, 36, 194, 242, 246; Chinese managers from, 40; source of clandestine trade, 42; emperor's merchant at, 49–50; limit on ships calling at, 57; in triangular trade, 60; ships to Japan from,

65; reopening of trade to, 71; rice deficiencies in, 77; source of rice relief for, 81; rice shipments to, 88, 90; merchants from, in rice imports, 103–105; transport of rice invited, 110, 120; attempt to monopolize foreign trade at, 128–129; co-hong system at, 131–132, 175, 247; Siamese tributary trade at, 140–142, 151, 155; power of viceroy at, 150; Chinese merchants trading in for Siam, 161, 168, 176; junks from in Siam, 195, 196; in coasting trade, 198

Capital: pooling of, 123; lack of in guilds, 124; and the yang-hang, 129; related to hang at Canton, 134; cost of outfitting a junk, 195; for foreign trade of Kwangtung, 197; fear of Western, 241

Cardamum, trade in, 183, 195, 202, 203

Catholic Church, in Japan, 17

Celebes, 188, 196

Chachoengsao, 179, 221

Chaiya: port in junk trade, 7, 159; Amoy trade with, 52; in rice trade, 72; Chinese population of, 215

Chakri reigns: see Rama I, II, III, IV

Champa, 189

Chang-chou: prefecture near Amoy, 43, 44; customs post at, 48; ships to Japan from, 65; rice shortages in, 75; in Sino-Siamese junk trade, 198

Chang-p'u, 166

Chang Te-ch'ang, 39

Chang Ts'uan, 161, 162

Ch'ang-lai, 71, 126

changkob (lit., "the rudder of a vessel"; kind of duty on carriers of cargo), 24; changkob rua, 25; changkob sinka, 25

Chang-lin (Chang-lim), 165, 175, 181, 188, 198, 205

Chantaburi, 171; port in junk trade, 7, 164, 174, 197; clandestine trade at, 42; shipbuilding at, 163; agriculture in, 178–179, 214; royal tribute ship at, 185; in Siamese coastal trade, 202; brig built at, 230

Chao-an, 130

Chao-kuang, 77

Chao-ta (Port Master), 20

Ch'ao-chou (Kwangtung prefecture), 44, 66, 189; shortage of rice in, 77, 177; rice relief for, 82; merchants from in rice importation, 103–105; commercial guild in, 132; men from in Sino-Siamese trade, 163; inland ports in, 165; immigrants to Siam from, 175, 213; agriculturalists from, 177–178, 211; increasing role of in Sino-Siamese trade, 189–190, 246; concentration of ships from in Southern Seas, 195–196, 197; in coasting trade, 198; junk-building by men from, 214

Ch'ao-chou *pang,* 124

Chaopraya Kosatibodi, 20

Chaopraya river, 16, 143, 172; junk-building on, 173, 180; agriculture along, 178; Chinese junks on, 195, 200

Chaopraya Sisuriyawong, 230, 241

Chatu-sadom (lit., "Four Pillars"; working departments), 20

Chekiang: anti-Manchu elements in, 28; foreign trade banned in, 29, 157; trade with Fukien, 44; customs post in, 48; Ningpo trade, 53–54; ban on ships from, 56; trade with Japan, 63; re-opening of trade to, 71; shortages of rice in, 78–79; rice to other provinces from, 79; "white-headed ships" from, 122; groupings of merchants in, 124; decline in trade with S. E. Asia, 130–131, 196; Siamese trade with, 170, 187; coasting trade to, 197

Ch'en (Tan), Chinese manager, 40

Ch'en Ch'ang-hsu, 137

Ch'en Chao-k'ua (Luang Chinchulisamut-pakdi), 61

Ch'en Chin, 165

Ch'en Ching-ho, 59

Ch'en Fen-jen, 84

Ch'en I-lao, 163

Ch'en K'un-wan, 168

Ch'en Ta-shou, 96

Cheng Ch'eng-kung (Koxinga), 13, 29; *hang* of, 44; threat to Ch'ing government, 45

Cheng Ching, 29; rebellion of, 43; on Formosa, 45

cheng-erh (revenue), 49

cheng-kung (regular tribute), 146, 148; vessel for, 140, 153, 155; tax status of, 156

cheng-kung ch'uan (main tribute ship), 31

Ch'eng-hai: merchants from in rice imports, 105; leader in Sino-Siamese rice trade, 109, 248; leniency toward Siamese ships, 157

Cheribon, 204

Chetsada-bodin, Prince, 187; *see also* Rama III

Chi-i hang, 134

chi-mi (loose rein), 1–2, 145; and dual aspect of tribute system, 151

Chi-shan, Canton Hoppo, 133, 135, 137

Chi Tseng-chun, 162

Chia-ch'ing emperor, xi, 153; on licenses for trips to Siam, 109; and the Wai-yang hang, 137; for curb on Chinese merchants in Siamese trade, 165, 166; porcelain industry under, 190; coasting trade during reign of, 197

Chiang-lin, 189

Chiang-men (Kiangmui), 188, 189; in coasting trade, 198

Chiang-yu, famine in, 78

chiao (*hang* or hong), 124

chieh-kung ch'uan (tribute-receiving ship), 32, 33, 38

Chieh-yang, 198

Chien-ning, 76

Ch'ien-che wei huan, er hou-che chi, hsun-huan lo-i, wu-yu hsiu-hsi (Hardly had the one ship before returned when another set sail), 154

Ch'ien-lung emperor, xi; trade under, 3, 122, 124, 136, 141, 246; shortages of rice during reign of, 74; measures to control shortage, 83, 90; rice imports during reign of, 91, 142; concessions to rice merchants by, 92, 107; on official vs. private import of rice, 97–98; *yang-hang* under,128; purchase of copper permitted by, 143; embassy from Taksin to, 145–150, 250; Rama I invested by, 153; restrictions on *t'an-kung* ships, 156–157; on Chinese residents abroad, 162

ch'ih-shu (imperial missives), 33

Chim-Cho-cho, 173

Chin, Amoy *nom de commerce,* 127–128, 195

Chin Hsieh-shun, 157, 158, 164

Chin hsieh shun, the, a vessel, 167–168

Chin luang (royal Chinese), 163

Chin Ruang, 163

chin-szu hang (guild at Hui-ch'eng), 132

Chin Yuan Feng, *Shang-hang* firm, 130
Chinese, in Siam: employment of in Siamese trade, 160, 185–189, 195, 203, 204; government attitude toward crews of, 161–162; artisans and craftsmen, 171, 173; encouraged by Siamese government, 173; in tin mining, 174, 211; composition of, 175; collection of taxes farmed out to, 177; agriculturalists, 178–179; in the Third Chakri Reign, 191–202; imports for, 200; management of Siamese regional trade by, 202; in trade with Singapore, 205; centered on temples, 211–212; laborers, 212; prolonged economic influence of, 233–235; after coming of Westerners, 240–241; *see also* Immigrants; Merchants, Chinese
Chinese Repository, 114
Ch'ing dynasty: foreign trade under, xi; Sino-Siamese trade during, 1; early problems of, 28; erratic trade policies of, 54–55; ban on S. E. Asian trade, 56–57; disdain for foreign trade, 123–124; inability to regulate perversion of tribute system, 158; Chinese managers for Siamese trade permitted by, 161–162; inability to stop emigration, 176; political decline of, 239; *see also* individual emperors by name
Ch'ing-fu, 91, 122
Ch'ing-lan, 198
Ch'ing-t'ou-ch'uan (blue-headed ships), 122
Ch'iu Shou-yuan, 162
Ch'iung-chou, *see* Hainan
Choisy, l'Abbé de, 51
Chou Hsiang, 47
Chou Hsueh-chien, 80
chou-p'an (second-class assistant), 102
chu-kung (auxiliary tribute), 34
chu-shang (chief merchant), 127
ch'u-chih-che (ones who put up the capital), 126
Ch'u Ta-chun, 51, 132
Chuan Han-sheng, 77
ch'uan-chang (shipmasters), 87, 126
Ch'uan-chou prefecture (Fukien), 40, 43, 44, 250; merchants from, in Canton, 50; rice shortages in, 75; rice from overseas to, 84

ch'uan-chu (shipmaster), 126
ch'uan hu (shipping firms), 56; and the *yang-hang,* 125–126
ch'uan-huo-shui (normal cargo duty), 91, 92, 93
ch'uan-t'ou (shipmaster), 60, 126
Ch'üan-Chang (Ch'üan-chou and Chang-chou) *pang,* 124
Chuang Bunnag, 192
Chula Chakrabongse, Prince, 194
Chulalongkom, Prince, 237; *see also* Rama V
Chumporn, 202
Ch'un-ying, secret-society group in Siam, 221
Chusan, 129
City, Department of (Vieng), 20
Civil Affairs, Ministry of (Mahattai), 20
Co-hong system, Canton: guilds as precursors of, 125; attempts to collectivize, 129; establishment of, 131–133; categories of, 133
Coastal trade, Siamese, 202–203
Coasting trade, Chinese: size of 197–198; value of, 198; ports of, 198–199; Bangkok chief foreign port, 200; cargoes traded, 200–202
Cochin China, 196; Japanese trade with, 15; Fukienese families in trade of, 43; Hainan trade with, 195; Siam's regional trade with, 203
Coins, in trade, 44, 45
"Commenda" system, 52–53, 127
Commercialism: Chinese disdain for, 1; informal indulgence in, 2
Conseequa, hong merchant, 111
Consoo fund, 131
Copper: trade in, 11, 13, 16; Japanese mining of, 16; Siamese import of, 22, 59, 149; sought in trade by China and Siam, 64; restrictions on, 66; from China, 67; purchase of as favor, 143, 145, 146, 154; in triangular trade, 251
Coromandel, 18, 228
Cotton: exported from Songkla, 63; goods, Chinese, 122, 191; goods, British, 205
Cowries, Siamese import of, 22
Crawfurd, John, 112, 123, 169; on shipbuilding, 180, 201; on Siamese royal

monopoly, 183, 184, 185; on Sino-Siamese trade, 186, 187–188, 189, 190, 191; on British disadvantages in Siam, 193, 229; on Siam's regional trade, 204, 205; mission of, 226–227

Crockery: imported by Siam from Japan, 59; from Ningpo, 190

Customs posts: establishment of, 48–49; personnel of, 49–50; at Amoy, 52

Daimyo (feudal lords), in Siamese trade, 16

Damrong Rajanubhab, Prince, 108, 232

Deerskin: trade in, 10, 16; exported to Japan, 63, 69

Defense, Ministry of (Kalahom), 20

Dit Bunnag, 185, 192, 216

Dutch East India Co., 9, 13, 170; failure of, 14

Dutch traders: in Siam, 9–15; anti-Chinese activities of, 11–12; losses of, 13–14; at Pattani, 62; at Songkla, 63; massacre of Chinese by, 91, 162, 170; in rice trade, 116

Duties, Chinese: Siamese rice exempt from, 89, 91; local merchants not exempt, 106–107; exemptions for rice shipments, 111; on ballast for rice shipments, 113–114; typical fees, 115

Duties, Siamese: kinds of, 24, 183–184; *changkob,* 24–25; as "gifts," 25–26; Chinese advantages in, 193; reduced by Rama IV for trade with West, 232–233; by Bowring Treaty, 238

Earl, George, 200, 201, 228

East Indies: on route of junk trade, 7; Dutch in, 14; Dutch massacre of Chinese in, 91, 162, 170; rice from Siam to, 120

Elephants' teeth: trade in, 4, 44, 48, 122, 174, 203, 215; royal monopoly in, 21; exported to Japan, 59

Embroidered fabrics, trade in, 122

Emperor's merchant (*huang-shang*), 49–50, 53

Eurin (Yu-lin), 195

Exports, Siamese: royal control of, 21; monopolies of Court, 21–22; pepper, 178; cane sugar, 179; in 19th century, 200–206; opium, 234

Extortion, by local officials, 250

Extraterritoriality, granted by Siam for British, 238

Fairbank, John K., 158, 159

Famine, 81; in Fukien, 75–76, 87, 88, 92; in Kwangtung, 77–78, 87, 88; in Chekiang, 78–79; in Siam, 107, 110; and emigration, 177

fan-shao (foreign crewmen), 87

Fang Hsien, 175

Fang Yung-li, 92, 93, 141, 161

Fatshan (Fo-shan), 43

Feng-shin hang, 134

Fifo, 203

Firearms, Western, royal import monopoly of, 22

First (Bangkok) Reign, *see* Rama I

Flint episode, 129

Foochow, 75; Ryukyu missions to, 38; ships to Japan from, 65, 66; rice prices in, 76; rice supplies in, 83

Formosa (Taiwan), 75, 175; Dutch in, 10, 13, 14; anti-Manchu elements in, 28; overseas trade to, 44; rice prices in, 76; relief rice to Fukien from, 80, 83; decline in sale of rice from, 118

France: in alliance with Siam, 12, 13; in trade with Formosa, 44

Frankfurter, O., 117

Free trade: not characteristic of Asian states, 18; Western pressure for, 223; as loss of revenue to king, 226, 253; incompatible with closed system of Sino-Siamese trade, 252

Fu-ch'ao hang (co-hong to handle trade by Ch'ao-chou and Fukien merchants), 133–134, 135, 175; precarious history of, 136, 137, 138

Fu-chou *pang,* 124

fu-kung vessel, 141, 155; tax status of, 156

Fu-le-hun (Furgun), 155

Fu-t'ien, 198

Fu Yuan-ch'u, 44

Fukien: anti-Manchu elements in, 28; foreign trade forbidden in, 29; clandestine trade at, 40, 42; customs post in, 48; ban on ships from, 56; trade with Japan, 63; reopened to trade, 71; rice shortages in, 75–76, 88; sources of rice relief for, 79–81; rice imports into, 91; attempts to encourage local merchants in foreign transport, 96; official vs. private importation of rice to, 97–98; encouragement plan for, 99, 108; decline in rice imports to, 105; rice trade renewed, 117; "green-headed ships" from, 122; groupings of merchants in, 124; mutual guarantee system in, 126; banned to foreigners, 157; inland ports in, 166; Siamese trade with, 170, 187, 235; dominance of in Siamese immigration, 174–175, 214, 235; coasting trade of, 198; extortion by officials of, 250

Gambage, trade in, 183, 195, 202, 203
Gambling, tax farming of, 215, 216, 219, 222
Gervaise, Nicholas, 58
Gia Long, 110
Gold, trade in, 13, 45, 174
Graham, W. A., 47, 238
Graphite, 126
Great Britian: tonnage of in S. E. Asia compared to Chinese, 180; dealings with Siam, 225–231; Chinese interpretation of treaties with, 232; concessions of Rama IV to, 233; tie with Siam, 237; see also British traders; Western trade
Green Standard (lu-ying), 76
Guilds, 124; tribute paid by, 126; transaction of trade managed by, 247; see also hongs
Gun, appointed Praya Rattanatibet, 185
Gützlaff, Charles, 2, 117, 189, 196

Hai-ch'eng, 166, 198
hai-chin (ban on overseas trade), 29, 31–32; limited success of, 45; see also Maritime ban, first; Maritime ban, second
Hai-feng district, ships from 195
Hai-k'ou, 188, 189; in coasting trade, 198
Hai-men, 198
Hainan (Ch'iung-chou), 77, 184, 188, 205; relief rice from 82; middle point in Canton-Siam trade, 51, 165; pirates in, 165; immigrants to Siam from, 175–176; trade with Siam, 188–189, 195, 235, 240, 246
Hai-nan hang, 132–134, 175

Hakkas: immigrants in Siam, 175–176; temple of, 212
hang (commercial firm), 44, 124, 247
Hangchow (Hang-chou), 44
Harris, Townsend, 231
Hatien, 135, 203; see also Pontameas
Hayakawa Junsaburo, 64
Hayes, J., 228
Heh-ch'ing, 141
Heilungkiang, 163
Herakamsamut, a royal tribute-bearing ship, 184
Hidetada, 17
Hideyoshi, 15
Hiokwan (Treasury), 59
Hirado: trade between Ayudhya and, 10; Chinese silks to, 11; and Siamese trade, 16
Hirase Minokichi, 136
ho-ku (partnership), 126
Holland, decline of as power, 14; see also Dutch traders
hong system, 50; see also hang
Hong Kong, 185; effect of on Siamese trade, 224
Hoppo, 86; appointment of, 48–49; traders of, 53
Horses, in trade, 90
hou-wang po-lai (lit., "coming light, returning heavy"), 37, 39, 145, 149
hsi-yang ("western ocean" route), 7
Hsia-men chih, 52, 109, 121, 129
Hsiang-shan, 198
Hsiao I-shan, 135
Hsieh Wen-pin, 40
Hsien-feng reign, xi, 236
Hsin-chu, 92
Hsin Shih-tuang, 136
hsing-che ju-hai chu-che fu-chih (those who manage enter the ocean; those who finance stay home), 126–127
Hsing-hua, 76
Hsu K'uan, 87, 162
Hsu Mou, 165
Hsu Shih-mei, 161
Hsu Szu-chang (Kor-si-chiang), 218
Hsueh Shih-lung, 93
Hu-chou (Hoochow), silk from, 44
hu-kung vessel (part of tribute embassy), 140, 155
hu-shih chu-kuo (trading states), 159

Huang-kang, 198
huang-shang (emperor's merchant, 49–50, 53
Huang Tung, 169
Hue, 203
Hughes, George, 52, 71
Hui-ch'eng, 132
Hui-chou prefecture (Kwangtung), 44, 77; rice relief for, 82; emigrants from, 175
hui-kuan (collective organization of ships and concerns), 124
Hui-lung hang, 137
Hui-tien (Ch'ing administrative code), 32
Hukuang (Hunan and Hupei), rice from, 79, 83
Hung-men, 221
hung-t'ou-ch'uan ("red-headed" ships), 122, 240
Hunter, Robert, 228
Hupei, cultivable land in, 75

I-ch'eng hang, 137
I-ho hang, 137
I-shun hong, 136
Ieyasu, Shogun, 15, 16
Immigrants, Chinese to Siam, 235; and the junk trade, 4; impact of on Siam, 4–5; competition among dialect groups, 220; transported in Western ships, 239; employed in public projects, 241; *see also* Chinese in Siam; Merchants, Chinese
Immigration: of Chinese to Siam, 173, 177–178, 244–245; from Fukien, 174–175; from Kwangtung, 175; other, 175–176; efforts to stop, 176; of agriculturalists, 177–179; rate of, 190; under Rama III, 210; and increase in trade, 245; Siamese rice as attraction, 249
Imperial Household (Nei-wu fu), 49
Imports, Siamese: royal monopolies in, 22; from China, 190; in 19th century, 200; from regional trade, 203, 205
India, 13, 226
Indian Archipelago, 72; in trade with Siam, 204–209, 243
Indo-China, Canton trade with, 51
Indonesia, spice trade of, 10
Industrial Revolution, effect of on Eastern trade, 224
Ingram, James, 85, 90, 118, 234

Inland ports, Chinese, 165–166
Intermarriage, of Chinese and Siamese in Siam, 5
Interprovincial sources of rice, 79–83; inadequacies of, 81
Iron: trade in, 39–40, 203; imported from Japan by Siam, 59; Siamese mines exhausted, 144; Siamese import of, 200
Iwao Sei'ichi, 59

Japan: in junk trade of Eastern Seas, 7, 47; Portuguese trade with, 9, 10; copper trade of, 11, 13; Dutch trade with, 14; trade with Siam, 15–17, 47; imposition of *sakoku,* 17, 58; Chinese trade with, 17, 44, 188; Canton trade with, 51; in triangular trade, 59–65; Chinese ships limited by, 65; rice from Siam to, 120; Shanghai trade to, 199
Java: Dutch in, 14; smuggling of rice to, 83; rice from, 112; Chinese junks to, 188, 196; in Siamese regional trade, 204
Johnson, a missionary, 197
Johore, 52, 122, 162, 174; in rice trade, 73
Ju-shun hang, 136
Juan Yuan, 113, 138, 169
Junk trade, Chinese: Siamese part in, 4, 7–8, 16, 188, 242; and Chinese emigration, 4–5, 211; official Chinese attitude toward, 5; defined, 7; and status of Chinese merchants, 23; basis of in Siamese trading structure, 27; beginning of, 45–55; Fukienese, 53; set-back to, 57; in triangular trade, 58, 62; in rice trade, 117; mutual cooperation in, 123; in 19th century, 123, 195; organization of, 127; to Singapore, 205; *see also* Sino-Siamese trade
Junk trade, Siamese, source of government income, 144, 152
Junkceylon (Phuket), 202, 211, 215; secret societies in, 221
Junks: Siamese construction of, 23–24, 180, 201, 214; sale of abroad, 56, 83; built abroad by Chinese, 96, 173; identification marks of, 122; value of, 123; Chinese style, owned by Siamese, 153; numbers of, 180, 186; cost of,

181, 202; in Hainan-Bangkok trade, 188–189; Siamese, under Rama III, 192–193; cost of outfitting, 195; in coasting trade, 197; as floating bazaars, 200; in Siamese regional trade, 206; decline of, 229–230; attempts to combine with brig, 230–231; small vs. large, 240

Ka-i hentai, xii–xiii, 62, 65
ka lim thong (golden stake fee), 24
ka pak rua (tax on application for construction of a junk), 24, 184
K'a-erh-chi-shan, 97, 98
Kaemper, Engelbert, 22
Kaew klang-samut (Ariel), a vessel, 230
Kalahom Krom-ta, 217, 218
Kamao, 203
kampan buey (inferior brig), 231
Kampongsom (Sihanoukville), 203
Kanemitsu Kanazawa, 62
K'ang-hsi emperor, xi; trade during reign of, 3; trade regulations of, 31–32, 33–34, 37, 44, 141; tribute presented to, 41; lifting of trade ban by, 48; ban reimposed by, 55–56; shortages of rice under, 79, 84; ban on Formosan rice by, 80; import of Siamese rice by, 85, 94, 107; on Chinese in Siamese ships, 161; porcelain industry during reign of, 190
kao (hang or hong), 124
Kao Ch'i-cho: Min-Che Governor-General, 70, 72; maritime trade promoted by, 73; on shortage of rice, 88; regulations proposed by, 121
Kao-chou, 66, 76; rice surplus in, 82; pirates in, 109; in Sino-Siamese trade, 189
Kedah (Queda), Malay sultanate, 186, 204; Burney mission on, 227
Kelamantan, 227
Kelantan, 201, 204, 206, 227
khlang klang, 213
khun (a rank), 217
Khun Ban (Khun Banbokburirat), 218
Khun Chaiyawari, 218
khun-nang chao pasi-akon (officials of taxation), 217
Khun Pitac, 217
Kiangnan (Chiang-nan): foreign trade

banned in, 29, 158; customs post in, 48; reopening of trade to, 71; "blue-headed" ships from, 122; Siamese trade in, 166, 170, 187
Kiangsi: porcelain from, 44; rice from, 79, 83
klang sinka (royal warehouses), 20
Koenig, Jean, 108, 172, 178
Koh Kong, 202
Koh Samui island, 189
Korea: trade with Japan, 17; tribute missions from, 39, 194; trade with Shanghai, 199
Koxinga, *see* Cheng Ch'eng-kung
Krisananon, Kularb, 40
Krom Na (Department of Agriculture), 110
Krom-ta (Office of Ports), 185, 192, 247; Krom-ta kwa, 19; Krom-ta sai, 19, 25, 172, 173, 176, 187; Krom-ta klang, 19–20
krom-ta chin (of the Chinese port department), 217
kromakanchin (officials in provincial towns), 219
Kuan-in-fen (the flour of the Goddess Kuan-in), 78
kuan-yun (official transporting), 97
Kuang-Chao *pang,* 124
Kuang-li hang, 137
kuchibune (mouth ships), 59, 66
kung (tribute), 34
kung-hang (central guild), 42
kung-kuo (tributaries), 159
kung-wai chih-kung (supplementary tribute), 146
Kung Yü-hsun, 88
kung-yun (official arrangement), 86; and Siamese rice, 88
Kuo I-kung, 161
Kwangsi, 71; source of relief rice for Kwangtung, 81–82
Kwangtung: anti-Manchu elements in, 28; foreign trade banned in, 29; trade with Fukien, 44; customs post in, 48; ban on ships from, 56; mines in, 64; shortage of rice in, 71, 76–78, 84, 88; sources of rice relief for, 81–82; rice imports into, 91; official vs. private imports, 98–99; encouragement plan for, 99–100, 103; awards to importers in, 104; active

trade with S. E. Asia, 122, 187, 196; "red-headed" ships from, 122; groupings of merchants in, 124; inland ports of, 165; Siamese trade with, 170, 235; immigrants to Siam from, 175–176, 235; extortion by officials of, 250

Kyoto, 15

Kyushu, 15, 65

Lan Ting-yuan, 73, 84

Land: cultivable in proportion to population, 75, 77, 81; for other crops vs. rice, 78

Land, department of (Na), 20

Langsuan, 222

Laos, 173, 182

Lead: trade in, 16, 18, 43, 45; exported to Japan, 59

Leang-Hae, 196

Leur, J. C. van, x, 52

Li Ch'u, 38

Li-ch'uan hang, 137

Li Kuang-t'ao, 37, 38, 147, 154

Li Shih-yao, 135, 144

Li Wei, 71

Liang-Kuang, 71

lien-huan-pao (mutual guarantee system), 121, 125–126

Ligor (Nakorn; Liu-k'un), 13; in junk trade, 7, 159, 174, 189; Portuguese in, 9; Japanese trade with, 15, 62; clandestine trade at, 42; Amoy trade with, 52, 72; and royal monopoly of pepper, 182–183; royal ships at, 185, 187; in Siamese coastal trade, 202, 204; Fukienese rule of, 214; trade via Bangkok, 215; in triangular trade, 251

Ligor ships, 64, 66

Lim Hoi (Lin Hai?), 186

Lin Ngou (Lin Wu?), 163, 172

Lin Tao-ch'ien, 62

Lin Tse-hsu, 116

Lin Yen, 162

Lin yung fa, 165

Linguists, fees collected by, 115

Linqua, 131

Liu Ho-hsin, 136

Liu Kuo-hsien, 68

Lottery, tax farming in, 216, 218, 222

Loubère, Simon de la, 21, 23, 65

Louis XIV, 12

Lower Siam, 53; trade at ports of, 62; Chinese influence in, 186; trade of, 186–187; Fukienese in, 214–215; influence of triangular trade on, 251–252; *see also* Ligor; Pattani; Songkla

lu-t'ou-ch'uan ("green-headed" ships), 122

luang (a rank), 217

Luang Ratcha-kapitan, 186

Luang Rattanasetti, *see* Hsu Szu-chang

Luang Surasakorn, 225

lucha (fee in recognition of interests belonging to private individual), 24

Lui-chou, 76; rice surplus in, 82; pirates in, 109

Lung-ch'i, 166, 168

Lung-tu, 165

Luzon, 44; smuggling of rice to, 55, 78, 83, piracy in, 56; in rice trade, 73; rice to Fukien from, 84; rice to Canton from, 110; Amoy trade to, 129

Ma-hsiang, 166

Ma Kuo-pao, 141

Macao, 43, 162, 189; Portuguese in, 9; Dutch attempt to capture, 10; customs post at, 48; base for S. E. Asian trade, 57; decline of trade at, 185; Hainan trade with, 195; in coasting trade, 198; contacts with Siam, 225

Macassa, 227

Machachai, 214

Maeklong river, 178

Maha uparat (Second King), 152, 177, 235

Mahattai (Ministry of Civil Affairs), 185, 217

Malacca, 174, 227; Portuguese capture of, 9; Dutch capture of, 10; Japanese copper at, 11; Canton trade with, 51; Siamese trade with, 187, 204, 205, 206

Malacca, Straits of, 204

Malapranakorn, royal tribute-bearing ship, 184

Malay peninsula, 184, 188; on route of junk trade, 7; Fukienese families in trade of, 43; in rice trade, 72; Chinese trade via Songkla, 174; in Siamese coastal trade, 202, 204; clash of Britain and Siam in, 225–226; decline of junk trade to, 227

Malaya, Great Britain in, 233
Malloch, D. C., 118, 119, 195, 207–209;
    on Chinese immigration, 210; on
    Chinese vs. Westerners in Siam, 229
Manchu Banners, 76
Manila: Chinese-Spanish trade at, 47, 170–
    171; Canton trade with, 51; rice to
    Canton from, 110, 117; junks in groups
    to, 126; sugar from, 201
Mao Wen-ch'uan, 73, 81
Maritime ban, first (hai-chin): imposition
    of, 29; limited success of, 45; lifted
    by K'ang-hsi, 48; relation of triangular
    trade to, 251
Maritime ban, second: imposed, 55–56;
    reasons for, 56–57; lifted, 70–71, 73;
    foreign trade during, 72; reasons for
    lifting, 248
Markevald, 120
Measurement fee: Chinese, 115; Siamese
    (changkob rua), 25
Medicine, trade in, 122
Merchants, Chinese: methods of in foreign
    trade, 8; Dutch competition with, 11,
    15; Siamese rewards for, 23; in clan-
    destine trade, 42; attempts by court to
    discourage from foreign trade, 95–96;
    encouragement of, in rice imports, 98–
    101, 248; privileges of, 106; decline in
    role of, 108–109; in illicit rice trade,
    118; prominence of in Siamese trade,
    161–164; swindles by, 164–165; efforts
    to curb, 164–169; continued employ-
    ment of, 169–170; efforts to exclude
    Westerners, 229; continued foreign
    trade of, 240–241; dependence of
    Siamese ruling class on, 243–244; see
    also Chinese in Siam; Immigrants
Metals: trade in, 122; tools, 51
Military, the, drain on rice supply, 76, 80
Min-Che (Fukien and Chekiang provinces),
    56, 70
Ming Mang period, 110
Ming dynasty: private trade during, 3, 29;
    trade regulations of, 30–33; Chinese
    management of tributary trade during,
    40
Ming-shu, secret-society group in Siam,
    221
Mohammedans, in Siamese trade, 48, 185,
    243

Moluccas, spice trade of, 10
Money economy, Siamese, role of Chinese
    labor in, 5, 245
Mongkut, King, see Rama IV
Monopoly, royal Siamese, 18–21, 242;
    under Rama II, 181–185, 202–203;
    under Rama III, 216, 228; tax farming
    as, 215–220; in sugar, 228
Morgan, John, 226
Morrison, J. R., 115, 201
Morrison, Robert, 221
Morse, H. B., 49, 53, 114; on co-hong
    system, 125, 131; on foreign trade in
    Canton, 132; on Chinese emigration,
    176
Moslem revolt, 120
Mowqua, on importation of rice, 111
Mu-t'eng-o, 153, 156
Mua Seng (Luang Apaipanit), 163, 173
Murgui, 9

Na (department of Land), 20
na Nakorn family, 214
Nagasaki: Dutch trading post, 10, 14, 17;
    Chinese silks from, 11; ship reports from,
    54, 55; in triangular trade, 58–59,
    247, 251; numbers of Siamese ships
    in, 60; trade from Lower Siam to, 62–
    64; limits on ships trading with, 65
nagegane (Japanese commenda system),
    127
nai (privileged class), 212
nai-hang (Siamese hong organization), 150
nakaokubune (middle-inner ships), 59
Nakorn, see Ligor
Nakorn Chaisi (Lung-tzu-ch'u), 178, 222
Nakorn Pathom, 120, 179, 234
Namoa (Nan-ao island), 47, 57, 165;
    stopping place in triangular trade, 60;
    troops on, 76; price of rice on, 77; in
    coasting trade, 198
nangke (jen-k'e, "guests"), 173
Nanhai (Namoi) district, 168
Nankeen: trade in, 43, 190; import of for
    Chinese in Siam, 200
Nanking, 65, 66
Nanking Treaty, 232
Narai, King: and unequal treaty of Dutch,
    12; trade monopoly of, 18–19; royal
    factories of, 20; control of exports by,
    21; tribute missions from, 31, 32, 33,

37, 253; exploitation of tributary trade by, 41; supposed stagnation of trade after, 46; three-way trade sponsored by, 58
Negishi Tadashi, 122
Nei-wu fu (Imperial Household), 49
Neo-Confucianism, and nonequality in foreign intercourse, 1
Nguyen Anh, 110
Nien revolt, 120
Nien-hsi-yao, 86
Ningpo, 189; Siamese ships at, 47; customs post at, 48; Siamese trade from, 53–54, 195; in trade with Japan, 65, 66, 135, 246, 251–252; rice imported by, 90; British attempt to trade at, 129; central guild at, 130; Siamese tributary trade at, 142, 148; exports from 190; in coastal trade, 198, 199
Ningpo *pang,* 124
Nishikawa Tadahide, 62, 64, 75

Okphra Sivepott, 41
okubune (Chinese-style junks from Southeast Asia), 59, 66
Ong Heng-chuan (Wang Hsing-ch'üan), 160, 161, 172
Ong Lai-hu, 160, 163, 164
Opium, 186; rice shipments a cloak for trade in, 114; trade in, 203, 204; and rise of secret societies, 221; legalized in Siam, 222; monopoly of Chinese in Siam, 234

Pa-chiao, secret-society group in Siam, 221
pa-tsung (sub-lieutenant), 102, 108
Pa-yen-san, 250
Paet-riu, 179, 222
Pahang, 204
Pai-ling, 166–167
pai-t'ou-ch'uan (white-headed" ships), 122
Palace, department of (Wang), 20
Palembang, 204
Pallegoix, Bishop Jean, 232, 234
P'an Chen-ch'eng (Puankhequa), 133, 138
P'an Chih-hsiang (Puankhequa "the Second"), 137
P'an Shih-chü, 97, 162
pang (groupings of merchants), 124
pao-chia (tithing), 126
pao shang (security merchants), 115, 133

Paper, Siamese import of, 200
Parker, J. S., 120
Passengers: China-Siam, 176, 190, 197, 210; integral part of junk trade, 244–245
Patronage: and tax farming, 217–219; of Siamese trade, 243, 245
Pattani (Pei-ta-nien), 206, 215, 250; port in junk trade, 7, 159; Portuguese in, 9; Dutch factories in, 9; English in, 10; Japanese trade with, 15, 16, 65; in triangular trade, 62, 251; Chinese gold prospectors in, 174; pepper from, 201
Pattani ships, 62–63, 66
Pearl River delta, 81
Pearl shells, imported from Japan, 59
Peking: included in tributary trade, 33; tribute missions to, 35; permission to trade in, 151
Pen-chiang hang (co-hong to manage Siam's tributary trade), 133–134, 146, 150, 175; trade of, 135; precarious history of, 136; dissolution of, 137; relations with other *hangs,* 138–139
Penang, 176, 186, 187, 196; in Siamese regional trade, 204, 205; secret societies in, 221; trade with India, 226
P'eng Tse-i, 132
Pepper: trade in, 4, 9, 44, 122, 141, 164, 195, 205; transshipment of, 174; cultivation of, 177, 178, 214; royal monopoly, 182–183, 203; as major export, 201, 204, 234
Perkins, Dwight, 74, 77–78
Persia, Dutch post closed in, 14
Pescadores, the, Dutch trading post, 10
Petracha, King, 13
Phaulcon, Constantin, 12
Philip II of Spain, 9
Philippines: on route of junk trade, 7; Portuguese trade lost, 10; non-Christian Chinese expelled from, 170; Chinese junks to, 188, 196
Phipps, John, 198, 199
Pickenpack Thies, 120
p'ing-tiao (traditional relief method), 79, 83
Pipat-kosa (official in charge of outfitting junks), 20
Piracy, 33; of Chinese in Luzon and Batavia, 56; and rice imports, 86;

implication of Ch'eng-hai traders in, 109; merchant collaboration in, 165; in Ch'ao-chou waters, 175; of secret societies, 222

Pitsanuloke, 184

Pontemeas (Kang-k'ou), 108; (Hatien), 174

Population: increase in, and rice shortages, 74, 81, 84, 94, 112, 120, 247; in Fukien, 108; Chinese, in Siam, 210–211

Porcelain: trade in, 4, 45, 122; Siamese import of, 22, 190, 200; from Canton, 51–52; development of industry, 190; profit on, 191

Ports: in Sino-Siamese trade, 189–191; in coastal trade, 198

Ports, Office of (Krom-ta), 19; sections of, 19–20

Portuguese traders: in Siam, 9; contested by Dutch, 10; on Formosa, 44; in rice trade, 116; in 19th-century Siam, 225

Potinak, 204

Pra Nangklao, 192; see also Rama III

Pra Petracha, 12–13; decline of trade under, 46

Pra Pichaiwari, 163

Pra Pinklao, 232, 235

Pra Sua, 46

prai (commoners; laborers), 212

prai-luang (commoners owing service directly to king), 212

prai suei (tax in lieu of corvée labor), 183

Praklang (Treasury), 18, 21, 176, 182, 247

Praklang maha-sombat (Royal Treasury), 216, 218

Praklang sin-ka (Royal Warehouses department), 182, 216

Pran, 222

Prasart Thong, 9; wealth of, 18; development of trading monopoly by, 19, 21–22

Praya Anumanrachaton, 230

Praya Chakri, see Rama I

Praya Choduk-ratchasetti, 192

Praya Pipat, 22

Praya Pisanponpanich, 239

Praya Praklang, 12, 20, 47–48, 138, 173; on hiring of Chinese merchants, 166, 168; appointments of, 185, 192

Praya Ratchamontri (Pu), 217, 218

Praya Tattanatibet, 185

Praya Sipipat, 217

Praya Sisahatep (Tung P'ing; Tong-peng), 219

Praya Sisuriyawongse (Chuang Bunnag), 192, 235

Praya Suriyawong-montri, 225

Prince of Wales Island, 206

Private trade: tributary replaced by, 46, 231; linked to tributary, 245

Profits, from trade with Siam, 122

pu-cheng shih (provincial treasurer), 30

Pu-cheng-shih ssu (provincial financial administration), 103

pu-kung ch'uan (supplementary tribute ship), 31, 32–33

P'u-ch'ien, 198

P'u-t'o-shan, 65

Puankhequa, see P'an Chen-ch'eng

Puankhequa "the Second," see P'an Chih-hsiang

Puiqua, hong merchant, 111

"Punkang," 138

Queda, 206

Raffles, Sir James, 204

Rama I (Praya Chakri), 109, 110, 144, 152, 153, 175; rice shipments during reign of, 112; tributary trade under, 153, 154; forbidden to put Chinese merchants in charge of tribute ships, 166; capital at Bangkok, 172; client-ships to Chinese from 174; taxes under 177

Rama II, 144, 171, 177; royal monopoly system of, 181–185, 202–203; employment of Chinese by, 185–187; coastal trade under, 202–203; contest with British in Malay peninsula, 226–227; exclusion of Westerners by, 229

Rama III, 117, 177, 191–202; growing Chinese population under, 210; tax farming by, 215–218, 223, 253; revenues of, 220; and trade with West, 227–228; gains for West during reign of, 229–230

Rama IV (King Mongkut), 2, 40, 144, 172, 177; growth of tax-farming under, 222, 240–241, 253; decline of junk trade, 223–224; disruption in reign of, 232–241; development of country by, 241

Rama V (Prince Chulalongkorn), 237

Ramkamhaeng, King, 25
Ranong, 214
Ratakosa-tibodi, in charge of outfitting
  junks for trade, 160
Rattanakosin era, xii
Rayong, 202
Red wood: gifts of, 150, 151; trade in, 195
Remi Schmidt, 120
Revenue, customs, kinds of, 49; *see also*
  Duties
Revolution of 1688, effect of on foreign
  trade, 46
Rhinoceros horns: trade in, 4, 44, 48, 195,
  250; exported to Japan, 59
Rhio, 188, 204
Rice: staple in Sino-Siamese trade, xi, xii,
  18, 43, 195, 247; royal monopoly, 22;
  smuggling of, 55; shortages of, and
  reopening of maritime trade, 70–71,
  72; quantities transported, 73; shortages
  linked to population increase, 74–79;
  military consumption of, 76, 80; prices
  of, 77, 94, 108, 118; interprovincial
  sources of, 79–83; import encouraged,
  83; amount imported from Siam, 90,
  94–101, 248; private vs. official management of, 97–98; decline in imports of,
  105–106, 116; trade in late 18th, early
  19th centuries, 107–120; obstacles to
  sale of, 114; for Chinese in Siam, 200;
  Siamese export of, 206, 233, 248; in
  Western ships, 239
Rites, Board of, 146, 166; on tax exemptions for rice, 89; Siamese presents to,
  151
Roberts, Edmund, 196; on junk-building,
  201; on tax farming, 220; commercial
  treaty of, 228
Rosewood: trade in, 59; gifts of, 151
Ruschenberger, Dr. W., 196
Russia, population increase in, 74
Ryukyus, the: on route of junk trade, 7,
  16; trading connected with tribute
  missions from, 39; tribute missions
  from, 194

Sa-nga Kanjanakapun, 21–22
Saigon: appeals for rice for, 110; Siamese
  trade with, 187, 203
Sakai, 15
sakdina rank, 217

sakoku, closing of country (Japan), 17
Saltpetre: trade in, 18, 45; royal monopoly
  in, 21; Siamese sources exhausted, 144
Samuhanayok, the, 185
Samutprakan, 221
San-ho-hui, 221
San-sui, 198
San-tien-hui, 221
Sapan wood: trade in, 4, 10, 14, 16, 18,
  43, 44, 157, 195; a royal monopoly,
  21, 183; exported to Japan, 59; presents
  of, 150, 151; Siamese export, 206
Savary brothers, 47, 51, 54
Schouten, Joost, 18
Screens, Chinese, Siamese import of, 22
Sea slugs (*biches de mer*): exported from
  Songkla, 63; trade in, 73
Secret societies, Chinese: and tax farms
  operated by Chinese, 220, 253; and
  rivalry among dialect groups, 220–221;
  linked to opium smuggling, 221; mob
  violence by, 222
Semarang, 204
Setti Ka-sampao (Wealthy Junk Trader),
  73
shabandar (trading agent), 225
Shang Chih-hsin, 29, 42, 43, 50
Shang-chou, 250
shang-ch'uan (commercial ships), 52, 128
Shang-hai hsien-chih, 190
shang-hang (commercial guilds), 128
Shang K'o-hsi, 29, 30, 31, 131; sponsor
  of tributary trade at Canton, 42
shang-ssu (imperial gifts), 33
Shanghai, 189; Siamese trade to, 195,
  246; coasting trade of, 197, 198;
  expansion of trade at, 199
Shantung: customs post in, 48; coasting
  trade to, 197
Shao-wu, 76
Shen-ch'uan, 198
Sheng Shang-ta (Hunshunquin), 42
shih (market), 34
shih-huo (market clerks), 127
Shih-lang, Manchu admiral, 52, 175
Shih-po-ssu (Bureau of Trading Junks),
  31
Shih-san hang (Thirteen Hong), 131
Shih-wan-ta-shan, 162
Shinra tōsen fusetsu (Reports from
  Siam's China ships), 60

Shotoku shinritsu (New regulations of the Shotoku reign), 66

Shrimp, dried, exported from Songkla, 63

shu-in (licenses), 15

shu-kuo (tributary state), 1

Shun, *nom de commerce,* 128

Shun-chih Emperor, 30, 34, 41

Siam, 122; position of in junk trade, 4, 7–9; early Western trade with, 9; Dutch trade with, 9–15; treaty imposed by Dutch, 11–12; court pro-Chinese, 14, 47–48; Japanese trade with, 15–17, 58, 243; supposed decline in trade of, 46; Canton trade with, 51; in triangular trade, 58–69; in rice trade, 73; 120; official transport of rice from, 84–101, 117, 119; decline in imports, 101, 105–106; rice a principal crop, 118; lack of guilds in, 125; Pen-chiang hong in trade to, 133–136; Chinese governmental leniency toward, 161–163; ship-building in, 180, 181; royal monopoly of trade in, 181–185, 202–203; employment of Chinese in, 185–189; value of trade to China, 191; part in Chinese coasting trade, 197–202; regional trade of, 202–209; effect of opening of Hong Kong on, 224; beginning of Western economic influence in, 225–231; development of country, 241; assets of, for trade with China, 243

sib porka mai tao nung praya liang (Ten merchants are not equal to the patronage of one nobleman), 218

Silk: trade in, 4, 11, 16; Siamese import of, 22, 43, 190, 194, 200; profit on, 51, 191; reshipped by Siam to Japan, 59, 61

Silver: trade in, 13, 45; Japanese mining of, 16; Siamese import of, 22, 145, 146, 149; sought in trade by China, 64; Siamese import of for specie, 200, 249–250; from China for purchase of goods in Siam, 239–240

Silviera, Don Carlos Manoel, 225

Singapore, 186; Siamese rice to, 113, 118; rice to China from, 116; Amoy trade to, 129; growing importance of, 187; Chinese junks to, 188, 196, 200; in trade with Siam, 193, 204; transshipment to from Siam, 200, 228; opening of, 204; growth as trading center, 205, 224, 228; Siamese ships at, 207, 235

Sino-Siamese-Japanese trade (triangular trade), 58–69; Siamese part of, 58–59; numbers of Siamese ships in, 60; stops at Chinese ports, 60–61; ships managed by Chinese, 61; part of Pattani in, 62–63; part of Songkla in, 63; part of Ligor in, 63–64; restrictions on, 65–67; profitability of, 67–69; taken over by Chinese, 69; significance of, 251–252

Sino-Siamese trade: phases of, xi; related to tribute, 1, 28; pragmatic attitudes toward, 2–3; lack of innovation in, 5–6; influence of Siamese trading structure on, 18; under early Ch'ing, 29; phase of tributary trade, 39–40, 244; Chinese management of, 40–41; illegal phases of, 42–57; beginning of junk trade, 45–55; Chinese ban on, 56–57, 72; resumption of, 70–71; linked to rice shipments, 85; rice trade of 18th and 19th centuries, 107–120; from Canton, 132; late tributary trade, 140; function of *t'an-kung* vessels, 141–142; value of, 151, 191, 194–195, 249, 250; effect on shipbuilding, 180; levy on vessels trading to Siam, 183–184; size of, 187, 195–196; Chinese junks in, 188; ports of, 189–191; decline of, 223; under threat of Western competition, 227–229; under Rama IV, 235; end of trading monopoly of, 238; significance of for Chakri kings, 251

Skinner, G. William, 19, 174, 178; on Hainan-Siam trade, 188; on Chinese population of Siam, 214

Smuggling: regulations to combat, 121; reaction to *yang-hang* monopoly, 128

Songkla (Sung-k'a), 35; port in junk trade, 7, 13, 62, 159, 187, 189; clandestine trade at, 42; Amoy trade with, 52, 72; in triangular trade, 63, 66, 251; center for Chinese Malay trade, 174; Fukienese rule of, 186, 214; in Siamese coastal trade, 202, 204

Songtham, King, 9, 16; control of exports by, 21

Soochow (Su-chou), 44; transshipment of rice from, 79, 83; (Sao-cheu), 189, 199

South Fukienese: in trade with Siam, 43, 246; in Canton co-hong, 131–132; in trade with S. E. Asia, 196

Southeast Asia: Chinese trade to banned, 56; burgeoning of trade to, 121–122; Amoy predominant in trade to, 125; 19th-century Chinese trade to, 195–197; British influence in, 227; Siamese trade with, 252; *see also* individual countries by name

Spanish Succession, wars of, 14

Spanish traders: on Formosa, 44; in rice trade, 116

Spice trade, 13

Spirits, manufacture and sale of: influence of on secret societies, 222; tax farming in, 215, 220, 222

Steamships, built by Siamese, 241

Sternstein, Larry, 7–8

Stic-lac, trade in, 203, 204, 206

Su-teng, 101; proposals for increasing imports of rice, 102

Suang nai Sit, 230, 232

suei (duty levied on concessions on "essentials"), 24

Sugar: trade in, 45, 51, 157, 176, 205; in triangular trade, 61, 63; cultivation of, 177, 233; switch to cane, 178, 214; Siamese export of, 201, 204, 206, 234; royal monopoly, 228

sui-kung (annual tribute presentation), 142; increase in, 153

Sukothai dynasty, 24

Sulu, 72, 122; Chinese employed in, 163

Sulu Seas islands, 188

Sumatra, 188, 196

Sun Shih-i, 156

Swankaloke crockery ware, 190

Swatow, 239

Sweetmeats, trade in, 51, 176

Swinton, George, 205

Szechwan: mines in, 64; rice from 79

Ta-ch'eng hang, 137

Ta-Ch'ing hui-tien, 147, 159

Ta-feng hang, 134

ta-k'u szu (head of Treasury), 20

ta-t'ou (chief), 26

Tachard, Father, 13

Taiping Rebellion, 120, 236, 239

Taisra, King, 46, 90, 149

Taiwan, *see* Formosa

Taksin, 107–108, 109; on trade with China, 143–144; embassy to China from, 145–151, 245, 250; deposed, 152; "royal Chinese" under, 163; aided by Chinese, 171; supported by Sino-Siamese trade, 172; Ch'ao-chou merchants favored by, 175, 220–221; shipbuilding by, 180

t'an-kung ch'uan (visiting tribute ship), 32, 33, 38, 155; rice brought by, 87; semi-official trade by, 141–142; taxation of, 156; under Chinese management, 160

Tao-kuang reign, xi, 169, 235; junk trade under, 4, 190; coasting trade under, 197, 199

Tartar-general, merchants of, 49, 53

Tax farming: monopoly of Chinese, 215, 234; and patronage, 217–219; profitability of, 219; government revenues from, 220, 229; competition among Chinese dialect groups for, 220–221; and decline in foreign trade, 223; after coming of Westerners, 240–241, 253

Taxation, Siamese: alternative to junk trade, 177, 215; under Rama II, 182; exemptions of Chinese from, 191; taxes farmed out, 216

Tea: trade in, 122; Siamese import of, 190, 200; profit on, 191

Teak: used in junks, 180; exported by China, 195

Teksia, 203

Tenasserim, Portuguese traders in, 9

Teng Chang-chieh, 136

Tha-mai, 214

Thajin Thachin, 178

Third Chakri Reign, *see* Rama III

Thompson, Joseph, 114

Thonburi, 108; port in junk trade, 7, 147; bricks for, 149; new capital at, 171; Hakkas in, 212

Three Feudatories, Revolt of, 42

"Three-year-maximum" rule, 121

t'ieh-kuo (iron pans), 42

T'ien Ju-k'ang, 5, 123, 197–198; on secret societies, 221

T'ien-ti-hui, 221

Tientsin, 189, 236, 237

Tin: trade in, 13, 14, 18, 44, 45, 174, 195, 205, 215; royal monopoly in, 21; exported to Japan, 59; from Songkla, 63; Chinese in mining of, 174

Ting-chou, 76

Tobacco: trade in, 203; cultivation of, 214

Tongkin [Tonkin], 66; Dutch post liquidated at, 14; Chinese junks to, 188, 196

tōsen: (Chinese), 17; (Chinese vessels), 58

Trad, 171, 178

Trade organizations: official markings of ships, 122–123; joint investment, 123–124; *pang,* 124; *hang* (hong), 124; *yanghang,* 125–130; Canton co-hongs, 131–138

Trading structure, Siamese: monopoly of ruler, 18–21; control of export and import, 21–22; arbitrary collection of duties, 22–23; construction of junks, 23–24; kinds of duties, 24–26

Trailokanat, King, 19

Trang, 215

Transportation, difficulties of for relief rice, 82

Treasury (Klang), department of, 20

Tree bark, trade in, 157

Triad societies, among Chinese in Siam, 221

Tributaries: Chinese attitude toward, 1; Ch'ing edict inviting, 30

Tributary trade: early Sino-Siamese, 28, 242; first phase of, 30–34; regulations for, 30–33; ballast cargo, 34–40, 244; Chinese management of, 40–41; replaced by private trade, 46, 231; size of, 72; and the guilds, 136–139; capitalization on commercial aspects of, 244; private trade protected by, 245

Tribute: to government officials from *yanghang,* 129; supplementary, 146, 148–149; gifts in return for, 150

Tribute missions: basis of Sino-Siamese trade, 1, 242; as form of commercial investment, 2–3, 151; official trade legitimized by, 3, 45, 181; and royal monopoly of trade, 19; accompanied by trade, 30, 145, 147; regulations for, 31; commercial worth of, 39; rice trade as part of, 87; typical instance of, 140; from Taksin to Ch'ien-lung, 145–151; restriction of, 153; Ch'ing regulation of, 154–155; succumbing to commercialism, 158–159; numbers under Rama III, 194, 231; decline under Rama IV, 223–224; termination of, 235–237

Tringganau, 72, 201, 204, 206, 227

tsai-kuan chiao-i (trade within the station), 30–31

Ts'ai Hsi-wang, 160

Ts'ai Hsin, 72

ts'ai-tung (financiers), 126

Ts'ai Wen, 161

Ts'ai Wen-hao, 92, 93

Ts'ai Yuan-ma, 175

Tsang Tzu-sheng, 160

ts'ao-mi (tribute rice), 120

Tseng Chi-tse, Marquis, 237

Tseng Tzu-sheng, 155

tso-sua (*cho-san;* one in position of philanthropist), 161

Tsūkō ichiran, 46, 64

tsung-shang (central guild), at Ningpo, 130

Tsushima, Korean trade at, 17

Tung-sh'uan district (Yunnan), copper from, 143

Tung-lung (of Ch'ao-chou prefecture), 157, 165, 176

Tung-pen-tao, the, cargoes and profits of, 68–69

Tung-sheng hang, 137

tung-yang ("eastern ocean" route), in junk trade, 7, 102

T'ung-an district, 128, 166, 198

T'ung-chih reign, rice imported during, 120

t'ung-shih (linguists), 87, 160, 169

T'ung-wen hang, Canton firm, 133, 137

T'ung-wen kuan, 33

Tungyai, 202, 204

Turpin, F. H., 107

Umbrellas, paper: trade in, 43, 190; import of for Chinese in Siam, 200

United States, treaty with Siam, 238; *see also* American traders

Van der Heide, Homan, 118, 119

Vella, Walter, 210

Vereeningte Oost Indische Compagnie (VOC), *see* Dutch East India Co.

Vietnam, 162; tribute missions from, 39, 194; Siamese rice to, 110

Wa-Kan senyo shu, 62

Wai-yang hang (outer-ocean guild), 132, 133, 137

Wakeman, Frederic, 132
Wales, H. G., 25, 219
Wan-ch'u hang, 136
Wang (Ong), Chinese manager, 40
Wang Chih-ch'un, 130
wang-lai mao-i (to-and-fro trade), 38
wang-shih mao-i (court-managed trade), 18
Wang Yeh-chien, 77
Wang yu chi, 165
Wang Yuan, 161
Wang Yuan-cheng, 92–93
Wat Sampreum-Sampeng, 172
Wei Yuan, 91, 111
Wen-te hang, 134
Weng Jih-sheng, 169
Wertheim, W. F., xv
Western shipping: junks pushed out by, 239; larger ports needed for, 252
Western trade in East Asia: conditions preceding, x; formal nature of, 8; Dutch, 9–15; Japanese, 15–17; unprofitable in Amoy and Ningpo, 53–54; centered in Canton, 131–135; levies on ships of, 184, 228, 233; Siamese reluctance in, 186; in sugar from Siam, 206; delayed by Chinese in Siam, 211; excluded by royal monopoly, 216; competition of, in 19th century, 223–227; missions to Siam, 227–229; gains for, 229–231; under Rama IV, 232–241; hiatus in, end of 17th century, 243; adverse effects of, 252; *see also* American traders; British traders; Portuguese traders, etc.
Whampoa, 111
White, George, 21, 40–41, 84
Wood, in trade, *see* Black wood; Redwood; Rose wood; Sapan wood; Teak
Wood, W. A. R., 13
Wu Ching, 168
Wu Hsing-tso, 50
Wu Hsiung-kuang, 109, 110, 157; on Chinese management of Siamese trade, 164, 167
Wu Shih-chin, 160
Wu Yang, 164, 186, 214

ya-ch'ang huo-wu (ballast cargo), 34
Yamada Nagamasa, 16
yang-ch'uan (ocean ships), 52, 125; from Amoy, 121–122
yang-hang sub-guild, 42; ocean guild, 102, 109; of Amoy, 125, 247; handling of local ships by, 125–128; competition of, 128; decline of, 128–130
yang-huo hang (firms of foreign goods), 132
Yang Kuei, 38
yang-kuei (ocean fee), 126
Yang Lin, 57
yang-mi (foreign rice), 74
Yang Ta-ch'eng, 163
Yang T'ing-chang, 101
Yang Ying-chü, 98
Yang Yu, 167
Yangtze valley: rice-growing region, 79, 81; effect of Taipings on, 120
Yeh Min-shen, 120
Yeh Shun-te, 161
Yen-p'ing, 76
yen-ts'ai (birds' nests), 126
Yi-hsing (Gee Hin), secret society group, 221
ying-yü (surplus quota), 49
Yu-lin, 198
yu-shih chih kung (missions dispatched with an aim), 152, 244
Yuan dynasty, 1
Yueh-tung, secret-society group, 221
Yung-cheng emperor: trade under, 3; junk trade of, 4; petitioned on trade ban, 70–71; rice trade permitted by, 72; shortages of rice during reign of, 74, 79, 82; prices of rice, 77; measures to control rice shortage, 83; and importation of foreign rice, 86–87, 89, 94, 107, 142; *yang-hang* organizations under, 128; purchase of copper by Siam permitted by, 143; on Chinese crews for Siamese ships, 161–162
Yunnan, mines in, 64, 143

Zeelandia, Dutch trading post, 10, 44

HARVARD EAST ASIAN MONOGRAPHS

1.   Liang Fang-chung, *The Single-Whip Method of Taxation in China*

2.   Harold C. Hinton, *The Grain Tribute System of China, 1845-1911*

3.   Ellsworth C. Carlson, *The Kaiping Mines, 1877-1912*

4.   Chao Kuo-chün, *Agrarian Policies of Mainland China: A Documentary Study, 1949-1956*

5.   Edgar Snow, *Random Notes on Red China, 1936–1945*

6.   Edwin George Beal, Jr., *The Origin of Likin, 1835-1864*

7.   Chao Kuo-chün, *Economic Planning and Organization in Mainland China: A Documentary Study, 1949-1957*

8.   John K. Fairbank, *Ch'ing Documents: An Introductory Syllabus*

9.   Helen Yin and Yi-chang Yin, *Economic Statistics of Mainland China, 1949-1957*

10.   Wolfgang Franke, *The Reform and Abolition of the Traditional Chinese Examination System*

11.   Albert Feuerwerker and S. Cheng, *Chinese Communist Studies of Modern Chinese History*

12.   C. John Stanley, *Late Ch'ing Finance: Hu Kuang-yung as an Innovator*

13.   S.M. Meng, *The Tsungli Yamen: Its Organization and Functions*

14.   Ssu-yü Teng, *Historiography of the Taiping Rebellion*

15.   Chun-Jo Liu, *Controversies in Modern Chinese Intellectual History: An Analytic Bibliography of Periodical Articles, Mainly of the May Fourth and Post-May Fourth Era*

16.   Edward J.M. Rhoads, *The Chinese Red Army, 1927-1963: An Annotated Bibliography*

17.   Andrew J. Nathan, *A History of the China International Famine Relief Commission*

18. Frank H. H. King (ed.) and Prescott Clarke, *A Research Guide to China-Coast Newspapers, 1822–1911*

19. Ellis Joffe, *Party and Army: Professionalism and Political Control in the Chinese Officer Corps, 1949–1964*

20. Toshio G. Tsukahira, *Feudal Control in Tokugawa Japan: The Sankin Kōtai System*

21. Kwang-Ching Liu, ed., *American Missionaries in China: Papers from Harvard Seminars*

22. George Moseley, *A Sino-Soviet Cultural Frontier: The Ili Kazakh Autonomous Chou*

23. Carl F. Nathan, *Plague Prevention and Politics in Manchuria, 1910–1931*

24. Adrian Arthur Bennett, *John Fryer: The Introduction of Western Science and Technology into Nineteenth-Century China*

25. Donald J. Friedman, *The Road from Isolation: The Campaign of the American Committee for Non-Participation in Japanese Aggression, 1938–1941*

26. Edward Le Fevour, *Western Enterprise in Late Ch'ing China: A Selective Survey of Jardine, Matheson and Company's Operations, 1842–1895*

27. Charles Neuhauser, *Third World Politics: China and the Afro-Asian People's Solidarity Organization, 1957–1967*

28. Kungtu C. Sun, assisted by Ralph W. Huenemann, *The Economic Development of Manchuria in the First Half of the Twentieth Century*

29. Shahid Javed Burki, *A Study of Chinese Communes, 1965*

30. John Carter Vincent, *The Extraterritorial System in China: Final Phase*

31. Madeleine Chi, *China Diplomacy, 1914–1918*

32. Clifton Jackson Phillips, *Protestant America and the Pagan World: The First Half Century of the American Board of Commissioners for Foreign Missions, 1810–1860*

33. James Pusey, *Wu Han: Attacking the Present through the Past*

34. Ying-wan Cheng, *Postal Communication in China and Its Modernization, 1860-1896*

35. Tuvia Blumenthal, *Saving in Postwar Japan*

36. Peter Frost, *The Bakumatsu Currency Crisis*

37. Stephen C. Lockwood, *Augustine Heard and Company, 1858-1862*

38. Robert R. Campbell, *James Duncan Campbell: A Memoir by His Son*

39. Jerome Alan Cohen, ed., *The Dynamics of China's Foreign Relations*

40. V.V. Vishnyakova-Akimova, *Two Years in Revolutionary China, 1925-1927,* tr. Steven I. Levine

41. Meron Medzini, *French Policy in Japan during the Closing Years of the Tokugawa Regime*

42. *The Cultural Revolution in the Provinces*

43. Sidney A. Forsythe, *An American Missionary Community in China, 1895-1905*

44. Benjamin I. Schwartz, ed., *Reflections on the May Fourth Movement: A Symposium*

45. Ching Young Choe, *The Rule of the Taewŏn'gun, 1864-1873: Restoration in Yi Korea*

46. W.P.J. Hall, *A Bibliographical Guide to Japanese Research on the Chinese Economy, 1958-1970*

47. Jack J. Gerson, *Horatio Nelson Lay and Sino-British Relations, 1854-1864*

48. Paul Richard Bohr, *Famine and the Missionary: Timothy Richard as Relief Administrator and Advocate of National Reform*

49. Endymion Wilkinson, *The History of Imperial China: A Research Guide*

50. Britten Dean, *China and Great Britain: The Diplomacy of Commercial Relations, 1860-1864*

51. Ellsworth C. Carlson, *The Foochow Missionaries, 1847-1880*

52. Yeh-chien Wang, *An Estimate of the Land-Tax Collection in China, 1753 and 1908*

53. Richard M. Pfeffer, *Understanding Business Contracts in China, 1949-1963*

54. Han-sheng Chuan and Richard Kraus, *Mid-Ch'ing Rice Markets and Trade, An Essay in Price History*

55. Ranbir Vohra, *Lao She and the Chinese Revolution*

56. Liang-lin Hsiao, *China's Foreign Trade Statistics, 1864-1949*

57. Lee-hsia Hsu Ting, *Government Control of the Press in Modern China, 1900-1949*

58. Edward W. Wagner, *The Literati Purges: Political Conflict in Early Yi Korea*

59. Joungwon A. Kim, *Divided Korea: The Politics of Development, 1945-1972*

60. Noriko Kamachi, John K. Fairbank, and Chūzō Ichiko, *Japanese Studies of Modern China Since 1953: A Bibliographical Guide to Historical and Social-Science Research on the Nineteenth and Twentieth Centuries, Supplementary Volume for 1953-1969*

61. Donald A. Gibbs and Yun-chen Li, *A Bibliography of Studies and Translations of Modern Chinese Literature, 1918-1942*

62. Robert H. Silin, *Leadership and Values: The Organization of Large-Scale Taiwanese Enterprises*

63. David Pong, *A Critical Guide to the Kwangtung Provincial Archives Deposited at the Public Record Office of London*

64. Fred W. Drake, *China Charts the World: Hsu Chi-yü and His Geography of 1848*

65. William A. Brown and Urgunge Onon, translators and annotators, *History of the Mongolian People's Republic*

66. Edward L. Farmer, *Early Ming Government: The Evolution of Dual Capitals*

67. Ralph C. Croizier, *Koxinga and Chinese Nationalism: History, Myth, and the Hero*

68. William Jefferson Tyler, translator, *The Psychological World of Natsumi Sōseki* by Dr. Takeo Doi.

69. Eric Widmer, *The Russian Ecclesiastical Mission in Peking during the Eighteenth Century*

70. Charlton M. Lewis, *Prologue to the Chinese Revolution: The Transformation of Ideas and Institutions in Hunan Province, 1891–1907*

71. Preston Torbert, *The Ch'ing Imperial Household Department: A Study of its Organization and Principal Functions, 1662–1796*

72. Paul A. Cohen and John E. Schrecker, eds. *Reform in Nineteenth-Century China*

73. Jon Sigurdson, *Rural Industrialization in China*

74. Kang Chao, *The Development of Cotton Textile Production in China*

75. Valentin H. Rabe, *The Home Base of American China Missions, 1880–1920*

76. Sarasin Viraphol, *Tribute and Profit: Sino-Siamese Trade, 1652–1853*

77. Ch'i-Ch'ing Hsiao, *The Military Establishment of the Yuan Dynasty*

78. Mei-hsi Tsai, *Bibliography of Contemporary Chinese Novels and Stories*

79. Wellington K. K. Chan, *Merchants, Mandarins, and Modern Enterprise in Late Ch'ing China*

80.   Endymion Wilkinson, translator, *Landlord and Labor in Late Imperial China: Case Studies from Shandong,* by Jing Su and Luo Lun

81.   Barry Keenan, *The Dewey Experiment in China: Educational Reform and Political Power in the Early Republic*

82.   George A. Hayden, translator, *Crime and Punishment in Medieval Chinese Drama: Three Judge Pao Plays*

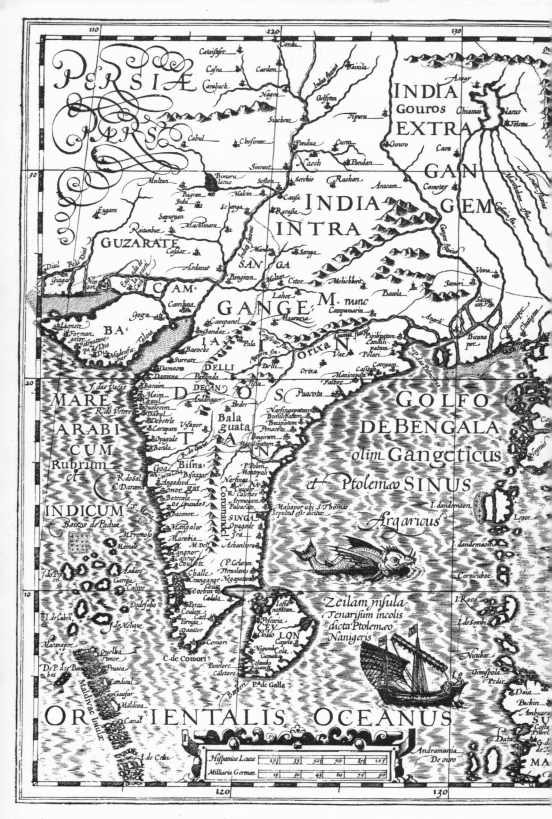

แผนที่ทวีปเอเชียตะวันออก โดยชาวเบลเยียมชื่อ ฮอนดีอุส ตีพิมพ์ในปี พ.ศ. 2156